Nigel Cawthorne is the author of *Military Commanders* and *Vietnam – A War Lost and Won*. His writing has appeared in over a hundred and fifty newspapers, magazines and part-works – from the *Sun* to the *Financial Times*, and from *Flatbush Life* to the *New York Tribune*. He lives in London.

THE MAMMOTH BOOK
OF NEW CSI

by
NIGEL CAWTHORNE

ROBINSON

RUNNING PRESS
PHILADELPHIA · LONDON

Constable & Robinson Ltd
55–56 Russell Square
London WC1B 4HP
www.constablerobinson.com

First published in the UK by Robinson,
an imprint of Constable & Robinson Ltd, 2012

A copy of the British Library Cataloguing in
Publication Data is available from the British Library

UK ISBN: 978-1-78033-002-0 (paperback)
UK ISBN: 978-1-78033-534-6 (ebook)

Printed and bound in the UK

1 3 5 7 9 10 8 6 4 2

First published in the United States in 2012 by Running Press Book Publishers,
A Member of the Perseus Books Group

Books published by Running Press are available at special discounts for bulk
purchases in the United States by corporations, institutions, and other organizations.
For more information, please contact the Special Markets Department at the
Perseus Books Group, 2300 Chestnut Street, Suite 200, Philadelphia, PA 19103,
or call (800) 810-4145, ext. 5000, or e-mail special.markets@perseusbooks.com.

US ISBN: 978-0-7624-4469-4
US Library of Congress Control Number: 2011930510

9 8 7 6 5 4 3 2 1
Digit on the right indicates the number of this printing

Running Press Book Publishers
2300 Chestnut Street
Philadelphia, PA 19103-4371

Visit us on the web!
www.runningpress.com

Printed and bound in the UK

CONTENTS

INTRODUCTION

T HE FATHER OF modern crime scene investigation was Alphonse Bertillon, who went to work for the Prefecture of Police in Paris as a clerk at the age of twenty-six in 1879. Three years later, he introduced a system known as anthropometry (also called Bertillonage) to identify criminals through the measurements of the head and body, which was adopted by the police in Britain and the United States. Although it was later superseded by fingerprinting, it remains in use as a means of furnishing a minutely detailed portrait, valuable to investigators. Bertillon's system brought with it the methodical collection of detailed criminal records and he took standard photographs of criminal suspects, full face and in profile, giving us the modern mug shot.

Bertillon also took his camera to the crime scene to photograph the evidence before it was disturbed. He employed a system he called "metric photography", mounting the camera on a high tripod and laying down maps with a grid printed on them so that the relative position of objects could be measured accurately. He also developed the science of ballistics, the casting of footprints to preserve them, the use of the dynamometer to measure the amount of force used in breaking and entering, and the forensic examination of documents. Bertillon was called as an expert witness in the Dreyfus affair in 1890s France, testifying that certain incriminating documents were written by Alfred Dreyfus. However, he was not a handwriting expert and, in this case, he was wrong and contributed to the conviction of Dreyfus, who was then sent to Devil's Island.

Nevertheless, Bertillon's scientific approach to crime scene investigation endured and was popularized by Sir Arthur Conan Doyle, who mentions Monsieur Bertillon in *The Hound of the Baskervilles* and the short story "The Naval Treaty", in which

Dr Watson says that Sherlock Holmes talked of the "Bertillon system of measurements" and "his enthusiastic admiration of the French savant".

Crime scene investigation has developed by leaps and bounds since Bertillon's day. In 1892, the world's first fingerprint bureau was set up in Argentina. That year, Francisca Rojas of Necochea, some 300 miles (482 km) south of Buenos Aires, was convicted of murdering her two sons on the strength of fingerprint evidence. A fingerprint bureau was established in Calcutta in 1897 where a system of classification was developed by Azizul Haque and Hem Chandra Bose. It was called the Henry Classification System after their supervisor Sir Edward Richard Henry and was adopted by Scotland Yard in 1901. The following year, Bertillon used it to identify a thief and murderer named Henri-Léon Scheffer.

Modern scientific equipment is used to study tiny fibres, hairs, poisons, pollen and dust. Murder weapons are subjected to minute scrutiny and pathologists make the most detailed study of dead bodies. But the greatest breakthrough came with DNA profiling, developed by British geneticist Alec Jeffreys of Leicester University in 1984. Using modern duplicating techniques, forensic scientists are now able to magnify samples, making it possible to identify an intruder from the tiny traces they leave behind.

Not only are the latest forensic techniques employed to solve current criminal cases, they are also used in historical investigations into, for instance, the fate of the Russian royal family killed by the Bolsheviks in 1918 or the murder of a man whose 5,000-year-old body was found in the Alps in 1991. However, crime scene investigation still has its limitations. So far, it has not been able to tell us what became of Madeleine McCann . . .

                                                        Nigel Cawthorne

MADELEINE McCANN

IN MAY 2007, Madeleine McCann was on holiday with her family in the Algarve region of southern Portugal. At around 6 p.m. on the evening of 3 May, just a few days before her fourth birthday, Madeleine's parents, Kate and Gerry McCann, put Madeleine and her two-year-old twin siblings, Sean and Amelie, to bed in the ground-floor bedroom of their holiday apartment in Praia da Luz. Madeleine was wearing a pair of pink pyjamas with the words "Sleepy Eeyore" on them. Before she went to sleep, Madeleine said to her mother: "Mummy, I've had the best day ever. I'm having lots and lots of fun."

At around 8.30 p.m., Kate and Gerry McCann left the children asleep in the apartment and went out to the tapas bar of the Mark Warner Ocean Summer Club. It was just 130 yards (120 m) away and part of the resort complex where they were staying. The McCanns and their fellow holidaymakers – Dr Matthew Oldfield and his wife Rachael, Russell O'Brien and Fiona Payne – agreed to take it in turns to check up on the children.

At 8.55 p.m., Dr Oldfield went to the apartment and listened outside the bedroom window to see whether he could hear any noise from the children. Ten minutes later, Gerry McCann went to check up on the children. Soon after Jane Tanner, another resident of the resort, noticed a man carrying a child but did not think anything of it. Gerry McCann had stopped to talk to Jeremy Wilkins, but did not notice Tanner as she walked past them to join the rest of the group.

Dr Oldfield checked on the children again at 9.30 p.m. This time he glanced through the open bedroom door. He only saw the twins, but had no reason to suspect anything was amiss with Madeleine. However, when Kate McCann took her turn to return to the apartment, she went inside. To her horror, Madeleine's bed was empty. The bedroom window was open and she was heard to scream: "They've taken her, they've taken her! Madeleine's gone!"

The police were called and, within ten minutes, were at the crime scene. Meanwhile, the staff and guests had begun searching the holiday complex. There was no sign of Madeleine and it soon became clear that the little girl had been abducted, so the police on the border with Spain were alerted, along with the authorities at all Portuguese and Spanish airports. Sniffer dogs were brought in. The local council searched the sewers and other waterways. But, after a week, they had found nothing.

The search was then widened. The Maritime Police combed the caves along the coast. Holidaymakers' photographs were examined for suspicious characters that may have been caught in the background. Even the Portuguese Secret Service was called in, in case there was some terrorist aspect to the abduction. Portuguese newspapers reported that a man with short brown hair, approximately 5 ft 7 in. (1.7 m) tall, was being sought. But otherwise the police drew a blank.

There were two initial theories about what had happened to Madeleine. One was that she had been kidnapped by a gang who would sell her for adoption. The other was that she had been snatched by a paedophile ring. A top forensic expert said that the layout of the Mark Warner holiday complex made it a "perverts' paradise" – with plenty of hidden corners where paedophiles could watch children unobserved. The police could not even say whether Madeleine was alive or not. Chief Inspector Olegário de Sousa said that so many people had been in the apartment that night, any forensic evidence the police might have gleaned from the crime scene had been lost. However, there would soon be plenty of work for crime scene investigators to do.

Lori Campbell, a journalist from Britain's *Sunday Mirror*, drew the attention of the police to Robert Murat, a dual British-Portuguese national who had been staying nearby at Casa Liliana, his mother's villa. He had been acting as a translator for the police and was said to be particularly concerned about the case because he had recently lost a custody battle over his own three-year-old daughter. Rachael Oldfield, Russell O'Brien and

Fiona Payne said that they had seen him in the Praia da Luz complex on the night Madeleine had disappeared, though his mother said that he had been at home with her.

On 14 May, Casa Liliana was sealed off. The swimming pool was drained and videotapes, mobile phones, computers and the two cars used by the Murats were taken away for forensic examination. There was speculation that the villa had a secret basement. A laptop and hard drives were also taken from twenty-two-year-old Sergey Malinka, an associate of Murat's who had set up a website for him. The two had been in frequent phone contact since Madeleine's disappearance. With no other clue to go on, this was found to be suspicious.

On 15 May, Robert Murat was named as an *arguido*, or official suspect, which, while falling short of actually charging him, granted him the right to remain silent. While Portuguese detectives flew to Britain to interview Murat's estranged wife, British detectives flew to Portugal with their own sniffer dog and hi-tech scanning equipment to search Casa Liliana once again. Desperate to find a clue, the vegetation was razed to the ground. Even so, no evidence linking Madeleine to Murat could be found. Nevertheless, it was ten months before his possessions were returned to him and, finally, four months after that, his *arguido* status was lifted.

By that time, the case had taken a shocking turn. On 7 September 2007, Kate and Gerry McCann were named as formal suspects and given *arguido* status. This was prompted by new crime scene evidence. Madeleine's blood, hair and other DNA evidence had been found in the car the McCanns had hired twenty-five days after Madeleine had disappeared. However, the Leicester Police who had been helping the Portuguese detectives with their enquiries said that the forensic evident was "very flaky".

"The preservation of the crime scenes carried out by the Portuguese police was very poor," a police source who had dealt with the British Forensic Science Service in Birmingham told the *Daily Mail*. "Every man and his dog has been to the crime scene at the apartment, and used the McCann's hire car. It means it's very hard to pin down where any fluids or other sources of DNA came from in the first place. And as for Madeleine's hair being found in the hire car – well, of course it could be. Hair stays around for ages, and sticks to clothes. So Madeleine's hair has been found in the boot? So what."

Another leading forensic scientist told the *Daily Telegraph*: "If they are spots of blood, it could not be from a car used by the McCanns twenty-five days later. That doesn't make sense. The blood would have dried and it would not transfer as spots unless the child is alive. It would be fragments, but that is not what the police are saying they have. This is the prevailing view among other forensic scientists I have spoken to."

There were other claims that analysis of the hair could show whether Madeleine had been drugged on the night she disappeared, supporting the theory then circulating that she had died after being heavily sedated. But toxicology could only show signs of drugs or medicines she had taken over the preceding months or years. It could not show what she had taken on the specific night. In the event, samples of Madeleine's hair were tested. They showed she had not received any medication for at least eight months. Her brother and sister were also tested and no traces of sedatives were found in their systems.

Naturally, the McCanns protested their innocence. Although they had not been charged, they paid for independent forensic tests to be performed on the hire car, which they had garaged in the home of tycoon John Geraghty nearby. However, British forensic experts considered a fresh examination of the car a waste of time.

"All of the evidence should have been taken out of it by the police," said Leicester Police. "But saying that, of course, in England the police would have kept the car as well, because we're so careful about preserving forensic evidence for potential court cases."

Sir Alec Jeffreys, the originator of DNA fingerprinting, offered his services as an expert witness to the McCanns. He pointed out that Madeleine's parents, brother and sister, who carried similar DNA, had all been in the hire car, so it would be nearly impossible to establish anything positive.

"There are no genetic characters in Madeleine that are not found in a least one other member of the family," he said. "So then you have an incomplete DNA profile that could raise a potential problem in assigning a profile to Madeleine, given that all other members of that family would have been in that car."

One of the useful clues from the crime scene was Madeleine's favourite cuddly toy, a pink cat. Kate McCann tucked Madeleine up with it, but later it was found on a shelf too high for Madeleine to have reached. This meant it had been handled by whoever took Madeleine and it might have yielded vital forensic evidence. Yet the police let the McCanns keep the pink cat. They used it as part of their "Find Madeleine" campaign and took it around Europe and North Africa as they followed up reported sightings. Many people had touched it when they visited the Vatican and the shrine of Our Lady of Fátima in Portugal. After one newspaper said that it looked a little grubby, Kate McCann put it in the washing machine. So any useful forensic evidence had long since been lost.

Then came news that a trace of blood had been found in another apartment at the Praia da Luz complex. The blood was sent to the Forensic Science Service in the UK, along with bloodstains found in the McCanns' original apartment. But it was impossible to assess its significance. Even if it had been Madeleine's blood, there could have been an innocent explanation, such as someone squashing a mosquito after Madeleine had been bitten by it.

The Leicester Police said the evidence collected by the Portuguese police against the McCanns was so insubstantial that it could not lead to their prosecution. Nevertheless, the case was passed to a local prosecutor who, in turn, passed it on to a judge who authorized the seizure of Kate McCann's diary and Gerry McCann's laptop. The Portuguese authorities were eager to read his emails and see what websites he had been visiting. But, again, this line of investigation met a dead end. Eventually, on 21 July 2008, the McCann's *arguido* status was lifted and it was decided to "close the file on the investigation concerning the disappearance of the minor Madeleine McCann due to lack of evidence that any crime was committed by the persons placed under formal investigation".

The files have been archived but they will be reviewed periodically and could be reopened if new evidence emerges, said Portugal's Attorney-General Fernando José Pinto Monteiro.

Again the case had moved on. In June 2007, it was revealed that another DNA sample had been retrieved from the McCanns' apartment that did not match anyone in the family. But by the time a British CSI team had been brought in with special ultraviolet equipment that could detect a spray of fine particles of blood, they found that the apartment had been cleaned up and reoccupied. The Portuguese authorities said they brought in a specially trained sniffer dog that could detect the scent of a dead body and had been in situ for two hours or more. It was said to have identified the presence of a corpse, but British police dog-handlers said that this was unlikely as the odour of death dissipated within a month.

In 2011, Kate McCann put the case back in the news with the publication of her book *Madeleine* to raise money for the search. As a result, Scotland Yard reopened the case and assigned thirty detectives to the investigation.

SNOWTOWN

O<small>N</small> 20 M<small>AY</small> 1999, the sleepy bush town of Snowtown in South Australia came to international attention. Some 75 miles (120 km) north of Adelaide, it had a population of just 600. On the corner of the High Street and Railway Terrace was a disused red-brick building that had once been the Snowtown branch of the State Bank of South Australia. Like many rural branches, it had been closed long ago. Even so, it attracted an unusual amount of visitors. In this quiet town, people had begun to notice vehicles belonging to strangers parked nearby. This eventually incited the interest of the police, who were involved in a year-long investigation of a growing number of missing-persons cases in the state. On 20 May 1999, they decided to take a look inside the bank. Behind the 4 in. (10 cm) steel door of the bank's vault they found six black plastic barrels that gave off a stomach-churning smell.

Detective Steve McCoy recalled: "The stench was unbearable. It was the stench of what I would say was rotting flesh, rotting bodies, human bodies. It was putrid. It permeated your hair, your clothing, everything you had on the stench got into. It was horrific."

The acid-filled drums contained partly dissolved human body parts. Among them were fifteen feet, leading the police to conclude that the drums contained the remains of at least eight murder victims. Worse, along with the corpses they found rubber gloves, a bloodstained saw, ropes, tape, handcuffs, knives and electrical equipment designed to give excruciating shocks. It seemed that the victims had been tortured before they were killed.

The following day, three homes in a blue-collar area of northern Adelaide were raided. Three men were arrested and charged with the murder of an unknown number of people between

1 August 1993 and 20 May 1999. The suspects were forty-year-old Mark Haydon of Smithfield Plains, thirty-two-year-old former abattoir worker John Justin Bunting of Craigmore and twenty-seven-year-old Robert Wagner of Elizabeth Grove. Given the horrific nature of the crimes of which they were accused, they were denied bail.

The missing-persons investigation had begun in November 1998 when Haydon's wife, thirty-seven-year-old Elizabeth, had gone missing. Her brother did not believe Haydon's inconsistent, even contradictory, stories of her disappearance. Nor did he believe that she would have voluntarily upped and left her two young sons. When her brother went to the police, they found it suspicious that her husband had not reported her missing. Then they noticed that she was connected to two other people who had disappeared – twenty-two-year-old Clinton Trezise, who had vanished in 1993, and his friend, the forty-year-old flamboyant transvestite and convicted paedophile Barry Lane, aka Vanessa, who had last been seen in October 1997. A missing-persons taskforce, codenamed Chart, was set up and Haydon's house was bugged. This provided evidence that was later used in court.

When it became clear that a good many more than three people had gone missing from Haydon's immediate circle, the taskforce swelled to thirty-three. They followed Haydon's car. It led them to Snowtown. As cars from out of town tend to attract attention in small outback towns like Snowtown, the sightings of the other unfamiliar vehicles led detectives to the other suspects.

The barrels found in Snowtown had done the rounds before ending up in the bank vault. They had first been stored in a shed behind Bunting's house in Murray Bridge in April 1998. Three were then moved to Haydon's house at Smithfield Plains. Later, one was stored in the back of a Mitsubishi Sigma at Murray Bridge, while five were kept in the back of a Toyota Land Cruiser at Hoyleton on the Adelaide Plains. The barrels had been moved to the bank, which Haydon had rented under the name "Mark Lawrence" about three months before they were discovered, after complaints about the smell. The accused had claimed that the barrels contained kangaroo meat.

Forensic scientists had the distasteful task of trying to identify the victims from their dental records and fingerprints. The killers had made the mistake of using hydrochloric, rather than sulphuric, acid. This tends to mummify bodies rather than dissolve them. Nevertheless, before they had been dunked in the acid, the bodies had been mutilated and dismembered, and were badly decomposed. So the then new and expensive technique of DNA profiling was used. Even body parts that had been marinated in acid for some time produce useful DNA. This could be extracted and compared with hair from combs or samples left on soiled clothing by suspected victims. Soon seven of the eight victims found in the bank vault had been identified.

It turned out that some of the victims had been on Disability Support Benefit. The authorities had not been informed of their deaths and the money was still being collected. Others, who had formally been declared dead, were still, apparently, drawing their benefits. It seemed that the prime reason for the murders was financial as the killers were drawing AUS$100,000 a year due to their dead victims. But there were other more personal motives for the killings. Robert Wagner, for example, was a neo-Nazi who, purportedly, hated Asians and gays. John Bunting, himself an abused child, had a pathological hatred of homosexuals and paedophiles. And the terrifying treatment that had been meted out to the victims in the run-up to their deaths indicated that the killers took a sadistic glee in their crimes.

As if eight victims were not enough, the police, convinced there were more bodies, continued their search. On 23 June, a taskforce of overalled crime scene officers arrived at Waterloo Corner Road in North Salisbury, the site of a semi-detached house where Bunting had once lived. It had since been demolished, but the police were convinced that the site might still yield vital evidence.

First they broke up a concrete slab in what had been the back garden and removed it. Then they used sophisticated ground-penetrating radar equipment, first developed to detect plastic landmines laid during the Falklands War. As the radar scanner moved over the exposed earth, ominous black shadows appeared on the TV monitor, showing that something lay beneath the soil. After digging down some six feet, the detectives found a corpse, wrapped in black plastic bags, which had been in the ground for more than three years. This was identified as forty-seven-year-old Suzanne Allen, a former lover of Bunting. He and Wagner claimed that she had died of a heart attack, but they had cut her up and buried her so they could continue to claim her benefits.

Below that they found a skeleton that was even older. This was twenty-six-year-old Ray Davies. In 1995, Suzanne Allen had rented a caravan to him. After Davies was accused of being a paedophile, Bunting and another of his lovers, Elizabeth Harvey, tortured and killed him, burying him in the garden. His disappearance was never reported. The death toll was now in double figures.

At the beginning of June 1999, a fourth suspect was arrested. This was nineteen-year-old James Vlassakis. He was the son of Elizabeth Harvey, who died of cancer soon after his arrest. Initially, Vlassakis was charged with just one murder that had taken place on 4 May 1999, though the name of the victim was suppressed. After his arrest Vlassakis repeatedly attempted suicide and was moved from prison to the secure wing of a psychiatric hospital. In a taped phone call played at the trial, he told his teenage girlfriend Amanda Warwick about the bodies in the barrels and said that he would soon be charged. She asked if he had anything to do with the murders. He replied: "It's too big, I can't tell you."

Another house in Murray Bridge was raided and an eleventh body was unearthed. The police then went through their unsolved crimes file and discovered that bones found in the field at Lower Light in 1994 belonged to Clinton Trezise. His head had been beaten in with a shovel by Bunting, after he had been invited into his home in Salisbury North.

The body of eighteen-year-old Thomas Trevilyan had been found hanging from a tree near Kersbrook in the Adelaide Hills in 1997. Initially, his death was thought to have been a suicide, but he was later implicated in the murder of Barry Lane. Gavin Porter, a missing man from the neighbouring state of Victoria, also appeared to be a victim. A heroin addict and friend of Vlassakis, he had been killed after Bunting had pricked himself on a discarded syringe and decided he must die.

More properties were raided in the wheat belt around Snowtown and along the Murray River. This led to press speculation that the gang extended much further than the four already in custody. Indeed, the gang had once been bigger. It became clear that some of the victims had earlier been perpetrators. The gang had turned in on itself and began killing its own. It was thought that the transvestite Barry Lane had a hand in the murder of his boyfriend Clinton Trezise, before he himself was killed. Lane had lived with Robert Wagner – despite his vociferous hatred of homosexuals – just a block away from Bunting's demolished house where two corpses were unearthed.

The four accused went on trial in November 2000. Bunting, Wagner and Haydon were charged with ten counts of murder, but remained silent and refused to plead. Vlassakis, who was then charged with five counts of murder, reserved his plea. The evidence given in court was deemed so gruesome that suppression orders were used to keep the horrific details from the public. The Snowtown murder case was subjected to over 150 suppression orders in all. However, in Britain, the *Daily Telegraph* ignored the ruling and revealed that the victims had been sadistically tortured. According to the medical testimony, some victims had burn marks on their bodies. Others were found with ropes around their necks. They were gagged. One victim died with his arms handcuffed behind his back and his legs tied together. Another had received electric shocks to the genitals. A burning sparkler had been pushed into his urethra. His nose and ears were burnt with cigarettes and his toes were crushed before he was left to choke to death on his gag. Another had been put in a bath and assaulted with clubs. He had been beaten around the genitals and had his toes crushed with pincers, before being garrotted with a length of rope and a tyre lever.

Victims' bodies had been mutilated and dismembered. The head and arms of Elizabeth Haydon had been cut off. Her torso had been stripped of its flesh and her breasts and genitals removed. The final victim, David Johnson, had been cooked and partially eaten.

Before they died, victims had been forced to call their tor-mentors "Lord Sir", "Chief Inspector", "Master" and "God". They had also been forced to record carefully scripted phrases, which were then left on the answerphones of friends and relatives to allay suspicion. Gang members then impersonated their vic-tims at benefit offices to collect the money due.

In July 2002, Vlassakis pleaded guilty to four counts of murder and was given a life sentence with the stipulation that he must serve twenty-six years before he was eligible for parole. He had struck a deal with the prosecution, otherwise he would have had to serve forty-two years before he was eligible. By then the charges against Bunting, Wagner and Haydon had increased to twelve counts of murder.

On 8 September 2003, after an eleven-month trial in front of the South Australian Supreme Court, Wagner was found guilty of the murder of seven people, on top of the three murders he had admitted earlier. Bunting was convicted of eleven murders. The jury was hung on a twelfth charge – the murder of forty-seven-year-old Suzanne Allen, whose body had been found wreathed in plastic under Bunting's demolished house. The defence claimed that she had died of natural causes.

Many of the charges against Haydon had been dropped due to lack of evidence. He was not convicted of any of the murders, but pleaded guilty to having helped dispose of the bodies. Both Wagner and Bunting refused to stand when the judgment was read, while Bunting protested loudly that details of the deal that Vlassakis had made to get a shorter sentence in return for giving evidence against them had not been revealed to the jury, some of whom had undergone counselling after hearing his testimony. Both were sentenced to life imprisonment without the possibility of parole.

Vlassakis's testimony alone had lasted thirty-two days. He claimed that he had been involved in the killing of his half-brother Troy Youde, stepbrother of the last Snowtown victim, David Johnson. He vomited when he recalled how he had found

Wagner cooking Johnson's flesh in a frying pan and been offered some.

The victims, Vlassakis said, were relentlessly tortured. The eighth victim, Fred Brooks, had been beaten in a bath and had lit cigarettes stuck in his ear and nose. Wagner and Bunting, the prosecution said, boasted that "the good ones" never screamed. Their targets, they maintained, were primarily homosexuals, who they claimed to loathe.

The murders have given Snowtown a terrible notoriety. With street hawkers selling Snowtown Snow Shakers featuring body parts and barrel-shaped fridge magnets bearing the logo "Snowtown – you'll have a barrel of fun", the inhabitants are worried that the town may never shake its sick image. There has even been a proposal to change the name to Rosetown. Few think it will help.

RACHEL NICKELL

O N THE MORNING of 15 July 1992, twenty-three-year-old part-time model Rachel Nickell was walking on Wimbledon Common, close to her home in south-west London, with her two-year-old son Alex and their pet labrador Molly. She was brutally attacked. A passer-by found Alex clinging to Rachel's blood-drenched body under a silver birch tree, crying: "Get up, Mummy." She had been stabbed repeatedly and raped. Her throat had been slit – all while her son looked on. A bungled investigation led to the wrong man being charged, while the killer went on to kill again. But crime scene evidence eventually led to the conviction of the murderer sixteen years later.

Apart from Alex, there were no witnesses to the attack, but one person saw a man carrying a dark holdall towards the spot where Rachel's body was found and another saw the killer washing his hands in a stream. The killing was thought to be a murderous escalation of the "Green Chain rapes", a series of 106 sexual assaults that had taken place near green spaces across south London in the early 1990s. The police had already been tipped off to a possible suspect when the mother of Ministry of Defence warehouseman Robert Napper called them, telling them that her son had admitted to a rape. However, she got the details wrong, saying that the assault had taken place on Plumstead Common when, in fact, it had happened in a house nearby. As the report did not match the record of any crime, the police did not act on the tip-off, though Napper had a previous conviction for carrying a loaded air gun in a public place.

By the time Rachel Nickell was killed, Robert Napper was suspected of four sexual assaults, three of which he has since been convicted for. They demonstrated an increasing use of violence. Napper admitted attempting to rape a seventeen-year-old girl who was walking to a friend's home on the Caldwell Estate in Hither Green, south-east London, not far from his home in Plumstead in 1992. Eight days later he sexually assaulted another teenage girl at knifepoint in a field in Mottingham. In May, he grabbed a twenty-two-year-old mother pushing her two-year-old daughter in a buggy along the Green Chain Walk, Eltham, in broad daylight. He put a ligature around her throat, battered her and raped her on the footway. Neither the daylight nor the presence of the child seemed to discourage him.

Rachel Nickell was attacked at between 10.20 and 10.35 a.m. on a bright, sunny day. Her son Alex was found with blood completely covering his face, chest and arms. He had put a piece of paper on his mother's head as a makeshift bandage. When examined, he was found to have linear abrasions and bruising on the forehead, cheeks and mouth. The consultant paediatrician who examined him said these injuries were consistent with the child being dragged across the ground face down. There were flakes of paint in his hair.

The sexual nature of the attack on his mother was palpable. Her jeans and underwear had been pulled down to just above her ankles to expose her buttocks. The pathologist later said that it appeared something, such as a finger or round object, had been inserted into her anus. There were knife cuts to the T-shirt and bra, and the left cup had been pulled down to expose the nipple.

A total of forty-nine stab wounds were found, mostly to the front and rear of the upper body. The most severe stab wounds were to the front and side of her neck. Her heart and left lung had been stabbed while she was alive, while the right lung and liver were penetrated after death. A defence wound was found on her left hand, showing that she had tried to fend off her attacker. The killer also left a sample of his DNA, which was collected by swab from her intimate areas.

In August 1992, an e-fit of the Green Chain rapist was issued. A neighbour called the police saying that Napper matched the description. The police arranged for him to give a sample of saliva and blood on 2 September, but he did not turn up. A second caller identified the e-fit as Bob Napper. Napper failed to turn up to provide DNA samples again on 8 September, but the police ruled him out of the investigation because he was 6 ft 2 in. (1.90 m). They were convinced they were looking for someone who was no taller than 5 ft 9 in. (1.75 m), even though one of the victims said the suspect was 6 ft 3 in. (1.94 m).

On 27 October, Napper was arrested for the possession of an unlicensed firearm and ammunition. Searching his home, the police discovered an A-Z map with marks showing the locations of the attacks. Napper said they were "just doodles" or points on his jogging route. One even appeared to show the site of the Rachel Nickell murder, though it turned out to be a printer's error. Napper was prosecuted for the firearm offences and spent two months in jail.

Early the following year, Napper was stopped by the police after being seen climbing the wall of a young mother's home, but he persuaded them that his actions were entirely innocent and they let him go. Later, a tin containing a gun with Napper's fingerprints on them were found on Winn's Common in Plumstead, but the police did nothing. In a search of the area, other boxes were found. One contained a "Big Swede" folding lock knife that Napper had bought a year earlier.

The police were not interested in Napper. They were after Colin Stagg, an unemployed man from nearby Roehampton known to walk his dog on Wimbledon Common. Although no forensic evidence linked him to the murder, they were convinced that he was their man thanks to the profiling of the killer by criminal psychologist Dr Paul Britton, who was called in just thirteen days after the killing. Dr Britton had made his name in the investigation of the murder of pet beautician Caroline Osbourne in 1984. She had been tied up and stabbed repeatedly. After 15,000 people had been interviewed and 80 men arrested and released, detectives turned to Dr Britton to give them an insight into what motivated the killer and how to identify the suspect.

From a study of the case files, Dr Britton deduced that the motive was sexual and carried out as an expression of "corrupt lust". He said that the killer would be a man in his early to mid-twenties, lonely, sexually immature, with poor social skills and probably living at home. He was probably a manual worker and lived near the murder scene. The following year Paul Bostock was arrested. He matched Dr Britton's profile exactly and was convicted of the murder of Caroline Osbourne in 1986.

From then on, Dr Britton's profiles were used on more than a hundred cases. Following the murder of Rachel Nickell, he came up with a seventeen-point profile that was remarkably similar to the one used in the Osbourne case. It fitted Colin Stagg perfectly. Britton then joined the undercover Operation Ezdell where a policewomen from the Metropolitan Police's Special Operations Group contacted Stagg under the pseudonym "Lizzie James", posing as the friend of a woman he had once contacted through a lonely hearts column. Over five months, through meetings, phone calls and letters, she dangled the prospect of a sexual relationship in front of him and tried to get him to divulge violent sexual fantasies. At one point, she even told him: "If only you had done the Wimbledon Common murder, if only you had killed her, it would be all right."

But Stagg replied: "I'm terribly sorry, but I haven't."

Although Stagg never came close to confessing, he was charged with Rachel's murder. But when the case reached the Old Bailey, the judge, Mr Justice Ognall, threw out all the prosecution evidence obtained from Stagg by what he called a "honeytrap". The case collapsed within a day and Stagg was acquitted. Nevertheless, Colin Stagg complained that most people still thought he had done it. He found it impossible to get a job and was spat at and abused. He eventually won £700,000 in compensation, eight times the amount Rachel's son Alex was awarded.

Just three months after Colin Stagg had been charged with Rachel Nickell's murder, an intruder broke into the basement flat of Samantha Bisset in Heathfield Terrace, Plumstead, through a patio door that had been left open. Samantha put up a desperate struggle for life as he raped and murdered her in the hallway. There were twenty stab wounds in the body, one so savage that it severed her spinal cord.

The killer then suffocated and sexually assaulted her four-year-old daughter, Jazmine-Jemima, nicknamed J. J., in her cabin bed surrounded by toys. He then set about mutilating Samantha's body in a shockingly similar way to Jack the Ripper in Whitechapel in 1888.

According to the prosecution, the killer "cut open her body from the top of her chest to the genitals. He peeled her skin back and in some areas, in particular the umbilicus, pubic and lower abdomen area, removed the flesh altogether. He pulled away her ribs, causing extensive splitting of the tissue, and once the internal organs were exposed he stabbed them many times . . . Secondly, he cut open the top of her right thigh and attempted to cut off her lower leg at the knee. He cut open her left leg from the hip to the lower thigh with an extensive cut. He eventually left the flat, taking with him a piece of Samantha Bisset's abdomen, presumably as a trophy."

Samantha's body was discovered by her boyfriend who let himself into the flat the following morning. It seems that the killer had been spying on them as they made love the previous evening, as Samantha had been laid out on some cushions in the same position. An experienced female police photographer, who was called to record the scene, was so traumatized by what she saw that she never worked again.

Fingerprints had been left at the scene. They belonged to Robert Napper. He admitted manslaughter due to diminished responsibility. He also pleaded guilty to attempting to rape the two seventeen-year-old girls and the rape of the twenty-two-year-old mother, mentioned earlier. In October 1995, he was detained under the Mental Health Act, on the grounds that he suffered from paranoid schizophrenia and Asperger's syndrome.

Sentencing Napper, Mr Justice Hooper said: "You are suffering from paranoid schizophrenia, characterized by marked thought disorder, paranoia and grandiose delusions. You may have also experienced tactile hallucinations and you feel you can read people's minds. Your mental illness is severe and directly linked to the offences of homicide and rape. You are highly dangerous as a result of that illness. You present a grave and immediate risk to the public. You will require detention in hospital for many years to come."

The officer in charge of the Bisset enquiry, Detective Super-intendent Michael Banks, said at the time that he and colleagues on the Nickell team "liaised closely". But despite the similarity between the two murders, the police continued the prosecution of Colin Stagg as Napper claimed to have been at work on the day that Rachel was killed.

After the Stagg case was thrown out, the police went to see Napper who was, by then, in Broadmoor high-security psychi-atric hospital. But Napper refused to confess to the Nickell murder unless there was some crime scene evidence tying him to the killing.

In 2002, the Rachel Nickell case was reopened as part of a review of cold cases in light of new advances in DNA profiling. A new technique known as Low Copy Numbers allowed a DNA profile to be obtained from much smaller samples. However, when the sample from the Rachel Nickell case was sent to the Forensic Science Service, it was returned with no match – though Napper's profile was then on the national database. It was only when the sample was retested three years later that the link with Napper was finally established.

On 18 December 2008, at the Old Bailey, Napper pleaded guilty to the manslaughter of Rachel Nickell on the grounds of diminished responsibility.

Napper's barrister David Fisher QC said: "He was convinced he had an MA in mathematics, that he had received a Nobel Peace Prize, that he had medals from the time he was fighting in Angola, that he and his family were listed in *Who's Who*, that he had millions of pounds in a bank in Sidcup, that he and others could transmit their thoughts by telepathy. He also believed that he was kneecapped by the IRA and that he had his fingers blown off by an IRA parcel bomb but, because he inhaled sparkle fumes, this resulted in his fingers being miraculously repaired."

Sentencing him to an indefinite stay in Broadmoor, Mr Justice Griffith Williams told Napper: "I am satisfied there are sufficient safeguards in place under the Mental Health Act to ensure you will never be released unless you are no longer a danger to the public. That is highly unlikely to ever happen. You are on any view a very dangerous man. You still present a very high risk of sexual homicide."

Scotland Yard apologized to Colin Stagg and the family of Rachel Nickell for the mistakes it had made during the course of the investigation. The police were criticized particularly for their overreliance on offender profiling. Dr Britton was placed under a charge by the British Psychological Society, but the case was eventually dismissed.

HADDEN CLARK

IT IS NOT known how many people Hadden Clark killed. He boasted of killing numerous young women and burying them in the sand dunes of Cape Cod when he worked there in the 1970s. But he was certainly guilty of murdering and cannibalizing six-year-old Michele Dorr, six-and-a-half years before he was caught for another unrelated murder by a single piece of crime scene evidence.

Divorced psychotherapist Penny Houghteling lived with her daughter Laura in Bethesda, Maryland, in the United States. Laura was gifted and beautiful. She was a student at Harvard and friends called the six-foot blonde Twiggy. One day she was going to be US president, it was said, before Clark killed her during a bizarre torture ritual.

Her mother had made the mistake of employing Clark, a well-known oddball, as a gardener. Penny liked to help the unfortunate and thought she was doing a good deed when she took on a homeless man from a local church organization early in 1992. Clark was a good worker. He tended her flowers and shrubs, and began to depend on Penny emotionally as if she was his mother. His own mother, Flavia, boasted that she could trace her roots back to Plymouth Rock. But both she and his father, though outwardly respectable, were irredeemable alcoholics. Both sides of the family had antecedents who had fought on the winning side in the War of Independence. Hadden's grandfather on his father's side had been the mayor of White Plains, New York.

Hadden's father had a PhD in chemistry as well as an MBA. He had developed a flame-resistant carpet, as well as cling film. Earning good money for his expertise, he moved from job to job in the tri-state area. While the Clarks were thought of highly by their neighbours, behind closed doors they had alcohol-fuelled rows in front of the children. This had a devastating effect. Born in 1950, Hadden's older brother Bradfield had turned to drugs as a teenager. One night in 1984, drink and drugs got the better of him and he killed his date, an attractive twenty-nine-year-old named Patricia Mak. He cut up her body in his bathtub, then barbecued her breasts and ate them. The rest of her remains were packed into plastic bags. He had intended to bury them, but his conscience got the better of him. After a failed suicide attempt, he turned himself into the police and was sentenced to fifteen years to life imprisonment in Pleasant Valley State Prison in California.

The Clarks' youngest child, Alison, ran away as a teenager and eventually broke all ties with her parents.

"I never had a family," she said.

Only Hadden's younger brother, Geoffrey, seemed to hold things together – to start with at least. After graduating from Ohio State University with a degree in microbiology, he married his childhood sweetheart and moved to Maryland, where he worked for the Food and Drug Administration. They lived a cosy suburban existence in Sudbury Road, Silver Spring, before they divorced. Geoffrey's wife accused him of physical abuse before they separated. He was convicted and given a suspended sentence.

Although Bradfield turned out to be a killer, he was not in the same league as Hadden who, from an early age, was deemed to have been "born evil". He enjoyed hurting people, lashing out at anyone who peeved him. Those who crossed him would find the headless corpse of their pet cat or dog deposited on their doorstep.

He maliciously pushed his brother Geoff off his bike while they were practising to ride "no hands", only to rush home to tell his mother that Geoff's bike had not been damaged, making no mention of his brother's injuries.

Hadden's father dismissed him as a "retard", while his mother told him she had wanted a daughter. She dressed him as a girl and called him "Kristen" when she was drunk. The only place he found any stability was when he stayed at his grandparents' retirement home on Cape Cod. Some noticed that he was any-thing but a retard, playing chess to near-genius standards.

When his mother enrolled him for a two-year chef's course at the celebrated Culinary Institute of America, he showed a genuine talent for producing ice sculptures. Even so, he reacted badly against any perceived slight, on one occasion retaliating by urinating in a vat of mashed potatoes. Nevertheless, he graduated as a chef in January 1974. He found employment in prestigious restaurants on Cape Cod. It was there, he claimed later, that he began killing.

His strange behaviour in the kitchen, such as drinking blood, frequently lost him his job. The word spread throughout the restaurant owners of Massachusetts. Unable to find work on shore, Clark went to work on the SS *Norway*, a cruise ship. After a year, he found a job on Long Island, then at Lake Placid, New York, during the 1980 Winter Olympics. By 1982, he had been through fourteen jobs in eight years. Meanwhile, his personal life collapsed. His grandfather died and his grandmother entered a nursing home in poor health, robbing him of his only stability. Then his parents divorced and his father was diagnosed with cancer.

His career on the slide, he enlisted in the US Navy as a below-deck cook. But his shipmates had little time for a man who wore women's panties under his uniform. He was bullied and beaten, and once locked in a meat freezer for three hours. He was moved to other duties, but the bullying did not stop. After suffering concussion from having his head beaten against the deck of an aircraft carrier, he was diagnosed as a paranoid schizophrenic and given a medical discharge. He then turned up on the doorstep of his brother Geoff, who took him in. But Hadden refused to take medicine prescribed to him. He was arrested for stealing women's underwear from a local department store – not for a girlfriend but to wear himself.

"I like my ladies' clothing," he told his mother, who had started him down that road. "Don't try and change me."

Geoff had to ask his brother to leave when Hadden was caught masturbating in front of his nephews and nieces. He moved into a room he rented 5 miles (8 km) from Geoff's house. This did not last. His landlord found him "crazy and evil" and evicted him, but not before he had trashed the house, stealing books, tools and even the vacuum cleaner. He sprayed black dye on the living-room carpet and hid rotting fish heads up the chimney, in the stove and in the family's piano. The smell permeated the house and was almost impossible to eradicate. He left dead cats in the fridge and on the welcome mat, then perched a ten-gallon can on top of a door, so it would spill when the door opened. This led to a conviction for the destruction of property and he was put on probation.

It also led to homelessness and to the job as a minimum-wage gardener with Penny Houghteling. He also worked in a fast-food outlet at night, so he had plenty of money, saving some $40,000 by 1990. His outgoings were minimal. He slept in his Datsun pickup, or set up camp in the woods just off the interstate high-way. But his general condition and behaviour were not quite bad enough to have him committed.

Penny Houghteling had no trouble with him. She trusted him and allowed him to make himself coffee in the kitchen and use the bathroom without permission. She may have been too trust-ing. Things began to go missing. First, it was a string of pearls, then it was her underwear, one piece at a time. She said nothing. But when some tools disappeared, she confronted him. He blew up and she backed down, believing that perhaps she had been too hard on him.

For Hadden, things got worse after Laura graduated from Harvard in the summer of 1992 and returned home. Viewing Penny as the mother he never had, he saw Laura as a rival for her affections. Understandably, Penny was closer to Laura than to Hadden. In Hadden's mind, something had to be done. Then an opportunity presented itself. Penny Houghteling told Hadden that she was going away for a conference from 17 to 25 October. The following day, he went to a hardware store and bought rope and two rolls of duct tape. In the left-corner of the cheque he used for the purchases, where there is a box for a "memo", he wrote the word "Laura".

On Saturday, 17 October, Laura was seen at a horse meet in nearby Middleburg, Virginia. There was a gala dinner afterwards. The following morning, she slept in. Then she went to watch a football game with her older brother, Warren, and his housemate. Laura had taken a temporary job in Washington, DC, while she made up her mind whether to train as a teacher or a lawyer. A big project was starting the following day, so she was in bed just after ten o'clock.

Around eight o'clock the next morning, a housekeeper with a child waiting for the school bus saw a woman she took to be Laura leaving the house. But she did not arrive at work. Her employer phoned the house. There was no reply. Knowing Laura to be a conscientious worker, she was worried and sent a young woman, a personal friend of Laura, around to the house. But no one answered the door and she called Warren.

After he arrived, he searched the house. Then he decided to walk the route Laura took to the bus stop. Along the way, he saw Hadden driving down the street in his pickup and tried to wave him down. Hadden stopped. As Warren walked over to his pick-up to ask Clark whether he knew anything about Laura's whereabouts, the gardener suddenly drove off at high speed. This struck Warren as strange, but he still did not call the police until that night. They told him not to worry.

When the police finally got on the case, they decided they wanted to speak to Hadden Clark. Both Warren and Penny Houghteling gave them a description. But Penny Houghteling dismissed the idea that Hadden had anything to do with the disappearance of her daughter.

"Hadden wouldn't hurt anyone," she said. "He's just a gardener."

In the higher echelons of the Montgomery County Police Department, bells began ringing. Clark had briefly been a suspect in the disappearance of Michele Dorr.

When six-year-old Michele disappeared on 31 May 1986, her father Carl Dorr had been the prime suspect.

"It's page one in the handbook," said Detective Mike Garvey, the first cop to interview Dorr. In 90 per cent of cases where a child disappears, the parent or carer knows what has happened – and Dorr certainly looked like their man.

Although he had degrees in psychology and economics, the economic downturn meant that he could only find employment in menial jobs. By the mid-1980s, he was doing casual work, spraying cars. He had married in 1978, but soon after Michele was born the marriage had descended into domestic warfare. Carl would beat his wife Dorothy in front of the child, who developed a stutter and ground her teeth when she slept.

"She had seen too much for a six-year-old," Dorothy later told the *Washington Post*. She also had damning evidence to give to the police.

Three months before Michele's disappearance, Carl Dorr had turned up at his estranged wife's house and refused to leave. If she tried to divorce him, he said he would lie under oath, saying she was an adulteress and an unfit mother to prevent her having custody of the child. If he lost the custody battle, he would kidnap Michele from the school bus. Then, Dorothy told the police, he hurled her against the wall and slapped her around, leaving her with bruises and cuts. She was sure that he was responsible for the disappearance of Michele, she told the cops. At the time, he was trying to get out of paying $400 a month child support.

After separating from his wife, Carl Dorr had taken lodgings two doors down from Geoffrey Clark in Sudbury Road. On the evening of Friday, 30 May 1986, he picked Michele up from her mother. He bought her a toy in a 7-Eleven. They ate in McDonald's, then went home with a kid's movie from the video store.

The following morning, it was hot – over 90°F (32°C). He filled a small plastic pool in the garden for her and, after promising to take her to a full-sized pool in the neighbourhood, he went inside to watch the Indianapolis 500 on television. During the race, he looked out of the window a couple of times. He could not see Michele and there were no ripples on the pool, but he was not worried. Silver Spring was a safe suburban area and, no doubt, Michele had gone down the street to play with her new friend Eliza Clark, Geoffrey's daughter.

It was not until 5.30 p.m. that Dorr went over to Clark's house. Geoffrey was barbecuing in the back garden. Eliza and the other two children from his first marriage were there, along with Geoffrey's new girlfriend. They had been out all day. There was no sign of Michele and they had not seen her. Dorr walked to the end of the street, then began knocking on doors. Making no progress, he went to the police and reported her missing. They soon arrived and he quickly became their prime suspect. After all, he was the last person to see her; he had been battling over her custody for years and had threatened to abduct her earlier that year.

Dorr agreed to take a polygraph test, but the examiner told the police that he might know more about the disappearance of his daughter than he let on. Indeed, Carl Dorr did have a guilty secret. Not wishing to appear a negligent parent, he had told the cops that the last time he had seen Michele was 2.10 p.m. In fact, he had not seen her since noon.

The police interviewed him for twenty-four hours, playing good cop, bad cop. His daughter was dead, they said, and he had failed a lie-detector test.

"We're going to find her," the cops told him. "When we do, we're coming to get you."

Dorr took another polygraph exam and passed easily. He submitted to hypnosis and took the "truth serum" sodium pentothal. Nothing convinced the cops.

Under the pressure he cracked and became psychotic. Hallucinating, he was taken into hospital for psychiatric observation. In this state, he even told a psychiatrist that he had abducted and killed his daughter. When he was released, the police took him in again for further questioning. The evidence that would have exonerated him was all there on the crime scene, if they had looked. But they had not even located the crime scene yet.

Briefly, there was another suspect in the case. The day after Michele Dorr went missing, Detective Wayne Farrell was driving down Sudbury Road when he saw Hadden Clark tinkering with his truck in the driveway of his brother's house. Thinking he might have found a valuable witness, Farrell asked Hadden whether he had been there yesterday.

Hadden said he had "for about two or three minutes".

Farrell told Mike Garvey, who discovered that Hadden Clark was the neighbourhood oddball. They called him in for questioning. He had punched in at the time clock in the nearby Chevy Chase country club where he worked as a chef at 2.46 p.m. on the afternoon Michele disappeared. Garvey and Farrell had already worked out that it would have been practically impossible for Clark to have abducted and murdered the child, hidden the body and driven the 10 miles (16 km) to the country club in the thirty-six minutes between 2.10 p.m., when Dorr said he had last seen his daughter, and the time Clark arrived at work. But they questioned him anyway.

After going softly on him at first, they began to ask him about the local children and Hadden almost gave himself away. The relationship was antagonistic. One boy had kicked him in the testicles, then he admitted to pinning one little girl to the ground.

"Is that what you did with Michele?" asked Garvey.

The cops produced a photo of her. Hadden refused to look at it. Tears welled in his eyes and he rocked back and forth in his chair.

"Is that what you did with Michele?" asked Garvey again.

"I feel sick," said Clark. "Do you have a bathroom?"

In the washroom, the police could hear Clark vomiting in a cubicle. But they did not let up.

"What did you do?" Garvey shouted. "The parents need to know. Tell me what happened. They need to bury their child. Was it an accident? Let's talk about it."

He even pushed the photo of Michele under the cubicle door.

Clark admitted to having blackouts. He did things, he said, that he did not remember. But he had been at work that day. It would still have been nearly impossible for Clark to have murdered Michele after 2.10 p.m. and been at work at 2.46 p.m. Besides, the police were convinced that the murder had been committed by Carl Dorr, who had unwittingly given his daughter's real killer an unshakeable alibi.

After the Michele Dorr enquiry, Clark came to the attention of the police on several occasions. Visiting his mother, who was then living in Rhode Island, in September 1988, he began stealing from her. When she confronted him, he knocked her down and kicked her, then tried to run her over with his truck. She charged him with assault and battery and he got a year's probation. Afterwards she wrote to him, saying that unless he sought help from a veterans' hospital, as far as she was concerned he was dead.

He did seek help from a local veterans' hospital. He was treated with the anti-psychotic drug Haldol, but left after a few days to return to the woods. It was clear, both to the doctors and to Clark, that he was a danger to others and to himself.

Stopped for speeding in Rhode Island, he was found to be carrying a .38-calibre handgun under his seat. Then there was a conviction for the destruction of property later that year.

In February 1989, he was arrested on fifteen counts of theft. Dressed as a woman, he would visit churches while choir practice was going on, slip into the cloakroom and steal women's possessions. One day, the police found him tinkering with his car on the shoulder of the road. Inside his truck, they found women's coats and handbags. Hadden claimed they were his.

"I am a woman," he said.

He stayed in jail for six weeks before he posted bail. It was February and no time to be sleeping in the woods. Most of the charges were dropped when he agreed to plead guilty on two counts. Again he was sentenced to probation. The judge recognized that Clark had serious mental problems. The public defender was also sympathetic. He wrote Clark a note to hand to the police office the next time he was arrested. It read:

TO ANY POLICE OFFICER:
I want the help of my lawyer, Donald P. Salzman, and I want my lawyer to be present before I answer any questions about my case or any other matters.

I do not wish to speak to anyone concerning any criminal charges pending against me or anyone else, or any criminal investigation regardless of whether I am charged.

I do not want to be in any line-up, or give any handwriting samples, or give any blood, hair, urine, or any other samples unless my lawyer is present.

My lawyer's address and phone number are:

Donald P. Salzman
Assistant Public Defender
Office of the Public Defender
27 Courthouse Square
Rockville, Maryland 20850
(301) 279-1372

To prove that I have read this statement to you or that you have read it, please sign here . . .

Hadden Clark viewed this as a "get out of jail free" card. But when Laura Houghteling went missing it did not work. When Garvey asked Robert Phillips, his boss, whether he should bring in Clark, Phillips exploded.

"Hadden Clark! Absolutely! Let's go!" he yelled. "Let's get him! That son of a bitch got away once!"

The cops called Clark, and got his voicemail, but he called back almost immediately. He said he would come into the police station the following day. Right then he was tired and wanted to go to sleep.

When he turned up, he was accompanied by Sue Snyder, head of the local help-the-homeless group. The night Laura had gone missing, Clark had been asleep in his truck, he said. No one could corroborate this, but there was little evidence against him, so they had to let him go. On their way out of the station Sue Snyder noticed that Hadden was crying and asked him why.

"I feel so bad for Penny and Warren," he said.

With no sign of Laura, the police began a search of the area. A sniffer dog led them to a wood near the Houghteling house that also bordered the church where Clark's truck had been parked the day before. There, the dog found one of Penny Houghteling's bras, a woman's blouse, a high-heeled shoe and a pillowcase from Laura's bed with a single fingerprint in blood on it. An initial test showed that the blood was the same type as that of Laura.

Clark was hauled in again. He complained of harassment.

"I'm just a homeless man," he said. "I don't have any friends. I'll be jobless after this."

But the police were adamant. Michele Dorr's killer still had not been found. They had been easy on Clark the last time. They were not going to make the same mistake again.

"We found the pillowcase in the woods," they told him. "It had a fingerprint on it. The print was yours."

It was a bluff. The fingerprint had not been identified yet. Again tears filled his eyes and he pulled his woollen hat down to hide them.

"What did you do with Laura Houghteling?" he was asked.

His pathetic answer was: "I don't remember."

But they still did not have enough to hold him. They found his campsite and searched it. They examined his bank records and found the cheque that he used in the hardware store with the name "Laura" on it. Then the lab finally identified the bloody fingerprint on the pillowcase as that of Clark. That night they found him asleep in the back of his truck with his arm around a one-eyed teddy bear.

Faced with overwhelming evidence, Clark confessed to second-degree murder and the full horrific tale came out. Around midnight on Sunday, 18 October, Clark had turned up at the Houghteling's house. He was in full drag. Wearing a woman's wig and a trench coat, he could feel Penny Houghteling's lingerie against his skin. Over it, he wore a blouse and slacks.

He went into the garden shed where a spare house key was kept. With it, he opened the door and moved silently towards Laura's bedroom. Once there, he pulled a .22-calibre rifle from under his trench coat and nudged Laura awake with it.

"Why are you in my bed?" he asked. "What are you doing in my bed?"

The startled Laura did not know how to reply.

"Why are you wearing my clothes?" he asked.

She began to cry.

"Tell me I'm Laura," he insisted.

"You're Laura," she said. "Please don't hurt me."

At gunpoint, he forced her to swear on the Bible that he was Laura. Then he made her undress and take a bath. His plan was, he said, to take her to the woods where he would introduce her to Hadden. He made her lie down again while he bound her wrists and ankles with duct tape. He covered her mouth with tape. This excited him so much that he covered her nose and eyes too. Soon after, Laura suffocated.

In an attempt to keep her alive, he tried to cut off the tape, but the scissors slipped and he gashed her neck, covering the sheets and pillowcase with blood. Next, he decided that he wanted her earrings. But he had trouble removing one, so he simply snipped off her earlobe with the scissors. More blood flowed. Then he sat quietly beside her bed, contemplating her naked body for about an hour. He admitted that he stroked her breasts, but did not attempt to rape her corpse or cannibalize it.

It was about three o'clock when he roused himself to wrap her body in the bloody sheet and carry her out to his truck over his shoulder. He went back into the house to gather up any other bloodstained bedding and some of her possessions that he wanted as personal souvenirs. Then he lay down on her bed and slept.

At eight in the morning, he left the house, still in full drag. It was Clark in women's clothing that the housekeeper had mistaken for Laura leaving for work. He then drove to the parking lot of the church where he went to sleep again, this time beside Laura's dead body.

When he awoke, he drove back towards the house to take some more of Laura's personal possessions, but on the way he was seen by Warren. He stopped, but then had second thoughts and sped off. Frightened, Clark decided that he would have to dispose of Laura's body. He had already picked out a spot, just across Highway 270 from his latest campsite. Her body was heavy. He carried it just 20 ft (6 m) from the road, where he dug a shallow grave. Bundling her into it, he covered her with dirt and leaves. It was not enough to protect her from the animals in the wood that would pick up her scent.

He then drove to Rhode Island where he hid the bloody bedding and the mementos he had stolen in a storage locker that he rented. He held on to the pillowcase so that he could bury his face in it to relive the events of the past night. Later, if he wanted a bigger thrill, he could return for the sheets. Then he went back to Maryland and parked in the church's parking lot.

When he received a call from the police, he dumped the bloody pillowcase at the base of a tree nearby. It was this that finally trapped him.

Hadden Clark was sentenced to thirty years for Laura Houghteling's murder in 1993. A few days later, he took the police to recover her body. Her legs and arms had appeared above the surface, forced out of the ground by heavy rain. And her body had been found by scavengers.

In jail, Clark began to boast that he had killed other people. Then he made the mistake of speaking about the murder of Michele Dorr. The story was chilling. Geoffrey's daughter Eliza had called him a "retard", just as his father had done. He was determined to have his revenge, so he returned to his brother's house on the hot afternoon of 31 March only to find everyone was out. He waited in the searing heat. Then along came Michele. Clark did not know her name, but he had seen her around several times and knew that she was a friend of his niece.

"Where's Eliza?" she asked.

"She's in the house," he said. "Upstairs in her room playing with dolls. You can go inside if you like."

He still had a key as he had yet to return to pick up the last boxes of his stuff. Letting Michele into the empty house, he heard her climb the stairs. Then he went back to his pickup where he kept a case of his chef's knives. Selecting a 12 in. (30 cm) blade that had been honed to an edge, he went back inside the house. Upstairs, he threw the little girl on the floor so fast that she had no time to scream. Then he slashed her across the chest in a Z shape. She fell back in shock, but she was not dead yet. When he put his hand over her mouth, she bit him. This was the final straw and he plunged the 12 in. blade through her throat.

Blood gushed all over the floor. Clark then tried to have sex with the six-year-old. When that failed, he wrapped her body in some plastic trash sacks and stuffed it in his old navy bag. Then he began mopping up the blood with rags. Everything with blood on it was stuffed into more trash sacks. Although none of the family spotted any signs of blood when they returned later, the forensic evidence was there to find if the police had ever examined the crime scene.

All the incriminating items were stuffed in the back of his truck and he drove off to work at the country club, which was over twenty minutes away. It was imperative that he was not late that day.

When he finished his shift, Clark drove to the nearby Bethesda Naval Hospital to get the wound on his hand dressed. He was an ex-serviceman, so got free medical help. Leaving at around midnight, he drove towards Baltimore along Old Columbia Pike. When he saw some woods, he pulled over – if the police came by, he would simply say that he was desperate for a pee. Taking a torch, the navy bag and a shovel, he climbed over the guard rail and down a ravine. At the foot of a tree he dug a deep grave and dropped her body in. But before he covered her over, he was overwhelmed with the urge to taste her flesh. That done, he shovelled the soil back into the hole and covered the gravesite with leaves and an old mattress he had found. Then he climbed back up to the road and drove home to the new room he had rented.

Prisoners do not like child killers. Several inmates turned him into the authorities and testified against him at his trial for the murder of Michele Dorr. He was given another thirty years. A further conviction for theft ensured that he would spend the rest of his life in prison.

In January 2000, he led the police to the spot in the woods where he had buried six-year-old Michele Dorr fourteen years before. He then confessed to up to a dozen more murders. On visits to prospective gravesites in Massachusetts, Connecticut, New Jersey and Pennsylvania, he was allowed to wear female clothing and a wig, and was accompanied by his fellow prisoner "Jesus", who bore a striking resemblance to Renaissance portraits of the Messiah.

Twenty years earlier, he told the police, he had killed a young woman on Cape Cod. He had buried her naked body in the sand dunes after first cutting off her hands to hamper identification. But over the years, the dunes have moved and the area has been developed. It is easy to dismiss Clark's claim of killing more hapless victims as the empty boasts of a man who will be confined to prison for the rest of his life. But he had evidence to back his story. A large bucket was recovered from his grandfather's estate. It contained some two hundred pieces of jewellery, taken, he said, from his victims. Some of them belonged to Laura Houghteling. One of them was a silver pin of a wood nymph taken, he said, from his first victim. Hadden Clark claims he was wearing it, pinned to Penny Houghteling's clothing, the night he murdered her daughter Laura.

COT DEATHS

THE PROBLEM WITH cases brought on CSI evidence is that they often rely on the expert witnesses and sometimes the experts can be wrong. One of the experts who has proved very wrong indeed is Professor Sir Samuel Roy Meadow, a British paediatrician whose misinterpretation of the evidence led to a series of miscarriages of justice.

Roy Meadow came to fame when he coined the term "Münchausen syndrome by proxy" in 1977. Sufferers, Meadows maintained in the British medical journal the *Lancet*, harmed those in their care – usually their children – or faked symptoms to get the attention and sympathy of medical staff. He based this theory on two cases: one where a mother, he claimed, had poisoned her child with an excessive amount of salt; another when a mother introduced her own blood into her child's urine sample.

In 1993, he appeared at the trial of Beverly Allitt, a psychiatric nurse who was accused of killing a number of patients in her care. When Allitt was found guilty, Meadow's theory seemed to have been vindicated. He went on to testify as an expert witness at a number of trials involving "cot death", or sudden infant death syndrome (SIDS). Meadow was convinced that in a number of these cases the child had actually been killed by its parents in an extreme example of Münchausen syndrome by proxy.

"There is no evidence that cot death runs in families," he said, "but there is plenty of evidence that child abuse does."

In his 1997 book, *The ABC of Child Abuse*, he went further, endorsing the dictum "one sudden infant death is a tragedy, two is suspicious and three is murder, until proved otherwise". This became known as "Meadow's Law", and a number of entirely innocent women fell foul of it.

In 1999, solicitor Sally Clark was convicted of murdering two of her sons, largely on the evidence of Professor Meadow. Her first son, Christopher, had been born on 22 September 1996. Although seemingly healthy, the child died suddenly at eleven weeks. His death was attributed to a respiratory infection and certified as "natural causes". It was only thought suspicious when Sally's second son, Harry, died after eight weeks. He had been born on 29 November 1997, three weeks premature. He was found dead with his head slumped forward. On both occasions Mrs Clark was at home alone with the child and, in both cases, there was evidence of trauma, which could have been caused by efforts to resuscitate the boys.

Both Mrs Clark and her husband Steve were arrested on 23 February 1998 on suspicion of having murdered their children. On the advice of her lawyer, Mrs Clark remained silent, only denying that she had killed the children. Her husband, who was also a solicitor, supported her throughout and she gave birth to a third son in 1999.

At her trial in Chester Crown Court, evidence was presented that Christopher had a slight cut on the lip and blood in the lungs, indicating that he might have been smothered, and had a bruise on his leg. Harry had injuries to the retina, indicating that he might have been shaken violently, and slight hypoxia – oxygen deficiency in the tissue – caused by suffocation. He also had a fractured rib.

Professor Meadow claimed that he had come across eighty-one cases of cot death that were, in fact, murder, though he had destroyed the data. He also said that the chances of two children suffering a cot death in a well-to-do, non-smoking family was one in seventy-three million. He arrived at the figure simply by multiplying the statistic for a single cot death – one in 8,500 – by itself. It was, he said, like backing an eighty-to-one outsider in the Grand National four years running and winning each time. She was convicted by a ten-to-two majority verdict on 9 November 1999 and sentenced to a mandatory life imprisonment.

Sent to Style women's prison in Wiltshire, then Bullwood Hall in Essex, she was given a hard time by fellow inmates, both as a child killer and because her father had been a senior police officer.

Meadow's double cot-death odds of seventy-three million to one was regularly quoted in the press to justify Clark's incarceration. However, the Royal Statistical Society issued a statement saying there was no mathematical basis for the figure. It was, they said, an example of "a medical expert witness making a serious statistical error". The society's president even wrote to the Lord Chancellor, Britain's leading law officer, expressing his concern.

The figure quoted essentially assumed guilt, rather than weighing the possibility of murder against that of a natural death. It also assumed that the two cot deaths were independent events, excluding the possibility that there may be a cot-death gene, or that the conditions that caused the first cot death might also produce a second. Taking into consideration genetic and environmental factors, it was estimated that the chance of a second cot death occurring in a family that has suffered a first was closer to 200 to one.

However, at the Court of Appeal in 2000, the judge dismissed the argument over statistics as a "sideshow", saying that the odds Meadow had quoted had no significant effect on the jury's decision and Clark's appeal was dismissed. Meadow had been vindicated again and responded to his critics in an article in the *British Medical Journal*, repeating his claim that "both children showed signs of both recent and past abuse".

It then came to light that microbiological tests done on the second child, Harry, had revealed a large population of *staphylococcus aureus*, the bacteria commonly responsible for food poisoning and other infections. This was known to the Home Office pathologist, Dr Alan Williams, but not to the defence, and was only discovered after Steve Clark combed through a thousand pages of medical records that were only handed to the defence team two years after Sally Clark was convicted. These medical records had been unearthed by campaigning lawyer Marilyn Stowe, who had offered her help to Steve Cark for free after she came to believe that Sally was innocent. Steve Clark discovered that a blood test had been performed on Harry that had not been produced at the trial. Stowe forced the records out of the local hospital, then passed them on to forensic experts who concluded that the blood test report proved conclusively that Harry was suffering from a form of meningitis.

Concerns about the statistics also persisted and the Criminal Cases Review Commission referred the case back to the Court of Appeal. Evidence was given by ambulance crew, nurses and hospital doctors that there were not any marks on either baby when they arrived at hospital. Christopher's cut lip could have been caused by attempts to resuscitate him. The blood in his lungs could have been caused by the respiratory infection originally thought to have been the cause of death, or even by a nosebleed he had suffered a week before his death. And the bruise on his leg was caused after death.

Harry's retinal injuries were also found to have been inflicted post-mortem. His broken rib was unexplained, but it was not unknown in young babies and was healing well. And the hypoxia, thought to have been evidence of smothering, was present in all cot deaths to some degree and is part of the dying process.

The motive that the prosecution had given – that Sally Clark was a career woman uncomfortable with the burdens of motherhood – was also called into question. Midwives, health visitors, neighbours, the nanny and Sally's husband all testified that there was a strong bond of love between Mrs Clark and her children. Dr Williams's pathology report was also found to be riddled with inconsistencies.

Sally Clark's second appeal succeeded and she was released in January 2003 having served more than three years. However, the ordeal and the loss of two of her children had taken a heavy toll. She succumbed to alcoholism and died in March 2007.

Despite doubts about Meadow's hypotheses concerning cot death, his testimony helped convict Angela Cannings of the murder of her seven-week-old son, Jason, who died in 1991, and of her eighteen-week-old son, Matthew, who died in 1999. Her first child, Gemma, had also suffered a cot death at the age of thirteen weeks in 1989, though no charges were brought.

No physical evidence of abuse was presented at her trial in 2001. The prosecution rested on what it called the "suspicious behaviour" of Mrs Cannings and Meadow's assertion that she suffered from Münchausen syndrome by proxy. He told the jury that the boys could not have been genuine cot-death victims because they were fit and healthy right up until the time of death. However, other experts maintain that this is typical of SIDS cases. The prosecution had also rejected any genetic explanation, saying that there was no family history of cot death. Meadow again asserted that a double cot death was extremely unlikely, though this time he did not quote figures. The jury convicted Mrs Cannings after nine hours of deliberation.

Professor Meadow was again called as an expert witness in the case against Trupti Patel, a Punjabi-born pharmacist from Berkshire who was accused of murdering three of her children. Her first child was born in 1995, but her second child, a boy named Amar, died unexpectedly at two months. In July 1999, her third child, Jamie, died after fifteen days. Again, a post-mortem revealed no cause of death, but when Mia, a girl, died after twenty-two days in June 2001, she was found to have four broken ribs. Trupti Patel maintained that this had been caused by attempts to resuscitate the child, while Meadow pointed to it as evidence of abuse.

Again the children had undergone several medical examinations shortly before their deaths and had been found to be well. Two key prosecution witnesses who had examined Mia's body disputed Trupti Patel's claim that the fractured ribs were caused by attempts at resuscitation. But at the trial they said that they were no longer sure. Paediatric pathologist Professor Rupert Risdon wrote to the judge saying that he had found evidence of rib fractures caused by resuscitation in three children that he had examined in the previous month alone, and a Home Office pathologist, Nathaniel Carey, said he could "no longer state categorically that the rib fractures were not due to resuscitation".

Meadow's assertion that "in general, sudden and unexpected death does not run in families" also came under attack. The jury heard evidence that Trupti Patel's maternal grandmother lost five children in infancy, but that her remaining seven children were "alive and well". They took ninety minutes to acquit her.

Following the acquittal of Sally Clark and Trupti Patel, the BBC investigated the Angela Cannings case and discovered that her paternal grandmother had lost two children to SIDS and her paternal great-grandmother one. Her appeal was "fast-tracked" and, in January 2004, the original conviction was found to be unsafe.

Professor Meadow was now under attack. Giving his reasons for allowing Angela Cannings's appeal, the Deputy Chief Justice, Lord Justice Judge, described Meadow's theory linking Münchausen syndrome by proxy and cot deaths as a "travesty of justice". A number of other convictions were quickly overturned.

Speaking in the House of Lords, the opposition spokesman for health Lord Howe said that Münchausen syndrome by proxy was "one of the most pernicious and ill-founded theories to have gained currency in childcare and social services in the past ten to fifteen years. It is a theory without science. There is no body of peer-reviewed research to underpin Münchausen syndrome by proxy. It rests instead on the assertions of its inventor. When challenged to produce his research papers to justify his original findings, the inventor of Münchausen syndrome by proxy stated, if you please, that he had destroyed them."

In July 2005, Meadow was struck off by the General Medical Council. Meadow appealed and the High Court reinstated him. This decision was overturned by the Appeal Court, though it was found, by a majority of two to one, that he was not guilty of serious professional misconduct.

Meadow's name was in the press again that year when a paper he had written on "Non-accident Salt Poisoning" was used in the trial of Ian and Angela Gay, who were accused of killing their adopted son Christian by force-feeding him excessive amounts of salt. Other medical experts insisted that the elevated level of salt in the boy's body could have been caused by a form of diabetes. But the couple spent fifteen months in jail before their conviction was quashed.

That is not to say that parents do not harm their children. There was the famous case of Kathleen Megan Marlborough in Australia. At the age of twenty, she married Craig Folbigg and the couple settled in Newcastle, New South Wales. Their first child, Caleb, was born in February 1989. The child had breathing difficulties. One night, Craig was woken by his wife's screams. He found her standing over the crib. The baby was dead. The cause of death was recorded as "Sudden Infant Death Syndrome".

In June 1990, Kathleen had a second son, Patrick. Soon after the baby arrived home, Craig was again woken by his wife's screams. She was standing over Patrick's cot. The child seemed inert, but Craig noticed faint signs of breathing and revived him. After he was rushed to hospital, it was found that Patrick was blind and suffering from epilepsy. In February 1991, he died while Craig was out at work. A post-mortem determined that he had suffocated while suffering an epileptic fit.

The couple moved to Thornton, New South Wales, and Kathleen fell pregnant again. In October 1992, she had a daughter, Sarah. At eleven months, the child caught a cold and had trouble sleeping. That night, Craig was woken by Kathleen's screams. Sarah was dead. According to the death certificate, it was another case of cot death.

The couple moved to Singleton where Kathleen gave birth to Laura in August 1997. At nineteen months, she caught a cold and died. Laura was considered too old to have succumbed to SIDS and, this time, the coroner ordered an investigation.

As the police began their enquiries, Kathleen left Craig. In a bedside drawer, he found her diaries, revealing a woman with enormously conflicting emotions, especially where it came to her children.

"My brain has too much happening, unstored and unrecalled memories just waiting. Heaven help the day they surface and I recall. That will be the day to lock me up and throw away the key. Something I'm sure will happen one day," she wrote on Wednesday, 11 June 1997.

The diary also revealed a terrible secret. In December 1969, Thomas Britton had stabbed his lover Kathleen Donovan to death in the Sydney suburb of Annandale. Britton allegedly told a witness: "I had to kill her because she had killed my child."

At the time, the couple had an eighteen-month-old daughter, also called Kathleen, who was sent to an orphanage before being adopted. Kathleen Marlborough was grown up before she learnt the truth. In her diary, for 14 October 1996 – with three of her children already dead – she wrote: "Obviously, I am my father's daughter."

On 19 April 2001, Kathleen Folbigg was arrested and charged with the murder of her four children. After a four-month trial, she was found guilty of all four murders and sentenced to forty years with a non-parole period of thirty years.

A few weeks after her conviction, Kathleen wrote to the *Sydney Morning Herald*, protesting that she had been convicted merely on circumstantial evidence and attacking her husband for betraying her.

Her appeal against the convictions was dismissed, but her sentence was reduced to thirty years with a non-parole period of twenty-five years. She is kept in protective custody due to the danger of violence from other inmates.

THE PIG FARM

THE PROSECUTION OF Canadian pig farmer Robert William "Willie" Pickton tested crime scene investigation to its limits. Charged with the murder of twenty-six women, he was only tried for the slaying of six. But the court was shown a videotape where Pickton boasted to an undercover policeman posing as a cellmate that he had actually killed forty-nine women.

"I got a murder charge," he said after he was first arrested, "and forty-eight more to come. Whoopee."

But he rued being stopped before he had made it fifty.

"Fifty?" asked the undercover cop, Sergeant Bill Fordy.

"I made my own grave by being sloppy," said Pickton. "Doesn't that kick you in the arse now? I was going to fucking do one more; make it even."

Even then his lust for murder would not be satisfied. He said he intended to let everything die down for a while, and then kill another twenty-five.

During the conversation Sergeant Fordy suggested that throwing corpses in the ocean was the best way to get rid of the evidence.

"I did better than that," said Pickton. "Rendering plant."

He did this so effectively that he created a massive problem for the forensic teams.

It had baffled the police, he bragged.

"They never seen anything like this before," he said, boasting he was "bigger than the Green River".

He was referring to the so-called Green River Killer, Gary Ridgway, who in 2003 had pleaded guilty to the murder of forty-nine prostitutes in Washington State – though he claimed to have killed many more – disposing of their bodies in wooded areas around King County and in the Green River itself.

Pickton was well aware that he was being videotaped. At one

point, he waved at the camera in his cell and said: "Hello!" Nevertheless, in court, he pleaded not guilty on all counts.

In fact, Pickton may well have killed more than the forty-nine he claimed. He was anything but systematic and well organized. He rarely knew the names of his victims, picking them from the hookers and drug addicts who inhabited Vancouver's Downtown Eastside area known as the "Low Track". During Pickton's rampage, at least sixty-five women disappeared from that area alone.

Women had begun to go missing from the Low Track in 1983. By 1997, the police began to fear that more than two dozen had been murdered, though no bodies ever turned up. However, they started to compile a list that would soon include the names of a number of women Pickton was later charged with murdering.

The police already had the first clue to the mystery. In March 1995, a roadside vendor found the right half of a woman's skull in a marshy area outside Mission, British Columbia, just off Highway 7 on a small hill overlooking a creek that runs into the Stave River. The area was searched by a police dog and divers trawled the creek, but nothing more was found. A pathologist, an entomologist and a coroner all examined the skull. None of them could give a reasonable explanation of how the skull got there or who the victim was. In the files she simply became Jane Doe.

Career cop Tim Sleigh was part of the investigation team. Although he was transferred to another detachment in 1996, he remained absorbed by the Jane Doe case. He even bought a house nearby and, from August 1997 to March 2000, walked the area hoping to find a clue that would tell him who she was. She could have been any one of the growing number of women who had gone missing from Downtown Eastside.

By September 1998, an aboriginal group complained that a number of First Nation women had gone missing from the Low Track area and had probably been murdered. They submitted a list. Detective Dave Dickson took an interest and drew up a list of his own. Soon, he had enough names to persuade his superiors to set up a cold-case taskforce. They began with forty cases from all parts of Vancouver dating back to 1971. But in an effort to discover a pattern, they narrowed the roster down to sixteen prostitutes from Low Track who had disappeared since 1995. By the time that Pickton was arrested, the list had grown to fifty-four women.

The taskforce's investigations were given a fresh impetus in March 1999 when Jamie Lee Hamilton, a transsexual and former prostitute who went on to become the director of a drop-in centre for sex-trade workers, called a news conference complaining of the police's lax attitude towards missing prostitutes. The problem was, despite Dickson's growing list of names, they had yet to prove that a serial killer was at work.

That May, Inspector Kim Rossmo began work on the case. He was the pioneer of "geographic profiling", then a new investigative technique. Using a computer system, he mapped unsolved crimes in an attempt to highlight any pattern or criminal signature overlooked by detectives working on individual cases. Most serial criminals, it seems, work around an "anchor point" – their home, workplace or other significant location. Using geographic profiling Rossmo maintained that the approximate location of an offender's home or workplace could be worked out by analysing the spatial patterns of the attacks. In one case, he traced a serial killer to within two-fifths of a mile (0.6 km) of his home.

Rossmo based his technique on research into the way that African lions hunt, believing that it matches the way serial killers work. Lions look for an animal that exhibits some indication of weakness – the old, the very young, the infirm, the vulnerable. They go to a watering hole and wait, knowing it is a draw for their victims.

"We see that all the time with criminal offenders," says Rossmo. "They go to target-rich environments to do their hunting. Spatial patterns are produced by serial killers as they search and attack. The system analyses the geography of these, the victim encounter, the attack, the murder and body dump sites."

However, in the Low Track investigation, his superiors questioned his theory and dismissed his conclusions. Rossmo resigned. Nevertheless, geographic profiling later became a respected technique used worldwide to track serial killers. The problem was that, at the time, Canada's Violent Crime Linkage

System did not track missing persons unless there was some evidence of foul play. In some cases, Dickson's taskforce did not even have a date when the woman had gone missing. Pimps and other prostitutes were reluctant to cooperate with officers who might put them in jail.

On 3 October 1996, twenty-two-year-old drug user and prostitute Tanya Holyk disappeared. Her family feared something had happened to her when she did not come home to see her son, who was about to turn one, after a night out with friends. However, they did not report her missing until 3 November. Pickton was later charged with her murder but, at the time, with no body, there was no murder investigation. It was just another missing-persons case that did not merit much police attention. And there was certainly no reason to connect her disappearance with Robert Pickton, a pig farmer at Port Coquitlam just outside Vancouver, although his name had already become familiar to the local police there.

In 1992, Robert Pickton's younger brother David had been convicted of sexual assault. He had attacked his victim in a trailer on the pig farm, but she had escaped. He was fined $1,000 and given thirty days' probation. Soon after, the two brothers converted one of the farm buildings into what they called the Piggy Palace. Parties were held there under the auspices of the Piggy Palace Good Times Society. This was a non-profit body set up to "organize, coordinate, manage and operate special events, functions, dances, shows and exhibitions on behalf of service organizations, sports organizations and other worthy groups". In fact, it was a drinking club for local bikers and prostitutes were shipped in from the Low Track to provide the entertainment for events that drew as many as 1,800 people. However, the Picktons fell foul of the zoning laws and, after a New Year's Eve party on 31 December 1998, they were served with an injunction banning future parties and the Piggy Palace Good Times Society was stripped of its non-profit status.

By then, Robert Pickton had already been charged with attempted murder. On 23 March 1997, Wendy Lynn Eistetter, a drug addict and prostitute with a wild and reckless past, had agreed to come out to the pig farm in exchange for $100. After they had sex, Pickton came up behind her and slipped a handcuff on her wrist. He then stabbed her repeatedly with a kitchen knife. But she managed to grab the knife and slashed him across the neck and arm, then bolted from the house. At 1.45 the following morning, she was picked up by a couple driving past. She was half naked and covered in blood. The handcuff was still on her wrist and she was carrying the knife.

They took her to a nearby hospital where Pickton also turned up to be treated for his wounds. He was found to be carrying a key that unlocked the handcuffs. His clothes were confiscated. Later they were found to be carrying the DNA of two women he was later charged with killing – twenty-seven-year-old sex worker and drug addict Andrea Fay Borhaven, of no fixed address, who went missing earlier that year, and twenty-five-year-old Cara Louise Ellis who was also last seen in 1997, though not reported missing until October 2002.

For the time being, however, Pickton was released on a $2,000 cash bond with the undertaking that he remained at the farm and did not have any contact with Ms Eistetter.

"You are to abstain completely from the use of alcohol and non-prescription drugs," ordered the judge.

"I don't take them," Pickton replied.

The farm was searched, but nothing untoward was found.

A trial date was set, but the charges were stayed – suspended – because the attorney-general's office decided "there was no likelihood of conviction", despite the grievous wounds Wendy Eistetter had suffered.

This brush with the law did not discourage Pickton. He was later convicted of the murder of twenty-seven-year-old Marnie Lee Frey who was last seen alive in August 1997, though was not reported missing until 4 September 1998. She had a baby at eighteen and asked her parents to adopt the child.

"She said: 'Mom, this is the only thing I can do for her. I love her dearly, but I know I can't look after her as a mom,'" her mother recalled.

Her parents pretended that the child, Brittney, was Marnie's younger sister but, in the light of the publicity surrounding the case, they were forced to tell the truth.

Twenty-three-year-old Jacqueline Michelle McDonnell disappeared in mid-January 1998 and was reported missing on 22 February 1999, and forty-six-year-old Inga Monique Hall was last seen alive in February 1998 and reported missing on 3 March. Pickton was charged with murdering both of them.

Twenty-nine-year-old Sarah Jane deVries was last seen on the corner of Princess and Hastings in Vancouver in the early morning of 14 April 1998 and reported missing by friends later the same day. Ex-boyfriend Wayne Leng said Sarah underwent "a lot of turmoil" in her twenty-nine years, particularly as an adopted child of mixed parentage in an all-white Westside family.

"This started when she was twelve," said her mother Pat. "She has HIV, she has hepatitis C. What I do for her now is look after her kids the best I can."

When Sarah went missing, her children were seven and two.

"It's very hard to tell a seven-year-old that somebody is missing," said Pat. "It's something you can't come to terms with, you can't work through, because there's never an end to it."

Nobody had seen or heard from her since – which was unprecedented as she always called home on her mother's birthday, Mother's Day and her own birthday. But as Sarah herself observed in the diary she left behind: "I think my hate is going to be my destination, my executioner."

Wayne Leng was so concerned about her disappearance that he put up posters, carrying Sarah's picture and details of a $1,000 reward, around Vancouver's Downtown Eastside. But three phone calls he got around midnight one Saturday night left him chilled.

"Sarah's dead," said a man's slightly slurred voice, with music pounding in the background. "So there will be more girls like her dead. There will be more prostitutes killed. There will be one every Friday night. At the busiest time."

The second message had the same voice and the same music playing in the background.

"You'll never find Sarah again," the man said. "So just stop looking for her, all right? She doesn't want to be seen and heard from again, all right? So, bye. She's dead."

The final message said: "This is in regard to Sarah. I just want to let you know that you'll never find her again alive because a friend of mine killed her and I was there."

Leng said the mystery caller knew things about Sarah deVries not known by many others. Pickton was charged with her murder.

Although Pickton had not been prosecuted, the stabbing of Wendy Eistetter had aroused the suspicions of one of his employees, thirty-seven-year-old Bill Hiscox. A relative of Robert Pickton's girlfriend, he worked for a salvage firm that the brothers owned in Surrey, south-east of Vancouver. On several occasions, Hiscox had to drive out to the pig farm to pick up his pay cheques and described it as "a creepy-looking place" that was guarded by a vicious 600 lb (272 kg) boar.

"I never saw a pig like that, who would chase you and bite at you," he told police. "It was running out with the dogs around the property."

Hiscox read a newspaper article about the missing women from the Low Track and put two and two together. He was particularly suspicious of Robert Pickton, who was "a pretty quiet guy" and drove a converted bus with heavily tinted windows. Towards the end of 1998, Hiscox went to the police, saying that Pickton "frequents the downtown area all the time, for girls". To back up his story, he said that the girls' "purses and IDs . . . are out there in his trailer".

Again the police searched the pig farm and found nothing. The Pickton brothers were now "persons of interest", but the farm was not put under surveillance. Meanwhile, the list of missing women grew longer. This was not just because women had continued to vanish from Low Track. Other women who had disappeared earlier were now coming to the attention of the authorities.

Forty-two-year-old Laura Mah was last seen on 1 August 1985, but was not reported missing until 3 August 1999. Mary

Ann Clark – aka Nancy Greek – was twenty-three when she was last seen on the evening of 22 August 1991 in Victoria, the capital of British Columbia on Vancouver Island, across the strait from the city of Vancouver itself. Concerns about Clark's well-being were raised the day after her disappearance because she had failed to return home to look after her two daughters, aged eight years and eight months. This was out of character.

"It was the birthday of her child that day and, for a sex street-worker, she was a bit of a homebody. That's what was suspicious at the start, because she would never have done that," said Victoria policeman Don Bland. However, he expressed doubts that she should be on the Low Track list as she had no connection to Vancouver and only worked the streets of the provincial capital. Nevertheless, Pickton was implicated in her disappearance, although he was never charged.

Forty-two-year-old Cynthia "Cindy" Feliks was last seen on 26 November 1997 and reported missing on 8 January 2001, while Sherry Leigh Irving was last seen in April 1997 and reported missing the following year. Pickton was charged with the murder of both Cynthia Feliks and Sherry Irving.

Native Americans Georgina Faith Papin and Jennifer Lynn Furminger vanished in 1999 along with Wendy Crawford, but did not make the list until March 2000. Pickton was convicted of the murder of Georgina Papin, and charged with the murders of Jennifer Furminger and Wendy Crawford.

Thirty-year-old Brenda Ann Wolfe, who went missing on 1 February 1999, made the list a month later. Tiffany Louise Drew was twenty-seven when she disappeared on 31 December 1999, but she was not reported missing until 8 February 2002. Pickton was convicted of Brenda Wolfe's murder, and charged with that of Tiffany Drew.

Publicity surrounding the list encouraged the reporting of more missing persons. Forty-two-year-old Dawn Teresa Crey was last seen on Main and Hastings on 1 November 2000 and was reported missing on 11 December. Pickton was implicated in her disappearance. Debra Lynn Jones, aged forty-three, disappeared on 21 December 2000 and was reported missing four days later on Christmas Day. Pickton was charged with her murder. Twenty-five-year-old Patricia Rose Johnson went missing from Main and Hastings on 3 March 2001, but took three months to make the list. Heather Kathleen Bottomley, aged twenty-four, made the list the same day she was last seen – 17 April 2001 – even though the police described her as a "violent suicide risk". But it was Tricia Johnson's disappearance that attracted the most attention. Shortly before she disappeared she had been befriended by photographer Lincoln Clarkes, who was recording the lives of the drug-addicted prostitutes of Low Track for his book, *Heroines*. She took time off from her revolving-door hustle for heroin and sex to talk to him about her world – how she had broken her boyfriend's heart, abandoning him and their two young children for heroin and crack cocaine.

Throughout the project Clarkes stayed close to Patricia Johnson, who was his original "heroine". They became friends. She tried to quit drugs for the sake of her kids, but her father's suicide sent her into a tailspin. She quit rehab and was repeatedly arrested for breaking and entering.

The last time Clarkes heard from Johnson was when she left a message on his home answering machine in February 2001.

"Hey, it's Tricia, Lincoln," she said in a sing-song voice. "Trying to get a hold of you, trying to find what's up! I wish I had a number you can call me back at, but I don't. So all I can do is keep trying."

Soon after, she stopped cashing her welfare cheques, stopped phoning her family and even stopped any contact with her two children. Her mother, Marion Bryce, spoke of the terrible warning she had given her daughter who had already survived five years on the streets.

"She was here on New Year's Day," she told reporters, "and I told her: 'Patty, you're not even going to see twenty-five if you keep on – you'll be missing like those women down there.'"

Marion Bryce also contacted Clarkes, who gave her a photo of Patricia with shoulder-length hair, wearing a leather jacket, her lips puffy, burnt by a crack pipe. Later, he brought her another portrait. Followed by a film crew, he was greeted by Bryce and her daughter Kathy.

Days after this blaze of publicity, Patricia Rose Johnson was listed as Missing Woman No. 44. Her last known possessions were recorded as "a book (title not given), a comb, condoms, water, a spoon, cigarettes, a lighter, belt, watch, rings and a chain".

Weeks after Johnson disappeared, the Royal Canadian Mounted Police (RCMP), the federal law enforcement agency, joined the case and promptly assembled a team of investigators. But that did nothing to stem the growth of the list. Six years later, Pickton was charged with the murder of Patricia Rose Johnson and that of Heather Kathleen Bottomley.

Thirty-three-year-old Yvonne Marie Boen, who sometimes used the surname England, was listed only five days after she disappeared on 16 March 2001. Her mother, Lynn Metin, began to worry when her daughter, who had three sons, failed to show up in March 2001 for a visit with her middle son Troy, whom Metin was raising.

"She was supposed to be here that Sunday to pick him up and she didn't show up," Metin told the *Vancouver Sun* in 2004. "She never contacted me. That just wasn't her. Every holiday, Troy's birthday, my birthday – it just wasn't like her not to phone."

Pickton was implicated in her disappearance.

Heather Gabriel Chinnock, age twenty-nine, vanished the following month. Pickton was charge with her murder. Then twenty-two-year-old Andrea Joesbury disappeared on 6 June 2001. Her grandfather Jack Cummer said Andrea was straightening out her life and providing a good home to her infant daughter in an East Vancouver apartment before she disappeared.

"She was working very hard, she needed a lot of things, but she was doing it all herself," Cummer told the *Vancouver Sun*. "Andrea was worn to a frazzle, but the baby was well cared for."

However, he said, social services received a complaint about the well-being of the girl and seized her, which sent his granddaughter into a downward spiral of drugs and prostitution.

"The thing is that she lost her whole reason to live," Cummer said.

The child was adopted and the Cummers were not able to see her. Andrea, he said, either didn't realize or wouldn't accept the finality of the adoption, and would tell her grandparents that she was going to try to get her daughter back.

"She decided that she was going to straighten up and her prime objective was to get the baby back. I didn't have the heart to tell her that she was never going to do that," he said.

Pickton was convicted for Andrea Joesbury's murder.

Twenty-nine-year-old Sereena Abotsway went missing on 1 August 2001. Adopted at the age of four, she had always been in trouble.

"She was sweet and bubbly but she was very disturbed," said her adoptive mother, Anna Draayers. "She gave her teachers a headache and we tried to teach her at home but there was not much you could do. At that time we did not have a name for the condition but it is now known as foetal alcohol syndrome."

The Draayers never lost contact with Sereena.

"She was our girl, and we loved her a lot," they said. "She phoned daily for thirteen years since she left our home at age seventeen."

And hope was at hand.

"She had come home in July," said Mrs Draayers, "and she agreed to come home and celebrate her thirtieth birthday on 20 August, but she never showed up."

Pickton was convicted of her murder.

Diane Rosemary Rock, aged thirty-four, was last seen on 19 October 2001 by the owner of the motel where she was living and was reported missing on 13 December. Diane, her husband and three children moved to British Columbia in 1992 for a fresh start in life. But in their new home, Rock's personal problems resurfaced and she was back using drugs again. After a while her marriage fell apart and she was on her own. The last member of the family to see her was her teenage daughter. That was in June 2001 when they met to celebrate the teenager's birthday. Pickton was charged with Diane Rock's murder.

Mona Lee Wilson, aged twenty-six, disappeared on 23 November 2001 and made the list a week later. She was the last to vanish. Her common-law husband Steve Ricks told reporters he had last seen her get into a car with two men.

"She told me many times she'd like to die," Ricks said. "She was sick of this hell, all the hooking and drugs."

Pickton was charged with her murder.

Then the police got a break. On 7 February 2002, Robert Pickton was arrested for the possession of illegal firearms. Meanwhile, the taskforce began scouring the pig farm once again. Pickton was released on bail, but arrested again on 22 February – this time on two counts of first-degree murder. The victims were identified as Sereena Abotsway and Mona Lee Wilson. On 8 March, it was revealed that DNA recovered from the farm had been conclusively identified as that of Sereena. Both had gone missing since Bill Hiscox had first reported his suspicions to the police.

Now a full-scale CSI investigation was in full swing and forensic experts began combing the pig farm for fingerprints, hair and the blood of the missing women. Now a top man in the RCMP's CSI department, Tim Sleigh, who had tramped the area two years earlier, was on the case and became concerned that the regular power failures caused by the equipment they were using would spoil any evidence contained in the farm's many freezers. He was particularly concerned about an old freezer in the back room of Pickton's workshop that was giving off a sickening smell. Although the crime scene investigation had been going on for two months already, the forensic team had not got around to it yet as a minute search of the slaughterhouse and Pickton's trailer was considered a higher priority.

The freezer's lid was held down by heavy weights, so Sleigh got RMCP Sergeant Fred Hicks to hold it open while he shone a torch inside. The beam picked out two buckets, one on top of the other. When he reached in to investigate, he found that the top bucket contained a human head that had been sawn in two, along with two hands and two feet. They belonged to Andrea

Joesbury. The second bucket contained the matching body parts of Sereena Abotsway.

A pathologist examined them and found that the heads had been sawn in half vertically by two cuts, one at the front and one at the back. When they had not quite met, the skull had been torn apart. Jane Doe's skull had also been cut in two in this unusual manner.

On 5 May 2002, Sleigh was called to the site of the old piggery. This had been attached to the slaughterhouse, but had collapsed some time earlier and was now a pile of rubble and garbage. In the trough on the floor of the old piggery, embedded in manure, was part of a lower jaw with some teeth in it. Using a toothbrush, Sleigh cleaned it off to reveal a filling. This matched the dental records of Brenda Wolfe.

A month later, on 4 June 2002, more garbage pails were found hidden behind some wooden braces between the pigpen and the main wall of the slaughterhouse. The bottom bucket contained the head, hands and feet of Mona Wilson. It was surrounded by other pails containing animal offal. Plainly, Mona Wilson has been butchered in the slaughterhouse like the pigs.

Her head, too, had been sawn in half. When a pathologist drew the cuts on a plastic head, they matched one another – and the half skull of Jane Doe – exactly. They had been sawn through with a reciprocated band saw like the one found in Pickton's slaughterhouse. The pathologist concluded that Andrea Joesbury, Sereena Abotsway and Mona Wilson had been killed by a bullet wound to the head. No bullet damage was found to Jane Doe's skull, but the other half has never been found.

Body parts were found in freezers used to store unsold pig meat. It is not clear whether human flesh was used to make the sausages that Pickton gave away to guests at the Piggy Palace. Investigators also found a wood chipper thought to have been used to turn victims into swill to feed to the pigs – which may explain why the police did not find anything when they first searched the farm in 1997 and again in 1998. The body parts of Andrea Joesbury and Sereena Abotsway had also been exposed to the elements before being returned to the freezer.

There were insects in the buckets in which their remains had been found.

At the beginning of July 2002, officers tore down a raised platform and a low wall by the pigpen. In the ground below was a rat's nest that contained a green toothbrush and fourteen hand bones. One at least appeared to have been hacked at with a knife. Some of them belonged to the left hand of Georgina Papin. None of her other remains or personal effects were ever found.

The task of searching the crime scene became so massive that the taskforce had to hire a hundred anthropology graduates and students. They were employed to search through the soil excavated from sites on the farm. Brienne DeForest-Rusnak was employed to monitor a conveyor belt that carried items sifted from the dirt. On 21 August, she found another partial jaw with three teeth in it. This belonged to Marnie Frey. Like Georgina Papin, none of her other remains or personnel effects were ever found. Both Brenda Wolfe and Marnie Frey's jaws had been sawn in half in a fashion that matched the skulls of Andrea Joesbury, Sereena Abotsway, Mona Wilson and Jane Doe.

Near where Marnie Frey's jaw had been unearthed, a rib bone and a part of a heel were found. DNA from their marrow matched Jane Doe's skull. No more of her was found. Although Sleigh now knew what had become of her, he was still left wondering why half her skull had been found several miles away.

Pickton was charged with the murder of Jane Doe, but the case was disallowed as she could not be identified. However, her remains did feature in the trial. Twenty of the prosecution's ninety-eight witnesses testified that the cuts on her bones resembled those in the six cases that did go ahead. In the end, however, Justice James Williams told the jurors to ignore everything they had heard about the Jane Doe case when it came to their deliberations about the guilt or innocence of Robert Pickton.

The crime scene investigation of the Pickton brothers' two properties in Port Coquitlam – the main farm on Dominion Avenue and the nearby multi-acre lot on Burns Road – continued for twenty months. Throughout it all, Pickton maintained his innocence, even expressing concern, as a taxpayer, at the expense of the investigation. It cost $70 million.

The Dominion Avenue site contained the brothers' farmhouse. In it was David Pickton's bedroom – also known as the "heirloom room" – where the police seized sex toys and lotions. At the Burns Road site, the CSI team focused its search on the building that had formerly housed the Piggy Palace, a smokehouse and other outbuildings, including the unfinished "Willie's House", along with a number of vehicles, including Robert Pickton's "Blue Phantom" bus.

So many items were seized that the police had to warehouse them. Some items had to wait for three or four years before officers got around to examining them thoroughly. Then, if necessary, they had to be sent out to one of the six RCMP labs across Canada.

In all, forensic evidence such as hair, blood, semen and other stains were removed from 235,000 items, creating a total of 600,000 exhibits to be tested. The search was so thorough that, the prosecutor said, even the lint tray from Pickton's clothes dryer was taken away for examination. However, the evidence linking Robert Pickton to the missing women all came from within a hundred metres of his motorhome. These included eleven items carrying Andrea Joesbury's DNA, such as her address book and jewellery, which were largely found in the slaughterhouse and Pickton's blood-smattered trailer; seven objects with Sereena Abotsway's DNA on them, including her shirt and inhaler; some forty objects carrying Mona Wilson's DNA, largely found in Pickton's trailer; and three items with Brenda Wolfe's DNA, including her leather jacket, which was found in Pickton's closet. Five of the sixty-one items linked to the missing women also carried DNA that linked them to Pickton, according to laboratory staff. However, the defence contested this, saying that Pickton was only a "possible contributor". Even a dildo (which Pickton said he used as a silencer for his gun) that carried Mona Wilson's DNA only had a "possible contribution" by Pickton. Mona Wilson's blood was also found soaked into Pickton's mattress.

The defence pointed out that there were at least nine items that linked the missing women to a second DNA person, not Pickton. DNA belonging to Pickton's friend Dinah Taylor was found on Mona Wilson's rosary, Andrea Joesbury's lipstick, and two lipsticks and the leather jacket belonging to Brenda Wolfe. Defence lawyer Marilyn Sandford claimed that the police had concentrated their crime scene investigation on evidence that connected Pickton to the missing women, while ignoring other suspects including Dinah Taylor, Pickton's younger brother David and fellow pig-butcher Pat Casanova, who could not be ruled out as a contributor to a stain on the slaughterhouse door, which was also thought to contain DNA from Mona Wilson.

There was no forensic evidence linking Pickton to the buckets that held the body parts and none of his guns or saws could be shown, conclusively, to have been used in the murders or dismemberments. Nor was it shown that the women's bodies had been dismembered in the method Pickton used when butchering pigs. The Crown maintained that Pickton was a butcher skilled enough to have dismembered the women in that way.

The DNA of people yet to be identified was also present at the crime scene. The DNA of two unknown men were found in the bucket containing the body parts of Andrea Joesbury, while the DNA of three unidentified people were found on the teeth of Joesbury and Sereena Abotsway. Defence lawyer Marilyn Sandford cited over eighty incidents where she maintained that DNA evidence had been contaminated before being sent to the laboratory.

One veteran crime scene investigator found a fingerprint on Pickton's freezer that contained the remains of Andrea Joesbury and Sereena Abotsway but did not match Pickton's prints, yet it was not compared to anyone else's who might have been involved. Head of the investigation Inspector Doug Adam said that the huge task of collecting the evidence had "stressed" the resources of the RCMP – to the point where every white contamination suit in the country was in use at the pig farm. More than 40,000 photographs were taken of the crime scene and testing 600,000 items "very much challenged" the lab system in

Canada. As a result, new robotic systems were brought in to handle the testing procedures very much more quickly than humans could do. However, when Pickton came to trial over six years after the crime scene investigation had begun, some items were still waiting to be tested.

The defence argued that, despite the vast mass of evidence that had been collected, the prosecution had found no smoking gun. The defence even sought to undermine the testimony of Pickton's friend Andrew Bellwood, who said that Pickton had told him that he had sex with women, then murdered them and fed hacked-off body parts to his pigs. Other remains were mixed up with the pigs' entrails and taken to a disposal plant. Pickton told him that he lured his victims out to the farm with the promise of drugs, then would have sex with the women when they were handcuffed and gagged. Finally, he garrotted them with a wire. Bellwood said that Pickton acted out the whole thing for him.

"It was like a play," he said. Nevertheless, he still sat down with Pickton afterwards and enjoyed a dinner of cooked pork.

Drugs were found among Pickton's effects, though he was not a user, and toxicologists identified traces of narcotics in the remains. Syringes full of windscreen-cleaning fluid were found in Pickton's office. He had once boasted of killing intravenous drug users with lethal injections of the substance, suggesting that police informer Scott Chubb use this method to get rid of Wendy Lynn Eistetter. He would pay him $1,000 for the favour.

Paul Casanova admitted that he had been given oral sex by Andrea Joesbury, who had been brought to the farm by Dinah Taylor, but denied any knowledge of her death. He also noticed items of clothing left by other victims. Lynn Ellingsen claimed to have seen Pickton skinning a woman hanging from a meat hook years earlier. She said she did not tell anyone about this out of fear for her life, perhaps understandably.

It took the jury nine days to reach a verdict. In the end they decided that Pickton was guilty of six counts of second-degree murder, but not guilty of six counts of first-degree murder, seemingly on the grounds that he had either not planned the murders or had not acted on his own.

THE PAPER TOWEL

T HE KILLER OF a sixteen-year-old girl was convicted twenty-six years after the crime by a trace of DNA left on a paper towel. On the evening of 30 October 1983, trainee hairdresser Colette Aram set out on the mile-long walk to her boyfriend Russell Godfrey's house in the village of Keyworth in Nottinghamshire, UK. He usually picked her up. Colette refused a lift from her mother, who was baking cakes that evening. The walk should have taken her about twenty minutes.

"She left my house, perfectly happy, a normal sixteen-year-old," said her mother. "She said: 'I will be fine, Mum.' That was it, I never saw her again."

At approximately 8.10 p.m., she turned into Nicker Hill. Witnesses reported hearing a woman's scream at around that time. Then a car drove off at speed. By 10.30 p.m., there were frantic phone calls between the Arams and the Godfreys, and friends and family set out to search the surrounding area. It was not until nine o'clock the next morning that Colette's brother Mark found her naked body in a field near Thurlby, around a mile-and-a-half (2.4 km) from where she had been abducted. She had been sexually assaulted and strangled. Her body had been left in an overtly sexual position.

The police spent months questioning 20,000 people during a house-to-house enquiry of Keyworth and the nearby villages. Some 2,200 statements were taken and 5,300 separate enquiries were made. The case also featured in the BBC's first *Crimewatch* television programme.

The investigation focused on a red Ford Fiesta belonging to the principal of a riding school in Lady Bay. It had been stolen from Adbolton Lane in Holme Pierrepoint at around 4.30 p.m. on the afternoon of the murder. It was seen again three hours later at Willow Brook in Keyworth, near Russell Godfrey's house.

One witness said that the man seen driving the car was carrying a knife.

Soon after Colette's abduction, the red Fiesta turned up outside the Generous Briton pub in the local village of Costock. The landlady, Sylvia Widdowson, said: "Around 9.30 p.m., this chap came in. He was a stranger, and the first thing I noticed was he had blood in the cracks of his fingers and under his fingernails."

Noticing that his hands were drawing attention, the man slipped away from the bar and went into the lavatory to wash his hands. He spent a long time in there. When he came out, he returned to the bar and ordered a pint of orange and lemonade, and a salad sandwich. He told the landlady he had driven up the M1 motorway to visit friends at Barton in Fabis, but they had not been in. But to Mrs Widdowson, the story did not make sense. Costock did not lie on any direct route from Barton in Fabis.

"He wasn't very talkative," she said. "I had to drag conversation out of him."

Mrs Widdowson said the man was clean-shaven. He had a baby face and short hair. Despite numerous witness statements, the man sitting in the Generous Briton pub that night was never traced nor eliminated from enquiries, leading police to believe he was Colette's killer. A police forensic team later took samples from the barroom.

Months later, a letter was sent to police. They believe it came from the killer and it taunted them for not catching him, even saying that he had returned to the village to watch them make their enquiries.

Written in an unusual style in capital letters with all "S"s replaced by exclamation marks, it claimed he had been hiding in a hut watching girls riding horses when he spotted the red Fiesta with the key left in. He claimed that he wore a Halloween mask so that he would not be recognized.

"Masks are common around haloween [sic]. No one knows what I look like. That is why you have not got me. I know I strangled her. I drove around and ended up at Keyworth. I left the key there to fool you and walked back across the fields . . . I go soon and then you will never get me."

Numerous appeals were made. In 1984, police called in language experts to help identify the suspect's accent, a hypnotist to help a key witness recall vital facts and even a medium to talk to Colette's mother.

At the time, twenty-five-year-old Paul Hutchinson lived only seven streets away from the Arams in Keyworth. To allay suspicion, he claimed he had cancer and shaved off his hair to give the impression he was having chemotherapy. Then he moved away. However, he moved back to south Nottinghamshire and led a seemingly normal life. He married twice and had four children. He worked as an electrician and held down jobs as a youth worker, helping children with learning disabilities, and with a local housing association. Later, he set up his own newspaper distribution business.

Soon after the murder, a young policeman named Kevin Flint interviewed Hutchinson as a "person of interest". In 2004, as a detective superintendent and head of homicide at Nottinghamshire police, he took over the enquiry, which was reinvigorated when officers began actively following up leads produced when the case was featured in the twentieth anniversary programme of *Crimewatch*. Over 1,500 suspects had been ruled out, including 800 men whose DNA had been compared to the profile made from a small sample left on a paper towel the suspect had used to dry his hands in the pub. Then, in 2008, Hutchinson's youngest son was arrested for a driving offence. A DNA sample was taken. It was entered on the national database and a match was made.

Hutchinson tried to blame his dead brother but, shortly before his trial, the police managed to find a sample of his brother's DNA and ruled him out. As a result, Hutchinson changed his plea.

According to the prosecutor, "Colette . . . was a sexually inexperienced girl and she sustained a blow to the head. However it may have been caused, it would not have been sufficient to render her unconscious, and she would have been alive and conscious when she was sexually assaulted in the car."

Sentencing Hutchinson to life imprisonment, Mr Justice Flaux described Colette's murder as a "truly horrendous attack".

"The terror and degradation that this poor girl must have suffered at the hands of a stranger in her last few moments are unimaginable," he said. "It's clear from the evidence before the court that you [Hutchinson] are a compulsive liar and fantasist. You have lived your life with your wife and children, who were completely ignorant of who you were."

Hutchinson's DNA had not been found at the scene of any other unsolved crimes, so it appears that he did not kill again.

On 17 October 2010, Hutchinson was found unconscious in a cell in Nottingham prison. Staff could not revive him and he died on his way to hospital.

MURDER IN PERUGIA

CRIME SCENE EVIDENCE played a crucial part in the controversial conviction of the American student Amanda Knox and her Italian boyfriend Raffaele Sollecito for the murder of twenty-one-year-old British exchange student Meredith Kercher in Perugia, Italy, on 1 November 2007.

It was All Saints' Day, a public holiday in Italy, and Meredith went to dinner with some British friends. She walked part of the way home with her friend Sophie Purton, parting company some 500 yards (460 m) from her upstairs flat at Via Pergola 7 at around 8.55 p.m. The Italian students that lived in the apartment below were out of town for the holiday, as were Meredith's Italian flatmates Filomena Romanelli and Laura Mezzetti. Her other flatmate, twenty-one-year-old Amanda Knox, said she was at her boyfriend's place. Knox was supposed to have gone to work that night at Le Chic restaurant-bar but her boss, thirty-eight-year-old Congolese-born musician and bar owner Diya "Patrick" Lumumba, sent her a text message saying that it was quiet and she would not be needed. She responded with a text that read: "OK see you later good evening" in Italian. At 8.45 p.m., a friend called at Sollecito's apartment. Knox answered the door.

At some point during the evening, Meredith Kercher's neighbour Nara Capezzali said she heard a woman's scream and the sound of "at least two people" running on the building's metal staircase. However, doubt was cast on this testimony, as the windows of Capezzali's apartment were double-glazed and too far away to have heard a scream from Kercher's flat. It was later reported that she was deaf and suffered from psychiatric problems.

At 12.07 p.m. the following afternoon, Knox called the mobile phone Meredith used to take calls from the UK. She always carried it, Knox later testified, because she was expecting calls about her mother who was ill back in Britain. Then she called Filomena, saying that she had returned to the apartment to find the front door open and blood in the bathroom. Knox called Filomena twice more, updating her. The window in Filomena's room had been broken and her room had been ransacked.

At 12.47 p.m., Knox called her mother in Seattle who told her to call the police. Knox called the Italian emergency number twice, reporting a break-in and mentioning that she had seen blood. She also said that her flatmate was missing and the door to her room was locked.

By the time the Carabinieri (the army police corps) had responded to these calls, the Italian Polizia postale e delle comunicazioni (Post and Communications Police) had turned up as Kercher's two mobile phones – one for UK calls, one for local calls – had been found in gardens half-a-mile (800 m) away. They found Knox and Sollecito standing outside the flat, saying they were waiting for the Carabinieri. Knox took the officers inside and showed them the broken window, bloodstains in the bathroom and Kercher's locked bedroom door. But the Polizia postale were reluctant to break it down, considering it outside their jurisdiction.

Filomena then turned up with three friends. One of them kicked Kercher's door in. Meredith's near-naked body was found lying on the floor, covered by a blood-soaked duvet. There was blood on the bed, the walls and the floor. The police then ordered everyone out of the flat as it was now a crime scene and forensic teams moved in.

Pathologists put the time of death at between nine and eleven the previous evening. Her body was covered in scratches and bruises. There were forty-three in all. An attempt had been made to strangle her, but she had actually been killed by multiple stab wounds to the throat. One had severed her superior thyroid artery and she died of suffocation due to inhalation of her own blood. The hyoid bone in her neck, which supports the tongue, was broken, indicating that she had been choked before she was stabbed. There were also the marks of three fingers and a thumb on Meredith's neck and knife wounds to her hands made when she tried to defend herself. There were also signs of sexual assault. Her body had been disrobed and moved some time after death. Two credit cards and money were missing.

On 5 November, twenty-four-year-old Sollecito was called to the police station in Perugia for questioning. Knox came, too, explaining later that she did not want to be alone. She sat on his knee and was told by police officer Giacinto Profazio that this was inappropriate behaviour in a murder investigation. He also said that they showed a "strange attitude" after their friend was found with her throat cut. Knox was said to have done the splits and cartwheels while waiting.

Monica Napoleone, head of the Perugia murder squad, said: "She had complained that she was feeling tired and at that stage I told her that she could go if she wanted. She said she wanted to stay; Sollecito was also at the station at the time and she said she wanted to wait for him. A few minutes later I walked past a room at the police station where she was waiting and I saw Amanda doing the splits and a cartwheel . . . She and Sollecito had had a bizarre attitude throughout the whole time – they were laughing, kissing and pulling faces at each other."

Napoleone said that she found their attitude very different from the others who had been brought in for questioning.

"When they were brought in after poor Meredith's body was found, the flatmates and the British friends were very upset," said Napoleone, "but Knox and Sollecito seemed to be more interested in each other. They were very indifferent to the situation and I found it quite disturbing considering that the body of a young girl had been found in such terrible circumstances."

It was later reported that Knox had gone shopping for lingerie with Sollecito the day after Meredith's murder. On the other hand, when one friend, Natalie Hayward, said she hoped Kercher did not suffer, Knox burst out: "What do you think? They cut her throat, Natalie. She fucking bled to death!"

Investigators were also struck by a gesture Knox made repeatedly in front of them over the next few days. "She'd press her hands to her temples and shake her head, as if she was trying to empty her brain of something she'd been through," one of them recalled.

Sollecito told the police he could not say for sure that Knox had stayed at his house on the night of the murder. He had passed the evening smoking marijuana and downloading cartoons on his computer. Knox said he used cocaine and acid. He said that Knox had been there, but she left. He could not remember when or if she came back. Computer experts for the prosecution say that the machine had been used to watch a film from around 6.30 p.m. that evening, but there was no activity on his computer between 9.10 on the evening of the murder and 5.32 the next morning – during the time he said he was downloading cartoons. But expert witnesses for the defence maintained that there were records of activity on his computer during the time he was at the police station, implying that his alibi had been tampered with. Curiously, at 9 p.m. on the night of the murder, both Sollecito and Knox's mobile phones had been switched off, something they did not normally do. Sollecito claimed that he phoned his father that night, but there is no record of the call. Pornography was also found in his apartment.

As Knox was on hand, the police decided to question her, too. Her interrogation began at 11 p.m. By 5.45 a.m., she had told the police that she was in the apartment when Kercher died. She had claimed earlier to have left her apartment at 5 p.m. on Thursday and returned only the next morning when Kercher's body was discovered. Now she said that on the evening of 1 November she met Lumumba at about 9 p.m. after their exchange of texts. She told police they had gone to the apartment.

"I don't remember if my friend Meredith was already there or whether she came later," she said. "What I can say is that they [Meredith and Patrick] went off together."

Apparently, their objective was to "have some fun".

"Patrick wanted her, and he had her," said Knox. "Patrick and Meredith went off together into Meredith's room while I think I stayed in the kitchen. I can't remember how long they were in the bedroom together, I can only say that at a certain point I heard

Meredith screaming and I was so frightened I put my fingers in my ears."

She also claimed she had drunk a lot of alcohol and fallen asleep.

"I'm not sure whether Raffaele was there too that evening but I do remember waking up at his house in his bed and that, in the morning, I went back to where I lived, where I found the door open."

Sollecito continued to claim he was not present on the evening of the murder. In his testimony he said that he had gone into town with Knox.

"I don't remember what we did," he said. "Amanda told me she was going to the Le Chic pub to meet friends."

Around 8.30 or 9 p.m., he had returned home, "smoked a joint", eaten dinner and then spoken to his father on the phone. After surfing the internet for a couple of hours he went to bed. Knox, he said, had returned at around 1 a.m. He said that Knox rose at 10 a.m. the next morning, before leaving to go to the apartment to change her clothes. She returned saying that she had seen blood there. The pair then went to investigate.

As result of Knox's testimony Lumumba was dragged from his home in front of his wife and children. He, Sollecito and Knox were then arrested.

The following morning, Knox wrote a five-page memorandum retracting everything she said: "In regards to this 'confession' that I made last night, I want to make clear that I'm very doubtful of the verity of my statements because they were made under the pressures of stress, shock and extreme exhaustion. Not only was I told I would be arrested and put in jail for thirty years, but I was also hit in the head when I didn't remember a fact correctly. I understand that the police are under a lot of stress, so I understand the treatment I received."

Sollecito had lied, she said. She was with him on the night of the murder.

"On Thursday, 1 November, I saw Meredith the last time at my house when she left around three or four in the afternoon. Raffaele was with me at the time. We, Raffaele and I, stayed at my house for a little while longer and around five in the evening we left to watch the movie *Amélie* at his house. After the movie I received a message from Patrik [*sic*], for whom I work at the pub 'Le Chic'. He told me in this message that it wasn't necessary for me to come into work for the evening because there was no one at my work . . . I told Raffaele that I didn't have to work and that I could remain at home for the evening. After that I believe we relaxed in his room together, perhaps I checked my email. Perhaps I read or studied or perhaps I made love to Raffaele. In fact, I think I did make love with him.

"However, I admit that this period of time is rather strange because I am not quite sure. I smoked marijuana with him and I might even have fallen asleep. These things I am not sure about and I know they are important to the case and to help myself, but in reality, I don't think I did much. One thing I do remember is that I took a shower with Raffaele and this might explain how we passed the time. In truth, I do not remember exactly what day it was, but I do remember that we had a shower and we washed ourselves for a long time. He cleaned my ears, he dried and combed my hair.

"One of the things I am sure that definitely happened the night on which Meredith was murdered was that Raffaele and I ate fairly late, I think around eleven in the evening, although I can't be sure because I didn't look at the clock. After dinner I noticed there was blood on Raffaele's hand, but I was under the impression that it was blood from the fish. After we ate Raffaele washed the dishes but the pipes under his sink broke and water flooded the floor. But because he didn't have a mop I said we could clean it up tomorrow because we (Meredith, Laura, Filomena and I) have a mop at home. I remember it was quite late because we were both very tired (though I can't say the time).

"The next thing I remember was waking up the morning of Friday, 2 November around 10 a.m. and I took a plastic bag to take back my dirty cloths [*sic*] to go back to my house. It was then that I arrived home alone that I found the door to my house was wide open and this all began . . ."

There was no lawyer present during Knox's interrogation and no audio tape was produced. In court, the defence managed to get reports of her verbal confession thrown out as evidence. So her memorandum stands as her account of the events. One lawyer compared Knox to the film's faux-naive heroine of the film *Amélie*, played by Audrey Tautou – had fish for dinner, smoked cannabis and made love.

Later, another piece of Knox's writing came to the attention of the prosecution. It was a short story, entitled "Baby Brother", that she had written for her creative writing class at the University of Washington in Seattle. It told of one young woman who had drugged and raped another young woman. One passage read: "She fell on the floor, she felt the blood on her mouth and swallowed it. She couldn't move her jaw and felt as if someone was moving a razor on the left side of her face." This could, perhaps, be dismissed as the product of an overactive imagination.

Patrick Lumumba was held for two weeks before being released due to lack of evidence. Witnesses testified that he was working at Le Chic on the night of the murder. Till receipts bore this out. Nevertheless, he lost Le Chic, which was closed as part of the investigation. It remained closed even after he was released and the business collapsed. For recompense he filed a $740,000 civil suit against Knox for defamation. Lumumba claimed that Knox had named him out of "revenge" because he had sacked her from his bar, where she worked on two evenings a week, for hitting on the customers. He said that he had offered the job to Meredith Kercher instead, and Knox had been jealous.

"She wanted to be the queen bee," he said. "She hated anyone stealing her limelight."

While it was true that there was some friction between Knox and Kercher over the sexual and hygienic habits of the American – symbolized by the "Rampant Rabbit" vibrator Knox kept in a transparent beauty case in their shared bathroom – witnesses said that the two girls got on. But Lumumba described Knox as irrational, vengeful and insanely jealous.

"I don't think she's evil," he said. "To be evil, you have to have a soul. Amanda doesn't. She's empty; dead inside. She's the ultimate actress, able to switch her emotions on and off in an instant."

In the end he said he had to sack her for excessive flirting with the customers and replace her with Kercher who was, he said, a "natural charmer". That is why Knox framed him.

"She was angry and wanted revenge," he said. "By the end, she hated me."

Others who knew Knox also said she was a "woman hater", possibly as the result of her mother having a string of affairs while she was growing up.

Sollecito said that Knox had "an almost non-existent contact with reality". In a letter from prison to his father, he wrote: "She lived life like a dream, reality didn't enter. Her only goal was the search for pleasure at all times."

He continues to deny any involvement in Kercher's murder, and believes that Knox is innocent, too, writing that even the thought that his girlfriend could be involved is "impossible".

Meanwhile, the police denied mistreating Knox.

"She was not hit or insulted at any point and . . . she was even taken for breakfast in the morning," said Napoleone. "She was given water, chamomile tea and breakfast as well, she was given cakes from a vending machine and then taken to the canteen at the police station for something to eat."

Knox has been charged with slandering the police in a case that will be tried separately.

However, blood and "organic substances" found on tissues recovered from Meredith's bedroom and the street outside matched none of those already in custody. A fourth suspect was sought. This turned out to be Rudy Guede, a drug dealer from the Côte d'Ivoire. He was the only one who admitted being at the apartment with Meredith on the night of the murder. Guede said he had sex with Meredith but insisted that he was not her "real killer". On the night of her murder he was seen in a local disco, then he fled and was eventually captured in Germany. Guede told the German police that he met Meredith shortly after 8.30 on the evening of the murder at her apartment and

had consensual sex. An Italian man he did not know had followed them and killed her while he was in the bathroom.

Later he told his lawyers that he had not had sex with
Meredith. His story was that they had met the night before at a
Halloween party, but the people with her said they had not seen
the pair talk. He maintained that they had arranged a "romantic"
date. She had invited him around for a drink and he had come to
the apartment to wait for her. When she turned up, she had
"flirted" with him but said they could not have sex as he did not
have a condom. Then he went to the bathroom because he had
eaten a "spicy kebab" that had given him stomach pains.

He said he failed to hear an intruder come into the house
because he had iPod earphones in his ears playing at full volume.
He had listened to three songs while in the bathroom, which
would have taken about twelve minutes. It was only at the end of
the third song had he heard Meredith scream. He emerged from
the bathroom to find a man "with brown hair and shorter than
me" holding a knife. Her throat had been slashed "by an Italian
lad with chestnut hair. We knocked into each other, I was also
injured, but I cannot remember clearly the face of that man".

They briefly fought, and Guede said he suffered a cut to the
palm of his right hand while trying to "protect himself". The
assailant then uttered "racist" insults as he left, saying in Italian:
"Trovato negro, trovato colpevole; andiamò" – "Found black man,
found guilty; let's go." Guede also said the man was accompanied by a woman whose voice he heard but whose face he
could not see.

"Then I ran away, I was scared," he said. "I am not the one
who killed her."

Guede also claimed that his efforts to save Meredith failed,
but he heard her dying words, which were either the initials
"A. F." or the sound "af". This has been interpreted as an
attempt to implicate Raffaele Sollecito. In court, he claimed that
it was Knox's voice he had heard arguing with Kercher in the
bedroom over some money that had gone missing. He also said
that when he glanced out of the window, he saw the silhouette of
Knox leaving the house.

Guede was tried separately because he had agreed to a fast-track trial where he exchanged his right to test the evidence for a more lenient sentence if he was found guilty. Certainly the crime scene evidence was stacked up again him.

DNA matching Guede's was found both on and in Meredith's body, and on her tampon. More was found on her blouse and bra, and in sweat left on her handbag. Inside there were traces of blood adding to the theory that theft was the motive. Meredith had withdrawn €200 to pay her rent just days before the murder. The money has not been found. She had also checked her bank balance online via her mobile phone on the night she died.

"The theory we are working on is that the killer rifled through Meredith's bag and took her rent money," said the police.

A bloody handprint matching Guede's was found on a pillow under the body and more DNA was found on a piece of toilet paper at the scene. His fingerprints were all over Kercher's bedroom and there were even pieces of his hair clenched in the dead girl's hands. The police said their tests showed that Meredith had not had "consensual sex" with Guede as he claimed, but had probably been held down. There was also evidence of an attempt to hide her body in a cupboard.

A witness has told police that a "coloured man" running from the direction of the house at about 10.30 p.m. barged so violently into her boyfriend that he nearly knocked him over. The police in Perugia painted Guede as a misfit who was "obsessed with foreign girls". He was recently involved in a stabbing incident in Perugia's main square, where students and local youngsters smoke cannabis and drink late at night.

The CSI evidence alone was enough to convict him for the sexual assault and murder of Meredith Kercher. He was sentenced to thirty years. The court of appeal upheld the verdict, but reduced his sentence to sixteen years as he was the only one of three people accused who offered their apologies to the Kercher family. A second appeal confirmed the verdict and the sentence.

The crime scene evidence in the prosecution of Knox and Sollecito was hotly disputed. Firstly, the experts who examined

Meredith's body maintained that she had been killed by more than one person due to the location and extent of her injuries. It was then said that she did not fight back as no skin or hair was found under her fingernails.

According to the lead prosecutor Giuliano Mignini, there was a deep hatred between Kercher and Knox because of Kercher's criticism of Knox's sexual promiscuity. Knox's diary listed seven sexual partners, four of whom she had slept with since arriving in Italy – including one she had had sex with on the train to Perugia. A great deal was made of the fact that she called herself "Foxy Knoxy" on her MySpace page, though the nickname came from her prowess on the soccer field rather than her activities in the bedroom.

Kercher, who was reading politics and language at Leeds University, introduced Knox, a gifted, Jesuit-educated student from Seattle, to her English friends. She showed her where to shop and they visited a chocolate festival together. But the relationship soon turned sour. According to friends, Meredith grew more and more exasperated by Knox's behaviour – she failed to flush the lavatory, kept strumming the same chord on her guitar and brought "strange men" to the apartment. According to the prosecution, it was Knox's sex life that really drove a wedge between the women.

Using blood-splatter analysis and other forensic techniques, Mignini pieced together what happened on the night of the murder. According to his reconstruction, shortly after Kercher arrived home, Knox turned up with Sollecito and Guede, who was strongly attracted to Knox. Mignini believes that Knox and Kercher then started rowing – either because Kercher was looking for some missing money or was annoyed by Knox bringing Sollecito and Guede to the flat. The row soon escalated. Mignini contends that Knox, Sollecito and Guede, "under the influence of drugs and maybe of alcohol, decided in any case to involve Kercher in a heavy sex game". The two young men took part "to please Knox, because they were competing to please her".

Mignini said that Knox grabbed Kercher by the throat and flung her against the cupboard in her bedroom. She then threatened her with a kitchen knife, while Sollecito grabbed Kercher's hair. Kercher fell between the bed and the cupboard and her jeans were pulled off. Forensic evidence indicated that Guede groped her and Mignini said that Sollecito produced a second knife and ripped off Kercher's bra.

Realizing that the violence was unstoppable, Kercher gave a desperate scream – a cry that was heard by Nara Capezzali, an elderly neighbour. To shut her up, Knox then stabbed Kercher, inflicting the deepest of three wounds to her neck.

As Kercher lay dying in agony – the autopsy found that it took her several minutes to die as she drowned in her own blood – Knox and Sollecito fled. Guede stayed and tried to stop the blood coming out of Kercher's neck with a couple of towels. He, too, then fled.

Professor Gianaristide Norelli testified that the multiple lesions on Meredith Kercher's body were consistent with being held and attacked by more than one person, and interpreted her stab wounds as having been inflicted as threats during a struggle. The wounds, mostly on the side of her neck, were possibly inflicted by two different knives, he said, but noted that one of the stab wounds was compatible with the alleged murder weapon.

The most potentially damning piece of crime scene evidence was the kitchen knife with a $6^1/_2$ in. blade (16.5 cm) found in Sollecito's apartment. This was the so-called "double DNA knife". Tests showed that it had Knox's DNA on the handle, which could have been left there when she had used it to cook. However, according to Italian forensic police expert Patrizia Stefanoni, Kercher's DNA was found in a groove on the blade. Witnesses for the defence conceded that the knife is compatible with at least one of the three wounds on Kercher's neck, but it was too large to have produced the other two. What's more, it did not match a knife print in blood that was left on Meredith's white bedsheet. More troubling for the prosecution was that, while the DNA on the handle was inarguably Knox's, the spot on the blade they attributed to Kercher was so small that Stefanoni could not double-test it as required by standard forensic protocols. She did not test it in front of the defence experts, although they had been offered the opportunity to attend. All the genetic material was used up in the test, so it cannot be repeated. Reviewing the evidence, two experts rejected the work of the police, saying "on that knife there was never enough to get biological material to get DNA profiles".

If Knox and Sollecito used this knife to kill Meredith, as the prosecution contended, why would they take it back to Sollecito's apartment and put it in a drawer with the regular utensils to be used for cooking. Testifying at the trial, an officer said he used "police intuition" when he picked out that knife from Sollecito's cutlery.

Officers testified that there was a strong smell of bleach in the apartment and that the knife looked exceptionally clean. Stefanoni testified that it had tiny scratches on the blade, compatible with intense scrubbing. However, no traces of bleach were found on the knife, so it had not been cleaned in the way police forensics experts said.

No DNA belonging to Knox was found in the room where Meredith had been killed. Both Knox's and Meredith's DNA was found in the bathroom they shared, as would be expected. Some was commingled in Meredith's blood, though. With the aid of Luminol – a white crystalline compound used in crime scene investigations that glows blue when it comes into contact with traces of blood even after it has been cleaned up – a spot of blood was found in Filomena Romanelli's bedroom. The prosecution maintained that Meredith was murdered when she refused to participate in a sado-masochistic sex game and the break-in was faked afterwards by Knox and Sollecito to cover up the crime. The window was broken from the outside with a large rock. This would have been a peculiar way to break into the house, according to Officer Profazio.

"I thought it strange as it would have needed a superhuman effort to climb up to it," he said. "There was a much easier way in at the back, via a terrace and a boiler [room]. There was a chair and table on the terrace and it would have been a lot easier to get in this way."

Filomena's room was ransacked, but nothing was taken – even though jewellery and expensive sunglasses were left in plain sight. A laptop, a video-camera and other valuables had not been stolen from the house.

"They were all items that would have been taken in a break-in," said Inspector Michele Battistelli of the Polizia postale.

Filomena testified that when she had first seen her room, she had thought: "What a stupid burglar." Clothes had been pulled from the draws of the dresser. Shards of glass were found on top of them, leading investigators to conclude that the window had been broken after the room had been ransacked, not before.

"Straightaway I thought it was an attempt to make it look like a burglary," said Inspector Battistelli. The defence did not counter this theory.

Another four spots of Kercher's blood mixed with Knox's DNA were found in the bathroom the women shared – on the sink, the bidet and on the side of a Q-tip box. Prosecutors argued that Knox washed Meredith's blood from her hands in the bathroom. But all this could be explained innocently enough and the defence did not contest any of the lab results, except to say that it is common to find mixed DNA from two people who shared a house. There were other reasons that Knox could have been bleeding. Originally she told police that her pierced ears were infected and her mother, Edda Mellas, told *Newsweek* magazine that she had been menstruating – though neither scenario was presented to the jury. Knox's supporters suggest that Meredith's blood had been dropped by Guede on a spot where Knox's dried blood or DNA already existed, even though Guede's DNA profile was not identified in any of the five spots.

No fingerprints from Knox were found in Meredith's bedroom. In fact, only one was found in the entire apartment – on a drinking glass in the kitchen sink. The lack of any witness or forensic evidence that placed Knox at the murder scene should have exonerated her. However, there were nineteen fingerprints in Meredith's room that had been smeared or were otherwise identifiable. They could have been those of Knox or Sollecito.

Luminol revealed Knox's footprint in the corridor outside Meredith's room. But, again, this is hardly damning evidence. Luminol reveals prints left in bleach and some acidic juices as well as blood. Knox also testified that when she came home, she had taken a shower, then seen the blood on the floor, so she might have trailed it unknowingly. However, this also invited the question: if she came home to find the front door open, why did she take a shower before investigating further?

A bloody footprint was found on the mat in one of the bathrooms. This was said to be "absolutely compatible" with Sollecito's foot by a forensic scientist testifying for the prosecution. An expert for the defence countered that it also matched Guede's foot. But experts for both sides agreed that the print was not a positive identification because it lacked the swirls of a toeprint that could be matched to a specific individual.

More bloody footprints were found in Meredith's bedroom, attributed to Sollecito by the prosecution. The defence said it belonged to Guede. A bloody footprint from a smaller shoe was found on a pillow beneath Meredith's head.

"A woman's shoeprint was found in Meredith's room, of a size ranging from 36 to 38, on a pillow placed under the body," said Monica Napoleoni, the head of Perugia's murder squad. "Amanda Knox wears 37."

Police forensic experts told her that the print came from a woman's shoe because of its shape and small size. But it has never been matched to any footwear owned by Knox. It could not be positively identified to any of the suspects and investigators do not know to whom the shoe belonged.

A fragment of Kercher's bra clasp is the strongest piece of evidence that links Sollecito to the murder. A small piece of the bra, with the hook on it, fell off when the bra was cut from Kercher's body by her assailant. Sollecito's DNA was found on the metal hook, at the very least placing him in the room, the prosecution contended. Or would have done if the crime scene evidence had been treated properly.

The clasp was identified and photographed when the forensic experts first examined the crime scene, but it was not collected as evidence until the third visit to the house nearly six weeks later when investigators realized it was missing. The house had been turned upside down in a police search in the meantime. Videos show that the clasp had been moved more than a metre from its original location and Sollecito's lawyers argued that the crime scene had been contaminated. The tiny clasp had picked up Sollecito's DNA in the mess, they say.

"How can you touch the hook without touching the cloth?" asked Sollecito's defence attorney.

However, the prosecution says that the apartment was sealed the entire time and contamination was impossible as DNA does not fly around the room. The only other DNA belonging to Sollecito found in the apartment was on a cigarette butt in another room. But forensic specialists have testified that the investigators did not change gloves between taking samples and made other grave errors in collecting evidence. And the defence contended that there were significant shortcomings in the lab work.

The bra clasp is the only evidence that places Sollecito in the room where Meredith was murdered, and not a single trace was found that puts Knox in the room – no fingerprints, no identifiable footprint nor DNA.

The only witness who put Knox and Sollecito anywhere near the murder scene was a homeless man named Antonio Curatolo, who slept on a bench outside the University for Foreigners in the Piazza Grimana. Curatolo, who has been a key witness in two other high-profile murder cases, said he saw Knox and Sollecito in an animated argument in the Piazza Grimana between 9.30 and 11.30 that night. He tied his memory to the presence of the shuttle buses that carry young people to the various discos outside of Perugia. However, it was pointed out that, on All Saints' Day, the discos were closed. Curatolo had been accompanied into the courtroom by prison guards. He was serving an eighteen-month sentence for selling cocaine.

With little firm evidence to rely on, the prosecution have also seen their theory called into question. They maintained that during a four-way sex game, Knox, Sollecito and Guede forced Meredith Kercher to submit to sex. They pushed her on to her knees and threatened her, then killed her. But Knox only knew Guede casually. Sollecito did not know him at all. Indeed, up to that point, Sollecito had only known Knox for six days. Would three people who barely knew each other conspire to commit a brutal, sexually motivated murder? Or did Rudy Guede, a known drug dealer and suspected thief, rape and murder Meredith on his own? While on the run in Germany, he made a call from an internet café via Skype, telling a friend that Knox had not been in the house at the time. He had spoken to Knox by mobile phone several times both before and after the murder. It was months after his arrest that he came up with the story about Knox and Kercher arguing over the rent and seeing a man who could have been Sollecito running from the house. And he refused to testify for the prosecution at the trial of Knox and Sollecito, though it would almost certainly have resulted in a reduction in his sentence.

Nevertheless, both Knox and Sollecito were found guilty of sexual assault, murder and other related crimes. Knox was sentenced to twenty-six years in prison; Sollecito to twenty-five. The verdict was unanimous. According to the judge, the court had determined that Knox and Sollecito had helped Guede subdue Kercher after she resisted his sexual advances. It was noted that Knox and Sollecito had smoked hashish and been reading sexually explicit and violent comics collected by Sollecito. These were alleged to have influenced their behaviour. The court ruled Knox and Sollecito acted without premeditation, and that they exhibited no particular malice against Meredith that motivated their crime.

The judges concluded that Knox and Sollecito had stabbed Kercher in the neck using two different knives, one of which had not been found. The bloody footprint found on a bathroom mat was made by Sollecito, the court stated, while the unidentified footprint in a bedroom had been made by Knox. Knox and Sollecito had then staged the apparent break-in at the house to make it appear that Kercher had been killed by an intruder. Knox had further attempted to shift the blame by falsely blaming Patrick Lumumba.

Plainly, the case was not going to end there and, in the run-up to an appeal, the crime scene evidence was examined again. The veracity of the "double DNA knife" was further undermined when two US experts wrote to the court expressing their concern. In the case of the knife, the letter says, contamination from other DNA present in the lab that did the analysis cannot be ruled out.

The technique used to examine the knife was standard at the time. A small sample of DNA is amplified by a polymerase chain reaction to create thousands of copies of the original segment. Then resulting segments are analysed using electrophoresis. A graph is produced that consists of a series of peaks whose heights represent how much of certain DNA snippets are present. Displayed on X-ray film, these peaks create a DNA "fingerprint" unique to an individual.

To minimize the risk of including peaks arising from contamination, most US labs only count peaks above a threshold of 150 relative fluorescence units (RFUs) and dismiss all those below fifty. According to Greg Hampikian of Boise State University in Idaho, who reviewed the DNA evidence, most of the peaks on the knife fell below fifty RFUs. This means contamination cannot be ruled out, the letter from the experts said. As the same lab may also have been running DNA profiles from other evidence in the case at the same time, tiny amounts of this could have contaminated the knife samples.

Significantly, no blood was found on the knife and it is thought unlikely that all chemically detectable traces of blood could be removed from the knife while leaving sufficient cells to produce a DNA profile.

"No credible scientific evidence has been presented to associate this kitchen knife with the murder of Meredith Kercher," the letter stated.

It went on to say that the evidence from the clasp is equally inconclusive. A mixture of different people's DNA was found on it, including, possibly, that of Sollecito. However, as Sollecito had visited the women's apartment several times before the murder, his DNA could have made its way on to the clasp "through several innocent means", the letter said.

Neither Knox's nor Sollecito's DNA was found on the rest of the bra, other items of Kercher's clothing, objects taken from Meredith's room or in samples from her body, the letter pointed out, although Guede's DNA was found everywhere.

The prosecution's star witness, Curatolo, plainly got his days mixed up. He later admitted he had seen the couple on the night of Halloween, as people were wearing masks. That was the night before the murder. However, he was also in the Piazza Grimana the day after the murder.

"Police and Carabinieri were coming and going, and I also saw the 'extraterrestrials', that would be the men in white overalls," Curatolo said. "I am really certain, just as certain as I am sitting here, that I saw those two youngsters the night before the men in white outfits."

According to Francesco Maresca, a lawyer representing the Kercher family, this supports his original story.

"What is key is that he is sure he saw them the night before the police came and that it was not raining," said Maresca. "It rained on the thirty-first but not on the first."

It seems in the Kercher case there was no smoking gun. But Knox did herself no favours in court. She failed to observe the strict decorum that Italians expect in the courtroom. She walked in like a beauty queen, pandering to the cameras and sometimes answered journalists' questions with a coy smile. On Valentine's Day, she also wore a "Let It Be" T-shirt and was seen winking at Sollecito and passing around chocolates. At times, she even lay her head down on the defence table. This was widely reported in the Italian press. The jury is not sequestered, so members were free to read about the case and were almost certainly exposed to stinging criticism of her conduct.

But when the jury delivered its guilty verdict after twelve hours of deliberation, Knox bowed her head and wept noiselessly, burying her head in her lawyer's chest. Then, as she was being led from the courtroom by armed guards, she cried: "No, no, no!"

At the appeal, she was far more serious and delivered a passionate speech to the jury.

"I am not the person the accusers say I am," she said. "They say I am dangerous, devilish, jealous, uncaring and violent. Their theories depend on this, but I was never that girl. People who know me can talk of my real past, not that which is recounted by the tabloids . . . I have seen justice fail me. The truth is not yet recognized and we are paying with our lives for a crime we did not commit . . . We deserve freedom like anyone here in this courtroom. I am innocent, Raffaele is innocent. We did not kill Meredith. Please believe that there has been an enormous mistake. There will be no justice for Meredith and her loved ones by taking our lives from us and making us pay for something we did not do."

Speaking Italian in a shaking voice and frequently comforted by her lawyers, Knox broke down as she claimed she was "honoured and grateful" to have known Meredith. Kercher's father had complained that his daughter had been forgotten while Knox was becoming "a celebrity". Knox attacked the issue head on, telling the court: "I want to say sorry to Meredith's family that she is no longer there . . . I can never know how you feel, but I have little sisters and the idea of their suffering and loss terrifies me."

On 3 October 2011, the appeal court in Perugia overturned the verdict against Amanda Knox and Raffaele Sollecito, and they were released.

LINDSAY HAWKER

TWENTY-TWO-YEAR-OLD Lindsay Hawker was taking a year off between graduating with a first-class honours degree in biology from Leeds University and beginning her Masters when she moved to Japan in October 2006 to teach English in the Koiwa International Language School in Tokyo. She shared a flat in the Funabashi area with two other female English teachers, one Canadian, the other Australian. Soon, she found she had a stalker.

On 20 March 2007, twenty-eight-year-old Tatsuya Ichihashi spotted her hanging out with friends in the Hippy Dippy Doo, an English pub in Chiba Gyotoku. She was a tall, good-looking Western girl, much beloved by Japanese men. He tailed her as she got on the train home, where he approached her. She related the incident by email to her boyfriend, BBC researcher Ryan Garside, back in Britain. Ichihashi had claimed that she was his English teacher, though she was not. But she did admit to being an English teacher, then set off home on her bicycle.

Ichihashi was obsessed with physical fitness. He attended the gym regularly and cycled 15 miles (25 km) a day. As Lindsay cycled home, he set off after her on foot. He kept up and, when they arrived at her doorstep, he said: "Do you remember me?"

He then asked for a glass of water. Lindsay felt sorry for Ichihashi and invited him in so that he could see she was living with two flatmates. Once inside, Ichihashi took out a felt-tipped pen and paper and drew a picture of her, signed it and added his telephone number and email address.

Later she emailed her boyfriend: "Love u lots – don't worry abt the guy who chased me home, its jus crazy Japan miss u xxxx."

Lindsay agreed to meet Ichihashi in a café five days later to give him an English lesson. The Nova Organization, who ran the Koiwa International Language School as part of a chain of language schools across Japan, allowed its teachers to give private lessons, but advised them to do so only in public places and always to leave a note of where they were going and who they were going to meet. Lindsay had given a private lesson before and was friendly with her students, talking with them in nearby cafés after school. Besides, she needed the extra money to pay for her flight home.

However, she left the café with Ichihashi and went with him by taxi to his apartment in the eastern suburb of Ichikawa. CCTV caught them getting out of the cab at around 10 a.m. on Sunday, 25 March 2005. Her father, Bill Hawker, said she appeared to be drugged, but no drugs were found in her body. It is not known how Ichihashi had persuaded her to come back to his apartment. The couple was also caught on CCTV in the Doutour café near Gyotoku station. After fifty minutes, Ichihashi was seen fumbling for money to pay for the coffees. Perhaps he said that he had left the fee for his English lesson behind in his flat. Her father thinks that he might have learnt of her ambition to become a GP and offered to introduce her to his father, who was a medical man. They also had a shared interest in botany.

She told the cab driver to wait. They would only be a minute. When she did not reappear after seven minutes, the cab driver took off on another job.

Just twenty minutes before Lindsay got out of the cab, a powerful earthquake hit Japan. Lindsay's mother Julia emailed to check that she was all right. There was no reply. Until then Lindsay had kept in close communication with the family, emailing, Skyping or calling several times a week. Julia grew worried. The whole family then tried calling, emailing and texting – to no avail.

In one email, Lindsay's elder sister, Lisa, wrote: "Mum has heard about an earthquake in Japan (I've told her that Japan is the most common place in the world to experience such phenomena) . . . she is v.v worried that you might have been injured . . . can you call or something? It's not good fun living with the worried one xxx."

In another her boyfriend, Ryan Garside, wrote: "Get in touch you fool! . . . Where is your moral support??"

Lindsay missed her classes on 25 and 26 March, something she had not done before. At around 2.30 p.m. on Monday 26th – the second day she had failed to turn up for work – Nova informed the police. Her flatmates had also tried to report her missing when she did not return home or answer her mobile phone, but the message had not been passed through the system. As advised by the college, Lindsay had left a note at the flat giving Ichihashi's name and address, so it was not hard to trace him. At 5.40 p.m. – three hours and ten minutes after the police had received that missing-persons report – they sent two officers from Funabashi station in Chiba prefecture to visit Ichihashi's apartment in Ichikawa City, one train stop from Lindsay's flat.

The police had already discovered that, although Ichihashi had no previous convictions, an allegation of "theft and injury" had been made against him. It seems he had assaulted a woman in the street during a robbery some years earlier, but Ichihashi's father had bought her off with one million yen. Then in 2006, he was given a police caution for following a female student at the university and stealing money from the coffee shop where she worked. These earlier offences immediately alerted the police to the fact that Lindsay may have been the victim of a crime. Nevertheless, the officers did not arrive at Ichihashi's apartment until 7 p.m.

They noticed that, while the lights were off, there was someone at home. But still they did not have "just cause" even to knock on the door. They called for backup and, by 7.45 p.m., there were nine officers on the scene, anticipating a hostage-taking situation.

They asked the neighbours if they had seen a foreign woman. They hadn't. Then they managed to gain entry into a flat that overlooked Ichihashi's balcony. By then it was dark and they could not see the bath on the balcony, filled with soil, with Lindsay's hand sticking out of it.

At 9.45 p.m., some police were standing outside Ichihashi's flat when he opened the door and came out, shutting the door behind him. He was barefoot and carrying a rucksack.

"Are you Mr Ichihashi?" one of them asked. The suspect confirmed that he was. "We want to talk to you about a foreign woman and we want to come in."

Ichihashi simply took out his key and turned to let himself back into his flat. The police said they could not "compulsorily restrain him" because they had not established the facts. But before he had opened the door, he turned and made a run for it. The police grabbed for his rucksack, which came off as Ichihashi sprinted away. The police had no walkie-talkies, so they could not alert other officers in the building. There were police at the bottom of the staircase, but Ichihashi simply vaulted the last few feet into the stairwell, made his escape and disappeared into the neighbourhood, which was dense with apartment blocks.

While the police searched for Ichihashi, he suddenly reappeared. He now had some running shoes, seemingly stolen from outside another apartment. He ran right past officers and disappeared into the maze of streets again.

Meanwhile, the father of one of Lindsay's fellow teachers called Julia and warned her to expect the worst. She eventually got in touch with another teacher who was outside Ichihashi's flat. This gave Julia the opportunity to talk to one of the police officers and she urged them to break in. Eventually, they did so.

Inside the flat, they found that Ichihashi had removed the bath from the bathroom. With Japanese plumbing, this is easily done. The taps are plumbed into the wall, but the bath is free-standing and can easily be shifted. The police think that this was done sometime on Sunday night and neighbours had heard the sounds of banging metal and something being dragged. He had put the bath, which measured $47 \times 27 \times 20$ in. ($120 \times 70 \times 50$ cm), out on the balcony. In it was the naked body of Lindsay Hawker. She was bound and gagged with scarves and the plastic cord used to tie plants, though first she had put up a terrific fight. She was 5 ft 10 in. and was trained in the martial arts. But Ichihashi was taller – 6 ft – and a black belt. Hardly an inch of her body was left unmarked by bruises or other injuries, even her feet. She had been the victim of a prolonged attack.

Egg-sized bruises on the left side of her face seemed to have been inflicted by a fist, while other marks on her upper body were the result of colliding with furniture during the struggle.

At first, Superintendent Yoshihiro Sugita, of the Chiba Prefecture Police said: "There was no sign of strangulation, and no sign that the body had been stabbed, but there were signs of violent assault – bruises on the face and in numerous places all over the body. We have found no traces of blood and there was no sign of a physical struggle. The victim was completely naked and her clothes were scattered around the apartment, although we don't know whether they were taken off by her or by the suspect."

Later the post-mortem report said that Lindsay had died when her assailant began strangling her, which he did so forcefully that he broke the cartilage of her neck. She was tied up and repeatedly beaten over several hours as the ligatures had tightened around her wrists.

"It would have been a long and terrifying time for her," a police officer said. "Judging by the bruising on her body and the fact that our examination showed she was tied up for a long period of time before her death suggests she went through a great deal of pain and fear before she died."

Detectives believed Lindsay was probably gagged during her ordeal as she would have screamed for help and neighbours had not reported hearing any cries. They concluded that Ichihashi might have used torture to force her to have sex with him.

It was widely reported that the bath was full of sand. In fact, Lindsay had been buried in a mixture of sand and compost soil, soaked in a chemical that the Japanese use to compact and decompose waste. A shopping trolley, which he may have used to transport the sand and compost bags, was removed from Ichihashi's building. Before he was interrupted by the police, Ichihashi had made six trips to a local hardware store for supplies. Plainly, he had been planning the murder for some time.

Lindsay's head was shaved after she was killed. Her hair was found in a bag in the apartment. Ichihashi had studied horticulture at university and would have known that hair takes longer to decompose than other tissue. The speculation was that, when

Ichihashi had finished filling the bath with soil, he was going to turn it into an ornamental flowerbed. Another source said he intended to cover her with concrete. The Hawkers feared that Lindsay may have been buried alive as, when the police found her, one arm was sticking out of the soil, but experts assured them that she would have been dead by then.

Bill Hawker flew to Tokyo to identify the body.

"I knew it was Lindsay because she was so tall and because she was my daughter, but she was so badly beaten," he said. "Her hair was wrapped in gauze, her body in a Japanese gown and they'd had to put a lot of make-up on her. They let me say goodbye and I just stayed there, holding her toe under the blanket. She was beautiful and to see her lying on a mortuary table like that . . . All I can say is that it's a very dangerous man that did this."

The apartment where she was found had originally belonged to Ichihashi's maternal grandmother, who had started a dental practice with her husband. They had one child, Ichihashi's mother, who was also a dentist. When she married a neuro-surgeon, they took over the apartment. Ichihashi and his sister were born and brought up there. But since his earlier assault on a woman, his sister was estranged, while his parents had gone to live in suburban comfort 200 miles (320 km) from Tokyo.

Lindsay's clothes and possessions, including her handbag and passport, were found strewn across the room. Otherwise, there was little in the apartment – a computer, a few hundred violent manga comics that featured scenes of rape and torture (it is thought that he may have tortured, raped and murdered her in imitation of a plotline) and a large number of empty cartons of pomegranate juice. There were also twelve portrait drawings of women – both Western and Japanese. Apparently, Ichihashi used his artistic ability as a pick-up. There were reports that he had often been asked to leave bars frequented by Western women for harassing the customers.

A number of wigs were found, leading the police to believe that Ichihashi was a "sister-boy", in Japanese parlance. However, he did have a Japanese girlfriend for about a year. He had been due to see her that Sunday night but had emailed to cancel. They were of a similar age and their relationship seemed normal enough. There was no evidence that he was bisexual or a transvestite except for one man's unsubstantiated claim to have had gay sex with Ichihashi, since his escape, in a club in Tokyo's gay quarter, Shinjuku. The other possibility was that he was trying on the wigs to look more Western.

The rucksack grabbed by the police at the crime scene contained Ichihashi's gym kit, clean underwear and Lindsay's shoes. The police believe that he was on his way to the gym to wash – after all, he no longer had a bath he could use. Clearly, he was not expecting to be greeted by the police. And, had Lindsay not written the note giving Ichihashi's name and address, her body might never have been found.

The police obtained an arrest warrant for Ichihashi – not for murder but for abandoning a body. Clues from the crime scene were brought into play in the manhunt. As pomegranate juice is so unusual in Japan, the police obtained a list of retailers and spoke to all of them. They took particular interest in sightings of Ichihashi in gay areas and issued a wanted poster with an image of the suspect disguised as a woman.

Ichihashi's passport had been left in the apartment so police investigated some 350,000 of the 700,000 passport applications made in the twenty months following his escape. The matter was complicated by the fact that Ichihashi spelt his surname in three different ways. There were rumours that he had fled to Canada, where he had once lived as a student in Edmonton, or the Philippines, a traditional haven for Japanese fugitives. There were reports that a man named Ichihashi, the same age as the suspect, had entered the Philippines. The 140 police officers investigating the case travelled widely in Japan, following up 5,200 reported sightings generated by the 4,000 wanted posters and 30,000 flyers they had distributed. They went from building to building in central Tokyo, to bars, to clubs and to hotels showing people a photograph of the suspect. They also followed up sightings in Hong Kong and Singapore.

It was also known that Ichihashi had little or no money. He did not work and lived on an allowance of 100,000 yen, or around

$1,000, a month. After he fled, he made no attempt to access his bank accounts. This led to the suspicion that he was being sheltered by his family. The Japanese police have limited powers of surveillance, but it was thought that his parents' communications were monitored. Otherwise, Ichihashi was a loner and had few friends he could call on. Other theories were that he was being protected by the Yakuza or that he had killed himself – though a man referred to as a "psychic dreamer" visited the scene of the crime and said that Ichihashi had escaped on a bicycle and was still alive. However, Ichihashi did not have a mobile phone or a credit card that might make him easier to trace.

Suspecting that the Japanese police were winding down their investigation, the Hawkers kept the case in the headlines by travelling to Japan and making direct appeals to the Japanese people. At the instigation of the British prime minister, a senior investigating officer from the Wiltshire Constabulary, Detective Chief Inspector Ally Wright, was assigned to liaise with the Japanese police. Travelling to Tokyo three times, Wright said he was convinced that the Japanese police's methodical approach would eventually pay dividends. As he put it, Ichihashi has to be lucky every day of his life but the police only need to be lucky once to catch him.

Two years after the murder, the Japanese National Police Agency raised the reward for Ichihashi from one million yen to ten million yen – over three times the normal top reward in serious cases. As it was, when Ichihashi was captured in November 2009, this had to be split between an employee at an Osaka construction company where Ichihashi had been employed for fourteen months, a cosmetic surgery clinic in Nagoya who had grown suspicious and given a photograph of his new appearance to the police, and an employee at the ferry terminal at Osaka where Ichihashi was arrested waiting for a ship to Okinawa. He was carrying a toy gun.

Ichihashi had undergone plastic surgery several times, after deliberately mutilating his own face to disguise his appearance. He had two moles on his cheek removed, a fold added to his eyelids to give him a more Western appearance, his lips made thinner and the height of his nose increased. This was paid for by his work at the construction company that earned him about one million yen. When arrested, he had to be identified by his fingerprints.

Ichihashi's fingerprints were found in a dormitory belonging to the firm, along with comics, an English dictionary and a passport application, leading police to believe he may have been planning to flee overseas. Colleagues said that he was learning French. He used the name and address of Kosuke Inoue, a dead man who had lived in the area.

Fellow workers described him as a quiet and hardworking man who spent his time reading comics and watching videos, and who mixed little with them. He wore a red cap and glasses and had a goatee beard.

His colleagues nicknamed him *"Dai-chan"*, or "Lanky", because of his height. When they persuaded him to go bowling in April, he hid behind a colleague when the group posed for a photograph.

"We gossiped that he was an odd guy, but I never thought that he was the suspect," said a former colleague. "It strikes me now that he was saving the money for cosmetic surgery."

Before he was caught, he was in a brawl with a fellow worker. Afterwards an acquaintance said to him: "If a grown man hits another like that someone could be killed." At this, he suddenly began weeping and apologized.

He disappeared after taking his last monthly pay packet of 100,000 yen. Two days later, he went to a clinic in Fukuoka and asked for surgery to alter the shape of his mouth. He was turned down because there were signs of previous operations to thin his lower lip. Ten days later he went to another clinic in Nagoya, where he requested another operation to raise the bridge of his nose. He paid in cash and told staff at the clinic that he was staying at local "love hotels", where couples rent rooms by the hour. Staff at the clinic grew suspicious and went to the police, who then released images of Ichihashi as he looked after his surgery. Workers at the construction company recognized their former colleague from the picture and contacted the police.

After being charged with abandoning the body, he remained silent. Subsequently he was charged with murder and rape – his DNA had been recovered from Lindsay's body, the police said. According to his lawyers, he later admitted to having been involved in her death, but said he had not meant to kill her and had attempted to revive her, but failed.

"In the early morning of the 26th, Lindsay repeatedly shouted she wanted to go home. So I choked her by putting my arm around her neck from behind. I didn't intend to kill her. I also tried artificial respiration," he was quoted as saying. His lawyer also said that Ichihashi had used scissors to cut the hair of Hawker because "adhesive tape came off (from the mouth) and it caught Lindsay's hair so I cut plucked hair". He said she was angry about her hair being cut, his lawyer reported.

According to the indictment, Ichihashi punched Hawker in the face and other parts of the body several times and tied her hands with binding at his apartment on or around 25 March 2007. He then strangled her to death and, in the meantime, he raped her, the indictment says.

Although forensic evidence indicates they had sex, Ichihashi denied rape and murder, though he admitted abandoning her body. The lack of a confession caused the prosecutors problems and delayed the course of justice. The bulk of convictions in Japan are secured on confessions. According to Ichihashi's lawyers, he was threatened with the death penalty if he did not talk, though usually only multiple murderers face hanging in Japan.

During his captivity, Ichihashi wrote the book, *Until I Was Arrested*, about his time on the run. In it, he claims he travelled the length of the country by train and ferry and spent some weeks on the remote Okinawan island of Oha. The island is less than 2 miles (3.2 km) in circumference and home to just four families. In drawings in the book, Ichihashi indicates that he lived rough in a concrete bunker and caught fish that he cooked over an open fire to survive.

The book makes no mention of Lindsay Hawker or the motive for the murder, but Ichihashi said that while on the run he had "apologized in his heart" to her. He wanted to donate the proceeds to her family, who expressed their disgust at the venture. In Japan, criminals are not permitted to profit from their crimes.

Returning to Japan after Ichihashi's arrest, Bill Hawker thanked Japan's press and public for the role they played in helping to catch Ichihashi.

"I'd like also to thank every single person in Japan who looked at the television, who looked at the newspaper and watched for Ichihashi," he said. "This has been a long, long investigation but it has been a team effort . . . and we thank you."

Holding up a photo of his smiling daughter, he added: "She came here, she loved the children of Japan. I now feel as if Japan has not let her down."

During his trial, Ichihashi admitted killing Lindsay, but denied murder. He tried to use a loophole in Japanese law to escape conviction by showing contrition to the family – he dropped to the floor of the courtroom and bowed repeatedly, clasping his hands and weeping. The ploy did not work. On 21 July 2011, Tatsuya Ichihashi was finally sentenced to life imprisonment for the murder of Lindsay Hawker.

SECRETS OF THE CELLAR

JOSEF FRITZL CONSTRUCTED his own crime scene. He painstakingly built a dungeon under his house where he imprisoned his daughter Elisabeth for twenty-four years, repeatedly raping her and giving her seven children, to which she had to give birth without assistance.

A convicted rapist, Fritzl had already served eight months in jail when, in 1978, he applied for a permit to turn his cellar into a nuclear shelter. Elisabeth was just twelve years old at the time. This was to be her prison. He had begun abusing his daughter the year before, when his wife Rosemarie and their other children were away on vacation in Italy. Fritzl had refused to let his wife take Elisabeth with her.

Building a nuclear shelter was not an unusual thing in the 1970s. The Cold War was at its height and the Fritzl home at Amstetten in Austria was barely thirty minutes' drive from the Iron Curtain that separated Czechoslovakia and the rest of the Communist bloc from the nations of Western Europe.

Fritzl was anything but discreet about the building work. Once, he fixed a heavy-duty industrial winch to the roof of the house to move massive concrete blocks, which he used to turn the cellar into an unbreachable fortress. In 1983, building inspectors came to inspect the bunker and gave it their seal of approval. They even gave him state funds towards the conversion.

By then Elisabeth was fifteen and had left school. She began running away from home. Although it was common knowledge that she was being raped by her father, the authorities tracked down Elisabeth and returned her home.

Elisabeth was eighteen when, on 28 August 1984, her father woke her and told her to come down to the cellar. He needed her help to fit a heavy steel door. It was a strange request, but her father often worked downstairs in the cellar at night and years of physical, emotional and sexual abuse had drilled absolute obedience into her. Once the heavy door was in place, he knocked her out with a towel drenched in ether. When she awoke, she found herself locked in and chained to a metal pole. After two days, she was put on a dog-leash that allowed her to reach a makeshift lavatory, but otherwise inhibited her movements. There was no escape. She banged on the walls and screamed for help, but her tiny prison was soundproof. Nobody could hear her cries for help. For the first few weeks, she was held in total darkness. Her father only visited to feed her, or to rape her. It soon became clear that either she submitted to rape or she would starve to death. In reality, it was no choice at all.

After two years of captivity, she had a miscarriage. Three years later, in 1989, a child, her daughter Kerstin, was born. Elisabeth had to cope without medical assistance, though Fritzl boasted that he bought her medical books, as well as towels, disinfectants and nappies. He did not even visit her much during that period. Apparently, he went off having sex with his daughter when she was heavily pregnant. The product of incest, Kerstin was sickly from the start.

The following year, she gave birth to a son, Stefan. Then in 1992, Lisa was born. But things were becoming a little cramped underground. At nine months, the child was found outside the family home in a cardboard box. A note was attached from their supposedly runaway daughter Elisabeth, begging her parents to take care of the infant. Josef and Rosemarie took her in and, eventually, adopted her as their own. The story was put out that Elisabeth had joined some strange religious sect where children were not welcome and she begged her parents not to look for her.

Two years later, ten-month-old Monika was found outside the front door and was taken in, too. This time there was a strange call from Elisabeth asking her mother to take care of the child. It seems to have been recorded. The authorities expressed surprise that Elisabeth knew her parents' new unlisted number.

By this time, the conditions were becoming dire below ground. Elisabeth helped her father extend the basement to give more room for her growing family. In 1996, Elisabeth gave birth to twins. One of the children, Michael, died after three days. Fritzl threw the infant's body in the household furnace. The surviving twin, Alexander, was found outside the Fritzl home at fifteen months.

Then, in 2002, Felix was born. He was kept in the cellar as Fritzl said his wife was too old to look after another child. Felix too would be condemned to life in a tiny cellar where adults could not stand upright, where there was no natural light and the ventilation was so bad the captives had to sit down and restrict their movements most of the day.

In 2008, Fritzl planned to release Elisabeth and his incestuous family in the basement. He had already forced his daughter to write a letter saying she was planning to leave the sect and would return home soon. The letter was in the same handwriting as previous notes, and DNA tests later confirmed that it came from Elisabeth.

But things began to go wrong with Fritzl's meticulous planning. Kerstin fell seriously ill. Fritzl treated her with aspirin and cough mixture. He had no medical training and his children downstairs had never seen a doctor. Kerstin had been ill before, but she had always recovered. Being deprived of sunlight and good air had taken its toll. She was also prey to genetic weaknesses. This time her condition worsened. She began to have fits. Blood spewed from her mouth and she fell into a coma.

Elisabeth begged her father to take Kerstin to hospital. Eventually, Fritzl relented. Rosemarie was on holiday in Italy again, so Elisabeth and her father carried the unconscious Kerstin upstairs. She was now nineteen and it was the first time she had been out of the cellar. By then, Elisabeth was forty-two. She had spent more than half her life incarcerated in the basement. After a few brief moments above ground, she was forced to return to her dungeon.

At 7 a.m. on Saturday, 19 April 2008, Fritzl called an ambulance. They collected the ghostlike teenager from the Fritzl home at 40 Ybbsstrasse in Amstetten and took her to the Mostviertel Red Cross hospital. Kerstin was in a coma and no one could tell what was wrong with her. An hour later the seventy-three-year-old Fritzl turned up at the hospital. He explained that the girl was his granddaughter. She had been left unconscious outside his front door.

The girl was pallid and malnourished. She had convulsions and was bleeding from the mouth. According to the doctor that treated her: "She hung in a state between life and death."

Fritzl handed the doctors a note, which he said he had found pinned to the unconscious child. It was, ostensibly, from her mother and said: "Wednesday, I gave her aspirin and cough medicine for the condition. Thursday, the cough worsened. Friday, the coughing gets even worse. She has been biting her lip as well as her tongue. Please, please help her! Kerstin is really terrified of other people, she was never in a hospital. If there are any problems please ask my father for help, he is the only person that she knows." A postscript, addressed to the girl, said: "Kerstin – please stay strong, until we see each other again! We will come back to you soon!"

This made her physician, Dr Albert Reiter suspicious. Fritzl told his well-rehearsed story about his daughter running off to a religious cult and dumping her unwanted children on his doorstep. Dr Reiter did not swallow it.

"I could not believe that a mother who wrote such a note and seemed so concerned would just vanish," he said.

Fritzl himself seemed unconcerned and, without even waiting for a diagnosis, he left. So Dr Reiter contacted the police. They visited 40 Ybbsstrasse where Fritzl repeated his bizarre story.

As Kerstin's condition deteriorated, Reiter launched a TV appeal for Kerstin's mother to get in touch. At the very least, he needed to know more about her medical history. Why, for example, had the teenager lost most of her teeth? She showed signs of severe neglect. Her body began to shut down. She was put on a respirator and a kidney dialysis machine. But without some idea of her medical history, Dr Reiter did not know what to do for the best.

After a week, Elisabeth re-emerged and she made her way to the hospital with her father. But the police had been tipped off. As Fritzl and his daughter reached the hospital grounds the police detained them. Elisabeth faced charges of criminal neglect.

They were taken to police headquarters in Amstetten, where they were questioned separately. At first, Elisabeth stuck to her story about running off to join a bizarre cult. But that did not explain Kerstin's condition. Nor did it explain the state that Elisabeth herself was in. Although she was only in her early forties, she looked like a woman of sixty. Prematurely grey, like her daughter, she had lost most of her teeth and had a deathly pallor.

After two hours of questioning, Elisabeth began to break down. Once the police assured her that neither she, nor her children, would have to see Fritzl again, she told a shocking tale. Her father, a retired electrical engineer and a pillar of the community, had kept her locked in a cellar and used her as a sex toy for twenty-four years. Although her story beggared belief, it was clear, from the look of her, that she had been through an appalling ordeal.

The police put these allegations to Fritzl. He denied them. He even produced the letter Elisabeth had written, saying that she was with a religious sect but would be returning home soon. The only way the police could tell who was telling the truth and who was lying was to examine the crime scene – for some crime had been committed, whether it was simply child neglect or a monstrous case of rape, incest and incarceration.

They took Fritzl back to 40 Ybbsstrasse. At the front, it was a typical Austrian townhouse on an ordinary street. But at the back it was an imposing concrete structure, not unlike a wartime bunker hidden behind high hedges. The police searched the house but failed to find the dungeon of which Elisabeth had talked. Then, sensing the game was up, Fritzl led them down the cellar stairs. He took them through five rooms, including his office and the boiler room containing the furnace where Michael's body had been burnt, before they reached his workshop. Behind a shelving unit stacked with tins of paint, there was a reinforced concrete door, so well concealed that the building inspectors had failed to notice it. It had an electronic lock. Fritzl handed over the remote control and, after some prompting, gave the police the code. The steel frame of the door had been sprayed with concrete and it was so heavy that it took four firemen to shift it. Fritzl moved it with the aid of an electric motor. If that had failed, the cellar family would have been trapped, sealed in their tomb for ever.

Fritzl had long taunted his daughter and their children that only he knew how to open the door. If they tried to kill him, they would be locked in their dungeon for ever and starve to death. He also told them that it was rigged so, if they tried to tamper with the door, it would release toxic gas. Fritzl told the police that the lock had a timer, so that, if he died or was otherwise incapacitated, it would open automatically. The police found no such mechanism.

The door was just 3 ft 3 in. (1 m) high. Beyond was a narrow corridor. At the end was a padded cell. Just 215 ft^2 (20 m^2), this was where Fritzl had held his daughter for the first nine years. It was soundproofed so that no scream, cry or sob could be heard in any other part of the building. A corridor just a foot (30 cm) wide – so narrow that you had to turn sideways to negotiate it – led on to a living area, where the police found eighteen-year-old Stefan and five-year-old Felix. They were pale and terrified by the intruders. The police were the only strangers they had ever seen. Stefan was stooped because there was nowhere he could stand upright. The maximum height of the ceilings was 5 ft 6 in. (1.7 m). Felix preferred to crawl, though he could walk with a strange apelike gait that he had copied from his fellow captives. The police took them upstairs into an alien world. They had never seen daylight before. The only things they knew from the world outside their prison was what they had seen on the TV, their only window on the world above.

In the living area of the dungeon, there was a rudimentary kitchen and bathroom. On the white tiled walls of the tiny shower cubicle, the inmates had painted a snail, a butterfly, an octopus and a flower in an attempt to brighten their lives. A toy elephant was perched on a mirrored medicine cabinet and there were scraps of paper and glue that the children had used to make toys. There were also pitiful drawings the children had made, portraying life as they knew it.

Along with the TV and video recorder there was a washing machine, a fridge and a freezer that Fritzl packed with food when he went off on extended sex tours of Thailand while they were left to fend for themselves. Among Elisabeth's clothing were skimpy clothes and sexy lingerie that Fritzl brought from Pattaya. A friend who accompanied him on his trips assumed he was buying the outfits for a mistress who Fritzl kept hidden away. So did Fritzl. In his mind, Elisabeth was no longer his daughter, but the mother of his second family.

Beyond the living area were two small bedrooms with two beds in each. They were lit by dim electric light bulbs. Elisabeth had begged Fritzl to provide vitamin D tablets and an ultraviolet light to prevent her children growing up deformed from being deprived of natural light. The dungeon was hermetically sealed. The only air came in through a small ventilation shaft. It did not provide enough oxygen for four people if they undertook any sort of activity. The place was also damp. The whole basement was just 376 ft^2 (35 m^2) – a tiny area in which four people had to live out all of their daily lives.

Confronted with the evidence, Fritzl confessed that he had imprisoned his daughter.

"Yes," he told the police. "I locked her up, but only to protect her from drugs. She was a difficult child."

While admitting to repeatedly raping Elisabeth, Fritzl rejected his daughter's claims that he had chained her to the cellar wall and kept her "like an animal". He claimed that he had been kind to the second family he kept in the cellar. He admitted that the children were his own, the offspring of his incest with his own daughter. DNA tests confirmed Fritzl was their father. They also confirmed that he was the only other person who had been in the cellar. He had no accomplice and was solely responsible for the imprisonment of his daughter and their offspring.

What staggered the police, given the extent of the crime scene, was that no one else knew. During the time Elisabeth was incarcerated, Fritzl had let rooms out in 40 Ybbsstrasse to over a hundred tenants. They had lived in the ugly three-storey extension to the house that Fritzl had built – directly above the cellar. One of them was a waiter named Joseph Leitner. He had been to the Amstetten Institute of Technology with a friend of Elisabeth's and knew that Elisabeth had been raped by her father before she had disappeared. But he still moved in.

Fritzl warned his tenants that the basement was strictly off limits. Anyone caught down there would be given their notice instantly. Although Fritzl also banned pets, Leitner kept a mongrel named Sam who barked every time he went past the door to the cellar.

"I thought he was just excited about going outside," said Leitner.

The dog would also wake in the middle of the night and start barking and getting agitated, though he slept soundly once they had moved out. Leitner believed that Sam could hear noises from the cellar below.

There was another curious thing about the bedsit that Leitner rented from Fritzl – the huge electricity bill. Each month he paid more than €400 although, as a waiter, he worked long hours and was barely ever there. He even got a friend from a cable TV company to check out the electrical system in the house. Even with everything unplugged, the electricity meter went round at a dizzying lick. He later learnt that the electricity used to run the lights, TV and other appliances in Elisabeth's dungeon just centimetres below his feet was being siphoned off from his apartment.

Eventually, Fritzl noticed that Sam was taking an inordinate interest in the door to the cellar and kicked Leitner out. That was fourteen years before Elisabeth's eventual release. Leitner later kicked himself for not following up on his suspicions.

Another tenant who had his suspicions was Alfred Dubanovsky, who lived there for twelve years. He had known Elisabeth at school and had known of her abuse. When she disappeared, he assumed, reasonably enough, that she had run away again.

Like Leitner, he was puzzled by Fritzl's blanket ban on anyone going near the cellar. Fritzl said that it was protected by a state-of-the-art electronic alarm. Both Leitner and Dubanovky also noticed Fritzl taking large amounts of food down there, usually at night. Tenants also noticed food went missing. If Fritzl had not had time to go on a shopping expedition – he bought provisions from supermarkets well away from Amstetten to allay suspicion – he would use his pass key to slip into his tenant's rooms and take food for Elisabeth and the children.

Dubanovsky also heard banging noises from the cellar below. He asked Fritzl about this, only to be told that the strange sounds came from the gas central heating. The cellar below was empty, Fritzl said. However, when Fritzl was still at work, he would go down to the cellar each evening. After he retired, Fritzl would go down there at 9 a.m. in the morning, ostensibly to work on some engineering plans, only to emerge long after his wife had gone to bed. Sometimes he stayed down there overnight. His wife was not even allowed to bring him a cup of coffee. He was not to be disturbed. A domestic tyrant, Fritzl banned questions about why he spent so long down there. However, he panicked at the merest mention of the police.

No one appeared to notice that, in order to extend the dungeon to accommodate Elisabeth's growing family, Fritzl had to remove an estimated 116 m^2 of earth – some 200 tons of it or the equivalent of seventeen truckloads without his tenants, the neighbours or his upstairs family noticing. The authorities did not notice that he was excavating a dungeon seven times the size of the nuclear shelter he had been given permission for, as well as violating all manner of building codes. The one thing he had not done was extend the ventilation system to provide Elisabeth and the children with an adequate supply of oxygen, as this would have risked noise from the cellar reaching the outside.

At the same time, he managed to smuggle tiles, bricks, wooden wall panels, a washing machine, a kitchen sink, beds and pipework into the underground cellar without anybody being any the wiser. He even installed a generator so that they had power if the electricity went off in the house. Although, even if it was vented, it is difficult to see how they could have used the generator without suffocating.

Fritzl was an electrical engineer so he could install the lighting and the power, but he needed help with the plumbing. Dubanovsky said that Fritzl once introduced him to a plumber who had come to fit a lavatory. The man was not thought to have been an accomplice, though he has never come forward or been identified.

Fritzl's various subterfuges worked so well that his son-in-law Jürgen Helm lived in the house for three years without noticing anything awry. To him, the cellar was just a place that Fritzl stored a lot of building materials and other junk.

Neighbours noticed nothing amiss either. They found Fritzl a little reclusive but he appeared to be the perfect family man, bringing up the children of his wayward daughter. They even talked to him about Elisabeth's disappearance, but had not the slightest inkling of what had really happened.

Fritzl's wife Rosemarie was unquestioning when children kept turning up on her doorstep. But on the one occasion she did try to leave her tyrannical husband, he burnt down the guest house they owned where she was staying, forcing her to return home. The social services did not even ask themselves why Elisabeth would foist her own children on her parents, who she found so unbearable that she had run away from them. Over the years, social workers paid at least twenty-one visits to the Fritzls' house and reported nothing unusual about the family. Josef and Rosemarie, they said, were "really loving and warm with their children".

Fritzl was even allowed to adopt, though he had a conviction for rape. However, under Austrian law, the conviction had long since been expunged from his record. After adopting Lisa, the Fritzls went on to foster Elisabeth's other two children who were allowed upstairs because it brought them a higher state benefit of €400 a month. Neighbours were sympathetic. Even the local press carried the story about the apparently uncaring mother who kept dropping off her unwanted kids on her parents' doorstep. They even interviewed Fritzl, who repeated the old story about his daughter being in the hands of some religious group.

After the third child arrived, Fritzl's sister-in-law Christine began to harbour some suspicions. She suggested to Fritzl that, maybe, he should try to find out about the sect that held such sway over Elisabeth. He said that there was "no point". Everyone was afraid of Fritzl and the matter was taken no further.

Short of money, Fritzl began an insurance scam, setting small fires around the house. The insurance company paid up. Loss adjusters did little more than a superficial assessment of the damage. A proper investigation would have unearthed the secret of the cellar.

Andrea Schmitt, who, as the girlfriend of Fritzl's friend Paul Hoera, once accompanied them to Thailand, noticed that Fritzl bought an awful lot of toys for the three children he had above-ground at home in Austria. Paul also noticed that the Fritzl children were never allowed downstairs near the cellar.

Fritzl's son-in-law Jürgen Helm had been down to the cellar, but had no reason to suspect there was a hidden doorway behind the shelves in the workshop. Fritzl's son by Rosemarie, Josef Jr, also had access to the cellar, but was rather slow on the uptake and was completely under the thumb of his father. Otherwise, the entire cellar area was strictly off-limits to members of the Fritzl family, friends and the tenants who lived upstairs.

It was only the suspicions of Dr Reiter that paid dividends. Fritzl's story of his daughter running off to join a bizarre sect, then dumping her sick daughter on her father's doorstep, did not ring true.

"I did not like his tone and something did not seem right," said Dr Reiter. "What made me particularly suspicious was that he did not seem to think it important to answer any of my questions, simply demanding we make Kerstin better so that he could take her away again."

In his effort to contact his patient's mother, he called the police. The case of Elisabeth Fritzl, who was still classified as missing, was reopened. The letter from Elisabeth, saying that she was coming home soon, was examined. In it, she mentioned Kerstin's illness, but also wrote that a second child, Felix, had also been ill and she had a third child with her, named Stefan. If these children were in the care of such a neglectful mother, they too were in danger. They had to be found – and fast.

The letter carried the postmark of the town of Kematen an der Krems, which is about 30 miles (48 km) from Amstetten. The police descended. None of the local doctors recalled a patient called Kerstin and no one remembered seeing a girl of her strange, ghostly appearance. No one knew anything about Elisabeth Fritzl and there was no indication that a bizarre sect had ever been in town.

The police then got on to the local diocese to find out what religious sects were at large in the area. The bishopric's expert on sects, Dr Manfred Wohlfahrt, said that there were none in the diocese or in any of the other dioceses of Lower Austria. He also examined the notes that had been found with the children and the letter Elisabeth had written, saying she was planning to come home. He noted that they had been written in a very deliberate hand, using formulated phrases, and concluded that they had been dictated.

Meanwhile, Dr Reiter made his television appeal, urging Elisabeth Fritzl to come forward. Journalists besieged 40 Ybbsstrasse. Instead of welcoming their help in finding his daughter, Fritzl was hostile and told them to clear off.

Enquiries were made at schools and social security offices, but nowhere was there any record of Elisabeth Fritzl or her children. She had not applied for a passport or a driver's licence and the births of Kerstin, Stefan and Felix had not been registered.

As the bureaucratic route seemed to be a blind alley, the police tried another tack. If they took DNA samples from Josef and Rosemarie Fritzl and the children Elisabeth had apparently left with them, they should be able to get a DNA profile of the children's father that might, perhaps, show up on the national database. But Fritzl proved less than helpful. He made several appointments to give a DNA sample, and then cancelled them, saying he had too much to do.

In her basement prison, Elisabeth saw Dr Reiter's appeal on the television. She managed to persuade her father to let her go to the hospital, promising to back his story that she had been with a religious sect for the past twenty-four years.

It seems they visited the hospital a couple of times, but Dr Reiter was not there. On the third occasion, Fritzl called ahead, saying that Elisabeth had returned home and wanted to see her daughter.

"We do not want any trouble," Fritzl said. "Do not call the police."

But the police were already involved and Dr Reiter called them anyway.

When father and daughter reached the hospital, they were arrested. Fritzl resisted and had to be handcuffed.

When Stefan and Felix were discovered, still imprisoned, they were suffering from vitamin D deficiency and anaemia, like their mother and older sister. Prolonged captivity had damaged their immune systems.

Neighbours looked on amazed as crime scene investigators removed boxes of belongings from the underground prison. With Fritzl refusing to answer any further questions, it was the forensic scientists' job to piece together what had gone on in the cell over the previous quarter of a century. It was gruelling task and the atmosphere in the cramped cellar was described as "oppressive".

Lower Austria's top criminal investigator, Colonel Franz Polzer, visited the dungeon.

"I went through it and was very glad to be able to leave," he said. "The environment in this room where the ceilings were kept very low, less than six foot at the highest point, was anything but pleasant. Everyday living, personal hygiene, etc., must have kept the level of humidity high."

Investigators found that even when the doors were opened, the air inside remained fetid and the crime scene investigators looked for another way to ventilate the bunker. Officers with years of experience on crime scenes found the working conditions intolerable. Polzer compared it to going down in a submarine. No fresh air could get in and no stale air or moisture could get out. Due to the damp, everything was covered in mildew. Consequently, Elisabeth and the children were found to be suffering from fungal infections and respiratory diseases. But for the crime scene investigators, it was not just the physical conditions that were unpleasant. They were also affected psychologically. Most affecting were the pitiful drawings made by the three children kept in this tiny space since their birth.

The cellar was lit only by dim electric bulbs. These were on a timer to give the illusion of night and day. The walls ran with condensation and water dripped from exposed pipes. From the very first room containing the kitchen and bathroom, investigators were overcome with nausea. The toilet was in a "catastrophic" state, investigators said, and the shower was covered in mould. The small bathroom contained a tiny bath. On the other side of a short partition was a hand basin. A cupboard above contained a toothbrush and other toiletry items. Beside it hung a hand towel and a hot-water bottle. Elisabeth's white bathrobe hung from a peg on the wall. Next to it was a small table covered with a plastic tablecloth and small hot plates for cooking.

A corridor led to two bedrooms, separated by a thin partition. Each contained two beds. No door or curtain separated the bedrooms – or any other room – which meant that Fritzl's sexual assaults on his daughter were in clear sight of their children. All other bodily functions also had to be performed in full view of the rest of the occupants.

The first part of the dungeon was padded and the whole vault soundproofed. But the basement was deep underground. No sound from the outside could be heard and no scream, however loud, could penetrate the thick concrete walls. The ventilation shaft was of the type designed for nuclear bunkers. It had filters to prevent fallout passing down it and baffles to deaden the blast. Consequently, the dungeon was an enclosed and silent world, completely isolated from anything outside it.

The filtration system would have restricted the air flow through it, reducing the supply of oxygen. But nuclear shelters were only designed to be occupied for a couple of weeks, not years on end. It would also have been unbearably hot. With little airflow and insulated walls, there would have been no escape from the heat generated by cooking, hot water, electrical appliances and four human bodies. The humidity produced by bathing, washing, cooking and breathing would have turned it into a sauna. The stench was almost unbearable, according to the police. However, Elisabeth had kept the place neat and tidy.

The forensic team had to comb the scene for weeks on end as their work rate was slow due to the lack of oxygen. They worked one-hour shifts and, if there were any more than four officers in the cellar at any one time, they found they could not breathe.

"Investigators wearing special clothes and masks can work there only one hour," said Polzer, "and during this hour they try, one team after the other, to gather everything available in this living space and search particularly for DNA traces to establish if the alleged criminal really committed this on his own. Not until then can we start with technical investigations like sonar probes, cavity and sound measurements, and also to comprehend all the electric and electronic systems."

DNA analysis of samples taken from the cellar confirmed that Fritzl worked alone. No traces of DNA belonging to anyone except Fritzl and his captive family were found, and Elisabeth said she never saw anyone else in the cellar. There was still the mystery of the plumber Alfred Dubanovsky had seen. Other experts were called in to examine the electrical, plumbing and security features of the dungeon to see whether Fritzl could have built it all himself.

Even a week after its discovery, Polzer said: "There are still areas we haven't found inside the dungeon and I expect it to take at least two weeks before we have answered all the questions we need to about how Fritzl controlled the areas and imprisoned the children."

It appeared that Fritzl had intended to extend the dungeon even further and crime scene investigators had to search further rooms filled with earth and rubble beyond the windowless living quarters they already knew about. Three weeks into the investigation, officers were breaking through walls to reach the hidden rooms.

Due to the death of Michael, Fritzl was the subject of a murder investigation and sniffer dogs were used to search the site for human remains. Forensic archaeologists were also brought in. They used ground-penetrating radar and sonar to scan the area around the house in case bodies or body parts were buried there.

The police concluded that Fritzl had worked alone and that he had begun his plan to imprison Elisabeth as early as 1978, soon after he began sexually abusing her. Rosemarie was living at the guest house they own at the time, so he could begin work on the bunker unhindered. It was no accident that Fritzl finally imprisoned Elisabeth at the time she met her first serious boyfriend.

"Today, we know for certain that part of the old cellar and the old house was kept back as a reserve, so to speak," said Colonel Polzer, "and that this new house suddenly gained a small space of 30 to 35 m² [320 to 375 ft²] without anyone noticing. We are now proceeding on the assumption that he had already settled on the plan to build his own personal *Reich* as early as 1978 and start a relationship with his pretty daughter Elisabeth in the cellar."

To begin with, she had no cooking area and no facilities for storing food, so she was completely dependent on her father's visits. The cooking area and the bedrooms were only added later. Before that, Elisabeth and the children would have had to eat, sleep and live in a single room with a low ceiling and a floor space of just 14 ft 6 in. by 14 ft 6 in. (4.5 × 4.5 m).

Extending the dungeon with Elisabeth and the children captive inside would have made their nightmare even worse. Their tiny living area would have been filled with dust and rubble. The work would have been rendered almost impossible due to the lack of oxygen and took years.

Fritzl was charged with incest, rape, false imprisonment, enslavement, grievous assault for threatening to gas his captives

if they disobeyed him and negligent homicide of the infant
Michael. At his trial in Sankt Pölten in Austria, he pleaded guilty
to all the charges except grievous assault and murder. On the
second day of the trial, Elisabeth appeared in court in disguise.
Fritzl recognized her, broke down and changed his plea to guilty
on all charges. He was sentenced to life imprisonment without
possibility of parole for fifteen years. He accepted the sentence
and said he would not appeal. He would serve out his sentence
in a former abbey converted into a prison, in the section for the
criminally insane.

VIKKI THOMPSON

A T 4 P.M. OF the afternoon of 12 August 1995, thirty-year-old part-time waitress and mother of two Vikki Thompson, who planned to study maths and computing at Oxford Brookes University, decided to take her dog, a collie named Daisy, for a walk near the picturesque village of Ascott-under-Wychwood in Oxfordshire. When the dog returned home without her mistress, Vikki's husband Jonathan put their children Matthew and Jenny, then aged eight and six, in the car and went out looking for her. Neighbours who joined the search found her lying on rocks at the bottom of an embankment near the Cotswold Railway line between 7.15 and 7.30 p.m. near where a farmer and three local residents had heard screams some hours earlier.

She had been bludgeoned and was covered in blood. When Mr Thompson reached her, she was barely conscious.

"I tried to talk to her to keep her coherent," he said. "I asked her a number of questions. One of them was the name of our son. She coherently replied, 'Matthew'. I asked her other questions like, 'Who did this to you?' I just got a mumbling. I couldn't work out what she was saying."

She then managed to get out the words, "It's all got too much," before lapsing into a coma.

Vikki Thompson had received three heavy blows to the back of the head and two to the face, fracturing her skull and causing brain damage. Rushed to John Radcliffe Hospital in Oxford, she was not able to say what had happened to her or who was responsible. She died there six days later when her brain ceased to function and the life-support machines were switched off.

Twenty-year-old odd-job man Mark Weston was arrested and charged with her murder. But at the trial it took the jury just fifty minutes to find him not guilty. Later the foreman of the jury wrote to him urging him to sue the police for wrongful arrest.

"I hope you are all getting on well now and hope you go ahead and get big compensation from the police as they had no evidence of any sort whatsoever," he said.

Weston's alibi was that he had gone fishing that morning and had worked in his parents' garden later that day.

The case was featured on BBC's *Crimewatch* and a £20,000 reward was posted for information. Then, in August 2005, on the tenth anniversary of Vikki's death, her mother, Margaret Simpson, issued a fresh appeal for information, saying that she would never rest until her daughter's killer was caught. "It's never too late," she said.

In March 2007, Thames Valley Police set up a team of eight detectives to review cold cases going back fifty years. A number of items found at the scene of Mrs Thompson's murder were sent for analysis in the light of advances in technology.

Since his acquittal, Weston, an alcoholic loner who lived with his parents in Ascott-under-Wychwood, had been convicted twice of harassing women, including the daughter of a police officer. In 1997, he admitted harassing village bobby PC Bob Salmon, who was involved in the murder enquiry, by making more than fifty silent phone calls to his home and harassing his wife and children. Weston was given a two-year conditional discharge. A year later, he admitted harassing neighbour Lucy Bull by putting notes through her door, shining a light into her house and making silent telephone calls. He also put posters up around the village saying "Lucy is a grass" and "Lucy is a police informer – don't trust her."

In 2003, his girlfriend, twenty-four-year-old Helen Rusher, claimed that he tried to strangle her shortly after she had given birth to their child. But when she reported him, police failed to act, even though she told them that Weston had also confessed to killing Mrs Thompson. She said that Weston often became tearful after he had been drinking and would claim to have been responsible for the murder. He also once boasted of duping police into believing he wore a different shoe size. However, in October 2009, following a re-examination of the crime scene evidence, Weston was rearrested and faced trial again in 2010.

Meanwhile, the crime scene investigation moved to his parents' home where police removed patio slabs and began digging in the back garden.

At his first trial, a plastic bag containing two bras stained with Weston's semen had not been admitted as evidence. The bag seemed to have been deposited in the area some time after the murder. This time it was deemed as admissible evidence. But the crucial piece of evidence that had been overlooked were two tiny specks of blood found on Weston's boots that had been retained after the first trial. In 2008, two scientists using microscopes and a type of halogen lamp not available in 1995 found tiny amounts of blood in the seams of both boots.

Alison Levitt, the principal legal adviser to the Director of Public Prosecutions, said: "It's not that techniques are different, but methods of examination have moved on. Looking for blood-stains of this kind is really, really difficult. It's a black boot with irregular surfaces and looking for bloodstains involves a combination of the naked eye, a microscope where you can, and dabbing areas with a reactive agent. I think it's accepted by everybody it's almost as much an art as it is a science."

The investigation into Mrs Thompson's murder was reopened in 2005 after a change in the Criminal Justice Act reformed the law on so-called "double jeopardy" cases by permitting retrials in very serious incidents where new and compelling evidence had emerged. Before this, no one convicted or acquitted of an offence could be retried for the same crime. But under the new legislation, prosecutors had to gain the Director of Public Prosecution's personal consent before applying to the Court of Appeal for an acquittal to be quashed and for a retrial to take place.

"The threshold is an extremely high one for the prosecution to reach," said Mrs Levitt, "because although the legislation permits it, it's accepted by everyone it's an exceptional step to take."

Describing how the new blood evidence was revealed, Detective Chief Inspector Peter Beirne, the head of Thames Valley Police's Major Crime Review Team, said: "We got it in three phone calls. The first one said 'we've found blood'. A week or two later, 'it's female blood', and then a week or two after that, 'it's Vikki Thompson's blood' and it was euphoria."

LGC Forensics, the UK's largest independent provider of forensic services, which had been working closely with Thames Valley Police on the reinvestigation into the death of Vikki Thompson, claimed that there was only a one-in-a-billion chance that someone other than Vikki would have the same DNA profile as the bloodstain on the boot. Weston had previously denied knowing Mrs Thompson or being on the scene that day. But he could not explain how the blood had got on his boots. Forensic scientists told the court that the blood was wet when it came into contact with Weston's boots, so accidental contamination could be excluded.

The prosecutor, John Price, told Reading Crown Court: "Important articles seized in the original investigation were re-submitted for further scientific examination. They included a pair of black boots belonging to Mark Weston, which had been seized from his home on the occasion of his first arrest. Found upon each of the boots, but which had been missed when they were first examined in 1995 and 1996, were very small blood-stains, the DNA profile of which was found to match that of Vikki Thompson to a degree which proves beyond question, the prosecution submit, that it is her blood . . .

"If Mark Weston is not the person who killed Vikki Thompson, how did her blood, as it is submitted it plainly is, get on to not just one but both of his boots, especially when it has to have been wet when it did so?"

Other cellular material on the boot stood a one-in-fifty-five-million chance of being from someone unrelated to Mrs Thompson. Price added: "In respect of certain criminal offences, including murder, the law now permits that a person previously acquitted may be retried if since that acquittal, there has emerged fresh evidence of his guilt."

According to the crime scene evidence, it seems that Mrs Thompson had caught Weston masturbating while watching her walking her dog. He chased after her as she ran screaming up the lane and struck her with a rock.

"You attacked her in the lane, dragged her across a field and finished her off in a railway embankment," said the judge. Evidence gathered at the post-mortem examination and at the scene of the crime suggested that, after the initial attack, Weston lifted her over a fence and dragged her across a field by her arms before dumping her. Police thought that it was Weston's intention to make it look like Vikki had been hit by a passing train.

Detective Chief Inspector Peter Beirne said: "This is the first time using double jeopardy legislation that new forensic evidence has been used to secure a conviction, so it is very significant."

It took the jury of seven men and five women just under four hours to return a guilty verdict this time. The judge, Mr Justice Bean, said the attack on Vikki was not premeditated but that by the time it ended Weston had "clearly intended" to kill her. He sentenced Weston to life, recommending that he serve at least thirteen years.

"It has taken fifteen years for justice to catch up with you, but it has done so at last today," he said.

Detective Superintendent Barry Halliday, head of Thames Valley Major Crime Review Team, said: "Weston was originally tried in 1996 and the jury returned a verdict of not guilty. Thanks to an intensive investigation by my team, working closely with the Crown Prosecution Service, LGC Forensics and the Forensic Science Service, new forensic evidence was uncovered which proved Weston's guilt and he has now been convicted of Vikki's murder. Weston pleaded not guilty and has still shown no remorse for his crime."

CLEARED AFTER A QUARTER OF A CENTURY

O N THE NIGHT of 4 December 1979, twenty-two-year-old gas-board clerk and part-time barmaid Teresa de Simone was working at the Tom Tackle pub in Commercial Road, Southampton. After finishing work at around 11 p.m., she went to a nearby disco with her friend Jenni Savage, where they drank only soft drinks. At around 1 a.m., Savage drove de Simone back to the pub to pick up her car, which was parked in the backyard. They sat chatting for a while, then de Simone waved goodbye and walked to her car. She was never seen alive again.

Shortly afterwards, a number of witnesses heard screaming and the banging of car doors. At about the same time, another witness saw a man near the scene of the murder who appeared to be vomiting near to some railings.

The following morning, de Simone's mother, Mary Sedotti, found that her daughter had not come home and sent her husband Michael, de Simone's stepfather, to investigate. He drove around to the pub and saw Teresa's car, but did not take a closer look. At around 10 a.m. the landlord was expecting a delivery and needed to move the car. He discovered de Simone's partially clothed body on the back seat of the vehicle and immediately called the police.

The pathologist arrived at 11.45 a.m. His crime scene report described "the deceased lying on her back, with her leg bent at the thigh and knee, with the knee resting against the back of the seat, and the left thigh running along the edge of the seat with the leg hanging over the edge. The body was naked from the waist down and her left breast was exposed. Part of a pair of tights was pulled down to the left ankle. The remainder of her underwear and the other part of her tights was found in the passenger well."

Six swabs were collected at the scene: a low and high vaginal swab, two anal swabs, a mouth swab and a control swab. Further swabs were taken from de Simone's clothing and the car.

The time of death was placed at between 1 and 2 a.m. that morning. In a statement issued at the time, Detective Superintendent John Porter said: "It is 99 per cent certain that the girl was murdered, attacked, chatted to or met by her killer in a matter of seconds after Jenni Savage left her. He could have been waiting, and seen Jenni leave. It is possible that he was actually sitting in Teresa's car, as we found the nearside door unlocked."

The pathologist found that the cause of death was strangulation. The air passages of the deceased were congested and contained abundant white frothy mucous. His evidence was that foam coming from the mouth of a victim of strangulation was not a feature of every strangulation, or even of most strangulations. It was a feature only of the long, slow strangulation from which this deceased had died.

On Teresa's neck were "a series of multiple, roughly horizontal, linear, bruised abrasions on the front of the neck [that] matched the description of a chain which the deceased had been said to be wearing that evening", which was probably used as a ligature. The gold chain carried a crucifix. As a result, the tabloid press began calling the murderer the "Crucifix Killer". The chain was not present when the body was discovered and has never been found.

There was no fingermark bruising on the deceased of the sort that is sometimes associated with manual strangulations. However, the abrasions were consistent with the clothing having been gripped and twisted against the neck.

Semen was found in the vaginal canal, "in sufficient concentration to indicate that it had been present no more than three to four hours before death". As Teresa's movements for the entire evening up to her death were known, no one suggested that the semen could have come from anyone else except her assailant. Evidence of bruising to the left outer lip of her vagina and a half-inch split in the posterior wall demonstrated that the inter-course was non-consensual. The anus was swollen and the lower margins intensely congested. The buttocks were stained with blood and dirt.

Blood in the semen was of blood group A. Teresa had blood group B. Tests performed on the high and low vaginal swabs also gave reactions for blood groups AB. So the assailant had either blood group A or AB. In addition, a bloodstain recovered from a J-cloth cleaning wipe, found on the front seat of the car, was of blood group A.

A black comb was found in the rear offside well. The victim's leather handbag and personal belongings, including a diary, were found scattered around the crime scene, but her car keys, Rotary wristwatch, two necklaces, three rings and a bracelet were miss-ing and have never been recovered. However, the police did not think that robbery was the motive for the murder. Teresa was the victim of a "vicious rape by a brutal and merciless killer", they said.

Two days later the police interviewed drink and drug addict Robert Graham "Sean" Hodgson, who had been arrested for stealing a car but claimed he had some information about the killing. He had arrived in Southampton on the night of the mur-der, but gave a statement implicating another individual. But the suspect had blood type O and was eliminated from the enquiry. Hodgson had numerous previous convictions for offences of dishonesty and deception, as well as many related to offences involving motor vehicles. He had one conviction for unlawful sexual intercourse and another for being in possession of an offensive weapon. He had no convictions for offences of violence, but it was known that he had a disturbed personality and a his-tory of significant self-harm. In 1978, he attended a clinic after several incidents of overdosing. There he was diagnosed as hav-ing "a severe personality disorder" and being a "compulsive liar".

Hodgson was found in possession of property from the car and was later convicted, but granted conditional bail after mak-ing a further statement about the man against whom he had made the earlier allegations. The following June, Hodgson was arrested in London's Trafalgar Square and charged with other offences. A set of keys were taken from him. At his trial he confessed to a large number of relatively minor offences, some of which he could not have committed as he was in custody at the time. He was sentenced to three years imprisonment. While serving time in Wandsworth Prison, he called the guards to his cell and said that he needed to see a priest. Though a protestant, he wanted to make a confession.

Father Frank Moran was called to speak to Hodgson, who confessed to the rape and murder of Teresa de Simone and wanted people do know what he had done. Hodgson said that he had been a drunk and had broken into cars to sleep it off. Later, at the trial at Winchester Crown Court, Father Moran told the jury: "He said he was sleeping in a car in Southampton about 2 a.m., when a woman got in and started to scream. He said to stop her screaming he put his hand over her mouth; he was frightened, and she was frightened."

The girl tried to scream again and Hodgson said he grabbed her around the neck. Then he remembered tearing at her clothes. Hodgson also told a prison officer he needed to confess because he could see a mental image of the girl screaming as he tore at her dress and beat her to death with a wine bottle. The face of the woman kept coming back to him, he said, particularly around the anniversary of her death.

The day after talking to Father Moran, and after seeing a solicitor, Hodgson told a prison officer that he had confessed to the Tom Tackle murder in Southampton to a priest. The prison officer made a note of what he said. According to this written record, Hodgson said that he had hit the girl to keep her quiet. He had later taken her by the throat. He had ripped her clothes and taken her oval-shaped wrist watch, which he sold in a public house the next day. He said that he had been questioned by the police in Southampton and had admitted other offences so that he would be taken away from the scene of the murder.

So there could be no mistake, Hodgson even made a written confession. In a note, he wrote: "After much deliberation and thought and confession with the priest here in Wandsworth, after all the trouble I have caused, not only to you, the police, but myself, the mental torture I have gone through, the family of the person concerned, I must for my own sanity and the punishment I will receive for this horrible crime, I wish now that it was me that was dead and not the person I killed at the Tom Tackle pub . . . I did the murder, why I don't know. So all I can say is let justice be done."

When interviewed by detectives, he repeated his confession, this time giving a long, detailed description of how he strangled Teresa after a desperate struggle. Information had been released that the victim's clothing had been torn, but not which items of clothing had been torn or that one leg of Teresa's tights had been torn away from the other. In one of his confessions, Hodgson appeared to describe these details.

He also said: "There was all foam coming from her mouth." This was consistent with what the pathologist had found, but was not publicized at the time. He ended by saying that he had to tell someone what he had done.

In further questioning that day, he described how the girl had "sat on the seat with her legs outside, and then as she swung them in, she pulled the door shut". That matched with her mother's description of how Teresa got into her car. Hodgson also described how afterwards her legs were left in "a funny position to describe" after the attack, but he said that he did not think that he had assaulted her sexually. However, he did describe the watch and broken chain.

When asked why he had made the earlier allegations against another man, he said: "To take the heat off me so that you wouldn't ask me questions. It's obvious, isn't it?"

Hodgson was then brought to Southampton and taken over the various routes he said he had used during the crucial days. Later, he identified a public house where he had sold the watch. This information had not been previously reported.

He described how he had thrown away the girl's diary and, in a sketch, showed a red brick wall and an area with a broken wall. This appeared to match the place where the victim's handbag and purse were found.

Hodgson said that he had twisted Teresa's clothing around her neck to strangle her, which was consistent with the marks on her neck. Again, the method of strangulation was not public knowledge. Also, it was never disclosed that she was injured in the vaginal area, or that there had been bleeding from the vaginal area and damage to the anal area, but he seemed to know about this.

After asking to see another prison officer, Hodgson dictated at great speed an account of how he had "done the murder and must face my punishment". Again, he provided a considerable mass of detail. He said, correctly, that the deceased's car had an "N" registration. He said that he had opened the empty car with his keys and started it. The bunch of keys taken from him after he was arrested in Trafalgar Square contained what he described as a "jiggler", which he said could unlock all Fords and start them. This was what he used to open Teresa's Escort. The police tried the key and it worked.

Hodgson said he moved the car a couple of yards and went to sleep. Then he described the struggle and the fact that her clothing was torn. He said that afterwards he had made his way from the yard and that he had been sick. However, in the sudden rush of words, the officer taking the notes thought that Hodgson had said that he had stabbed the girl in the lower part of her body with something he had found in her car.

Two days later the appellant handed two exercise books and six pieces of paper to another police officer. In these accounts he asserted that he knew his victim, who had spurned him. The account in the first exercise book contained less detail, but asserted that he had asked, time and time again, for someone "to help me put this statement in my own words . . . I would like the truth to be known. So, please, can I have help?"

The next exercise book asserts that he "did the murder" and that there was nothing he could do himself to bring her "back to life. What am I to do to punish myself for this appalling crime?"

However, no assessment was made of the mental competence of the prisoner. Hodgson also confessed to two other murders – that of a newspaper seller in Covent Garden and "a homosexual in a flat in North London at the end of '78 or '79". Investigations showed that the confessions were false and neither of the crimes had actually happened. But even though two of the three "murders" appeared to be figments of Mr Hodgson's imagination, police were certain he was the Crucifix Killer.

In letters found by a prison officer, Hodgson claimed that "since 1964" he had "led a very bad path of crime, killing, maiming, all for drugs and drink".

In January 1981, in front of his solicitor, Hodgson made a further statement. In it, he asked whether the police had "the jacket which had slime from her vagina on it and pubic hair – bits and pieces from down there, and blood, I think?" After describing the strangulation, he said that he had tried to rape his victim. Later he spoke of trying to have sex with her again, that is, after he had forced her to have sex with him, when he had ejaculated. He said that he had tried to push a tyre lever inside her vagina. By the end of the incident "one of her legs seemed to be up on the back parcel shelf and the other one was down behind the driver's seat". Again this accorded with the crime scene and, although it had been reported that Teresa was half naked in the back of the car, no details of her exact position were given. The interview was recorded and the statement was signed by Hodgson, with his solicitor adding that he had advised his client not to make the statement.

He was then asked about the other two murders he had admitted to and was told that these incidents were not known to the police and probably had not occurred. Asked why he admitted them, he said he wanted to clear things up. He said that he had been told about the death of the victim of the first murder, who had actually died of a heart attack. He wondered if it was the same man he had "gone over the cubicle to". As to the second, he had "done a homosexual over", though he did not know if he had killed the man and he was worried in case he had died.

Later he described how, after killing Teresa, he was left gasping for breath, heaving, trying to be sick and crying with no tears. Then a light came on and somebody looked out of the window of flats above a shop. That was consistent with the evidence of a witness who, after hearing sobbing, turned on her bedroom light before looking out to see a man, sobbing and vomiting or trying to vomit. This had not been reported at the time.

After the interview, Hodgson wrote two letters to the investigating officers. The first expressed his concern that his confessions might not be admissible. In the second he said he wanted to be charged because he felt so much remorse over the whole affair. He would never forgive himself for killing Teresa. He just wanted to be charged. He would plead guilty and take whatever punishment was meted out to him.

"Nobody in their right mind would hold their hands up to murder as I have done with the thought of a life sentence," he said, "but I did because I did it. So can you do what you can to sort things out and get the wheels in motion, as they say."

Shown the black comb found at the crime scene, he examined it closely for scratch marks, then identified it as his. He said that it was a prison-issue comb with his initials scratched on it, pointing to some scratches and said they were "R" and "H". He said that he last saw the comb on the night of the murder but did not know what had happened to it. The comb was of a type issued by the Home Office for distribution in prisons and microscopic examination of the scratches on it confirmed that they had been made deliberately.

Asked about a red Ladbroke's pen found near the scene, he claimed that it was his. A matching green pen was found with his property. He said he had last seen the red pen the day before the murder.

These confessions seemed to corroborate everything at the crime scene and Hodgson appeared to have personal knowledge of details of the crime that had not been reported in the press. However, when he came to trial in 1982, Hodgson changed his mind and claimed to have made them up. Nor would he take the stand.

"I would like to tell the members of the jury why I cannot go into the witness box," he said in an unsworn statement. "Firstly, it is because I am a pathological liar. Secondly, I did not kill Teresa de Simone. Thirdly, every time I have been nicked by the law and that has been many times, I have made false confessions to crimes I have not committed, and this is the reason why I am not going into the box."

Without going into the witness box, Hodgson had no opportunity to explain how he knew significant details of the crime that had been withheld from the public, while the confessions he had made about the murders that had not occurred contained no such details. Nor could he explain why he had made the confessions at all, nor his movements and whereabouts at the time of the killing.

The prosecution maintained that Hodgson, "under the influence of drink, broke into the deceased's car, intending to steal it, but then fell asleep on the back seat. When the deceased returned to her car, she put her handbag on to the back seat and brushed against [him]. He seized her by the back of her jumper, twisted it and strangled her, and when she was dead or dying he raped her, removing her underwear and tights with such force that one leg of the tights was torn from the other. Thereafter he made away from the scene after taking various items from the deceased."

DNA profiling was not available at the time – it was first used in a UK court in Leicester in 1986 – and the only crime scene evidence against him was blood analysis, which showed the killer had blood group A or AB. Hodgson was in that category, along with a third of the male population. The police said that Hodgson gave them details of the killing unknown to the public, which tallied with the crime scene investigation. These included the way Teresa died, the body's position in the car and the whereabouts of her clothing in undergrowth. The prosecution relied heavily on Hodgson's confessions and there was no reason to think that those who heard them were mistaken or lying, or that Hodgson had been coerced or pressurized into making them. They were made voluntarily.

The defence maintained that Hodgson was a compulsive liar. He had confessed to 200 different crimes, including murders, that not only had he not committed, but had not happened at all.

After a fifteen-day trial, Hodgson was convicted by a unanimous verdict. It took the jury just three-and-a-quarter hours to reach a verdict. The judge, Mr Justice Sheldon, said: "It is a verdict with which I entirely agree. I have no doubt whatsoever that you were guilty of this appalling, horrible crime of killing that girl." Hodgson was refused leave to appeal.

In prison, Hodgson maintained that he was innocent of the crime. However, it was only after he had served twenty-six years that a new team of "no win, no fee" lawyers took his denials seriously.

"We looked at it and thought we were on to something," said solicitor Julian Young. "We went to see him in prison and he continually denied he had killed her. He has repeatedly denied he was the killer throughout his time in prison."

He was surprised that the case had not been re-examined before.

"I don't know if he had made any other attempts to officially plead his innocence since his attempted appeal was turned down," said Young. "I can't say why his case wasn't looked at before now, but he has been in a psychiatric ward for much of the time since then, and maybe it was just that nobody listened to him.

"He was aware DNA evidence existed but my colleague decided it was the ideal case to take forward, particularly when we're looking at old samples because science has moved on fantastically in the last few years."

Young's team wrote to the Crown Prosecution Service and Hampshire Constabulary in July 2008 to ask for the evidence in the case to be reviewed. The police had kept swabs of the semen found on de Simone's body, though in 1998 the Forensic Science Service (FSS) said they did not have it. Despite previous claims that no forensic evidence from the case had been retained, the Crown Prosecution Service agreed to resubmit all the evidence to the FSS. It was only a question of finding it.

Rag Chand, a barrister who worked pro bono (without charge) on the case, spent four months looking for the evidence. The police said there were no surviving papers in the case. Instead, Chand trawled through local newspaper cuttings to piece together what had happened. When it came to seeking the exhibits that the legal team wanted to submit for DNA testing, he was repeatedly told – like the legal team in 1998 – that they no longer existed.

"The search was the most difficult thing I have encountered in my personal and professional life," he said. "It was like finding a needle in a haystack. But I persevered because I had a gut feeling that something was wrong."

Chand's tenacity paid off when his information led the FSS to an archive of evidence on an industrial estate in the Midlands, which they appeared to have forgotten about. There they discovered exhibits from the original investigation in 1979, which included swabs taken from de Simone's body, her clothes and the seats of her Ford Escort car.

The DNA testing could then take place and the FSS revealed that the semen from the vaginal and anal swabs, and, indeed, none of the twenty samples from de Simone's car, clothes and body, carried Hodgson's DNA. All the samples then had to be retested before Hodgson was told that he was going to go free.

The papers were sent to the Criminal Cases Review Commission, who referred the case to the Court of Appeal and his conviction was quashed. This left Teresa's family mortified. For years, they had thought that her murderer was safely behind bars. Hodgson was one of the longest-serving victims of a miscarriage of justice in the UK.

"The conviction will be quashed for the simple reason that advances in the science of DNA, long after the end of the trial, have proved a fact which, if it had been known at the time would, notwithstanding the remaining evidence in the case, have resulted in quite a different investigation and a completely different trial," said Lord Judge, the Lord Chief Justice of England and Wales.

He said that swabs taken from the dead girl had been examined and there were sufficient remnants of sperm on them for proper DNA analysis, resulting in the conclusion that the sample on the swabs did not come from the appellant.

"Whoever raped her – on these findings, it can't be the appellant," he continued. "The Crown's case was that whoever raped her also killed her, so the new DNA evidence has demolished the case for the prosecution."

Granting the appeal, Lord Judge concluded: "The decision leaves some important, unanswered questions. Perhaps the most important is that we do not know who raped and killed the dead girl. We can but hope for the sake of the appellant and the family of the murdered girl that her killer may yet be identified and brought to justice. But for now all we can do is to quash the conviction. It is accordingly quashed. The appellant will be discharged. There will be no new trial."

Hodgson's barrister at the original trial, Robin Grey QC, was there to shake his hand as he was released.

"As a human being I feel glad that we no longer have capital punishment," he said. "As a defence barrister I didn't get him off, and I have bitter feelings of guilt about that."

The DNA from the swabs also failed to match anyone on the national database. But the case was reopened.

"Hampshire Constabulary have started a reinvestigation into the murder of Teresa de Simone in 1979," said Detective Chief Inspector Phil McTavish, head of Hampshire Constabulary's performance and review unit. "This is aimed at identifying the owner of the new DNA profile. The fact that we have this DNA also means that we are able to eliminate people from our enquiry. The original investigation and evidence is now being revisited with the benefit of the DNA evidence and will utilize advances in forensic science."

The first job was to track down the original police files. They then found that, in the twelve months following the barmaid's murder, the police had interviewed 30,000 people, taken 2,500 statements and traced 500 people who were in the area on the night of the murder. At one point, the list of possible suspects totalled 300 men, whom the police started to track down all over again.

"A number of key witnesses have been located, interviewed and are assisting the investigation," he said. "All persons screened to date have been eliminated against the DNA profile. We will screen as many people as we consider necessary."

The police had their work cut out. Back in December 1979, they received two anonymous letters containing "certain information" about the murder and appealed for whoever wrote them to come forward. However, their appeal met a wall of silence and whoever penned the letters never came forward. During the court case it emerged that these letters, posted on 12 December and 27 December in Southampton, had given police false information about where they should look for the killer. Those letters would need to be re-examined, if they still existed.

Then there was the sobbing man seen trying to vomit, just yards from where Teresa's body was found, at 2 a.m. on the night she was murdered. He was described as aged between twenty-five and thirty, and 5 ft 9 in. (1.75 m) tall. And there was a blood-stained man who went into Threshers in Lodge Road, Portswood, to buy alcohol at around the time of Teresa's murder. At Hodgson's trial, shop manager Hilde Hutchings said he was about thirty and spoke with a north-country accent.

"He seemed agitated, aware of where he was," she said. "He knew what he wanted, and that was a bottle of drink. He had blood on his hair and his hands were shaking. He had grazed knuckles and his nails were not very clean."

There were eight other mystery men in the area at the time who were never traced or didn't respond to witness appeals. Any one of them might hold the vital clue to the murderer's identity, where he hid before the murder, where he went afterwards and what he did with Teresa's jewellery.

The first man was seen in a light-coloured car at 12.30 a.m. on 5 December 1979, parked at the rear of the Tom Tackle, just yards from Teresa's Ford Escort. The second was seen "acting suspiciously" for about ten minutes in darkness by the Gaumont Theatre entrance, within 50 yards (45 m) of the crime scene at about 1 a.m. on 5 December. He was in his early twenties, 5 ft 10 in. (1.78 m), thin with a slight stoop, a dark complexion and dark, straight, shoulder-length hair.

A third man was seen in Commercial Road at about midnight and again ten minutes later, this time carrying a small attaché case or woman's weekend case, heading past the Gaumont Theatre from the direction of the Tom Tackle. He was aged about thirty, 5 ft 10 in., with a medium build, dark hair and wearing a grey, flecked, knee-length coat.

The fourth man was seen at about 4.15 a.m. on 5 December driving "at very fast speed" from Blechynden Terrace, left into Commercial Road. Witnesses said the driver was sitting "low in the driving seat of the car". Two youths were seen running from the direction of the murder scene after what eyewitnesses described as "a noise and some brief shouting" at about the time of Teresa's death. Earlier in the evening they had been turned away from Friday's discotheque because of their clothing. Two other men flagged a taxi down in Blechynden Terrace at about 1.15 a.m. on 5 December and asked to be taken to Millbrook.

An appeal was also made for the taxi driver who took a man from the Civic Centre to the Blenheim Avenue, Oakmount Avenue or Brookvale Road area of Portswood sometime after 1 a.m. on 5 December 1979. Although fifty drivers contacted police, the driver who took this fare never came forward.

One man quickly ruled out of the investigation thanks to DNA evidence was the former landlord of the Tom Tackle, Anthony Pocock, who was accused of having an affair with Teresa, and then murdering her after she had been raped by someone else. The accusation proved groundless.

In August 2009, a body was exhumed at Kingston Cemetery in Portsmouth and DNA was taken. It belonged to David Lace who, although not one of the original suspects, confessed to the killing in 1983, eighteen months after Sean Hodgson had been convicted. He had been just seventeen at the time of the crime. This statement was filed alongside those of five other people who claimed to have been involved in the murder.

According to DCI McTavish: "David Lace was in custody for a series of burglaries in Portsmouth on 16 September 1983. Whilst being interviewed by local officers in relation to these offences he stated that he wished to tell them about a murder he had committed. He stated that he could no longer live with what he had done and he was better off in prison. They interviewed him and, realizing that he was referring to the murder of Teresa de Simone, they duly notified officers involved with that investigation.

"He then submitted to a more detailed interview by officers from the investigation during which he disclosed the following and this detail is taken from a record of that interview conducted with David Lace on 17 September 1983. He stated that he had stolen a rucksack and cash from his lodgings in Portsmouth on 4 December 1979, the day before Teresa's murder. That matter was reported to police in Portsmouth at the time and he was subsequently arrested and charged with these matters on 10 December. He made no disclosure at that time in relation to the murder in Southampton.

"He then walked to Southampton, arriving at some point in the evening, possibly after the pubs had closed and was present at the rear of the Tom Tackle pub in the early hours of 5 December when Teresa was dropped back at her car by a friend. He approached the car and knocked on the window, asking Teresa the time. He then forced his way into the driver's seat beside her and locked the doors to prevent her escape.

"He described Teresa, her clothing and how he used violence to subdue her. She struggled, he sexually assaulted her and strangled her using the passenger seatbelt in the car. He admitted subjecting Teresa to a violent attack and sensed that he had killed her. He removed her handbag and items of jewellery, concealing the handbag in bushes nearby. He kept cash from the handbag, and he kept the jewellery.

"He left Teresa lying across the back seat of her car. He hid for approximately ten minutes before going to Southampton railway station and catching a train back to Portsmouth. There is a note at the foot of the interview indicating that David Lace described his background and inability to cope with life and that he wished to be locked up."

Despite this fulsome confession, the police did not believe him, dismissing him as a fantasist. Details of his account – the clothes the victim was wearing, the colour of the car, the number of doors it had and the injuries he had inflicted – failed to match the crime scene. Besides, they already had Hodgson behind bars.

In 1983, the police failed to take a blood sample from Lace, which would have shown that he had the same blood type as the killer, or pass his file to the Director of Public Prosecutions. They simply dismissed him from the investigation.

However, Lace was still of interest to the police. He was already a seasoned criminal. A loner with an aggressive temper, he was convicted of a minor burglary in November 1977. The following year he was given a care order for snatching a woman's handbag. With Teresa, too, he claimed he only meant to rob her, but ended up raping and strangling her.

There were four convictions recorded against David Lace after the murder of Teresa de Simone in December 1979. In January 1980, he was convicted of stealing cash and property from his lodgings on the night before Teresa's murder. Then on 19 September, he was convicted for a series of burglaries in Portsmouth and served nine months of an eighteen-month sentence in prison. On 8 June 1984, he was convicted of a robbery at a post office in Swanwick. After threatening the shopkeeper with a knife, he took money from the till and made his escape, but he was chased and caught not far from the scene. This time he was sentenced to five years and nine months imprisonment.

On his release from Dartmoor prison in July 1987, David Lace moved to Brixham in Devon where he later worked on fishing boats. He had little or no contact with his family until the autumn on 1988, when he paid a visit to Portsmouth. Family members whom he visited said they felt that he had come to say goodbye. He made one disclosure at this time to the effect that he had done some bad things in his time, such as the post office robbery. He was also responsible for killing someone in Southampton when things got out of hand some years before when he was young.

In December 1988, just after the ninth anniversary of Teresa de Simone's murder, Lace quit his job and gave away all his possessions. He told friends he was leaving and said goodbye. At 4 p.m. on Friday, 9 December 1988, his landlord found Lace dead in his bed. There was evidence of superficial attempts to cut his wrist. He had also taken painkillers and there was a plastic bag over his head. He died of suffocation, leaving no note.

His body was buried in Portsmouth and his DNA was hidden away in a grave for the next twenty years.

When the case was reopened after Hodgson's acquittal, a partial match was made between the sperm sample from Teresa's body and the DNA of Lace's sister. This led the police to exhume his body. The DNA from the corpse then produced a billion-to-one match. The police had finally found their man.

"The evidence overwhelmingly bears out Lace's involvement in the rape and murder of Teresa de Simone," said DCI McTavish, "and we are not seeking anyone else in relation to this matter."

However, the Senior Crown Prosecutor Alastair Nisbet urged caution: "The CPS has advised Hampshire Constabulary that the evidence would have been sufficient to prosecute David Lace, if he were alive, with the offences of the rape and murder of Teresa de Simone. But this is in no sense a declaration that he was guilty of the offences. Had Mr Lace lived, our decision would merely have authorized the police to begin the legal process by charging him. Only after trial does a jury decide whether a person is guilty or not, on a higher standard of proof – beyond reasonable doubt."

Even so, the crime scene investigation team went into action again. Wearing protective clothing and using a range of gardening equipment, they searched an 80 ft (25 m) stretch of land alongside a railway embankment beneath Copnor Bridge in Portsmouth where Lace said he had thrown Teresa's cross and chain, her necklace bearing her name, three rings, a bracelet and her keys. They dug down several inches below the surface, but their efforts proved fruitless.

"Since Teresa's murder there has been a lot of disturbance and redevelopment around the railway track," said DCI McTavish, "but there was still a possibility that items may have lay undisturbed. Although we have not been able to recover any items linked to either Teresa or the suspect, it was important we did everything to explore this final aspect of the case."

Meanwhile, the forensic scientists at the FSS were kept busy with testing old crime scene samples using the latest DNA-profiling techniques.

LOCKERBIE CRIME SCENE

A T 6.25 P.M. ON 21 December 1988, Pan Am Flight 103 took off from London's Heathrow Airport twenty-five minutes behind schedule. The Boeing 747 was carrying 243 passengers and sixteen crew members.

The plane was heading for New York and on board were both Britons and Americans heading for the United States for the Christmas holiday, among them thirty-five of a party of thirty-eight students from Syracuse University who had been studying abroad and were going home to spend the holiday with their families. Others were on more serious business. Bernt Carlsson, a Swede and chief administrative officer for the United Nations' Council for Namibia, was flying to New York to sign an accord on Namibia's independence.

Thirty-seven minutes after take-off, Flight 103 was cruising at 31,000 ft – 6 miles (9.7 km) high – over the Scottish border. The plane was flying at 434 knots (500 miles an hour). James MacQuarrie, the fifty-five-year-old American pilot, and his fifty-two-year-old co-pilot Raymond Wagner, switched on the autopilot and settled down for a routine transatlantic flight. As they gave their instruments one final check, the air traffic controller at Shanwick gave them radio clearance for their flight over the Atlantic.

Outside it was cold and dark. During the climb, intermittent rain had splattered against the cockpit's reinforced windscreen. Now the 115-knot jet stream was creating light turbulence. Below them, clouds at around 16,000 ft covered the Scottish landscape.

A precisely 7.02 and 50 seconds in the evening, over the tiny village of Castlemilk 3 miles (4.8 km) south of Lockerbie, a terrorist bomb planted in a radio-cassette player in the plane's baggage hold exploded. It weighed less than a pound.

The baggage hold was in front of the plane's left wing. The bomb went off just 25 in. (64 cm) from the skin of the fuselage. The shock wave punched a hole in the side of the plane sending burning baggage out into the freezing air. It ripped through the jumbo's main electrical cables. Captain MacQuarrie had no chance to make a Mayday call. The flight recorder only captured the sound of the explosion before its power failed.

Then came the full force of the blast. It stretched the fuselage skin. Within a second, it blistered and busted. Around the five-foot hole, the edges "petalled" outwards in a starburst. The blast was also channelled upwards causing the passenger compartment to buckle and break. Everyone on broad had heard the explosion. Shock waves also travelled down the air conditioning, reverberating through the cabin. Those in the forward section and those on the left-hand side of the first-class section on the upper deck suffered minor injuries from the blast.

People sitting directly over the left wing felt the plane disintegrating beneath them. The starburst around the hole was rapidly unzipping. One petal tore back as far as the wing. A second ripped forward 43 ft (13 m) and a third tore around under the belly of the plane almost up to the windows on the starboard side. A passenger plane is only held together by its thin skin. It does not have a metal chassis like a car. With such severe damage, the forces on it will rip it apart.

Amid the sound of tearing metal and popping rivets, the aircraft nosedived. The flight-control cables had been severed by the explosion and it rolled to the left. The left side of the forward fuselage ripped open and the entire nose section twisted upwards and to the right. The cockpit turned all the way around until it was facing the back of the plane, then broke way. It hit the right wing, knocking the inner engine off its stanchion. The nose hit the tailplane causing extensive damage. From there the body of the plane travelled in an increasingly steep flight path until, by 19,000 ft, it was travelling vertically downwards.

On the way down, both the nose and the fuselage spilled their contents. The aerodynamic effects of the plane's steep dive tore the remaining three engines off the wings. Around 9,000 feet, the rear of the cabin broke away and disintegrated, scattering bits of the cabin floor, the rear baggage hold and the landing gear across the fields and houses below.

It was a quiet Wednesday evening in the small Scottish village of Lockerbie when Myra Bell looked out of the window of her flat. As she looked out of the southern edge of the village, she saw a huge black object falling from the sky. She realized that it was a passenger plane and all the people on board were going to die.

A wing filled with more than 200,000 lbs (90,000 kg) of aviation fuel crashed into Sherwood Crescent at 200 mph (322 km/h). It crashed into the houses at the end of the crescent, leaving a huge crater 100 ft long and 30 ft deep (30 × 9 m). The fireball could be seen 6 miles (10 km) away. Those in the rest of the crescent felt the terrible heat and air being sucked out of their houses. The force of the blast sent Robert Jardine flying across his living room. When he looked out of the window he saw that the home of his neighbours, the Flannigan family, had disappeared. The body of ten-year-old Joanne Flannigan was found in the wreckage of their home. Those of her parents, forty-four-year-old Thomas and forty-one-year-old Kathleen, were never found. The home of John and Rosaleen Somerville and their children, thirteen-year-old Paul and ten-year-old Lyndsey, had disappeared too. Their bodies had been vaporized in the impact. Eleven residents of Lockerbie died in the disaster.

The main body of the fuselage landed 350 yards (320 m) from the Townfoot service station, which went up in flames. The ball of fire that had been number three engine hit the town. The nose section buried itself in a hilltop 3 miles (4.8 km) from the east of the Lockerbie. The other engines hit the Netherplace area. One hit the water main.

Nearby, the seismic station belonging to the British Geological Survey registered 1.6 on the Richter scale. The main impacts occurred at 7.03 p.m., 36.5 and 46 seconds after the bomb had gone off. Some local residents thought there had been an earth-quake; others thought that two low-flying fighters had collided. Keith Paterson thought that the Chapelcross nuclear power station had exploded. He only discovered what had really happened when he grabbed a torch and went outside. In the dark, he saw two eyes looking up at him. They belonged to a dead body. All 259 people on board Flight 103 were dead – or soon would be. It was later discovered that some people had miraculously survived the crash and may have lived for some time after they hit the ground, but by the time they were found it was too late.

The first fire engine arrived at 7.10 p.m., eight minutes after the bomb went off. Rescuers were soon combing the area for survivors. It was an impossible task. Wreckage from the plane was spread over an arc 80 miles (130 km) long. The local police and volunteers, including a police surgeon from Yorkshire named Dr Fieldhouse, continued the search for survivors for twenty-four hours. All those they found where dead. Captain MacQuarrie's body was found on the grass outside the cockpit. Inside the nose section rescuers found another fifteen bodies, nearly all of them cabin crew or first-class passengers.

Christine Copeland found the body of a young woman in her garden. It turned black before her eyes. The body of a young man landed on the front doorstep of Esther Galloway. For the next three days she had to step over it while the accident investigators went about their work. But most of the bodies were not intact and the emergency services had to set about the grim task of finding body parts.

Every body part had to be examined by a doctor, photographed, numbered and tagged before it could be removed. Some pieces had to be dug out of the rubble or cut out of the wreckage of the aircraft. This was a gruesome and laborious business. Some bodies were not removed until five nights after the crash.

From the beginning, it was clear that the crash site was also a crime scene. One week before Flight 103 was blown from the skies, the American Embassy in Finland received a message from an anonymous caller saying: "There will be a bombing attempt against a Pan American aircraft flying from Frankfurt to the United States."

Flight 103 had originated in Frankfurt. Passengers from Germany travelled on a 727 to London, but the flight used the same number. At Heathrow, the passengers and luggage were transferred to the 747, along with more passengers from Britain and others on connecting flights from elsewhere.

The warning was forwarded to the American embassy in Germany. Embassy staff actually cancelled their reservations with Pan Am. Surveillance was stepped up, but the general public was not alerted.

Other warnings were received. One was accompanied by a photograph of a bomb inside a Toshiba radio-cassette player wired to a barometric time switch. It was similar to one found in West Germany, just two months before Flight 103 was downed, when Hafez Kassem Dalkamoni was arrested while visiting an electrical shop in Frankfurt. He was the right-hand man of Ahmed Jibril, a former Syrian Army captain and leader of the Damascus-based Popular Front for the Liberation of Palestine – General Command (PFLP-GC), a splinter group that hired itself out to states that sponsored terrorism. Accompanying Dalkamoni was known bomb-maker Marwan Khreesat. The radio-cassette bomb was found in the trunk of their car. It had Semtex plastic explosive moulded to fit inside the case, a time-delay switch and a simple barometric switch that activated the bomb when the air pressure dropped with altitude. It usually took seven or eight minutes for the plane to reach the height that tripped the barometric switch, then a timer detonated the bomb half-an-hour later. It was between thirty-seven and thirty-eight minutes after Flight 103 left Heathrow that it was blown from the skies over Lockerbie.

Dalkamoni admitted that he has supervised Khreesat when he had built bombs into the Toshiba radio-cassette player, two radio tuners and a TV monitor. He also said that a second Toshiba radio-cassette bomb had been made. While Dalkamoni was prosecuted in Germany, Khreesat was released. Later it became clear that he was working undercover for a Jordanian intelligence organization, which itself had been set up by the CIA.

It was known that the four other bombs Dalkamoni and Khreesat had built were somewhere at large. On 9 November 1988, Interpol circulated warnings. At Heathrow Airport, security staff were told to be extra vigilant when "screening or searching radios, radio-cassette players and other electrical equipment".

At the time, the motive for the crime seemed all too obvious. In July 1988, the US battleship *Vincennes* had shot down Iran Air Flight 655 in the Persian Gulf. There were 290 passengers on board, many of them pilgrims on their way to Mecca. No one survived. A TV crew were on board at the time, so the incident was screened worldwide. President Reagan then claimed the *Vincennes* was under attack and decorated the ship's commander and crew.

Meanwhile, Tehran Radio said that the passengers and crew would be avenged in "blood-splattered skies". The US Air Force Command warned that the Iranians would strike back in a "tit for tat fashion" producing "mass casualties". The warning went on to say: "We believe Europe is the likely target for a retaliatory attack . . . due to the large concentration of Americans and the established terrorist infrastructures in place." Soon after, the CIA noted that Ahmed Jibril met with Iranian officials and offered the services of the PFLP-GC.

As a crime scene, the Lockerbie crash site was impossible to manage. Covering 850 square miles (2,200 km²), it was impossible to seal off. Immediately, it was scoured by the rescue services, the army, the police and emergency volunteers looking for survivors, as well as accident investigators and airline personnel. And people lived there. Residents reported men wearing the insignia of the FBI and Pan Am, though some of them were clearly not airline staff at all. There were other men wearing no insignia. Unmarked helicopters flew overhead, carrying men with rifles and telescopic sights.

There were clear signs of interference with the evidence. A suitcase belonging to Major Charles McKee, a Defense

Intelligence Agency operative flying back to the United States to report his misgivings about condoning the couriering of drugs to entrap dealers in the United States, was found to have had a hole cut in the side after the explosion, while the clothes inside carried no trace of explosives. A Scottish farmer found a suitcase full of white powder – heroin, a local police officer told him. There is no record of any heroin being recovered. More disturbingly, all but two of the labels that Dr Fieldhouse had put on the bodies he had found had gone missing.

As a crime scene, the crash site was in the jurisdiction of Dumfries and Galloway Constabulary, the smallest police force in the UK. So officers from all over Scotland and northern England were drafted in. Over a thousand police officers and soldiers carried out a fingertip search of the crash site for evidence. This lasted for months. Divided into groups of eight or ten, they were told: "If it isn't growing and it isn't a rock, pick it up." They were asked to pay particularly attention to items that were charred as they might have been close to an explosion.

High-resolution satellite photographs were used to locate the wreckage and helicopters carrying thermographic cameras scoured the local woods. Every item picked up was tagged, placed in a clear plastic bag, labelled and taken to the gymnasium of a local school. There, everything was X-rayed and checked for explosive residue with a gas chromatograph, after which the information was entered into the Home Office Large Major Enquiry System. In all, searchers retrieved more than 10,000 items from the fields and forests of southern Scotland.

A week after the crash, the Air Accidents Investigation Branch (AAIB) announced that it had found traces of high explosives, indicating that Flight 103 had been brought down by a bomb. After examining the wreckage of the aircraft at a hangar in Longtown, Cumbria, the air accident investigators began the mammoth task of partially reconstructing the fuselage. They found that at the left side of the forward cargo hold, directly under the aircraft's navigation and communications system, there was a small area less than 3 ft^2 (0.26 m^2) that had been completely shattered. The metal there was sooted and pitted, and the skin of the fuselage had petalled out in a starburst, a clear sign of an explosion.

The cargo hold had carried baggage containers made of aluminium or fibreglass and filled with suitcases. Most of these baggage containers showed damage consistent with falling from 31,000 ft (9,400 m). However, two of them showed other damage likely to have been caused by a bomb. These were the aluminium container AVE 4041 PA and the fibreglass container AVN 7511 PA. They were found at the southern end of the wreckage trail, indicating that they had fallen from the plane early on in the break-up.

From the loading plan, investigators saw that AVE 4041 PA had been situated slightly above the starburst-patterned hole in the fuselage and inboard of it, with AVN 7511 PA right next to it. The containers were then reconstruction on wooden frames. Around 85 per cent of AVE 4041 PA had been recovered. It showed blacking, pitting and other damage consistent with a blast. A buckled section of the skin was found to contain the remnants of a Toshiba radio-cassette player.

Although the floor of the container was damaged, it showed no blackening or pitting. From the distribution of sooting and pitting elsewhere, investigators deduced that the suitcase containing the bomb had been near the floor, but had been on top of another case. From the damage to AVN 7511 PA, it was possible to calculate that the explosion had occurred some 13 in. (330 mm) from the floor of AVE 4041 PA, 8 in. (200 mm) from the left side of the container and about 25 in. (640 mm) from the skin of the fuselage. It was also concluded that the blast damage to the forward face of container AVN 7511 PA was not caused by a second bomb, but occurred as a direct result of hot gases and blast fragments escaping from the aft face of container AVE 4041 PA. No other containers exhibited blast damage and there was no evidence to suggest that more than one bomb had exploded on Flight 103.

Meanwhile, in the United States, the Federal Aviation Administration began a series of tests detonating plastic explosives placed into a Toshiba radio-cassette player inside a suitcase packed with clothes that was, itself, in a baggage container. These confirmed the AAIB's theory about the positioning of the bomb. The FBI and a forensic team from Britain's Defence Evaluation and Research Agency analysed the carbon deposits left on the two containers and concluded that the bomb contained between 12 and 16 oz (340 and 450 g) of plastic explosive. Analysis of traces from the metal strips of AVE 4041 PA found penta-erythritol tetranitrate and cyclotrimethylene trinitramine, components of Semtex-H, a high-performance plastic explosive manufactured in the Czech Republic. It was later revealed that a large consignment of Semtex had recently been supplied to the Libyan government by a company called Omnipol.

During the fingertip searches around Lockerbie, fifty-six fragments of a suitcase were found that showed extensive, close-range blast damage. With the help of luggage manufacturers, it was determined that the fragments had been part of a brown, hard-shell, Samsonite suitcase of the 26 in. (660 mm) Silhouette 4000 range. The damage indicated that the bomb had gone off inside it. A further twenty-four items of luggage were found to have been within a very close range of the suitcase when it exploded.

Clothing was found containing more fragments from the Toshiba radio-cassette player. These included a white Abanderado-brand T-shirt, striped pyjamas, a herringbone jacket and brown herringbone trousers. Fragments of the owner's manual of a Toshiba RT-SF 16 BomBeat radio-cassette player were also found in two different Slalom brand shirts, a Babygro and a pair of tartan checked trousers, along with fragments thought to come from an RT-SF 16 itself. During October 1988, 20,000 black Toshiba RT-SF 16 radio-cassettes were shipped to Libya. In fact, of the total worldwide sales of that model, 76 per cent were sold to General Electric Company of Libya whose chair-man was Said Rashid. He was also head of the Operations Administration of Libya's External Security Organization.

A singed page from the instruction manual for the Toshiba radio-cassette player had been found in a field 60 miles (100 km) from Lockerbie by Gwendoline Horton the day after the crash. However, at the trial, Mrs Horton could not positively identify the official exhibit, as the page she had found had been intact, while the exhibit was in pieces. The police said the paper was damaged during a battery of forensic tests.

Material from the white T-shirt and the tartan trousers, and fragments of a black umbrella, carried blue and white fibres matching those from the Babygro. The Babygro itself came from Primark. Two fragments of the label were found. Together they read: "Made in Malta". The trousers also carried a label. It identified them as Yorkie-brand, size thirty-four. The Yorkie Clothing company manufactures in Ireland and Malta.

In August 1989, British police officers visited Malta in an attempt to trace the source of these items. After a visit to Yorkie Clothing, they went to a shop called Mary's House, run by the Gauci family in Sliema. Tony Gauci recalled a particular sale about a fortnight before Christmas 1988, although he could not remember the exact date. His recollection was that the Christmas lights were just being put up. It was midweek, possibly a Wednesday. At about 6.30 in the evening, a man who Gauci recognized as a Libyan came into the shop. Their conversation took place in a mixture of Arabic, English and Maltese. Many Libyans visit his shop, and Gauci said he could tell the difference between a Libyan and a Tunisian or an Egyptian.

The customer bought an assortment of clothing, though the nature of what he was buying did not seem to be of any importance. Among the items that Gauci remembered him buying were two pairs of Yorkie trousers, two pairs of striped pyjamas of the same brand as the fragment found, a tweed jacket, a blue Babygro, two Slalom shirts with collar size sixteen, two cardigans, one brown and one blue, and an umbrella. The order number seen on the fragment of one of the pairs of Yorkie trousers was 1705, and the delivery note for this order showed that it was delivered to Gauci's store on 18 November 1988.

The police then obtained, either from Gauci or from the manufacturers, samples of all of these items, so that forensic scientists could compare them with the fragments. They matched.

Towards the end of 1989, the *Sunday Times* reported that the police were closing in on the Lockerbie suspects, saying categorically that the bombing had been carried out by the German PFLP-GC cell led by Dalkamoni under orders from Ahmed Jibril with a bomb made by Khreesat. It was also revealed that a member of Dalkamoni's cell, Abu Talb, who was awaiting trial for other terrorist offences in Sweden, had visited Malta. Gauci identified Abu Talb as the man who had brought the clothes from him in Mary's House. However, in court, he identified the defendant Abdelbaset Ali al-Megrahi, who later went on trial for the Lockerbie bombing along with his one-time business partner, Al-Amin Khalifa Fhimah.

It was thought that the bomb had been on a flight in Malta. It was then flown to Frankfurt were it joined the luggage of Flight 103 being carried to London. In that case, a simple barometric trigger could not have been used to initiate the explosion, otherwise it would have gone off in the first leg of the flight. There must have been another device that overrode it.

The mystery was solved by a tiny fragment of debris found in January 1989 by two policemen on the outer reaches of the search area. It was initially labelled as "cloth (charred)" and later "debris". On 12 May 1989, Thomas Hayes, a forensic scientist at the Royal Armament Research and Development Establishment, got round to examining it. The material came from the neckband of a Slalom-brand shirt. In it there were fragments of the Toshiba RT-SF 16 and its owner's manual. But he also testified that he found a fragment of a green circuit board no bigger than a fingernail.

But there is a mystery surrounding this piece of circuit board. Hayes did not make a drawing of the fragment and where it was positioned when he found it, though this was his usual practice. Nor was a photograph taken, which was standard procedure. A month later he was assigning to other evidence lower identification numbers than the PT/35(b) he gave to the circuit-board fragment. The details of the fragment appeared on page fifty-one of his notes. But the pages originally numbered fifty-one to fifty-five were renumbered fifty-two to fifty-six. He offered no explanation of the repagination.

He had not tested the circuit board for explosive residue, claiming that it was too small, though he admitted that smaller samples had been tested in other cases. His expertise would soon come into question. He had been involved in a case against the Maguire Seven, who were convicted in 1976 for supplying explosives used by the Irish Republican Army in a number of pub bombings on the forensic evidence that they had handled nitroglycerine. The convictions were eventually quashed in 1991, but not before one of the convicted, Giuseppe Conlon, had died in prison.

On 15 September 1989, Hayes's colleague Alan Feraday sent a Polaroid picture of the fragment to the police officer leading the investigation, Detective Chief Inspector William Williamson, with a note saying: "Willy, enclosed are some Polaroid photographs of the green circuit board. Sorry about the quality, it is the best I can do in such a short time" – even though the fragment had been found back in May. He continued: "I feel this fragment could be potentially most important so any light your lads or lasses can shed on the problem of identifying it will be most welcome." If it was so important, why wasn't it looked at four months earlier?

Feraday had also been involved in three early cases where convictions secured on his forensic evidence were overturned. He had no relevant academic qualifications other than a higher national certificate in physics and electronics that was thirty years old. He has subsequently been banned from appearing as an expert witness.

Thomas Thurman of the FBI forensics laboratory identified the fragment as coming from a timer similar to the one seized from a Libyan intelligence agent, Mohammad al-Marzouk, who had been arrested in Dakar airport ten months before Flight 103. He was also carrying 9.5 lbs (4.3 kg) of Semtex, several packets of TNT and ten detonators. The timer was an MST-13 made by a Swiss company called Mebo. Thurman said on TV: "I made the identification and I knew at that point what it meant. And because, if you will, I am an investigator as well as a forensic examiner, I knew where that would go. At that point we had no conclusive proof of the type of timing mechanism that was used in the bombing of 103. When that identification was made of the timer I knew that we had it."

In 1997, the US Inspector General Michael Bromwich issued a damning report on Thurman's investigations of terrorist cases after Dr Frederic Whitehurst, a former FBI chemist who had worked alongside Thurman for five years, filed a complaint. He was barred from the FBI labs and from being called as an expert witness. It appears that he, too, had no scientific qualifications and according to a former colleague he had been "circumventing procedures and protocols, testifying to areas of expertise that he had no qualifications in . . . therefore fabricating evidence". Inspector General Bromwich found that in a number of cases, other than Lockerbie, Thurman rewrote lab reports, making them more favourable to the prosecution. He was not present at the trial of al-Megrahi. Nor did he appear in court in Paris in 1999 when six Libyans were convicted in absentia for the bombing of UTA Flight 772, which he also investigated. Again, among thousands of pieces of debris, a fragment of a circuit board was found. Again, Thurman identified the manufacturer as Mebo.

Mebo was short for Meister & Bollier, an electronics firm in Zürich. According to co-owner Edwin Bollier, he had sold the MST-13 timers exclusively to Libya at the request of Ezzadin Hinshin, the director of the Central Security Organization of the Libyan External Security Organisation (ESO), and Said Rashid, head of the Operations Administration of the ESO. When Bollier delivered the first batch, he said he met Abdelbaset Ali al-Megrahi, who he thought was a major in the Libyan Army and a relative of Colonel Muammar Gaddafi, the Libyan leader. After that meeting, Bollier said that al-Megrahi and Al-Amin Khalifa Fhimah had set up a travel business together in the Mebo offices in Zürich. Fhimah later went on to become the station manager at Luqa Airport in Malta for Libyan Arab Airlines, where al-Megrahi was head of security.

When al-Megrahi and Fhimah came to court, Bollier was described by al-Megrahi's barrister as an "illegitimate arms dealer with morals to match". Even before the case came to trial it was discovered that the timer had been sold elsewhere. Some were delivered to the East German secret police, the Stasi, who supplied terrorist groups. The judge said that Bollier's testimony was "inconsistent" and "self-contradictory".

As part of the investigation, the police were tracing every piece of luggage found at the crime scene through the baggage-handling system. Records from Frankfurt showed that an unaccompanied bag had been routed from Air Malta Flight KM 180 out of Luqa Airport to Frankfurt, where it had been loaded on to Pan Am 103A, the feeder flight to London. A properly marked Air Malta baggage tag would have routed the suitcase through the so-called interline system from Malta to Frankfurt, Frankfurt to London, and London to New York.

Detectives discovered that the baggage for Air Malta Flight KM 180 was processed at the same time as the bags for Libyan Arab Airlines Flight 147 to Tripoli. They later discovered that al-Megrahi had been a passenger on this flight, having arrived in Malta two days earlier on a false passport. As he did not take the stand during his trial, his explanation for his presence in Malta was never heard.

Once the connection between Edwin Bollier of Mebo and Fhimah had been established, the Scottish police obtained permission to search Fhimah's office in Malta. They found a diary where he reminded himself, on 15 December 1988, to "take taggs [sic] from Air Malta". However, Air Malta issued a statement in 1989, denying that an unaccompanied suitcase could have been carried on Flight KM 180. All the passengers were identified and all the baggage was accounted for.

In November 1990, it was discovered that the US Drug Enforcement Agency (DEA) often used Flight 103 to fly informants and suitcases of heroin seized in the Middle East back to the United States. Pan Am staff were used to loading these cases without the usual security checks. One of the DEA men involved in this operation, Detroit-resident Nazir Khalid Jaafar, was on board the downed flight and it was thought that he might have unwittingly put the bomb on board the plane. There was also a report that Pan Am's baggage area at Heathrow had been broken into seventeen hours before the flight.

Although Scotland Yard concluded that the bomb had been planted by Iranians or groups sympathetic to Iran, Prime Minister Margaret Thatcher was told by US President George Bush Sr to keep the Lockerbie investigation "low key" to avoid prejudicing negotiations with Syrian and Iranian-backed groups holding hostages in Lebanon. Soon after, Britain and the United States needed the backing of Syria and Iran during the First Gulf War. So it was decided that Libya was to blame. The theory put forward was that the attack was done in retaliation for the 1986 bombing of Libya by American planes that had taken off from bases in Britain. The United States and Britain asked the government in Tripoli to extradite Fhimah and al-Megrahi. But Colonel Gaddafi refused to send them aboard for trial.

In 1992, Britain and the United States went to the United Nations and asked for economic sanctions to be imposed on Libya, if Gaddafi did not hand over the two men. In late March, the United Nations Security Council gave the Colonel two weeks to hand over the suspects, or flights in and out of Libya would be banned and the country would be shunned as a diplomatic pariah. In response, Gaddafi threatened to cut off oil supplies to those countries supporting the resolution. There was a surplus of oil on the world market at the time so no one took any notice.

But, by 1998, Gaddafi was tired of being an international outcast. South Africa's President Nelson Mandela flew to Tripoli and brokered a deal. In 1999, the two men were sent to the Netherlands where they went on trial in a special terrorist-proof military compound called Camp Zeist and were tried under Scottish law. The *Sunday Times* claimed that Colonel Gaddafi himself should have been on trial alongside his henchmen: it was he who gave the order, as the British government knew, but it remained silent because of lucrative contracts negotiated between the UK and Libya.

During the trial, 621 pieces of crime scene evidence were produced, the largest of which was the reconstruction of the aircraft. That was the only one not conveyed to the court. It remained at the Air Accident Investigation Branch premises at Farnborough in England.

On 31 January 2001, al-Megrahi was convicted of the murder of 270 people – 259 on the plane and eleven on the ground – largely on forensic evidence from the crime scene. He was sentenced to life imprisonment with a recommendation that he serve at least twenty years before he was considered eligible for parole. The verdict found that he was "a member of the Libyan Intelligence Services . . . while acting in concert with others, formed a criminal purpose to destroy a civil passenger aircraft and murder the occupants in furtherance of the purposes of the . . . Libyan Intelligence Services". Fhimah had an airtight alibi. He was in Sweden at the time of the sabotage. He was found not guilty and acquitted.

The judgment stated: "From the evidence which we have discussed so far, we are satisfied that it has been proved that the primary suitcase containing the explosive device was dispatched from Malta, passed through Frankfurt and was loaded on to PA103 at Heathrow. It is, as we have said, clear that with one exception the clothing in the primary suitcase was the clothing purchased in Mr Gauci's shop on 7 December 1988. The purchaser was, on Mr Gauci's evidence, a Libyan. The trigger for the explosion was an MST-13 timer of the single solder mask variety. A substantial quantity of such timers had been supplied to Libya. We cannot say that it is impossible that the clothing might have been taken from Malta, united somewhere with a timer from some source other than Libya and introduced into the airline baggage system at Frankfurt or Heathrow. When, however, the evidence regarding the clothing, the purchaser and the timer is taken with the evidence that an unaccompanied bag was taken from KM180 to PA103A, the inference that that was the primary suitcase becomes, in our view, irresistible. As we have also said, the absence of an explanation as to how the suitcase was taken into the system at Luqa is a major difficulty for the Crown case but after taking full account of that difficulty, we remain of the view that the primary suitcase began its journey at Luqa. The clear inference which we draw from this evidence is that the conception, planning and execution of the plot which led to the planting of the explosive device was of Libyan origin. While no doubt organizations such as the PFLP-GC and the PPSF [Palestine Popular Struggle Front] were also engaged in terrorist activities during the same period, we are satisfied that there was no evidence from which we could infer that they were involved in this particular act of terrorism, and the evidence relating to their activities does not create a reasonable doubt in our minds about the Libyan origin of this crime."

Al-Megrahi's first appeal was refused in 2002 and his application to the European Court of Human Rights was declared inadmissible. In 2003, Libya accepted civil responsibility for the bombing and paid compensation to the victim's families. However, Hans Köchler, the United Nations observer at the trial, called it a "spectacular miscarriage of justice". He pointed to the role of intelligence services in the trial and stated that proper judicial proceedings could not be conducted under conditions in which extrajudicial forces are allowed to intervene. If the CIA had been able to dictate what was disclosed and what was not, as it seems they did, then the entire proceedings had been "perverted to a kind of intelligence operation, the purpose of which is not to search for the truth, but the obfuscation of reality".

In 2007, after a three-year review of the case, the Scottish Criminal Cases Review Commission granted al-Megrahi a second appeal against conviction. At a preliminary hearing in Edinburgh on 7 October, his lawyers claimed that vital CIA documents that relate to the Mebo timer that allegedly detonated the Lockerbie bomb had been withheld from the defence team at the trial. Edwin Bollier has said that the FBI offered him $4 million to testify that the timer fragment found near the scene of the crash was part of a Mebo MST-13 timer supplied to Libya. Tony Gauci had allegedly been paid $2 million to testify against al-Megrahi. And a former employee of Mebo, Ulrich Lumpert, swore an affidavit in July 2007 that he had given false evidence at the trial concerning the MST-13 timer. He claimed that he stole a "non-operational" timing board from Mebo and gave it to "a person officially investigating in the Lockerbie case".

There are doubts that if the MST-13 timer had triggered the explosion on board Flight 103, even a fragment of it would have survived. The UN's European consultant on explosives, John Wyatt, told the BBC's *Newsnight* programme that he had recreated the suitcase bomb that had destroyed the plane, using the same type of radio-cassette player, the explosives and timer circuit board, along with the same kind of clothes that were packed around it. When it was set off, the circuit board was totally obliterated, indicating that such a fragment could not have survived a mid-air explosion.

"I do find it quite extraordinary and I think highly improbable and most unlikely that you would find a fragment like that – it is unbelievable," he said. "We carried out twenty tests, we didn't carry out a hundred or a thousand, but in those twenty tests we found absolutely nothing at all – so I found it highly improbable that you would find anything like that, particularly at 10,000 feet when bits are dropping into long wet grass over hundreds of miles."

Even Bollier has expressed his misgivings about the timer.

"The fragments kept changing," he said. "The procurator fiscal showed me one fragment then the police showed me a fragment in two parts – one was green, one was brown. Later in the witness box I was shown a screen and the smaller piece was completely carbonized – you could not even see the colour. It had been manipulated, but when I tried to say that the judge cut me off."

He says he made repeated requests to examine the fragment itself, in person. The Scottish authorities said no, citing "the need to protect the integrity of the evidence", as police put it in a letter to Bollier. Instead, he was shown a blown-up photograph of the fragment. He noted the fragment's unfinished edge and a white line with wavy edges that he says prove it was made by hand and not a machine.

"This fragment of PC board is from a prototype timer," Bollier says, not part of the batch sold to the Libyans. "It was made by Mr Lumpert, an engineer here in our labs. Two of these

PC boards eventually became complete timers, and these two I took to what at the time was East Germany."

Finally, in September of 1999, with a trial approaching, the Scottish prosecutors who had refused for eight years to show Bollier the circuit board fragment suddenly invited him to Scotland. As Bollier tells it, a prosecutor, surrounded by four policemen, brought in the fragment in an unmarked plastic sleeve and placed it before him on a table. He says he'd brought his own magnifying glass – "I was surprised at how small it was."

Bollier says the fragment, just 2 × 3 mm in size, was different from the one the FBI displayed on television back in 1991. This one, he claims, was machine-made, like the ones he sold to the Libyan government, but now had a new problem: it didn't show traces of solder, which Bollier says should have been present if an electrical relay had ever been attached to the circuit board. In other words, he says, the fragment could never have been used in a bomb.

"As far as I'm concerned, this is a manufactured fragment," Bollier says. "A fabricated fragment, never from a complete, functional timer." Bollier insisted on making a written statement to that effect; the statement was signed by Scottish police witnesses.

The next day, Bollier says, prosecutors brought out the fragment again. This time, he says, it had the soldering traces one would expect on a used timer. The soldering points had apparently been added overnight.

"It was different," he says. "I'm not crazy. It was different!"

But none of this evidence will be tested in court. The second appeal was dropped when al-Megrahi was released on humanitarian grounds in 2009. He was suffering from terminal cancer, it was claimed. However, he says that he has evidence that will clear him after he is dead.

SATAN ON THE SCENE

On 30 June 2003, fourteen-year-old Jodi Jones was brutally murdered near her home at Easthouses in Scotland. Her naked body was found behind a wall along a well-known short-cut between Easthouses and Newbattle known as Roan's Dyke, leading the police to suspect a local man had been responsible. Her throat had been cut and her body savagely mutilated.

Detective Superintendent Craig Dobbie, of Lothian and Borders Police, said Jodi's murder was "one of the most violent crimes I have experienced in my twenty-eight years as a police officer". Police said that Jodi suffered a "high level of violence" and there was evidence that she had put up "quite a struggle" with her attacker before she was overpowered. Detective Superintendent Dobbie said that it was possible that the killer was heavily bloodstained as a result of the attack.

That evening, Jodi had arranged to meet her boyfriend Luke Mitchell, also fourteen, after school. Meeting at St David's High School in Dalkeith, the couple had started seeing each other in March and spent time together most nights and at weekends. Rebellious teenagers, they experimented with drugs, sex and alternative music. Jodi was a fan of Nirvana and they both wore baggy clothes. But Mitchell was fascinated by the darker side of youth culture. Although they were both underage, Mitchell admitted that they had sex just two days before Jodi's murder. There was evidence that he was sexually involved with another girl, a fifteen-year-old, at the same time. Nevertheless, Jodi seemed happy with her first boyfriend and, in her diary, said that she loved him.

Roan's Dyke path was around half a mile (800 m) long. Jodi lived around 300 yards (275 m) from the east end of the path; Mitchell about 600 yards (550 m) from the west end. The journey between their two homes took about fifteen minutes.

Mitchell would sometimes collect Jodi from her house. On other occasions they would meet at the east end of the path. Jodi had been told by her mother that she was not to walk along the path on her own.

For much of its length, a high stone wall, which had fallen into disrepair, ran along the north side of the path. To the north of the wall was an area of wooded ground bounded by a park and a golf course. A number of gaps in the wall provide access to the wooded area. The first, as the path runs westwards from Easthouses, was marked by graffiti. The second gap forms a "V" shape in the wall and is about two-thirds of the distance from its eastern end. There are a number of bushes at this point and over-hanging trees, which form a canopy over the path.

In statements to the police, Mitchell claimed that he saw Jodi at lunchtime on the day of the murder. She had taken the bus home after school and he had walked. He said he had not seen her alive after that point. He had returned home at around 4 or 4.05 p.m. and Jodi had texted him soon afterwards, asking if he was coming out. He had replied that he would do so later on, as he had to make dinner first. They made arrangements for Jodi to come down to the Newbattle area. At no time had they agreed to meet along the way, he said.

Jodi had been grounded by her mother in the weeks before her death, but the restrictions had been lifted on the afternoon of the murder. She arrived home from school at around 4.05 p.m. At 4.35 p.m. she used her mother's mobile phone to send a text message to Mitchell. He responded a minute later. A further text was sent to him by Jodi at 4.38 p.m. After that, Mitchell said, he had listened to music while cooking dinner. His mother arrived home at 5.15 p.m. Mitchell said he waited at home for Jodi, leaving at around 5.30 or 5.40 p.m. when she had not arrived.

Jodi had left home at about 4.50 p.m., telling her mother that she was going to meet Mitchell and would be "mucking about up there". At 4.54 p.m. a call was made from Mitchell's mobile tele-phone to the speaking clock.

Between about 5.05 and 5.20 p.m., Leonard Kelly was cycling along the path from the west to the east end, and heard a noise, which he described as "a strangling sort of sound, a human thing", coming from the far side of the wall. John Ferris and Gordon Dickie rode a moped along the path at about the same time. They did not hear anything of the sort described by Kelly and they did not see him. Nor did he see them.

Mitchell called Jodi's home at 5.32 p.m., but got no reply. At 5.40 p.m., he phoned Jodi's home again. This time Jodi's mother's boyfriend, Alan Ovens, answered and Mitchell asked if Jodi was there. He was told that she had already left to meet him. Mitchell replied: "OK, cool."

When she failed to return at 10 p.m., her mother sent a text to Mitchell's mobile phone, telling her daughter to come home. Mitchell replied with a call, saying he had not seen Jodi. At 11 p.m., a search party was formed, which included Jodi's seventeen-year-old sister Janine and Janine's boyfriend, nineteen-year-old Stephen Kelly, and their sixty-seven-year-old grandmother, Alice Walker. They began down the path from the Easthouses end, while Mitchell, with the family dog Mia, began from Newbattle. They met up near the east end of the path, then headed back west.

The search was conducted at night and the weather was poor. Nevertheless, Mitchell and Mia soon found Jodi's body between 11 p.m. and midnight. He said that he had walked some 20 yards (18 m) past a V-shaped hole in the wall when Mia, who had been trained as a tracker dog, remained behind clawing at the wall, alerting him to something suspicious. For a month, the other members of the search party corroborated this. But later they claimed that he had not walked past the "V" in the wall before climbing over and finding Jodi's body, which was well hidden by vegetation. The prosecution maintained that this constituted "guilty knowledge" – no one but the murderer could have known the exact location of Jodi's remains.

Jodi's body was found naked apart from her socks. Her trousers had been used to tie her hands behind her back. Other items of clothing were strewn around and had been extensively cut and torn with a sharp, bladed implement such as a knife. There was no sign of a struggle except in the area around the body. Carrying out the post-mortem, Professor Anthony Busuttil found that the deceased had suffered "a prolonged assault with extensive blunt force injury and that a stout, sharp-pointed, bladed weapon had been used against her several times before and after death".

A series of incised wounds across her neck had cut through the neck muscles, windpipe, jugular vein and carotid artery. Cutting the artery would have caused unconsciousness within seconds and death within two minutes. This, Professor Busuttil determined, was the cause of death. There had been between twelve and twenty cuts to the neck. Extensive injuries to the face, chin, neck and head were consistent with punches, kicks or blows with a blunt weapon. One was severe enough to produce a contusion on the brain. There were signs of "mechanical asphyxia" – strangulation – possibly involving the use of clothing as a ligature. There were penetrating injuries to the forehead and tonsils, the latter caused by the introduction of a sharp object into the mouth. There was also a deep cut to the face.

Cutting injuries around the eyes and deep cuts to the breast, arm and abdomen had been inflicted after death. Extensive bruising and cuts to the hands and arms indicated that the deceased had tried to defend herself. There were no signs of a sexual assault, it was said. Professor Busuttil said that he had been involved in many homicide cases and had not come across mutilation as extensive as this, or had done so only infrequently. Mutilation was quite uncommon, he said, especially where there was no sexual element in the attack.

It was also noted that there were no signs of a struggle beyond the immediate scene of the crime, particularly on the path side of the wall. This led to the inference that Jodi had crossed to the wooded side voluntarily, possibly with someone she knew.

"There has to be an element of local knowledge given the location of the finding of the body," said Detective Inspector Tom Martin. "It would be perhaps somewhat strange for a complete stranger to happen upon this walkway, which is a shortcut for kids and used by local people. To us, that would depend on some kind of local knowledge."

More than forty officers carried out door-to-door enquiries and forensic teams engaged in a more detailed examination of the crime scene. The area of examination was repeatedly extended in the hope of discovering the murder weapon.

"There is a strong likelihood, given previous experience, that this could be found in reasonable proximity to where the body was found," said Detective Inspector Martin.

Suspicion had already fallen on Luke Mitchell by the time of Jodi's memorial service on 3 September 2003. Her family begged him to stay away, but he turned up and gave an interview to Sky News, who were covering the service.

Asked if he had killed his girlfriend he replied coolly: "No. I never, I wouldn't . . . In all the time we were going out, we never had one argument at all. Never fell out or anything."

He was filmed laying flowers at Jodi's grave. They were later flung back at his front door by a distraught member of her family.

But the police did not rush to conclusions. They took over 3,000 statements during their enquiry.

"We interviewed everyone possible," said Detective Superintendent Dobbie. "We interviewed every male who had been viewed with general suspicion. That group included any males known to Jodi – both relatives and friends. Luke was one, and, at first, he was no different from the rest of them. We were just trying to eliminate people from that group."

School friends said that Mitchell carried a knife. He told another teenage that he knew the way "to slit someone's throat". A classmate recalled him saying: "I can just imagine myself going out and getting stoned and killing somebody and how funny it would be."

A witness named Andrina Bryson claimed she had seen Mitchell with a female at the Easthouses end of Roan's Dyke between 4.50 and 4.55 p.m. on the day Jodi was killed. She recognized Mitchell from a book of photographs and noted he was wearing a khaki green, hip-length, fishing-style jacket, identified by others as a parka. Its collar was up and a pocket was bulging. She was unable to identify the female, but gave a description of someone with black, shoulder-length hair, combed back into a ponytail. She was wearing a navy-blue jumper with a hood and a pair of lighter trousers, which Bryson took to be a pair of jeans. The couple had been seen together smoking cannabis in the woods.

Two other women identified Mitchell as the young man they saw at the Newbattle end of the path about fifty minutes later. One of them, Lorraine Fleming, said that it appeared he had been "up to no good". But it was the difference between his account of finding the body and everyone else's that troubled the police.

"We couldn't get away from this conflict in versions," said Detective Superintendent Dobbie. "We tried to eliminate Luke from our enquiries but we just couldn't."

The next inconsistency in his story concerned the wood burning stove in the Mitchell's back garden that was in use between 6.30 and 7.30 that night. Neighbours said that they had smelt a strange smell emanating from it around 10 p.m. Mitchell was seen returning home around that time. He told the police that his mother Corinne and brother Shane were using the stove that night. Corinne said it was not being used and Shane was not able to say either way.

"We also had reports from neighbours saying they had smelled burning coming from the Mitchell's back garden that night," said Detective Superintendent Dobbie. "Then there was the parka jacket. We spoke to friends, school teachers and others who knew Mitchell and established he had a parka jacket. The eyewitnesses had also made references to a long parka-style jacket. His mother said he had never owned one."

But others were adamant that he had one. The police then searched Mitchell's house and could not find it. Then they made a connection between the missing parka and the wood burner, "and we started to paint a picture," said Dobbie.

However, they did not want to make any further moves against Mitchell until the test results of the DNA collected at the crime scene had come back from the lab.

"When the results came back there was not one DNA profile which could not be accounted for," said Dobbie. "Every profile belonged to people who knew Jodi, including Luke. However, what we didn't have was DNA from someone unknown, which ruled out anyone unknown as the killer."

In August, the police called Mitchell in for further questioning. They searched his house again and his father's house, but still found no evidence of the parka or the knife he was reputed to have carried – a 4 in. (10 cm) lock knife, or "skunting" knife, which came with a pouch. But they did find cannabis – he boasted that he smoked hundreds of joints a week – and twenty bottles of urine.

"At this stage, unless Luke gave us a confession or took us to the knife, we did not want to arrest him," said Dobbie. "We did not want to go down that road unless we were 100 per cent confident the circumstantial evidence we had was correct."

It was not until October that the police believed that they had enough evidence to report Mitchell to the procurator fiscal. Senior detectives called on the FBI for help with the crime scene evidence in January 2004 and a warrant for Mitchell's arrest was issued in April 2004, ten months after the murder.

His mother, forty-five-year-old Corinne Mitchell, and twenty-two-year-old brother Shane were arrested and charged with attempting to pervert the course of justice when Mitchell claimed them as an alibi. He had been at home with Shane at the time of the murder, while his mother insisted that Luke was at home cooking tea at the time and denied all knowledge of the green jacket he was seen wearing. But Shane then admitted he had been looking at porn on the internet on the evening of Jodi's death, something he would not have done if anyone else had been in the house. The charges against Mitchell's mother and brother were dropped, but the prosecution further sought to undermine Corinne Mitchell's credibility as a witness by showing that she had signed a consent form confirming that Mitchell was over eighteen when he went to get a tattoo on his fifteenth birthday in October 2003. The tattoo showed a skull with flames coming from it. Mrs Mitchell told members of staff at the tattoo parlour: "That's really him."

On the day he was arrested, Mitchell's house was searched again. This time the police found a knife pouch with the inscription "JJ 1989–2003" and the numbers 666 written on it, along with "The finest day I ever had was when tomorrow never came" – said to be one of Jodi's favourite quotes from Nirvana's lead singer Kurt Cobain.

"It was like some kind of memorial to Jodi," said Dobbie. "We made enquiries and discovered that Mrs Mitchell had bought a knife which came with a pouch identical to this one in December 2003. She said she had bought it for him to go on a camping trip. But why purchase that knife? It seemed bizarre, bearing in mind Jodi had been killed and that her son was a suspect. We started to question whether that knife was a replacement to one he had previously."

Mitchell described himself as a goth and admitted stubbing out cigarettes on his hand as a "party trick". He also scratched the numbers 666 on his upper-right forearm with a compass and covered his schoolbooks with satanic symbols. On one of them he wrote: "I have tasted the Devil's green blood." On another were: "Evil is the way" and "Depression is only a stage in my life so fuck off and stay out of my mind".

He wrote an essay saying: "If you ask me, God is just a futile excuse at most for a bunch of fools to go around annoying others who want nothing to do with him. Are these people insane? People like you need Satanic people like me to keep the balance. Once you shake hands with the Devil you then have truly experienced life."

In another essay, he wrote: "So what if I am a goth in a Catholic school? So what if I dress in baggy clothes? Just because I am more violent than others and cut myself, does that justify some pompous git of a teacher to refer me to a psychiatrist? Just because I have chosen to follow the teachings of Satan doesn't mean I need psychiatric help."

However, some of these "satanic references" were not as sinister as they first appeared. It was later discovered that they were lines from the popular computer game *Max Payne*. Mitchell was said to have been a fan of musician and artist Marilyn Manson. And the prosecution claimed that Mitchell took a keen interest in the "Black Dahlia" case, an unsolved homicide where aspiring young actress Elizabeth Short was found murdered and mutilated in Los Angeles in 1947. Manson painted a picture of Short's corpse, showing massive injuries to her face, breast and torso. The crown suggested that there was a similarity between Jodi and Elizabeth's injuries. But a BBC documentary in 2007 revealed that Mitchell only owned one DVD by Manson. He bought *The Golden Age of Grotesque* two days after Jodi's death.

An extensive search of his home and computer hard disk produced no evidence that Mitchell knew of the Black Dahlia case until after Jodi was dead. In the BBC documentary Professor Anthony Busuttil, when asked about the similarities between Jodi and Elizabeth's injuries, said that "there were major dissimilarities" between Jodi Jones's injuries and those of Elizabeth Short.

At the trial that began in Edinburgh on 11 November 2004, the prosecution maintained that Mitchell had repeatedly hit Jodi, tied her arms and stabbed her time after time both before and after she died. Her throat was slashed up to twenty times, severing her windpipe and the main artery in her neck. He stripped her dead body, tied her wrists with her trousers, slit her eyelids and slashed her right arm, left cheek and left breast. He cut her stomach open in three places and thrust the knife through her mouth.

However, they produced no murder weapon or clothes belonging to Mitchell covered in blood – despite the gruesome nature of the murder. There was no damning DNA evidence. Even the wood burner yielded no forensic evidence showing that his parka had been burnt. And all the eyewitness testimony was purely circumstantial. Nevertheless, on 21 January 2005, Luke Mitchell was found guilty of the murder of Jodi Jones.

The judge, Lord Nimmo Smith, described the sixteen-year-old defendant as "truly wicked".

"You subjected Jodi to a horrible death and one can only hope mercifully quick," he said. "She still had her full life ahead of her and you snuffed it out. She was loved by her family and you have left them bereft."

Mitchell was also convicted on an unrelated charge of supplying cannabis. He was said to be a heavy user of the drug.

During the trial, the police came under criticism for their handling of the crime scene. Jodi's body was left uncovered and exposed to the elements for eight hours after it was first discovered, possibly risking the destruction of vital DNA evidence in the rain. The schoolgirl's body and the objects around it had been moved before the forensic team started work.

Crime scene investigator Derek Scrimger admitted that it was "not an ideally managed crime scene from the very start". A tent should have been erected over the scene, he said. Scrimger's CSI work was further delayed because a female colleague had arrived at the scene, but could not get over the wall to get to the body because she had a bad back.

However, Detective Superintendent Dobbie insisted that the crime scene was one of the "finest I have ever seen" and every care was taken to recover every single piece of evidence that was there. Crime scene photographs showed the initials L. M. and J. J. were found carved into the bark of a tree near to the body. However, even though the knife used to murder Jodi had not been found, the bins in the area were emptied before a thorough search could be carried out.

The way police carried out a virtual identity parade, presenting photographs of Luke and other youths to one witness, was also criticized during the forty-two-day trial. The defence claimed that "a tactical decision" had been taken not to treat the boy fairly. At just fifteen, Mitchell was interviewed without a lawyer being present in an "overbearing and hostile" fashion in an attempt to wring a confession out of him.

"We are driven to the conclusion that some of the questions put by the interviewing police officer can only be described as outrageous," appeal court judge Lord Hamilton said later. "Such conduct, particularly where the interviewee was a fifteen-year-old youth, can only be deplored."

Detective Superintendent Dobbie admitted that the case against Luke Mitchell was purely circumstantial, but insisted Lothian and Borders Police Force had done a good job.

"We have been scrutinized by one of the finest defence lawyers in the country, but not one point has been inadmissible," he said. "I am open to suggestions as to where we could have made improvements in the investigation, but I can't think of anything obvious."

However, early in the investigation the police were hoping that their crime scene investigation would lead to a breakthrough in the case.

"We're hoping we may get something forensically to stand up or knock down our thoughts," said a police source. "It's no longer the old detective thing about experienced interviewers breaking down someone's alibi. The work on hairs, fibres and microbiology, the dependence of the major enquiry on forensic science, has grown."

That evidence never emerged.

According to forensic scientist Professor Allan Jamieson, who oversaw the crime scene evidence in the case: "There was a prolific amount of scientific work in the Jodi Jones case with zero result. One of the things you don't see happening much is much being made of the absence of evidence where one might expect to find it. If someone is supposed to have been involved in a violent assault involving transfer of fibres and body fluids and these are not found on the suspect, that is rarely used as evidence [that the suspect was not guilty]. But forensic science is still a relatively new science – that may well change."

Even so, the jury took just five hours to reach its decision in what was the longest trial of a single accused in Scottish history. The defence bill alone came to £452,687, the biggest ever paid by taxpayers for a murder trial in Scotland. Luke Mitchell was sentenced to life, serving a minimum of twenty years before parole. This was the longest sentence ever given to a youth.

While 122 items were taken from the murder scene, including hairs and saliva on Jodi's body and clothing, attempts to discover the killer's DNA profile proved unsuccessful, the prosecution said. However, the new defence team brought in to fight Mitchell's conviction said that the original police forensic service laboratory report contradicted the prosecution case that the murder did not have a sexual motive as semen was found on Jodi's body. The report is also said to show that a blood sample found on Jodi produced a full DNA match with a named individual and a second full DNA profile, for an unknown male, was retrieved from a condom found near the body.

The latter individual was identified three years later when he committed a crime and provided a match on the DNA database. Mitchell's new solicitor, John Carroll, said: "The DNA evidence could put two people, two associated people, at the locus in circumstances that require an explanation."

Mitchell's original defence team had a copy of the reports but never raised them in court because of issues over who would pay for an expert opinion, according to Sandra Lean, an author studying wrongful convictions who has been campaigning on Mitchell's behalf.

Two appeals have already been turned down.

Dismissing an appeal in 2008, the Lord Justice General said that the identification of Mitchell along the path "not only destroyed the appellant's alibi (that he was in his home during that period) but also put him in the company of Jodi Jones at a point of time which on other evidence may well have been shortly before she met her death. Further, it rendered the place of her death on the general route which the appellant would have had to take to proceed from one locality where he was sighted to the other. The absence of any signs of struggle on the path side of the wall which ran along the northern side of the Roan's Dyke Path suggests that, if Jodi Jones went through the break in the wall close to where she met her death with someone, she did so with someone she knew – such as the appellant, whom she had gone expressly to meet that evening. The manner of her death was also significant, as was the unexplained disappearance of a knife which the appellant was in the habit of carrying and of the jacket which he may have been wearing on that day. The appellant's conduct later that evening was also significant – not least in the apparent ease with which he was able to identify the location of the body in relatively dense woodland on the far side of the wall . . . there was sufficient evidence in law, in our opinion, to allow the jury, if they accepted it, to draw the inference of guilt."

DARLIE ROUTIER – CHILD-KILLER?

A T 2.31 A.M. ON 6 June 1996, the emergency phone rang at the Police Department in Rowlett, Texas. The night dispatcher Doris Trammell picked up the phone to find a hysterical woman on the line.

"Somebody came here . . . they broke in," she screamed.

"Ma'am?" said Trammell.

"They just stabbed me and my children," said the caller.

"What?"

"They just stabbed me and my kids, my little boys."

"Who did?" said Trammell, trying to calm the woman. It was her job to get the details down in as orderly a manner as possible. But the caller began screaming: "My little boy is dying! Oh my God, my babies are dying!"

Trammell punched the button for the main police unit and said: "Stand by for medical emergency, woman and children stabbed!"

Then she advised the woman caller that she was calling an ambulance. The woman was now sobbing.

"My babies are dying! My babies are dying!" she cried. Then she said: "My baby's dead."

"Ma'am, please calm down," said Trammell. "Tell me what's happened!"

But by then the woman was incoherent. Trammell turned to her computer screen and traced the caller ID to a number at 5801 Eagle Drive, the residence of Darin and Darlie Routier. It was in the peaceful suburb of Dalrock Heights Addition.

The caller identified herself as Darlie. Eventually, she calmed down enough to give the dispatcher some of the details.

"While I was sleeping . . ." she said haltingly, "me and my little boys were sleeping downstairs . . . someone came in . . . stabbed my babies . . . stabbed me . . . I woke up . . . I was fighting . . . he ran out through the garage . . . threw the knife down . . ."

"How old are your boys?" asked Trammell.

Damon was five; Devon six. By then an ambulance and a squad car were on their way.

Awakened by Darlie's screams, her husband, twenty-eight-year-old Darin Routier, who had been asleep upstairs, rushed down to the living room. When he had gone to bed some hours earlier, the boys were lying on the floor watching their big screen television, while Darlie lay on the sofa in a sexy Victoria's Secret nightshirt. Now all three of them were covered in blood.

There were two huge gashes in Devon's chest where the six-year-old had been stabbed. Darin checked for a pulse. There was none. Devon's lifeless eyes were wide open and stared vacantly back at him. He turned to five-year-old Damon, who was lying against the wall with his back to the room. Blood was oozing through the back of his shorts and his lungs rattled as he struggled to suck in air. But he was, at least, alive.

Darin turned back to Devon and began to give him the kiss of life. But as he placed his hand over Devon's nose and breathed into the child's mouth, blood sprayed back into his face.

The first policeman on the scene was Officer David Waddell. He was struck by the overpowering smell of blood. He had not come across such a scene of carnage during his career as a lawman in sleepy Rowlett. Quickly assessing the situation, he instructed Darlie to get towels, cover Damon's wounds and apply pressure. But she ignored him, screaming that the intruder might still be in the garage where he had fled.

Waddell was soon joined by Sergeant Matthew Walling and paramedics Brian Koschak and Jack Kolbye. They found one child dead, another dying and their mother drenched in blood with a bloody rag pressed to her throat. Quickly they radioed for backup.

While the casualties were being attended to, Officer Waddell and Sergeant Walling followed the trail of blood that ran through the house. From the living room, it led through the kitchen and a small utility room into the garage. Their flashlights lit the scene as they moved forward with pistols drawn. But there was no one there. However, the screen on a side window of the garage had a slash down the centre where an intruder could have got in or out.

The attacker may still have been in the house, so they went back into the kitchen. It was a mess. There was blood on the tiled floor. The vacuum cleaner had been knocked over and there was a bloody butcher's knife on the island countertop. Next to it was a woman's purse and some expensive jewellery. The motive for the crime was not, apparently, robbery.

They continued their search. Upstairs they found a third child, an infant, whimpering in its crib. Sergeant Walling gently lifted up the baby boy and examined him for bruises. There were none. This was the Routiers' youngest son, Drake. He was just six months old.

Three more paramedics turned up – Rick Coleman, Larry Byford and Eric Zimmerman. They noted the two large gashes in the boys' chest, which had penetrated the children's lungs. Devon was beyond help, but Damon was still alive. Coleman quickly installed an IV tube to sustain the boy until they reached hospital. Paramedic Kolbye scooped Damon in his arms to carry him to the stretcher. It was then that he thought he heard the boy's death rattle as his lungs expelled what little air they contained.

Once they had the boy on the stretcher, Kolbye and Coleman performed chest compressions in an attempt to keep the boy alive. Then they headed across town to the Baylor Medical Center, but the child had died before they got there.

Meanwhile, the hunt for the intruder was on. A canine unit had arrived at Eagle Drive. The dogs were unmuzzled and went sniffing for scent. The paramedics had staunched Darlie Routier's bleeding neck with gauze. Out on the front porch, Sergeant Walling managed to calm her. She told him she had awoken to find an intruder straddling her on the sofa. She screamed. There was a struggle. She managed to ward off his blows and he fled towards the garage. Then she noticed her two boys. Apparently, while she was still sleeping, the intruder had butchered them. She had heard and seen nothing.

Byford and Koschak put an IV line into Darlie's arm and placed Steri-Strips across a shallow but ugly cut to her throat. Afterwards, she continued talking to Sergeant Walling, describing her attacker as a man who was medium to tall and wearing black jeans, a black T-shirt and a black baseball cap.

At 3 a.m., Sergeant Walling concluded his interview. The paramedics then escorted Darlie to the ambulance and took her to Baylor Medical Center for further treatment. Too shaken to drive, Darin called on his neighbour Tom Neal to take him there, while Neal's wife Karen stayed to babysit Drake.

More policemen arrived and threw a cordon around the Routiers' house. Neighbours awoke to find their quiet cul-de-sac full of flashing lights. Lieutenant Grant Jack, commander of the Investigative Division, arrived at Eagle Drive shortly after three. In the hallway of 5801, he met Detective Jimmy Patterson, a veteran of the Crimes Against Persons Division. Together they examined Devon, who was lying under a blanket. Patterson explained that the child's mother claimed a stranger had attacked her and the children. The butcher's knife still lay where the police found it on the kitchen counter. The mother, said Patterson, had put it there after picking it up off the floor where the killer had dropped it.

Other police began searching the house for clues. On the landing, a yapping white Pomeranian nipped Patrolman Mark Wyman's trouser leg. Karen Neal called the dog off.

"It's Karen, Domain, Karen! Now leave the policemen alone and get in your corner!" she said. She explained to the policemen that the dog did not like strangers. This immediately begged the question, what was the dog doing when the intruder broke in?

A veteran of twenty years on the force, Lieutenant Jack said he had never seen such a slaughter. Later, when he saw Damon in the morgue, he turned away in tears. For months after that, when he went into the bedroom of his own sleeping five-year-old to check on him, the image of Damon in the morgue and Devon on the living-room floor flashed before his eyes.

"I just couldn't shake the vision," he said.

It was not just the physical horror of the scene that got to him. Both Jack and Patterson felt that there was something very wrong here.

As the crime scene investigation got into full swing, the Routier home was filled by CSI men and women taking photographs, dusting for fingerprints and making notes. Sergeant Nabors's job was to examine the patterns of blood. In the kitchen, he noticed that the sink was spotless but the edge of the countertop around it was smudged with blood. It seemed as if someone had tried to clean the sink of blood.

He sprayed the area with Luminol. When the lights were turned off, the entire sink and surrounding counter glowed in the dark. There had, indeed, been blood in the sink that someone had tried to wash away.

On the leatherette sofa, he found a small child's handprint near the edge where Damon had been stabbed. Like the blood in the sink, someone had wiped it away. Why?

Crime scene consultant James Cron began checking out Darlie Routier's testimony. She said that the killer had entered and left through the garage. True, the screen on the side window had been slashed. But it showed no sign of having been pushed in or out by someone passing through the netting. Indeed, the frame of the screen was easily removable if someone had wanted to get through. Even the stupidest criminal would have simply taken it down. Besides, there were no footprints in the ground outside the window, which was soft and damp. It had not been disturbed. Cron figured that Darlie Routier must have been wrong. The intruder must have entered and left by another route. He went around the house looking for signs of a forcible entry or exit, but found none.

Curiously, the trail of blood led to the garage window. But the dust on the window sill had not been disturbed. And there were no handprints around the window. This was doubly odd as someone would have had to hang on to the wall to maintain their balance while forcing their way through the screen.

He then checked for traces of blood outside the house. Presumably, the fleeing attacker would have been dripping with gore – he had left enough of it in the trail up to the garage window. But outside there were no further traces. There was none on the undisturbed earth below the window, none on the manicured lawn, none on the six-foot fence that surrounded the yard, none in the alley outside. All the blood was in the house.

Darlie Routier said that she had fought off the attacker in the living room. But there was little sign of a struggle. A lampshade was askew and an expensive flower arrangement had been overturned. But the stems of the flowers were unbroken. It was as if the arrangement had not been knocked over, but had been placed there.

In the kitchen, only the bloody footprints of Darlie were visible – no one else's. Pieces of a shattered wineglass lay among the prints and the vacuum cleaner had been knocked over. But the blood underneath them indicated that they had been deposited afterwards.

She also said that she had run barefoot through the kitchen pursuing the intruder, but there were no cuts to her feet from the broken glass.

At the Baylor Medical Center, the staff were puzzled by Darlie Routier's behaviour. While she seemed outwardly agitated and repeated over and over, "Who could have done this to my boys?", they found her manner to be artificial and insincere.

According to the testimony of trauma nurse Jody Fitts, "Darlie was wheeled by Trauma Room 1, where her dead child was. She glanced over there, and I was very concerned she would get more upset. His physical condition alone was disconcerting. He was nude and covered head to toe in blood. Tubes were still held in place with tape, and brown bags had been placed around his little-bitty hands to preserve any possible evidence. It was a very stressful and horrible sight . . . I'll never forget it. She saw him. She had absolutely no response, just turned her head back and stared straight ahead – cold as ice."

While Darlie was covered with blood, her wounds were superficial. Even the ugly gash in her throat was not life-threatening. The platysma, the muscle fibres protecting the jugular vein, was intact. Nevertheless, the doctors decided to keep her in the hospital for observation.

Lieutenant Jack put Patterson and his partner, Chris Frosch, in charge of the investigation. The day after the murders, they went to the hospital to interview Mrs Routier. Again, she told them of her attack, but this time the details were slightly different.

"I woke up hearing my son Damon saying, 'Mommy, Mommy,' as he tugged on my nightshirt," she said. "I opened my eyes and felt a man get off me. I got up to chase after him. As I flipped the light in the kitchen on, I saw him open his hand and let the knife drop to the floor. Then he ran out through the garage. I went over and picked up the knife. I shouldn't have picked it up. I probably covered up the fingerprints. I shouldn't have picked it up. I looked over and saw my two babies with blood all over them. I didn't realize my own throat had been cut until I saw myself in a mirror. I screamed out to my husband."

During the interview, Patterson mentioned that her dog, Domain, had tried to bite a patrolman.

"Oh, he always goes off like that when someone he doesn't know walks in the door," she said.

Patterson made a note of the remark and later repeated it to Lieutenant Jack.

Nurse Christopher Wielgosz was present during the interview. He noted that Darlie repeatedly admonished herself, then and on other occasions, for picking up the knife and erasing the intruder's fingerprints. She seemed to be deliberately driving home the point.

Others noted how cold she was. Nurse Jody Cotner said: "Her mother, Darlie Kee, and her little sister, God bless their hearts . . . they were hysterical. I probably held her sister I don't know how long. They were all sobbing. All except Darlie."

Cotner had worked with trauma patients for more than a decade and concedes that people who lose their children go through a wide range of emotions.

"Mothers are always inconsolable, but in my entire nursing experience I have never seen a reaction like Darlie's."

Another nurse, Paige Campbell, concurs: "People react differently, but there is a commonality when someone . . . sees someone they love die. But I had never seen a reaction like Darlie's before. There were tissues by the bed, but she never took one."

Denise Faulk, who looked after Darlie on her first night and washed the blood off her feet, expected her to break down. Instead, she displayed complete indifference. Faulk was so struck by this that, when she went off duty, she sat down and recorded her observations.

On 8 June, Dr Santos discharged Darlie. She and her husband Darin were taken to the police station by Patterson and Frosch to make written statements. In this version she said that Damon was still standing on his feet when he said, "Mommy, Mommy"; before, she said that he had been on the floor.

That evening, Darlie and Darin went to the Rest Haven Funeral Home. In the chapel, the boys were laid out in tiny tuxedos in separate walnut caskets, surrounded by white and red roses. Darlie knelt at their sides and Detective Frosch said he overheard her whisper to them, "I'm sorry." Then she wailed, "Who could have done this to my children?"

After Darin calmed her down, Helina Czaban, who sometimes performed general housekeeping duties for the Routiers, stepped forward to express her condolences, adding, ". . . and now this expensive funeral to add to your problems".

"I'm not worried," Darlie replied. "I'll get five thousand dollars each for both of the boys."

The following day there was an hour-long funeral service. Darlie did not cry or wipe her eyes. Instead, she comforted others and made a note of who had sent flowers, saying that she would send them thank-you notes. It was the proper thing to do. The family put down Darlie's lack of emotion to the Xanax pills the doctor had prescribed.

With no crime scene leads to the intruder, the investigator focused on Darlie herself. She had been born in Altoona, Pennsylvania, on 4 January 1970, the first child of Darlie and Larry Peck. When she was seven, her parents divorced. The following year, her mother married a man named Dennis Stahl and, with her two sisters and two step sisters, she moved to Lubbock, Texas. However, the new marriage was soon on the rocks with the couple occasionally involved in violent fights.

A shy child, Darlie blossomed into a showy teenager. She was blonde and hazel-eyed, and attracted the boys, including one named Darin Routier. He worked as a busboy in a Western Sizzler restaurant alongside Darlie's mother. He was bright and ambitious, a good catch for her eldest daughter, so she introduced them. Apparently, it was love at first sight. They dated at high school and continued writing to each other when Darin went to technical college in Dallas.

There was a strange incident at Darin's going-away party. According to a friend, Darlie found she was not getting enough attention, so she left the party and returned in a frantic state, claiming that someone had tried to rape her. It did the trick.

After graduating from high school, Darlie joined Darin in Dallas where he now worked as a technician at a computer-chip company. Darlie landed a job with the same firm. The couple lived together and, in August 1988, they married.

The computer-chip industry was booming. Within the year, they moved to a small house in Rowlett. Then Darin started his own company, Testnec, that tested circuit boards for computers. He ran it out of their home.

Their first child Devon was born on 14 June 1989, followed by Damon on 19 February 1991. Meanwhile, Darin's company grew so fast that it moved into an upscale office building. Earning a small fortune, Darin had a house built for his growing family in Dalrock Heights Addition, an affluent new suburb of Rowlett. The two-storey Georgian-style mansion cost $130,000. Darin also bought a Jaguar that sat waxed and gleaming in the circular driveway.

Darlie was happy. She was a doting mother, who went overboard with decorations at Christmas and Halloween, and threw extravagant parties for Thanksgiving and the boys' birthdays. But neighbours noticed that she often left Devon and Damon, who were little more than toddlers, unsupervised. When she did look after them, she appeared short-tempered.

She was attracted by all that was gaudy and showy. When she treated herself to breast implants, she opted for EE, the size favoured by soft-porn models. To show them off, she bought skimpy, attention-grabbing outfits. Her clothing bills soared. But for the Routiers it was spend, spend, spend. They even bought a $24,000, 27 ft (8.2 m) cabin cruiser and a mooring space at the exclusive Lake Ray Hubbard Marina nearby.

This outward display papered over marital problems. There were rumours that both partners were seeing other people and there was a violent row at a Christmas party when Darin decided that Darlie had danced too many times with another man.

Nevertheless, Darlie fell pregnant again in early 1995. Friends hoped that the new child would bring the couple together. But, after Drake was born on 18 October 1995, Darlie suffered from post-natal depression. She also found it difficult to shed the weight she had put on during her pregnancy. It was a sore point that Darin used against her when they argued.

While Testnec was making good profits, Darin was not earning enough to fund their extravagant lifestyle. Ends did not meet. Cost-cutting measures failed. Suddenly, Testnec was losing money and Darin was unable to pay himself the salary he needed. Nor could he pay Darlie for doing the books, which increased her depression. Creditors hounded them and, five days before the murders, their bank denied them a much-needed loan.

Darlie became suicidal and recorded her state of mind in a diary. On 3 May 1996, she wrote: "Devon, Damon and Drake, I hope you will forgive me for what I am about to do. My life has been such a hard fight for a long time, and I just can't find the strength to keep fighting anymore. I love you three more than anything else in this world and I want all three of you to be healthy and happy and I don't want you to see a miserable person every time you look at me . . ."

Darin walked in while she was writing and noticed the tears welling in her eyes. She broke down and confessed that she was contemplating suicide. He held her and they talked long into the afternoon. By the end of the conversation, she had calmed. For one afternoon, they loved each other again. This moment of happiness was followed by tragedy.

After the boys' funeral, Darlie, Darin and Drake did not return home. Instead, they went to stay at her mother's house 10 miles (16 km) away in Plano. A few days later, she needed some clothes and got her friend Mercedes Adams to drive her to Eagle Drive.

Mercedes expected Darlie to break down when she returned home. Instead, confronted with the scene of the murder, she cried: "Look at this mess! It'll cost us a fortune to fix this shit!"

Standing on the spot where the two boys had been killed, Mercedes put her hands on Darlie's shoulders and voiced what others were already thinking. She said: "Darlie, look me in the eye and tell me you didn't kill the boys."

According to Mercedes, Darlie did look her in the eye and said: "I'm gonna get new carpet, new drapes, and fix this room all up."

"I couldn't believe it," Mercedes said later.

At Rowlett Police Department, they took a more analytical approach. There were a number of things about the crime scene that simply did not add up. What was the motive for the murders? If it was a robbery, why had Darlie's purse and jewellery been left untouched? Why had an intruder killed two children before killing the adults, who posed a more serious threat? The killer had no scruples when it came to killing two small boys, so why had he backed off when Darlie awoke, leaving a witness alive to identify him? Why would he drop the knife on the floor, giving his pursuer a weapon she could use against him while leaving himself defenceless? Why would he have used the Routiers' butcher's knife in the first place? If he had broken into the house intent on robbery or worse, why had he not come already armed? Even the cut in the screen appeared to have been made by the Routier's bread knife, which carried microscopic particles from the screen. If that was the way he came in, how had he got the bread knife in the first place? But most telling of all: why were there no physical traces of an intruder – no footprints, handprints, fingerprints, no drops of blood outside the house after he had made his escape? In fact, the only sign that the intruder had been there at all were two dead boys and the gash to Darlie's throat.

Detective Patterson consulted the coroner Janice Townsend-Parchman, who had examined the wounds Darlie had allegedly received by the hand of the phantom intruder. While the boys had been attacked forcefully and maliciously, her wounds were superficial. The gash in her neck showed the signs of what doctors call a "hesitation wound". That is, the blade had been introduced slowly, anticipating pain. Then when the pain is encountered, the perpetrator pulls back by reflex action. In other words, the wound appeared self-inflicted.

For a second opinion, Rowlett police turned to the FBI's Center for Analysis of Violent Crime in Quantico, Virginia. After studying the doctors' and coroner's reports, Al Brantley of the FBI's Investigative Support Unit concurred. The children's and mother's wounds were hugely different – Damon's and Devon's massive and mortal; Darlie's superficial. Brantley also said that the attack on the children was personal.

"The killer focused on their chests, almost as if going for their heart," he said. "That indicates extreme anger toward them."

Brantley also made other observations about the crime scene.

"For a violent struggle to take place as the mother claimed, no real breakage occurred," he noted. "After looking at the crime scene photographs, it appeared to me that the intruder who committed this crime had a strong connection to the material items in the home. The living room was fairly small and compressed. Two adults fighting would have resulted in a lot more broken things. A lot of fragile items in the living room that should have taken the brunt of a struggle were not broken."

His conclusion was that Devon and Damon's killer was someone who knew them and knew the house. The entire scenario had been planned in advance – and it had been staged.

Devon's birthday fell just eight days after his murder. Bizarrely, the Routiers decided to celebrate with a party at his graveside. Darlie and Darin Routier, baby Drake, Darlie's sixteen-year-old sister Dana, her mother and a few invited personal friends attended, along with a news crew from local television station KXAS-TV. It was, at the very least, in shockingly bad taste.

Patterson's men were also filming the event with a hidden camcorder. A concealed microphone had also been planted nearby to catch any remark that could be interpreted as a confession. With the TV cameras there, this was hardly necessary.

The proceedings opened with a pastor delivering a eulogy. Darlie, who was laughing and chewing gum, sprayed a can of Silly String over the grave. She sang "Happy Birthday" and cried: "I love you, Devon and Damon!"

Afterwards, she told reporter Joe Munoz: "If you knew my sons, you'd know that they are up there in heaven having the biggest birthday party we could ever imagine. And though our hearts are breaking, they wouldn't want us to be unhappy. But they'll be a part of us always."

She was then asked about the boy's mysterious killing and said: "The only thing that keeps me going is the hope that they will find that person. I have faith in God. I believe He will direct the police to that man."

Four days later, Darlie Routier was arrested for the murder of her two children. After the televised birthday party, this caused a nationwide sensation. News crews and network anchors descended on Rowlett.

Darlie insisted on being given a polygraph test, but withdrew the request when she was told that her husband could not be in the room while the test was being administered. Later, the defence team renewed the request, provided she was allowed to take a test in private first. The result was never released, but Darlie and her mother were seen crying afterwards.

Darlie remained in custody while a grand jury indicted her on two counts of capital murder. That same day, 28 June, Judge Mark Tolle, who would preside at her trial, issued a gag warrant, barring both the defence and prosecution from discussing the case with the media. Meanwhile, Darlie's court-appointed lawyer Doug Parks requested the trial be moved out of Dallas County where bad publicity might prejudice the jury. Judge Tolle agreed and it was moved to Kerrville in neighbouring Bexar County.

State Prosecutor Greg Davis announced he would seek the death penalty – though the last woman to be executed in Texas had been hanged during the Civil War. Nevertheless, the Routiers dropped the court-appointed lawyers. Their in-laws mortgaged their homes to pay for top lawyer Doug Mulder, formerly of the district attorney's office. He assembled a top-rank team that included a retired FBI investigator. Meanwhile, Darin abandoned the house in Eagle Drive, leaving the mortgage in arrears. It was repossessed.

Jury selection took nearly a month. Eventually, a panel of five men and seven women were selected. By this time, press speculation was at fever pitch. When the trial began on 6 January 1997, crowds descended on the tiny courthouse. Visitors had to pass through a metal-detector gate, while purses and briefcases were searched. No tape recorders, cameras or newspapers were allowed in.

The prosecution decided only to proceed on one murder charge, that of Damon, holding the murder indictment on Devon in reserve in case Darlie was acquitted or, in the state prosecutor's eyes, escaped with a life sentence. She pleaded not guilty.

In his opening remarks, State Prosecutor Davis said: "The evidence will show you, ladies and gentlemen, that Darlie Routier is a self-centred, materialistic woman cold enough to murder two precious children." He would, he said, prove that the crime scene evidence found by experts did not match her story of what happened in her home on the night of the killings.

For the defence, Mulder said that Darlie was a caring mother, though, like any many another housewife, had her own personal problems and concerns.

"The State wants you to believe she became a psychotic killer in the blink of an eye," he said. "Well, folks, that's just absurd!"

The first witness for the State was Dr Joanie McLaine from the medical examiner's office. She drew the jury's attention to two defence wounds on Damon's body. These indicated that he had struggled with his attacker before he died. Then Dr

Townsend-Parchman described the differences between the children's savage wounds and Darlie's hesitation wounds and suggested that Darlie inflicted her wounds on herself.

Officer Waddell described the crime scene that confronted him on 6 June and the jury were shown the crime scene photographs. Paramedic Jack Kolbye told of the efforts made to save Damon's life. Then fellow paramedic Larry Byford, who was with Darlie in the ambulance, testified that during the entire trip to the hospital she did not once ask about her children.

In the second week of the trial, Officer David Maynes introduced the material evidence uncovered from the crime scene, including a section of white carpet that bore Damon's bloody handprint. Then fingerprint expert Charles Hamilton told the jury that the only prints uncovered at the scene were those of Darlie and the two boys.

Crime scene investigator James Cron described following the path of the supposed intruder's flight through the Routier home and garage. During this detailed scientific trek, he failed to turn up any sign that there ever had been an intruder.

"After my initial walk-through, I thought someone in the family had committed the murders and staged the scene," he said. "The further I got into my investigation, the more convinced I became."

Charles Linch, an analyst for the Southwestern Institute of Forensic Sciences, agreed that it was impossible for any intruder to have left the crime scene without leaving a trail of blood. Then blood-splatter expert Tom Bevel discussed patterns of blood found on Darlie's nightshirt. Both boys' blood was found, indicating, at the very least, that she was close to them while they were being stabbed. There was also blood on the shoulder and back of the nightshirt. This came from the knife, he maintained, while she was making the upswing. That is to say, she was doing the stabbing.

There was very little blood on the sofa, where Darlie said she had been stabbed, and the slash on Darlie's throat was made by a knife coming down at a forty-five-degree angle, consistent with her inflicting the wound herself.

FBI special agent Al Brantley also dismissed the idea that there had been an intruder. Anyone breaking into the house would not have cut the screen, but removed it. And the position of the Routiers' house, behind a high fence in a cul-de-sac, would have discouraged a burglar or rapist.

A thief would have taken Darlie's purse and jewellery, while a rapist would not have killed the children but used them to force her to submit. The ferocity of the assault on the boys led him to believe that the attack was personal and had been done in extreme anger.

"Someone who knew those children very well murdered them," Brantley concluded.

The prosecution case, which depended almost totally on crime scene evidence, was damning.

The defence countered with relatives, neighbours and friends who testified to Darlie's good character. The Reverend David Rogers, who officiated at the funeral, said Darlie was "grieving appropriately". Neighbour Karen Neal, who had stepped in to babysit Drake on the night of the murders, said Darlie's grief was real, not artificial as the prosecution was suggesting. Darlie's friend, Cara Byford, talked of her kindness. She said that Darlie came to her for consolation as Cara had lost a four-month-old boy previously.

Darin Routier testified that Darlie had been devastated by their boys' deaths. He also recounted administrating CPR to Damon.

"Darlie was running back and forth getting wet towels, going, 'Oh, my God! Oh, my God, he's dead!'" he said. "I blew two or three times. She was over him trying to hold the gaps in his chest together. I knew he was dead in three minutes. I screamed at Officer Waddell, and Darlie tried to get him to go to the garage. All three of us were in shock."

However, Darin's presence in the witness box allowed the family's financial problems to be aired.

To counter the prosecution's testimony about Darlie's "hesitation wounds", the defence called Bexar County's medical examiner Dr Vincent DiMaio, a professor of forensic pathology.

The gash to her throat, he said, came within 2 mm of the carotid artery. And bruises on her arms were caused by a blunt instrument and could not be self-inflicted.

Forensic psychologist Dr Lisa Clayton was called to explain that people who had gone through some traumatic event were often unable to give a clear account of it afterwards. And Darlie exhibited the typical blackout and distorted-memory symptoms of those who had lived through trauma.

Finally, against the advice of her counsel, Darlie took the stand. Mulder took her through her life story and painted her as the dedicated stay-at-home mother of three. He got her to read from her diary to show that she was not the shallow, thoughtless person she had been portrayed as. The Silly String used at the graveside during Devon's posthumous birthday party was brought by her younger sister, Dana, not her, she explained. It was a symbol of the fun the little boys would have had, had they been alive. As for the inconsistencies in her account of the murder: deep in shock, she simply could not remember things clearly.

The prosecution would not accept this. They took her through the various contradictions she had made in her interviews with the police. Why had she told one policeman one thing, another something else? Why didn't her dog bark when the intruder entered the house? Why had she washed the blood out of the kitchen sink? The prosecution suggested she had gashed her throat over the sink and washed the blood down. Why had she lied and lied and lied? They left her a broken, sobbing woman.

On 1 February 1997, the jury found Darlie Routier guilty of the murder of her son Damon. Three days later, Judge Tolle handed down his sentence. It was death. However, there remained some doubts about her guilt.

A special episode of ABC's investigative TV show *20/20*, entitled "Her Flesh and Blood", aired on 3 February 2000. It reviewed the Routier case and found that the jury may not have been shown photographs of bruises on Darlie's arms, which may have revealed that she had fought off an attacker. Nor had they seen the police surveillance videotape of Devon's graveside birthday party that showed Darlie and her family sincerely grieving over the children. Audio tapes presented at the trial were incomplete and there were errors and omissions in the court transcript. One juror claimed he was pressured into giving a guilty vote.

Barbara Davis, who wrote the book *Precious Angels* about the case, discovered that there was a latent, bloody fingerprint found on the Routier living-room table. According to two New York City police fingerprint experts, the print did not match Darlie nor Darin, nor any of the officers at the scene. Another finger-print expert, Dr Richard Jantz, said that the unidentified bloody fingerprint left at the crime scene is "consistent with an adult" rather than a child, so lends new credence to the intruder story. Another unidentified print was found on the door of the garage. An unidentified pubic hair was found at the scene of the crime and a bloodstained sock was found in an alley a few houses away.

On 25 July 2001, the Dallas *Morning News* reported that Darlie's lawyers had filed an appeal, citing thirteen trial errors and a possible conflict of interest. The defence counsel was also representing Darin Routier, another potential suspect in the crime. Indeed, the Routiers had dropped the public defender Douglas Parks after they heard that he intended to portray Darin as the guilty party. They had then taken on Doug Mulder on the understanding that he would not "go after" Darin.

In June 2002, the *Morning News* reported that, months before the murder, Darin Routier had asked his father-in-law, Robbie Gene Kee, whether he knew anyone who would burgle his home as part of an insurance scam. He may have mentioned this to others, making the house a target. Neighbours said they saw men in a black car watching the house before the Routier boys were killed. Darin Routier later admitted that he had looked for some-one to burgle the house, but that he planned to have it done when the family was not at home.

As the prosecution case had depended almost totally on crime scene evidence, in July 2002, Darlie's lawyers asked prosecutors to hand it over for new forensic tests. They were particularly keen to have Darlie's nightgown, believing that they could use it to demonstrate that her wounds were not self-inflicted. They also wanted to test the butcher's knife, the samples of bloodstained carpet and the window screen. But on 10 September 2008, the Texas Court of Criminal Appeals rejected her attorney's motion for a second chance to make their case for more DNA testing. They fight on in the federal courts. Meanwhile, Darlie Routier sits on Texas's death row. She continues to protest her innocence.

A STAGED SUICIDE?

W HEN THE POLICE found Paula Gilfoyle hanging in the garage
of the family home in the Wirral, Cheshire, they thought she
had committed suicide. But when experts examined the crime
scene, they concluded she had been murdered. Her husband
Eddie was convicted of the offence in 1993, but the dispute about
the interpretation of the evidence runs on. Even though he was
released on licence after serving eighteen years of his life sentence,
Gilfoyle is still determined to prove his innocence.

Eddie Gilfoyle was a veteran of the Royal Army Medical
Corps. He left the army in 1986. In January 1991, he started
work as a theatre technician at Murrayfield BUPA Hospital in
the Wirral where his job was to sterilize and prepare surgical
instruments before operations.

He had met Paula Carbert at the wedding of his sister
Christine in June 1988. A year after they met, they married and
moved into a modest terraced house in Sherlock Lane, Wallasey.
But then things began to go wrong. In June 1991, the couple
bought a substantial three-bedroom, semi-detached house in
Grafton Drive, a quiet residential area, close to Upton Village. It
became a bone of contention.

At the time, Paula worked on the assembly line at the local
Champion Spark Plug factory and ran a mail-order business
from home. Their new house needed a good deal of renovation,
so the couple moved into the home of Paula's parents while the
work was being done. This did not suit Eddie and after two
months he moved into Grafton Drive, even though the renovation was not complete. Although the remaining work was largely
cosmetic, Paula refused to move into the house with him and
made it clear that she would not move in at all until the house
was completely finished.

While Eddie continued working on the house, Paula went on

holiday to Turkey with her mother, Joan Carbert, and her best friend, Julie Poole, who was accompanied by her young child. Eddie was put out. He thought the money would be better spent on their new home.

When Paula returned, she went back to her parents' home while Eddie continued to live at the new house in Grafton Drive. To speed up the work, Eddie paid his friend, David Mallion, to do various jobs in the house while his own father, Norman Gilfoyle, lent a hand decorating.

But the relationship had not broken down altogether. Paula would call in for an hour or so after she had finished work to see how the decorating was progressing. The couple would occasionally have a night out together and, very occasionally, Eddie would stay overnight with Paula at her parents' home. Nevertheless, their relationship continued to deteriorate. Even though Eddie and his father managed to complete one bedroom, the living room, the kitchen and the bathroom, Paula still refused to move in. She remained at her parents' for another three months.

During this time Eddie began a relationship with Sandra Davies, who worked in the canteen at Murrayfield Hospital. They both maintain that this was not a physical relationship. Sandra was having problems with her own marriage and it seems that, in each other, they found a shoulder to cry on. Eddie still did everything he could to get Paula to move into their new home – even, at one point, threatening to go to a solicitor to formalize their separation. It did no good.

Towards the end of October 1991, Eddie had given up all hope of Paula returning to the marriage, so he asked Sandra to move into the house at Grafton Drive with him. She agreed, so Eddie asked Paula to come to Grafton Drive and collect her belongings. When she arrived at Grafton Drive, she announced that she was pregnant. It seemed like a golden opportunity for a new beginning, so Eddie phoned Sandra and told her of his wife's pregnancy. Sandra was understandably upset as she had been led to believe that Eddie's relationship with his wife was at an end. But now, under the new circumstances, Eddie explained that he intended to try and make his marriage work. Paula also called Sandra and told her to keep away from her husband.

For a while it seemed that Eddie and Paula had patched up their differences and Paula moved into Grafton Drive. However, on 11 February 1992, Eddie sent Sandra a birthday card, followed by a Valentine's Day card. More shocks were to come. In April, Paula wrote Eddie a letter saying that the baby she was carrying was not Eddie's. She stated that she had been having an affair for the past fourteen months with a man called "Nigel", who was the father of the child. Furthermore, she intended to leave Eddie to go and live abroad with Nigel. The letter also urged him "to try and pick up the pieces with Sandra". However, there is no evidence that this man existed, or that she was having a relationship with anyone other than Eddie.

At work, Eddie showed the letter to Sandra, who read it and returned it to Eddie, saying she was not prepared to become involved in Eddie's marital problems. With nobody else to turn to, Eddie asked his boss if he could go home. When asked what was wrong, Eddie broke down and explained that his wife had told him the baby she was having was not his.

However, Paula did not leave and go abroad with Nigel. On more than one occasion, she set a date, but when the day came she did not leave. Gradually, Eddie came to believe that Paula was not telling him the truth about Nigel. Strangely, Paula had not told anyone else of her plans to leave the country with Nigel, and asked Eddie to also keep quiet about her plans. He reluctantly agreed. In the meantime, he tried every way he could to make Paula happy in the hope that she would stay with him. The longer she stayed with him, the more he felt that his attempts to keep her were going to be successful. But on 2 June, Paula dropped another bombshell. She said that the father of the child was not the fictional Nigel, but her brother-in-law Peter Glover, who was married to her sister Margaret. Again, Paula swore Eddie to secrecy. Besides, she said, there was a chance that the baby was Eddie's as they had slept together around Eddie's birthday, which was when the baby was conceived. However, she thought it was more likely that the father was Peter Glover.

Naturally, Paula was in an emotional state when she revealed this. They talked late into the night. Eddie said that he loved Paula. He would stay with her and bring up the child as his own. However, under the circumstances, they would have to move further away from Paula's family. In pursuance of this, Eddie rang his brother, David Gilfoyle, who was a hotel manager in Bournemouth. He asked David if he could arrange accommodation for a couple he knew who were moving into the Bournemouth area in a few weeks. They had a young baby and he also asked David if he could help find a job for his friend. David said he would do what he could to help, unaware that the accommodation was intended to be for Eddie, Paula and their child, and the job for Eddie himself.

When Paula told Eddie about her affair with Glover, she said that was why she had initially wanted to move from their previous home in Sherlock Lane, which was just a short walk from Glover's house. Glover could not drive: Grafton Drive was further away and he would not be able to drop around. This made sense to Eddie. He recalled an occasion when, at the last minute, he had taken the day off work. About half an hour after Eddie would have normally left for work, Glover turned up. As it was, Glover helped Eddie paint the back gate. He asked Eddie not to mention this to his wife, who thought he was at work. Paula had also insisted that Glover should be the best man at their wedding, though the choice of best man was traditionally that of the groom. However, DNA testing subsequently showed that Paula's child was Eddie's and Glover denied any impropriety with his sister-in-law.

On 3 June, the day after Paula's revelation about her affair with Glover, Eddie arrived home from work early and tried to get Paula to continue their discussion. But Paula said, before she would talk more about Glover, she had to speak to her other sister, Susan Dubost. That evening Eddie drove Paula to Susan's house. But Susan had visitors and Paula was unable to speak to her sister privately, so they left after ten minutes.

At about 4.40 p.m. the following day, 4 June 1991, Eddie arrived home from work to find a letter from Paula in the kitchen. After reading the first few lines, Eddie said he thought Paula was finally leaving him. Without reading the rest of it, he jumped into his car and drove to his parents' house. It transpires that the letter was, in fact, a suicide note.

When Eddie arrived at his parents' house in Claughton Drive, Wallasey, his father was not there. But his mother, Jessie, read the letter. She understood its significance, but told Eddie that it was probably a cry for help and Paula had no real intention of committing suicide.

Eddie's father, Norman, did not get home until 6.10 p.m. that day. After he read the letter, the three of them drove to Grafton Drive. They searched the house but there was no sign of Paula. Norman then began to call Paula's family and friends. When this drew a blank, he rang his son-in-law, Paul Caddick, who was a sergeant at the local police station in Upton. He arrived at Grafton Drive at around 7.10 p.m. After reading the suicide note, he decided that they should make a formal call to the police. He rang Upton Police Station and spoke to his colleague, Constable Tosney.

When Constable Tosney arrived at Grafton Drive, they began searching the outbuildings and found that the garage was locked. Caddick asked Eddie for the keys. Eddie gave him a bunch of keys from the kitchen that belonged to Paula. None of them fitted the garage. Eddie then picked up the mat in the porch and gave Caddick two single keys, one of which he used to open the Yale lock of the garage. Caddick and Tosney said the two keys were identical. Later, Eddie said that there should have been a garage key on Paula's key ring, but no other garage key was found inside the garage or elsewhere.

In the garage, they found Paula hanging by a rope from a roof beam. A set of small aluminium ladders was near her. It was clear that she was dead. The coroner's officer, the CID, the police surgeon, the scene-of-crime officer and the local undertakers were all informed. At the time, it was assumed that the incident was a straightforward suicide by hanging. The suicide note made it plain that she intended to kill herself. Paula had left a diary and other written material showing that she was at a low ebb.

However, three of Paula's friends – Diane Mallion, Julie Poole and Christine Jackson – had misgivings and made statements to the police. They said that Paula had told them that Eddie was doing a course on suicide at work. As part of it, he had asked her to write suicide notes. This had worried and frightened her. They said that Eddie had also taken Paula into the garage to show her how to put up a rope. These statements caused the police to reconsider their initial assumption that the death was a suicide and began to investigate the possibility of murder.

Key to their investigation was Paula's state of mind. Three weeks before the baby was due, she had a leaving party at work where she was described as "radiant". Seventeen witnesses described her as being happy and looking forward to the birth of the child, despite misgivings about the birth itself. Her gynaecologist and her GP, whom she visited regularly and who saw her last a week before her death, both described her as fit and positive about the birth. She had no history of depression. She had prepared a nursery and had bought two sets of baby equipment so that one could be left with her mother, who was going to look after the baby when she returned to work. She had talked about the christening with the local vicar. Two days before her death, she had been to the library and borrowed six books on childcare and names.

On the morning of 3 June, she appeared happy and normal. That afternoon she had a conversation with a friend about a man whom they both knew who had recently hanged himself. Paula had said: "How could someone hang themselves? How could you get so low? His wife will feel guilty for the rest of her life."

That evening, again, she was her usual happy self. There was nothing in her personality or behaviour to suggest that she was about to take her own life.

The following morning, a market researcher doing a wine survey called at the house and spoke to Paula and Eddie. She was there for about fifteen to twenty minutes. She was unclear about the time, but thought the visit was between 11 a.m. and noon.

According to Eddie, she had left by 11.15 a.m. He left for work about 11.25 a.m. Then, at 11.50 a.m., a courier for Freemans catalogue company called to deliver a package, but got no reply. Other people called at the house between 2 and 2.30 p.m. They, too, got no reply. At 2 p.m. Paula had an antenatal appointment, which she missed. She had not missed any appointments previously.

Eddie's shift at work began at 12.30 p.m. and he was seen by Sandra Davies reading a paper in the canteen from about 11.30 a.m. to 12.20 p.m. His shift was due to end at 8.30 p.m., but he asked for time off and was allowed to leave at 4.30 p.m. There was no evidence that he had been absent from work between 11.30 a.m. and 4.30 p.m. Eddie said he got home at about 4.40 p.m., noticed his wife was missing and found a suicide note in the kitchen. As a result of reading it, he said he panicked and went straight to his parents' house, arriving there at about 4.50 p.m. But this was not confirmed by his mother. The courier from Freemans said she returned at about 5.30 p.m. and found Eddie in the drive. He signed the delivery note and manifest in his wife's name, though it has been suggested that the courier got the date wrong. However, a neighbour said she saw Eddie in his drive at about 5.30 p.m. She fixed the day and time by reference to her children's music lessons. Another neighbour said he saw Eddie going into a shop in Upton at about 5.50 p.m.

The timeline was confused, so the crime scene evidence was crucial to deciding whether Paula had committed suicide or been murdered. Unfortunately, no photographs were taken of the body before it was cut down. And there were no pictures of the rope on the beam. As no foul play was suspected, the temperature of the body was not taken. When the police surgeon, Dr Roberts, arrived at 8.20 p.m., he took three photographs of the body on the floor of the garage. At that stage, he and Dr Burns, the pathologist who carried out a second post-mortem, estimated the time of death as having been between three and eight hours before Dr Roberts had examined the body. Both acknowledged that the margin of error could be considerable.

Post-mortem examination confirmed that the cause of death was hanging. There was a single ligature mark and, apart from two small scratches immediately above it, no other injury to the body. There was no sign of drugs or alcohol in Paula's system.

Paula was 5 ft 8 in. (1.73 m) tall. Her total reach was 7 ft 2 in. (2.18 m). But the distance from the top platform of the ladder to the underside of the beam was 7 ft 4 in. (2.23 m) and to the top-side of the beam 7 ft 10 in. (2.39 m). Her legs were crossed and bent at the knee, with one foot resting on the bottom rung of the aluminium ladder. According to the coroner's officer, the rope had been wrapped round the beam three times with a knot halfway up the side of the beam. He was 6 ft 1 in. (1.85 m) tall and the knot was only just within his reach when standing on the platform of the ladder.

After the body was cut down, a mortuary technician removed the ligature from around the neck and, as the coroner had decided there were no suspicious circumstances, threw it away. The technician subsequently reconstructed the two knots on the ligature, one on top of the other, as he remembered them. This would have permitted the ligature to tighten under the weight of the body.

The end of the rope that had been attached to the beam had been preserved. But there was no evidence concerning the exact length of the rope, or where the knot was positioned on the beam, or the exact distance of the deceased's feet from the floor. However, it was later estimated that her knees were about 15 in. (38 cm) from the floor, so that her feet would have touched the floor had her legs not been bent.

In a drawer in the house, another noose was found. This was thought to have been a practice noose, but there was no evidence about who had been practising. However, the prosecution contended that Eddie Gilfoyle had killed his wife and had dressed up her murder to make it look like suicide. He had tricked his wife into writing the suicide note, which he said he had found after her death, then persuaded her to take part in a lethal experiment. He had got her to put her head into a noose, then suddenly knocked her off her feet, giving her no time to struggle. The ligature tightened under the weight of her body, quickly causing her death. The pathologist Dr Burns noted two small parallel scratches on the deceased's neck above the ligature. These could be interpreted as the deceased's attempts to release the ligature. He said that in twelve years, seeing about ten suicide cases a year, he had not seen one in which there was a scratch mark on the neck.

Dr Burns conceded that, while most suicide victims had their feet well above the ground, in many cases the feet were on the ground and there were successful suicides when the victim was sitting, kneeling or even lying down. The coroner's officer said the body touched the floor in about half of the many hanging deaths he had seen. But the prosecution said that Paula was not tall enough to put the rope round the beam several times and tie it at the side of the beam when standing on the aluminium stepladder. She was also was too heavily pregnant to have done this. Had she been set on suicide, there were loose timbers at about head height that were far more obvious and accessible.

A longer wooden stepladder was found in a storeroom. She could have used it to rig up the noose, but in that case why would she have returned the ladder to the storeroom before committing suicide? However, her husband could have used the wooden stepladder to rig up the rope in advance and then put the ladder away. Neighbours heard a noise from the garage at around 4 a.m. on 4 June. The prosecution claimed that Gilfoyle was preparing the noose at that time. He then removed his wife's garage key from her key ring in case she went into the garage and saw it.

When interviewed by the police, Gilfoyle denied murdering his wife and maintained that she had committed suicide or killed herself accidentally while making a grand gesture. He said she had not been herself for several days and was terrified of giving birth. Suicide was on her mind. She had been talking about it for a week or so before she died. He thought she may have written the Nigel letter to stir emotion in him and she may have told him she was having an affair with Peter Glover for the same reason.

The defence contended that the position of the body was consistent with suicide and that it was not uncommon in suicide to find the feet within reach of the ground. There was no indication of any struggle having taken place in the garage and the two scratches on Paula's neck could be explained as the instinctive reaction of the hands, bringing them to the neck as the ligature tightened. Gilfoyle maintained that it was ridiculous to suggest he had persuaded his wife to go into the garage and let him tie a rope round her neck. There were bound to have been signs of a struggle. It was possible she had tied the rope to the beam with no intention of taking her own life, but something had gone wrong and she had died by accident. Besides, Gilfoyle was looking forward to the birth of their child. He maintained he did not have the opportunity to kill his wife between the departure of the market researcher and leaving to go to work. The courier from Freemans and the neighbours who said they had seen him at home that afternoon were mistaken. The jury did not believe Gilfoyle and he was convicted.

In 1998, Professor Crane, a distinguished pathologist from Northern Ireland, produced a report for the Criminal Cases Review Commission. Unlike Dr Burns, he said he had seen scratch marks in cases of suicide, and said that one might expect more severe or extensive marks in a case of homicide. He had personal knowledge of a case where a pregnant woman had committed suicide.

He accepted that homicidal hanging could occur with a compliant victim. This was relatively easy to effect as the pressure required on the neck was small. He attached no significance to the fact that the deceased's feet were on the ladder and believed that death could have occurred whether the deceased had been standing on a lower or higher step. He disagreed with Dr Burns who had said that, in the majority of suicides by hanging, the feet are well above the ground.

Dr West, a highly experienced pathologist, prepared another report in 2000. He had personally been involved in the cases of the murder or attempted murder by hanging of three compliant victims in prison. He agreed that it would not be necessary for the victim's feet to be off the ground. All that was required was pressure to the front of the neck, which, if it constricts the arterial flow, leads to loss of consciousness within seconds. This could have been achieved by pushing the deceased in the back when her neck was in a loose ligature. Homicide and suicide would produce the same mechanical effect, namely the body moving forward against a ligature, whether that person was standing or sitting on the steps of the ladder. If the legs had been held he would have expected the ligature mark to be much broader, with signs of the ligature being in more than one position. In this case, he concluded, the pathological evidence does not help in determining whether the death was homicide or suicide. The scratch marks did not help either, because they were found in 5 per cent of suicide cases.

The Criminal Cases Review Commission also heard from Mr Ide, a forensic scientist for thirty years and a specialist in knots and ligatures. His conclusion was that the deceased could not have been standing on the floor when the noose was put round her neck. Initially, she would have needed to be at a higher level in order to finish with her knees 15 in. (38 cm) above the floor as the rope would have stretched and the individual knots and the noose would have tightened. His conclusion was that she would have needed to have been standing on the ladder somewhere near the top. She would not have been high enough if she was sitting. While the knots and rope did not provide unambiguous evidence to indicate whether her death was murder or suicide, he concluded that "this evidence provides slightly more to support the hypothesis that Mrs Gilfoyle had been murdered rather than that she had killed herself", as it would have been difficult, if not impossible, for the deceased to tie a knot at the side of the beam. While it would have been technically possible, it would have been very difficult for her to have wrapped the rope several times round the beam. If a knot had been tied after the rope had been wrapped round, it would have had to have been higher than where it was found. However, his evidence did contradict Dr Burns's evidence at the trial that Paula had been standing on the floor with the noose around her neck – before Gilfoyle had knocked her off her feet, thereby killing her.

The dispute between the pathologists went on through two appeals and a review by the Criminal Cases Review Commission, which again upheld the original verdict. It was not for the Crown to show how Eddie had killed his wife, the Commission said, only that he had. Eddie Gilfoyle has protested his innocence throughout and in 2010 was released on licence by the parole board.

KILLERS FOR THE KLAN

O<small>N</small> 7 J<small>UNE</small> 1998, in Jasper, Texas, three white men offered a ride to a forty-nine-year-old handicapped black man named James Byrd Jr, who was hitchhiking home from his niece's bridal shower. Instead of taking him home, they drove to a wooded area where they beat, kicked and tortured him simply because of the colour of his skin. They stripped him and spray-painted his face black before wrapping a heavy logging chain around his ankles, which was tied to the back of their truck. Then they took off down an isolated road, dragging him for nearly 3 miles (4.8 km) as the truck swerved from side to side. Forensic evidence showed that he tried keeping his head up, and the autopsy showed that he remained alive for most of the ordeal. His skin was torn off, his bones broken and his elbows shattered to the bone. When his head hit a culvert, it was ripped off, along with his right arm.

"It was my opinion that Mr Byrd was alive up to the point he hit the culvert," said forensic pathologist Dr Thomas J. Brown. "He was alive when the head, shoulder and right arm were separated."

What was left of his shredded torso was dumped in front of a church for its black congregation to find. The three men went on to a barbecue.

The following morning, James Byrd's limbs were found scattered along a trail of blood down the seldom-used road. The police found remains at seventy-five places along the route. They also found a lighter carrying a Ku Klux Klan symbol and the name "Possum", the prison nickname of twenty-three-year-old white supremacist John William King, and a wrench with the name "Berry" on it. This led them to twenty-four-year-old Shawn Allen Berry and thirty-one-year-old Lawrence Russell Brewer, who had met King in prison. The three were room-mates in

Jasper, a small town with a population of 8,000, and an equal number of blacks and whites.

King was unrepentant about his crime, though he knew he faced the death penalty.

"Regardless of the outcome of this, we have made history. Death before dishonour. *Sieg Heil!*" he wrote from jail.

His body carried tattoos showing a black man being lynched, the insignia of the white supremacist prison gang, the Confederate Knights of America, Nazi symbols and the words "Aryan Pride". He said he joined the group for self-protection after being gang-raped by black inmates in jail. He was accused of beating Byrd with a bat as well as kidnapping and murdering him. Convicted by a jury of eleven whites and one African-American, he was sentenced to death.

Prior to Byrd's murder, Brewer had served a prison sentence for drug possession and burglary. Paroled in 1991, he was returned to prison in 1994 after violating his parole conditions. According to his court testimony, he joined the Confederate Knights of America with King in prison in order to protect himself from other inmates. A psychiatrist testified that Brewer did not appear repentant for his crimes. He was convicted and sentenced to death.

Although Berry drove the truck, he claimed that King and Brewer were solely responsible for the murder. Brewer claimed that Berry had cut Byrd's throat before he was tied to the truck, but the jury decided that there was little evidence to support this claim. There was no evidence that Berry was a racist. Consequently, he was spared the death penalty and sentenced to life imprisonment. He will be eligible for parole on 7 June 2038, when he will be sixty-four. It is thought that Berry knew Byrd; they shared the same parole officer.

"MAD DOG" MURDERS

O N 29 June 2008, the fire brigade were called to a ground-floor flat in Sterling Gardens, New Cross, south London, when neighbours phoned 999 after an explosion at the premises. The blast blew the windows out and ignited a blaze shortly after 10 p.m. One neighbour described hearing several loud bangs before seeing flames coming from the windows of the ground-floor flat.

"I went outside to see what was going on and there were other residents banging on the door and shouting to see if anyone was in," said a thirty-two-year-old man who lived above the flat. "People were throwing water through the windows to try to put the fire out. Because there was no answer we thought there was no one in."

A white man was seen running from the flat moments after the explosion, but he was nowhere to be seen.

Once the fire had been extinguished, two dead bodies were found in the burnt-out apartment. It soon became clear that the victims – Laurent Bonomo and Gabriel Ferez – had been dead before the fire took hold. Laurent had spoken to his fiancée on the phone at around 1 a.m. on that morning. After that, no one but the killers heard from or saw Bonomo or Ferez again.

It soon became clear that the twenty-three-year-old bio-chemistry students had been bound, gagged and tortured for three hours, then killed by frenzied knife attack. A post-mortem at Greenwich mortuary revealed that both died from stab wounds to the head, neck and chest. Bonomo had been stabbed 196 times; Ferez forty-seven. They had then been doused with flammable liquid and set on fire. The ferocity of the attack led them to be described at the "Tarantino murders".

"This attack was horrific," said Detective Chief Inspector Mick Duthie. "Everyone working on this case, including myself, has been deeply shocked by what we've seen . . . We believe that anyone involved in this scene would have been bloodstained when they left the area."

An inventory of the crime scene revealed that two Sony PSP games consoles and the victim's mobile phones and bank cards were missing. Six days earlier the flat had been burgled and a laptop computer had been stolen. On that occasion, the burglar had fled after he was disturbed by Bonomo, who heard a noise while he was in the shower. Police believed the earlier burglary could be linked to the double murder as forensic experts had found no evidence of forced entry, suggesting that a stolen set of keys may have been used.

The robbers had returned at 5.30 a.m. on 29 June, over-powered and bound the two victims, then demanded their bank cards and PIN numbers. The two students thought it best to cooperate. The thieves managed to withdraw £360 from an ATM using Bonomo's card, but when they tried to take money from Ferez's account at around 7.22 a.m., the cash machine retained the card. It had blood on it. They returned to the flat to take "revenge" on the French students.

Twenty-three-year-old Daniel "Dano" Sonnex, a wanted criminal who had been left at large in error, was seen on CCTV withdrawing cash from an ATM using one of the stolen bank cards. His palmprint was also found on the frame of a foldaway bed at the crime scene.

An artist's impression of another suspect, seen running from Sterling Gardens just after 10 p.m. on the night of the fire, was circulated. He was described as "white, thirty to forty years of age, of slight or slim build and wearing a light-coloured baseball cap, a dark top with the word 'Junfan' on, blue jeans and white trainers".

Soon after, Sonnex's flatmate, thirty-three-year-old Nigel Edward Farmer, handed himself in to the police in Lewisham and confessed to being the killer. He had third-degree burns to his face and hands, but was told by a civilian worker at the police station that he must wait his turn.

Twenty-seven-year-old Lucy Downer, who was sitting in the police station with the man while waiting to pay a motoring fine, said: "We were sitting on a row of seats when this skinny bloke walked in. He looked really out of it. His hands were bright red and his face was peeling badly. There were booths just to the right of the front door and he went into the first one and spoke with a reception officer. Then he came back out, sat down next to my cousin and started looking at her very strangely. I got a bit worried and changed places with her. Then this bloke got out a tub of antiseptic cream and rubbed it into his hands for the next few minutes. He then stood up, put his hands in the air and said: 'I've got third-degree fucking burns and they are not doing anything about it.'"

Ms Downer said she asked the man to repeat what he had said and then mouthed the word "help" to a nearby policeman. She added: "The guy could have had second thoughts about giving himself up and scarpered at any point. He was off his head but he looked like he was very serious about what he said."

Police took him to hospital before questioning him. Farmer was then charged with two counts of murder, arson and attempting to pervert the course of justice by destroying the crime scene. As it was, the crime scene investigation took several weeks.

Two days later, armed police arrested Sonnex at his brother's council house in Deptford, south-east London, just ten minutes' walk from the scene of the crime, after his brother had gone to the police. The police alert described Sonnex as being 6 ft 3 in. (1.90 m) tall and "extremely dangerous". He had a previous conviction for inflicting grievous bodily harm with intent for a stabbing he carried out at the age of sixteen.

As helicopters hovered overhead, officers smashed their way into the house at 3.40 a.m., screaming at neighbours: "Keep away from your windows." Sonnex was charged with murder and perverting the course of justice.

Farmer was a drug addict who had checked into a psychiatric hospital in Woolwich a month before the murders but left after four days, complaining about not getting the "right help".

The prosecutor, Crispin Aylett QC, told the jury at the Old Bailey: "What the firemen found was a scene of almost unimaginable horror."

"To take revenge for the fact that they had been unable to steal money from Mr Ferez, both men were murdered in a way that can only be described as inhuman," he said. "The two men, dressed only in their underpants, had been tied up. They had been bound at the ankles and the wrists. Their heads had been wrapped with towels. They had been subjected to an attack of brutal and sustained ferocity . . . Both of them had been repeatedly stabbed in the head. In some instances, a knife had been used with such force that the skull had been penetrated and damage caused to the brain."

The jury were told to brace themselves before being shown the crime scene photographs.

The prosecution said that the defendants had left at around 8.15 a.m., after subjecting the students to an ordeal that had lasted nearly three hours. Bonomo, Farmer said later, "just wouldn't die". That evening he had returned to the flat to set it on fire.

Sonnex and Farmer denied murder, arson, false imprisonment and trying to pervert the course of justice. However, Sonnex pleaded guilty to burglary at the property on the same date as the murders, admitting taking a bank card, credit card, the two Sony PSP games consoles and two mobile phones. Farmer denied the burglary.

On 4 June 2009, they were both found guilty of murder. Sonnex was sentenced to life, serving a minimum of forty years in prison. Farmer was told he would serve at least thirty-five years.

In sentencing, trial judge Mr Justice Saunders said: "I am satisfied that the only possible reason for the number of stab wounds is that the killings were sadistic. The killers got pleasure from what they were doing."

Sonnex should have been in prison at the time of the murders but had been set free due to a series of administrative errors. He had been jailed for a previous knife attack and had been released on licence. In a robbery in 2007, he had chained up his half-sister Louise Shine, who was pregnant, and her boyfriend Robert Sentongo and threatened them with various weapons to extort money. If they had made a formal complaint he would have been returned to jail. As it was, he was given a verbal warning by his probation officer instead.

He was then bailed for handling stolen goods when he should have been remanded in custody by magistrates. Further blunders delayed his recall to prison, and it took thirty-three days for the administrative process to be completed. It was a further sixteen days before the police went to Sonnex's house to arrest him. By that time the two young French students were dead.

O. J. SIMPSON REVISITED

A T 12.13 A.M. ON 13 June 1994, a black-and-white patrol car carrying Officers Robert Riske and Miguel Terrazas arrived at 875 South Bundy Drive in the Brentwood area of Los Angeles, California. The off-white stucco, three-level condominium was the home of Nicole Brown Simpson, ex-wife of pro-football star, actor and TV sports presenter O. J. Simpson. Nicole and O. J. had divorced two years earlier.

As the two policemen approached the house, they saw a large pool of blood. It came from the body of a female, later identified as Nicole Brown Simpson. She lay about 15 ft (4.7 m) from the sidewalk with her back towards the steps to her front door. The left side of her face was pressed against the walkway. She was wearing a short black dress. Nicole had been stabbed multiple times through the throat to the point she had nearly been decapitated, with her vertebrae almost severed. Blood from the wounds drenched her entire body.

Shortly after, the officers discovered the body of a male, later identified as waiter, part-time model and would-be actor, Ronald Goldman, behind an agapanthus bush to Simpson's right. He was fully clothed and lay sprawled out on his right side against the garden fence. His eyes were open. His light-brown shirt and blue jeans were saturated in blood and his body perforated with stab wounds. In between Goldman and Simpson lay a beeper, a knitted cap, a set of keys, a bloody left-hand glove and a white envelope. Bloody footprints and blood drops led away from the bodies to the back of the property.

After establishing that both victims were dead, Riske and Terrazas radioed for backup. Within minutes, Sergeant Martin Coon and Officers Edward McGowan and Richard Walker arrived and secured the crime scene. At 12.45 a.m., paramedics from a nearby fire station arrived and confirmed that the man and woman lying near the entrance of the condominium were dead. By then, Riske had established that the woman was probably Nicole Brown Simpson, the owner of the townhouse. Upstairs, they found her two young children, five-year-old Justin and eight-year-old Sydney, still fast asleep. The officers woke them and got them dressed, then arranged for them to be taken to the West Los Angeles Division where they would wait until they were collected by a family member. An animal control officer picked up Nicole's Akita dog, Kato, which first alerted neighbours to the slaughter. It was taken to a pound in West Los Angeles.

At 2.10 a.m., West Los Angeles Division Homicide Detective Supervisor Ron Phillips arrived at South Bundy Drive, accompanied by Detective Mark Fuhrman. They made a visual inspection of the crime scene. Fuhrman's partner Brad Roberts logged in at 2.30 a.m. on the sign-in sheet set up by Officer Terrazas. There were eighteen police officers on the scene by this time. A police photographer arrived at 3.25 a.m.

Detective Phillips was notified that the investigation had been handed over to the Homicide Special Section of the LAPD's Robbery-Homicide Division. Division Head Captain William O. Gartland assigned Detectives Tom Lange and Philip Vannatter as the lead investigators. They arrived at the crime scene at 4.05 and 4.25 a.m. respectively.

Detective Phillips briefed Vannatter and walked him through the crime scene. They saw the set of keys, dark-blue knit cap, beeper, blood-spattered white envelope and bloodstained leather glove lying under the agapanthus plant only a few inches from Nicole's body and the trail of blood that led towards the back of the property.

Commander Keith Bushey, chief of operations for the LAPD West Bureau, sent word that they should contact O. J. Simpson in person to make arrangements to collect his children. Fuhrman mentioned that, as a patrol officer, he had visited the Simpson residence in Rockingham Avenue, which was about 2 miles (3.2 km) away. On that occasion, back in 1985, the newly married Nicole, pregnant with her first child, had called the police. Simpson had attacked her car with a baseball bar, but no charges were brought by Nicole or the police.

Detectives Fuhrman, Roberts, Lange and Vannatter drove over to the Simpson residence, but no one answered the entry phone. Fuhrman drew Lange's attention to blood on the driver's door of Simpson's white Ford Bronco. Fearing that Simpson had also become victim of murder, Fuhrman climbed over the stone wall and unlocked the gate from the inside. At 5.45 a.m., the four detectives walked up to the front door, rang the bell and started knocking. Getting no response, they walked around the side of the property to a row of three guest houses. In the first one, they roused Brian "Kato" Kaelin, a bit-part actor and family friend who was a house guest – the children had named the dog after Kaelin. In the next bungalow, they woke an attractive young woman who identified herself as Arnelle Simpson, Simpson's daughter from his first marriage. With the help of Kaelin and Arnelle Simpson, they traced Simpson to the Chicago O'Hare Plaza Hotel. Phillips called Simpson there and told him of the murders. Apparently distraught at the news, Simpson said that he would catch the next available flight back to Los Angeles.

At 6.21 a.m., Lange called Nicole's parents to break the news. In the background, he heard a woman's voice screaming and wailing: "O. J. did it! O. J. killed her! I knew that son of a bitch was going to kill her!" The voice belonged to Denise, Nicole's sister.

A few moments later, Detective Fuhrman returned to the house after an absence of ten or fifteen minutes. He led Vannatter out into the garden to show him, on the leaf-covered walkway behind the guest house occupied by Kato Kaelin, a bloodstained leather glove like the one in the garden back at South Bundy Drive. Vannatter found more blood and decided that the Rockingham Avenue estate qualified as another crime scene.

At 7 a.m., Fuhrman returned with his partner and a police photographer who had been shooting at the South Bundy crime scene. At 7.10 a.m., Dennis Fung, a LAPD criminalist, and his assistant, Andrea Mazzola, arrived to begin the collection and documentation of evidence. Leaving Fuhrman in charge of the

Rockingham Avenue crime scene, Vannatter returned to join Lange at South Bundy, then went to West Los Angeles station to prepare a warrant to enter, search and seize any relevant evidence at O. J. Simpson's home.

Inside, investigators found blood spatters in the foyer, master bedroom, the shower and the sink. Among the items taken as evidence was a pair of socks. Much later, bloodstains were discovered on them. Investigators had packaged these socks together rather than individually. Inside the Bronco, they found multiple spatters of blood and a bloody footprint. Two sets of keys to Nicole's condominium were found in Simpson's possession. Nicole had reported a set missing a few weeks before the slaying.

At 10.15 a.m., Dennis Fung and his assistant arrived at South Bundy Drive, having completed their work at Simpson's home. They and the coroner's investigators completed their examination of Nicole's body, photographing it from every angle and recording its position relative to all other objects and the other body. Then they turned their attention to Goldman. He was lying on his right side, his body bent at the waist. His face showed scrape marks. Blood from his nose and left ear had dried in crusty rivulets. His light-brown shirt had been pulled up and was bunched around the back, indicating that the killer may have grabbed him and swung him around in the fight. Or, perhaps, he had been killed on the walkway, and then his attacker had dragged his body beneath the bush. He had stab wounds to his body and upper left thigh, and his throat appeared to have been slashed. In the back pocket of his jeans, they found his driver's licence, giving them a positive ID.

The medical examiners then took the bodies away to conduct autopsies. They were both found to have been slain with a knife approximately 6 in. (15 cm) long. Nicole had received four deep wounds. One of them, a slash across the neck, had almost beheaded her. She also had a large contusion to the back of the head, indicating blunt-force trauma. There were cuts to her hands, defence wounds showing that she had tried to fend off the attack. Analysing the wounds, the pathologist concluded that the attacker was probably right-handed and slit her throat, left to right, from behind.

Ronald Goldman also had a large contusion on the back of the head, which suggested he also might have been struck from behind. There were six wounds found on his face and neck and several more on his body, a total of nineteen in all. Some of the wounds intersected, indicating a frenzied attack; four of the lacerations were lethal penetration wounds, fatally damaging internal organs. Hairs were taken from Goldman's shirt. The shirt itself and cap were also taken as evidence, but they were packaged together in the same bag. Investigators swabbed blood from the various blood pools with wet cotton swatches, which were then sealed in plastic bags before being consigned to a truck.

Meanwhile, investigators took pictures of footprints leading from the bodies. There was a single set, leading them to conclude that there was a lone assailant. Several coins were found along with fresh blood drops behind Nicole's condo, in the area where the cars were parked – indicating that the attacker had left that way.

After Vannatter returned to the Rockingham Avenue estate, O. J. Simpson had arrived home only to be handcuffed by Patrol Officer Don Thompson and Detective Brad Roberts, Fuhrman's partner. Vannatter quickly released him, noticing as he did so a bandage on the middle finger of Simpson's left hand. Once Simpson was arrested, Vannatter would only have forty-eight hours to file charges. As yet, they had little evidence against him. The police needed his cooperation, firstly to get a blood sample from him. Simpson complied, and Detective Philip Vannatter received the vial at 3.45 p.m. However, the vial would not make it into the hands of Dennis Fung, who was responsible for recording the evidence, until 5.30 p.m.

At the Parker Center headquarters of the LAPD, Vannatter interviewed Simpson for thirty-seven minutes. During that time, Simpson gave contradictory accounts of the times he had used his Ford Bronco and how he cut his hand. On one occasion he said that he had cut his hand on a broken glass in his hotel room in Chicago. On another, he said that he had cut his hand in Los Angeles and reopened the wound on the glass in Chicago.

On 16 June, Nicole Brown Simpson was buried in Lake Forest Cemetery, Mission Viejo, in Orange County. Nicole's mother recalled how, at the wake the day before, Simpson had leant over the open coffin, kissed Nicole on the lips and murmured: "I'm so sorry, Nicki, I'm so sorry."

Later that day, the police filed a formal complaint. Simpson's lawyers convinced the Los Angeles Police Department to allow Simpson to turn himself in at 11 a.m. on 17 June 1994, even though the double murder charge meant there was no possibility of bail. It also meant that Simpson could face a death sentence if convicted.

Over a thousand reporters waited at the police station for Simpson, but he did not show up. Simpson had been staying at the house of Robert Kardashian, one of Simpson's defence lawyers and a personal friend, in the San Fernando Valley. Three patrol cars were sent to Kardashian's house to get him. The police then learnt that Simpson had left with his close friend Al Cowling in a white Ford Bronco.

At 2 p.m., the LAPD issued an all-points bulletin. At 5 p.m., Kardashian read a letter from Simpson to the media. It said: "First everyone understand I have nothing to do with Nicole's murder." It also sent greetings to twenty-four friends and concluded: "Don't feel sorry for me. I've had a great life."

Simpson's psychiatrists thought that the letter could be a suicide note. He said later that he was "just gonna go with Nicole". Another of Simpson's lawyers, Robert Shapiro, made a television appeal to Simpson to surrender.

The police traced calls from the phone in Simpson's Bronco, which was then in Orange County. At 6.45 p.m., a police officer saw the Bronco going north on Interstate 405. At the wheel was Al Cowling. When the officer approached the vehicle, Cowling dialled 911 and said that Simpson was suicidal and had a gun to his head. The officer backed off and Simpson's Bronco headed off at 35 mph (56 km/h). Soon there were twenty police cars following him in a low-speed chase.

Over twenty helicopters carrying news crews joined the pursuit, providing live coverage that was broadcast worldwide.

Former University of Southern California American football coach John McKay broadcast an appeal to Simpson to pull over and let himself be arrested, rather than commit suicide.

The chase ended at 8 p.m. at Simpson's home in Brentwood, having covered 50 miles (80 km). His son Jason ran out of the house to greet him. Simpson remained in the Bronco for another forty-five minutes. Then Simpson was allowed to go inside where he talked to his mother for about an hour. Shapiro arrived at the house and, a few minutes later, Simpson surrendered. A search of the Bronco found $8,000 in cash, a loaded .357 Magnum, a passport, family pictures, a change of clothing and a false beard.

On 20 June, Simpson was arraigned on two counts of first-degree murder and pleaded not guilty to both. The following day, a grand jury was called to determine whether to indict him, but had to be dismissed two days later due to excessive media coverage. It was thought that this might influence its decision. The grand jury had heard from Brentwood resident Jill Shively, who testified that she saw Simpson speeding away from the area of Nicole's house on the night of the murders. She said that the Bronco almost collided with a Nissan at the intersection of Bundy and San Vicente Boulevard.

Another witness to the grand jury was Jose Camacho, a knife salesman at Ross Cutlery. He said that, three weeks before the murders, he had sold Simpson a 15 in. (38 cm) German-made knife. Neither Shively nor Camacho appeared at the criminal trial as, in the meantime, they had sold their stories to the media. Shively had got $5,000 to talk to the tabloid TV show *Hard Copy*, while Camacho had got $12,500 from the *National Enquirer*.

After a week-long court hearing, the California Superior Court found that there was enough evidence to bring Simpson to trial for the murders. At his second court arraignment on 29 July, when asked how he intended to plea, Simpson said: "Absolutely, 100 per cent, not guilty."

After the preliminary hearings, the trial was moved from Santa Monica to the Criminal Courts Building in downtown Los

Angeles where there were more African-Americans, Asian-Americans, Latinos and blue-collar workers than in the jury pool in Santa Monica. When the jury was selected, it comprised eight African-Americans, two of mixed descent, one Hispanic and one white. The alternate jury was made up of seven African-Americans, one Hispanic and four white people.

The judge took the jury to visit the crime scene at South Bundy Drive and the Rockingham Avenue estate. Although the legal ruling was that both had to remain as close to their condition on the night of the murder as possible, the defence had been to work on Simpson's home. All the pictures of scantily clad white females, including a nude photograph of Paula Barbieri, Simpson's girlfriend at the time of the killings, had been taken down, along with those of his white golfing buddies. These had been replaced by decorous images – photographs of his mother and Martin Luther King, and a print of a famous school integration painting by Norman Rockwell. There was even a Bible on the bedside table in Simpson's bedroom.

The jurors from downtown LA were not prepared for the opulence of Simpson's surroundings. He had bought the 6,200 ft² (576 m²) property for $650,000 in 1977 and spent another $2 million upgrading it over the years. It had seven bathrooms, a tennis court and an Olympic-sized pool, surrounded by waterfalls.

The outcome of the trial was anything but a foregone conclusion. The prosecution had no murder weapon, no good fingerprints and no eyewitnesses to the murders. However, they felt they had enough DNA and crime scene evidence to convict. According to Deputy District Attorney Marcia Clark, the "trail of blood from Bundy through his own Ford Bronco and into his house in Rockingham is devastating proof of his guilt".

From the physical evidence the police collected, the prosecution contended that Simpson drove over to Nicole's house on the evening of 12 June with the clear intention of killing her. After putting the two children to bed, Nicole opened the front door, either in reply to a knock or after hearing a noise outside. Simpson then grabbed her before she could scream and silenced her with a knife. Forensic evidence from the Los Angeles County coroner suggested that Ron Goldman arrived at the front gate to the townhouse sometime during the attack. Simpson then turned on him, grabbed him a choke-hold and stabbed him repeatedly in the neck and chest with the other hand.

According to the prosecution, Nicole was then lying face down and, after he finished with Goldman, Simpson put his foot on her back, pulled her head back by her hair and slit her throat, severing her carotid artery. Simpson then left a trail of blood from the townhouse into the alley behind. There was also testimony that three drops of blood were found on the driveway near the gate to his house on Rockingham Avenue.

Nicole's pet Akita had led a neighbour to the crime scene at 11 p.m., leading investigators to conclude that the murders had taken place between 10.15 and 10.40 p.m. The dog had not barked earlier, at the approach of the murderer, suggesting that it knew the killer – further evidence that it was O. J.

Simpson had last been seen in public before the murders at 9.36 p.m. when he returned to the front gate of his house with Kato Kaelin. They had been to a McDonald's in Santa Monica. Simpson was not seen again until 10.54 p.m., when he left his house in a limousine hired to take him to Los Angeles International Airport on his way to a Hertz convention in Chicago. As it took just five minutes to drive from Nicole's condo to Simpson's house, there was plenty of time for him to have carried out the murders, which both the prosecution and defence agreed took place between 10.15 and 10.40 p.m. What's more, a car similar to Simpson's white Bronco was seen speeding away from the South Bundy Drive area at 10.35 p.m.

When driver Allan Park arrived with the limousine at the Rockingham Avenue entrance to Simpson's estate at 10.25 p.m., he said he did not see Simpson's white Bronco parked there. Park testified that he had been looking for the house number. Next morning, the Bronco was found parked next to the house number – implying that Park would certainly have noticed the Bronco if it had been there at that time. Simpson maintained that it had been parked there for hours. Rose Lopez, a neighbour's housekeeper, said that she had seen Simpson's Bronco there but, under cross-examination, was force to admit that she could not remember the precise time. Her testimony was not presented to the jury.

Park pulled up opposite the entrance in Ashford Street, then drove back to the Rockingham Avenue entrance, checking to see which driveway would have best access for the limo. Deciding that the Rockingham entrance was too narrow, he drove back to the Ashford gate. A 10.40 p.m., he buzzed the intercom but got no answer. He looked though the gate and saw that the house was dark except for a dim light coming from a second-storey window – Simpson's bedroom. Park then made a series of calls from his mobile in an attempt to get the phone number for Simpson's house.

At the time, Kato Kaelin was on the phone to Rachel Ferrara. At around 10.50 p.m., he heard three thumps against the outside wall of the guest house. Kaelin hung up the phone and went outside to investigate. Instead of venturing directly down the dark pathway where the thumps came from, he walked to the front of the property where he saw Park's limousine outside the Ashford gate.

At the same time as Park saw Kaelin, he said he saw "a tall black man" of Simpson's height and build enter the front door of the house from the driveway. Then the lights went on. Simpson finally answered the intercom and explained that he had overslept. He would be at the front gate soon, he said. Kaelin opened the gate to let Park in, and Simpson came out of his house through the front door a few minutes later. His luggage was already outside the front door. Park and Kaelin helped load it into the trunk. Kaelin said that Simpson told him not to touch a small black bag, which he loaded into the limousine himself. Prosecutors believed that the bag contained bloody clothes and the murder weapon. Park testified he saw five bags loaded into the car before Simpson left Rockingham Avenue, but the airport porter, skycap James Williams, counted only three bags when Simpson got out of the car. He said he noticed Simpson standing by a trash can afterwards, which led prosecutors to speculate that Simpson stuffed the small bag into the bin. It was never found.

Both Park and Kaelin testified that Simpson looked agitated. Park said he was sweating profusely and insisted on keeping the air conditioning on all the way to the airport. But other witnesses, such as the ticket clerk at Los Angeles International Airport who checked Simpson in and a flight attendant on the plane, said that Simpson acted perfectly normally. He even signed autographs, the defence said. Detective Ron Phillips testified that, when he called Simpson in Chicago to tell him of the murder of his ex-wife, he sounded shocked and upset, but was strangely uninterested in the way she died. Nor did he enquire about the safety of his children.

Defence lawyer Johnnie Cochran said that Simpson was not sleeping when Park arrived. He was, in fact, packing for the trip to Chicago. Then he went out into the grounds and hit a few golf balls. Those caused the thumps Kaelin had heard when they bounced off the wall of the guest house.

The defence claimed that Simpson was not physically capable of the murders. Ronald Goldman was a fit young man who put up a tremendous struggle against his assailant. Simpson was then a forty-six-year-old whose injuries as a football player had left him with scars on his knees and chronic arthritis. But Deputy District Attorney Marcia Clark introduced an exercise video Simpson had made two years earlier that showed Simpson was anything but frail. And Nicole's sister Denise testified that, during fights in the 1980s, she had seen Simpson physically pick up Nicole, hurl her against a wall and throw her out of the house. Officers found arrest records indicating that Simpson was charged with beating his wife and photographs of Nicole's bruised and battered face were shown in court. Simpson denied beating his wife, even though he had pleaded *nolo contendere* – "no contest" – to charges in 1989. He did acknowledge that they had "physical altercations" and that they engaged in what he repeatedly referred to as "rassling". But he denied causing her bruises. Most nights, he said, the skin of her face would appear reddened as she picked her pimples. But Nicole's friends insisted that Simpson physically abused her and that she was afraid that he was going to kill her. He had a short temper and was a jealous man. There were even reports that he was stalking her.

In preparation for what appeared to be an assignation, Nicole had run a bath and lit burning candles just before her murder. Prosecutor Chris Darden maintained that Simpson spied on his ex-wife, saw Nicole lighting candles, realized that she had a date and killed her in a jealous rage.

Karen Lee Crawford, the manager of the Mezzaluna restaurant where Nicole ate that night, testified that Nicole's mother phoned the restaurant at 9.37 p.m., asking about a pair of glasses her daughter had lost. Karen found them and put them in an envelope. When waiter Ron Goldman left at the end of his shift at 9.50 p.m., he said he would drop them off at Nicole's home.

Nicole's neighbour, Pablo Fenives, testified that he had heard a dog barking and the "plaintive wail" of a dog at around ten to fifteen minutes after the beginning of the 10 o'clock news. Another neighbour, Eva Stein testified that she heard a loud and persistent barking at around 10.15 p.m. that prevented her from sleeping. Neighbour Steven Schwab testified that, while he was walking his dog in the area near Nicole's house at around 10.30 p.m., he noticed the Akita trailing its leash. The animal was agitated and had blood on its paws. However, a quick examination showed it was uninjured. Schwab took the dog to his friend Sukru Boztepe, who let the dog into his home and noticed it was agitated. Boztepe took the Akita for a walk at around 11 p.m. He testified that the dog tugged on its leash and led him to Nicole's dead body. He then flagged down a passing patrol car.

The first police officer on the crime scene, Robert Riske, said he found a woman lying face down in a pool of blood on the walkway that led to her house. She was barefoot and wearing a black dress. Goldman's body was lying on its side beside a tree. Beside him was his bleeper and a white envelope, which contained Nicole's glasses. Riske also testified that there was a dark-blue knit ski cap and a black leather glove on the ground near the bodies.

Detective Tom Lange testified that the bottom of Nicole's feet were clean, which indicated she had probably been killed first, before any blood had flowed. This vital piece of crime scene evidence implied that Simpson had set out to kill Nicole, while Goldman inadvertently stumbled upon the killing, forcing Simpson to turn on him, too. In cross-examining, Defence Attorney Johnnie Cochran proposed two alternative hypotheses as to what had happened at the murder scene. He suggested that one, or more, drug dealers had come to the house looking for Nicole's house guest, Faye Resnick, an admitted cocaine user. Or that the "assassin, or assassins" had followed Goldman to the house to kill him.

But it was the DNA evidence found at the crime scene and Simpson's home that the prosecution thought would convict him. Socks found in Simpson's bedroom had over twenty bloodstains on them. DNA analysis showed the blood to be that of Nicole. The odds against it being hers were approximately one in 9.7 billion, rising to one in 21 billion when compiling results of testing done at the separate DNA laboratories.

However, the bloodstains showed a similar pattern on both sides of the socks. Dr Henry Lee of the Connecticut State Police Forensic Science Laboratory, called by the defence, testified that the only way such a pattern could appear was if the socks were lying flat. The blood would have to be wet at the time, and it was estimated that if Simpson had killed Nicole and splashed blood on his socks, it would have dried by the time he got home. The defence also contended that the chemical preservative ethylenediaminetetraacetic acid, or EDTA, was found in the stain. The victims' blood samples were stored at the LAPD laboratory in tubes that contained EDTA, implying that the stains were planted.

DNA analysis of the blood found in and on Simpson's Bronco and where it was parked in his driveway showed traces of Simpson's blood and that of both of the victims. Strands of African-American hair were found on Goldman's shirt and in the knitted cap found at the crime scene, along with fibres from the carpet of Simpson's Bronco. Dark-blue cotton fibres were also found on Goldman, and the prosecution presented a witness who said Simpson wore a similarly coloured sweatsuit that night.

The matching sweatsuit itself was never found. The defence also pointed out that the hair could have come from any African-American – about 10 per cent of the population of Los Angeles is black. The hair appeared to have no dandruff, while Simpson's hair did. As to the fibres, the defence contended that the whole crime scene had been contaminated when a detective unfurled a blanket from Nicole's home to cover her body.

Bloody footprints leading from the crime scene were identified by FBI shoe expert William Bodziak as having been an exclusive type of Italian Bruno Magli shoes, size twelve. A similar impression was left on the floor of the Bronco. Only 299 pairs in that size had been sold in the United States. They were on sale in Bloomingdale's where Simpson sometimes shopped and twelve was Simpson's shoe size. The defence claimed that there was no proof that Simpson had ever bought such shoes. After the trial, the *National Enquirer* published a photograph that appeared to show Simpson wearing a pair of these shoes taken by a freelance photographer in 1993. While Simpson's defence team claimed the photograph was faked, other similar photographs were circulated. But no such shoes were ever found. DNA taken from bloody footprints at the scene of the crime and spots found in the driveway of the Rockingham estate also matched Simpson's, the prosecution contended.

The defence had its own team of DNA experts who contested this and the cross-examination of the police criminalist Dennis Fung, who had gathered the evidence, lasted eight days. He admitted to "having missed a few drops of blood on a fence near the bodies". On the stand he said that he "returned several weeks afterwards to collect them".

Most of the blood samples from the crime scene were collected on 13 June 1994, immediately after the discovery of the murders, but the three bloodstains on the rear gate of Nicole's house were not collected until 3 July. The defence maintained that these stains were not collected the day after the crime because they were not there at that time. A photograph taken the day after the crime shows no blood in the area of the rear gate where the largest and most prominent stain was later found.

"Where is it, Mr Fung?" asked defence attorney Barry Scheck.

Fung had no answer. The implication was that it had been planted.

Further, Fung admitted that he had not used rubber gloves when collecting some of the evidence. Also, when he collected Simpson's socks from his bedroom he did not notice the bloodstain, though it was the size of a quarter and he was looking for blood in Simpson's home at the time. The socks were examined twice more at the crime laboratory and no blood was found. It was over six weeks later that the bloodstain was noticed. If Nicole's blood had been planted on the sock, her blood and that of Goldman and Simpson could have been planted elsewhere, the defence reasoned.

Why had Fung and his assistant been at both sites, introducing the possibility of contamination? A crime scene photograph showed an ungloved hand holding the blood-spattered envelope containing Nicole's glasses. Fung also admitted to placing blood samples into plastic bags. Fung claimed this was purely a temporary measure and admitted that doing so could foster bacteria growth, which, in turn, could distort test results.

LAPD Detective Philip Vannatter testified that he saw photographs of press personnel leaning on Simpson's Bronco before evidence was collected. It also transpired that Andrea Mazzola, Dennis Fung's assistant who collected much of the evidence, was a trainee. She was working without supervision and was captured on camera dropping several bloody swabs and wiping tweezers with dirty hands. She had also carried a vial containing blood collected from Simpson in the pocket of her lab coat for nearly a day, increasing the chances of contamination. Samples of blood taken from the crime scene were handled by a technician wearing gloves already flecked by the sample of blood Simpson had given. And the LA County District Attorney's Office and the Medical Examiner's Office could not explain why 1.5 ml of the original 8 ml of blood taken from Simpson were missing.

LAPD criminologist Collin Yamauchi admitted that he spilled some of Simpson's blood from a reference vial while working in the evidence processing room. Shortly afterwards, he handled the glove from the Rockingham Avenue estate and the cotton swatches containing the blood from outside Nicole's house. He was wearing the same gloves at the time. The defence contended that some of Simpson's blood was inadvertently transferred via Yamauchi's gloves or instruments, contaminating the evidence.

DNA of the person who left the blood drops – possibly the true perpetrator – could not be detected, the defence argued, because it was degraded and destroyed due to mishandling of the samples from outside Nicole's townhouse. LAPD crime scene investigators collected the blood drops by swabbing them with wet cotton swatches. The swabs were then put in plastic bags and left in a hot truck for several hours. The prosecution's expert witnesses all acknowledged that DNA degrades rapidly when blood samples are left in a moist, warm environment. This degradation can make the DNA untypeable and that subsequent contamination of the sample by a second person's DNA can produce a false match. The quantity of DNA found in the samples was consistent with such contamination. And at the crime laboratory, the swabs were put into bundles before they had been left to dry, leading to contamination, the defence said.

Detective Vannatter, who led the investigation, also had access to Simpson's blood, the defence pointed out. Thano Peratis, the nurse who took Simpson's blood, put the tube in an unsealed envelope and passed it to Vannatter. Instead of booking it as evidence straightaway, he took it with him across town to the Rockingham estate, where he handed it to Dennis Fung a couple of hours later. Clearly, he was in sole possession of the blood tube long enough to have planted DNA evidence.

Dr Robin Cotton of Cellmark Diagnostics, one of the companies that tested the DNA, was on the stand for six days. It was revealed that Cellmark had made two errors in DNA tests in 1988 and 1989 – finding DNA in mock crime scenes where none was present – though no further mistakes had been made since. In fact, one of the testing companies consulted by the defence had also made a similar mistake in 1988. But, generally, it was shown that the prosecution's handling of the DNA evidence was lax, undermining its credibility. Vials of the victims' blood used for reference sent to other laboratories for further tests were found to be contaminated with Simpson's DNA.

The prosecution said that they had made DNA samples available for the defence to do their own testing, but they had not done so. It also pointed out that substrate controls – test samples taken from unstained areas adjacent to the blood drops – were negative. That is, they contained no detectable DNA. The defence pointed out that the substrate controls were not tested in parallel with the crime scene samples and, consequently, did not pick up the cross-contamination.

According to the DNA tests, blood from both Simpson and the victims was found on the black leather glove at the scene of the crime, though no other drops of blood were found near the glove. Fibres from the carpet of the Bronco were also found on it. A matching glove was found outside the guest house on Simpson's estate near where Kato Kaelin had heard the thumps on the night of the murders. This glove, too, according to the prosecution, carried the DNA of O. J. Simpson, Nicole Brown Simpson and Ronald Goldman, along with a long strand of blonde hair similar to that of Nicole. Hair consistent with that of Goldman was also found. The type of glove was Aris Light, size XL. Nicole had bought Simpson two pairs of gloves of this type from Bloomingdale's back in 1990, before they divorced. A photograph was produced showing Simpson wearing the same type of gloves.

In court, Cochran asked Simpson to try on the leather glove found at the scene of the crime. It was plainly too tight. However, it had to fit over a latex glove worn to prevent the evidence being further contaminated. Assistant prosecutor Christopher Darden said that Simpson "has arthritis and we looked at the medication he takes and some of it is anti-inflammatory and we are told he has not taken the stuff for a day and it caused swelling in the joints and inflammation in his hands". The prosecution also claimed that the glove had shrunk because it had been soaked in blood, then repeatedly frozen and unfrozen in the lab. But the defence adopted the slogan: "If it don't fit, you must acquit."

At least two of the jury were not impressed by this demonstration. One said: "Those gloves fit. He wasn't putting them on right . . . I do believe the gloves fit. I have no doubt about that. The glove demo didn't impress me at all. Not one iota."

Prosecutors contended that the presence of Simpson's blood at the crime scene came from a cut on the middle finger of his left hand. Police noted his wounds on the day of the murder, believing that they had been incurred during the attack on Ronald Goldman. But no cuts were found on the gloves and both prosecution and defence witnesses, including Kato Kaelin, testified that they had not seen cuts or wounds of any kind on Simpson's hands in the hours after the murders had taken place. The defence contended that Simpson had cut himself later, first while retrieving a mobile phone from the Bronco and again on a glass in a Chicago hotel, which he broke on hearing of the death of his ex-wife.

The glove on Simpson's Rockingham Avenue estate had been found by LAPD detective Mark Fuhrman. He also found the drops of blood in the driveway there. However, Fuhrman had a chequered career with the LAPD. In 1983, he had made a disability claim for work-related stress. He told Dr Ira Brent that he blacked out, became a wild man and beat-up suspects. The following year, Fuhrman stopped a young African-American male for jaywalking, put him in a choke hold and threatened to kill him. It happened in front of a movie theatre in a predominately white area. There were several witnesses. Fuhrman was fined a day's pay.

It was put to Fuhrman that he was a racist. On the stand, he denied that he was racist or had used the word "nigger" to describe black people in the previous ten years. Later, the defence played audio tapes made by screenwriter Laura McKinny, who had interviewed Fuhrman for a screenplay she was developing about the police. In them Fuhrman used the word forty-one times. This destroyed Fuhrman's credibility as a witness. Later, he was indicted for perjury and pleaded *nolo contendere* – "no contest". The LAPD already had a reputation for racism. Riots followed the acquittal of four white cops who had been caught on video beating black motorist Rodney King just two years earlier.

The defence alleged that Fuhrman had taken the glove from the crime scene and planted it at Simpson's house. The prosecution said that officers had been at the crime scene for more than two hours by the time Fuhrman arrived and none of them had noticed a second glove. It was also suggested that Fuhrman was responsible for the blood from Nicole found in Simpson's Bronco. He could have swiped the glove inside the Bronco in order to plant the victims' blood there. Detectives testified that the Bronco was locked when they first saw it and denied that anyone had opened the doors while it was at Simpson's residence. But the defence produced evidence suggesting that Fuhrman had opened the door of the Bronco. In his testimony, Fuhrman reported seeing bloodstains on the lower sill of the Bronco's door. Photographs of the Bronco showed that there were stains where Fuhrman reported them, but they could be seen only when the door was open.

Even if Fuhrman did not swipe the glove in the Bronco, he might have transferred the victims' DNA there unintentionally as he had already visited the crime scene. A photograph taken at South Bundy Drive showed Fuhrman standing in a pool of the victims' blood pointing at a glove. Afterwards, Fuhrman went with the other detectives to Rockingham Avenue. If Fuhrman then entered the Bronco looking for evidence, the blood on his shoes could have been deposited on the carpet. Fuhrman or another officer who had some of the victims' blood on a sleeve or shirt cuff could have accidentally swiped it on to the Bronco's steering wheel and dashboard while looking for evidence.

The blood could also have arrived on the dashboard when the Bronco was in storage. On 14 June 1994, Dennis Fung first collected blood from the Bronco. The general practice, when swabbing blood, was to collect the entire sample. Three witnesses testified that they had been in the Bronco after 14 June and saw no blood. But when the Bronco was inspected again on 26 August 1994, blood was found on the dashboard in the same place that Fung had collected the initial samples. In the meantime, the Bronco had been left at an unsecured storage facility where a large number of people had access to it and two unauthorized people were known to have entered looking for souvenirs.

Fuhrman's credibility was further undermined. When first asked whether he had planted evidence at Simpson's home, he replied: "No." Asked the question a second time, he took the Fifth Amendment that permits witnesses to remain silent, rather than give testimony against themselves.

The jury took just four hours to return a verdict of not guilty. One juror blamed Fuhrman and his possible "racial vendetta" against Simpson for their decision to acquit.

"There wasn't enough evidence," she said.

"There was a problem with what was being presented to prosecutors for testing from LAPD," another maintained. "We felt there were a lot of opportunities for . . . contamination of evidence, samples being mixed or stored together."

It was all down to the crime scene evidence.

"As far as I'm concerned, Mr Simpson would have been behind bars if the police work had been done properly," said a third.

Later, the Goldman and Brown families brought a civil suit against Simpson. In civil proceedings, Simpson could not take the Fifth Amendment and was forced to testify. The standard of proof was also lower. While in a criminal suit the case has to be proved "beyond a reasonable doubt", in a civil suit the case is decided on the "preponderance of the evidence". This time the venue was the Santa Monica courthouse and the jury comprised one African-American, one Hispanic, one Asian and nine whites. The civil suit took four months to hear, rather than the nine months of the criminal trial. The jury spent six days on its deliberation – rather than four hours – and found against Simpson. It awarded $8.5 million in compensatory damages to Fred Goldman and his ex-wife Sharon Rufo for the loss of their son. A few days later, they awarded punitive damages of $25 million to be shared between Nicole's children and Fred Goldman. However, by then, Simpson was broke. His money had gone in legal fees and back taxes. He was now deeply in debt. The mortgage on the Rockingham Avenue estate was in arrears and it was repossessed. Simpson moved to Florida where future earnings would not be seized to pay the damages, as they would in California.

"It will be a cold day in hell before I pay a penny," said Simpson.

Then in October 2008, Simpson was convicted of kidnapping and armed robbery after he entered a room at the Palace Station hotel-casino in Las Vegas and took sports memorabilia that he claimed had been stolen from him. He was sentenced to thirty-three years in jail, without possibility of parole for nine. His earning potential gone, it seems he will be proved right and never pay a penny in damages to the families of Nicole Brown Simpson and Ronald Goodman.

DR DAVID KELLY

ON 18 JULY 2003, Dr David Kelly, an expert on biological warfare and a former UN weapons inspector in Iraq, was found dead in a wood in Oxfordshire. Normally in the case of a person who had met a violent death there would be an inquest. However, as the case was politically sensitive, the government set up a judicial inquiry under Lord Hutton. Critics pointed out that this had fewer legal powers than a normal coroner's court. Witnesses could not be compelled to appear and did not have to testify under oath. The Hutton Inquiry duly concluded that Dr Kelly had committed suicide. Others were not convinced. Crucial, as always, was the crime scene evidence.

David Kelly was in Iraq after the end of the First Gulf War. In 2002, he was working for Britain's Defence Intelligence Staff when the Joint Intelligence Committee was compiling a dossier on the weapons of mass destruction possessed by Iraq. The purpose of the dossier was to convince the British Parliament and people to join the American-led invasion of Iraq in 2003. Although Kelly did believe that Iraq had retained some weapons of mass destruction after the First Gulf War, he had some doubts about the claims made in the dossier – particularly the controversial claim that the Iraqis could deploy chemical and biological weapons within forty-five minutes.

After the invasion of Iraq that toppled Saddam Hussein, Kelly returned as a weapons inspector. He went to see what the British government alleged were two mobile germ-warfare laboratories and decided that they were no such thing. He told the *Observer* this, off the record.

On 22 May 2003, back in London, he met BBC journalist Andrew Gilligan, who wanted to ask him about the validity of the dossier that claimed that Saddam Hussein had weapons of mass destruction when none had been found. Kelly agreed to talk on a non-attributable basis – the BBC could report what he said, but not who had said it. BBC Radio Four's prestigious *Today* programme reported that the forty-five-minute claim had found its way into the dossier even though the government knew it was dubious. In a subsequent article in the *Mail on Sunday*, Gilligan reported that Tony Blair's director of communications, Alastair Campbell, was responsible. This caused a political storm.

Kelly admitted to his bosses at the Ministry of Defence that he had talked to Gilligan, but added: "I am convinced that I am not his primary source of information."

Eventually, the Ministry of Defence announced that one of its employees was the source for Gilligan's story. It did not name Kelly, but gave enough clues for other journalists to identify him. To avoid the press, Kelly and his wife went to stay in Cornwall. However, he was required to appear before two committees of the House of Commons. On 15 July, he appeared before the Commons Foreign Affairs Committee where he expected to be chastised for saying too much to Andrew Gilligan. Instead, he was asked whether he had briefed Susan Watts from *Newsnight*. A long quote was read from Watts's piece. Dr Kelly denied all knowledge, but Watts had recorded the interview with him. He compounded the falsehood by denying having briefed the BBC's Gavin Hewitt.

Once he was found out, he knew is reputation would be in tatters. At the time, his marriage was on the rocks. In Iraq, he had become close to Mai Pedersen, a US Air Force interpreter. Coming up to retirement at the age of sixty, he had to decide whether to leave his wife and take a job with a think-tank in California, near to where Pederson lived. He asked a friend for advice about the matter.

On the morning of 17 July 2003, Dr Kelly was working at home in Oxfordshire, largely answering emails of support from journalists and friends. In one email to Judith Miller of the *New York Times*, he said that he would wait until the end of the week before judging how his appearance before the House of Commons' committees had gone and talked of "many dark actors playing games". Then an email came from the Ministry of

Defence asking for details of all his contacts with journalists. At 3 p.m., as usual, Dr Kelly told his wife Janice he was going for a walk. When he did not return, she went to look for him. Later she was joined in the search by two of their three daughters. They drove around the lanes where they knew their father liked to walk. No trace of him could be found.

At twenty minutes past midnight they called the police. A police dog and a helicopter with thermal imaging equipment were brought in. Assistant Chief Constable Michael Page had a meeting with key personnel at Abingdon Police Station at 5.15 a.m. By 7.30 a.m., forty police officers were engaged in the search, which centred on Harrowdown Hill, an area where Dr Kelly often walked. Members of the South East Berkshire Emergency Volunteers and the Lowland Search Dogs Association also joined the search.

Paul Chapman and Louise Holmes, along with Holmes's trained search dog, arrived in the area at 8 a.m. Her dog picked up a scent. It returned barking, indicating that it had found something, and led her to the body of a man. He was lying on the ground at the foot of a tree with his head and shoulders slumped back against it. His legs were straight in front of him. His right arm was at his side and his left arm had a lot of blood on it and was bent back in a strange position. It was clear that the man was dead and he matched the description of Dr Kelly that she had been given by the police.

Chapman made a 999 call to Abingdon police, then Chapman and Holmes made their way back to their car where they met three police officers who were involved in the search. Chapman then took Detective Constable Coe to show him where the body was lying some 75 yards (69 m) in from the edge of the wood. DC Coe saw that there was blood around the left wrist, and a knife and a watch on the left side of the body. He remained some seven or eight feet from the body for the next thirty minutes until two other police officers arrived to tape off the area. At around 9.55 a.m., two members of an ambulance crew arrived at the scene. They checked the body for signs of life. Four electrodes were placed on his chest and a heart monitor showed that there was no cardiac activity. Dr Kelly was dead.

When Assistant Chief Constable Page heard that a body had been found, he initiated an investigation. Home Office forensic pathologist Dr Nicholas Hunt was called. He arrived on the scene at 12.10 p.m. At 12.35 p.m., he again confirmed that Dr Kelly was dead. He then waited until the police had finished a fingertip search of the approach path to the body, before beginning his examination at about 2.10 p.m.

Kelly was wearing a green Barbour-type wax jacket; the zip and the buttons at the front had been undone. In the bellows pocket on the lower part of the jacket, Dr Hunt found a mobile telephone and a pair of bifocal spectacles. There was also a key fob and three blister packs of the drug Coproxamol. Each of those packs originally contained ten tablets. Of the thirty tablets, only one was left.

Kelly's face appeared pale and vomit had run from corners of the mouth, streaking the face. To Hunt, this suggested that Kelly had tried to vomit while he was lying on his back. Next to the body there was a Barbour-style flat cap with some blood on the lining and the peak, which was near his left shoulder. Lying on the grass near his left hand there was a digital watch, which was also bloodstained. It had a black resin strap. Next to the watch was a Sandvig gardening knife with a little hook or a lip near the tip of the blade for pruning. There was blood on the handle and the blade.

Nearby there was a half-litre bottle of Evian with some water left in it. The bottle was lying propped against some broken branches to the left, about a foot away from his left elbow. There were smears of blood on the bottle and the bottle top, indicated that Dr Kelly had been bleeding when he place the bottle in its final position. More blood was found spread across the soil and undergrowth up to 3 ft (1 m) from the body.

Dr Hunt could see that there were at least five cuts in the creased area to the front of Dr Kelly's left wrist. Later, Dr Kelly's daughter Sian confirmed that her father was right-handed.

A fingertip search was made of an area of up to 30 ft (10 m) from the body. This lasted from 12.50 p.m. to 4.45 p.m. One of those involved was Constable Sawyer. He said: "When I first saw Dr Kelly I was very aware of the serious nature of the search and I was looking for signs of perhaps a struggle; but all the vegetation that was surrounding Dr Kelly's body was standing upright and there were no signs of any form of struggle at all."

At 7.19 p.m., Dr Hunt ended his initial, on-scene examination of the body and it was moved to the John Radcliffe Hospital in Oxford where Dr Hunt began a post-mortem examination. This started at 9.20 p.m. and ended at 12.15 a.m. the following morning. After the corpse was removed, the police conducted a fingertip search of the ground under the body. Nothing of significance was found in the searches.

In his post-mortem report, Dr Hunt wrote: "There was a series of incised wounds, cuts, of varying depth over the front of the left wrist and they extended in total over about 8 by 5 centimetres on the front of the wrist. The largest of the wounds and the deepest lay towards the top end or the elbow end of that complex of injuries and it showed a series of notches and some crushing of its edges. That wound had actually severed an artery on the little finger aspect of the front of the wrist, called the ulnar artery. The other main artery on the wrist on the thumb aspect was intact. There were a number of other incisions of varying depth and many smaller scratch-like injuries over the wrist. The appearance that they gave was of what are called tentative or hesitation marks, which are commonly seen prior to a deep cut being made into somebody's skin if they are making the incision themselves."

There were no defensive injuries to the fingers or palms of the hands that would result from the victim trying to grab a knife or other bladed weapon, or to the outer part of the arm if the victim was trying to parry a blow.

The temperature of the body was measured using a rectal thermometer and death was estimated to have occurred between eighteen and twenty-seven hours earlier. This put the time of death between 4.15 p.m. on 17 July to 1.15 a.m. on 18 July.

According to Dr Hunt: "Dr Kelly was an apparently adequately nourished man in whom there was no evidence of natural disease that could of itself have caused death directly at the macroscopic or naked eye level. He had evidence of a significant incised wound to his left wrist, in the depths of which his left ulnar artery had been completely severed. That wound was in the context of multiple incised wounds over the front of his left wrist of varying length and depth. The arterial injury had resulted in the loss of a significant volume of blood as noted at the scene. The complex of incised wounds over the left wrist is entirely consistent with having been inflicted by a bladed weapon, most likely candidate for which would have been a knife. Furthermore, the knife present at the scene would be a suitable candidate for causing such injuries."

The orientation and arrangement of the wounds over the left wrist were typical of self-inflicted injuries. Also typical was the presence of small, so-called tentative or hesitation marks. Dr Hunt noted that Dr Kelly's watch appeared to have been removed deliberately to allow access to the wrist.

"The removal of the watch in that way and indeed the removal of the spectacles are features pointing towards this being an act of self-harm," he said. "Other features at the scene which would tend to support this impression include the relatively passive distribution of the blood, the neat way in which the water bottle and its top were placed, the lack of obvious signs of trampling of the undergrowth or damage to the clothing. To my mind, the location of the death is also of interest in this respect because it was clearly a very pleasant and relatively private spot of the type that is sometimes chosen by people intent upon self-harm."

Many of the injuries to the left wrist showed evidence of a "well-developed vital reaction"– that is, the body showed some signs of trying to heal itself – so Dr Hunt believed that they had been inflicted over a period of minutes, rather than seconds or hours, before death. This "vital reaction" manifests itself chiefly in the form of reddening and swelling around the affected area.

Dr Hunt again remarked on the total lack of classical defence wounds against sharp-weapon attack.

"Such wounds are typically seen in the palm aspects of the hands or over the outer aspects of the forearms," he said. "It was noted that he has a significant degree of coronary artery disease and this may have played some small part in the rapidity of death but not the major part in the cause of death."

Given that blister packs of Coproxamol tablets were found in the coat pocket and vomit was found on the ground, Dr Hunt said it was an entirely reasonable supposition that he may have consumed a quantity of these tablets either on the way to or at the scene itself. The toxicology report also indicated that he had consumed a "significant quantity of tablets".

There was also a minor injury to the inner lip and small abrasions to the head "consistent with scraping against rough undergrowth such as small twigs, branches and stones which were present at the scene". There was no sign that Dr Kelly had been knocked out by a volatile liquid such as chloroform before his death or been subject to a violent attack. There were no indications that he had been restrained by the wrists or ankles, or had been strangled either manually or by a ligature.

Dr Hunt concluded that Dr Kelly had died from the loss of blood from the wound in his left wrist. His death was hastened by the ingestion of dextropropoxyphene and the weakness of his coronary arteries.

"There was no pathological evidence to indicate the involvement of a third party in Dr Kelly's death," said Dr Hunt. "Rather, the features are quite typical . . . of self-inflicted injury if one ignores all the other features of the case."

Forensic biologist Roy Green arrived at the scene where the body was lying at 2 p.m. on 18 July. He examined the scene with particular reference to the bloodstaining in the area and found that most of the staining came from blood spurting from about a foot (33 cm) above the ground, though the highest came from 20 in. (50 cm). This meant that most of the injuries took place while Dr Kelly was sitting or lying down. When Green first viewed the body, Dr Kelly was lying down with his wrist curled back. There were bloodstains on his right elbow, the tops of his thighs, his right shoulder and the sleeve of his Barbour jacket.

Green described the bloodstain on the right knee of Kelly's jeans as a "contact bloodstain" – meaning that the stain had come from direct contact with a source of blood, rather than blood being splashed on it. Probably Dr Kelly had knelt in a pool of blood after he was bleeding.

"The jeans . . . with this large contact stain, did not appear to have any larger downward drops on them," said Green. "There were a few stains and so forth but it did not have any staining that would suggest to me that his injuries, or his major injuries if you like, were caused while he was standing up, and there was not any – there did not appear to be any blood underneath where he was found, and the body was later moved which all suggested those injuries were caused while he was sat or lying down."

The smear of blood on the Evian bottle indicated that Dr Kelly had become thirsty – "when people are injured and losing blood they will become thirsty," said Green, because they are losing fluid.

The forensic toxicologist Dr Alexander Allan examined blood and urine samples as well as the contents of Dr Kelly's stomach sent to him by Dr Hunt. These also contained paracetamol and dextropropoxyphene. The prescription medicine Coproxamol contains 325 mg of paracetamol and 32.5 mg of dextropropoxyphene. It is a mild to moderate painkiller, typically used to alleviate a bad back or period pain. The concentrations of the drugs he found represented "quite a large overdose of Coproxamol".

Dextropropoxyphene is an opioid analgesic drug which causes symptoms typical of opiate drugs in overdose, such as drowsiness, sedation and ultimately coma, respiratory depression and heart failure. It is known, in certain circumstances, to cause disruption to the rhythm of the heart and it can cause death by that process in some cases of overdose, while paracetamol does not cause drowsiness or sedation in overdose, but if enough is taken it can cause damage to the liver. Dextropropoxyphene was present in the blood at a concentration of one microgram per millilitre; paracetamol in a concentration of 97 micrograms per millilitre. These levels were much higher than would be found in therapeutic use.

"Typically, therapeutic use would represent one tenth of these concentrations," said Dr Allen. "They clearly represent an overdose. But they are somewhat lower than what I would normally expect to encounter in cases of death due to an overdose of Coproxamol."

When asked what concentration he would expect to see in a case where dextropropoxyphene resulted in death, Dr Allan said: "There are two surveys reported I am aware of. One reports a concentration of 2.8 micrograms per millilitre of blood of dextropropoxyphene in a series of fatal overdose cases. Another one reports an average concentration of 4.7 micrograms per millilitre of blood. You can say that they are several fold larger than the level I found."

Paracetamol was found in concentrations five or ten times higher than would normally be expected in therapeutic use, but lower than expected if it was the cause of death.

"I think if you can get the blood reasonably shortly after the incident," said Dr Allan, "and the person does not die slowly in hospital due to liver failure, perhaps typically three to four hundred micrograms per millilitre of blood."

The levels of paracetamol and dextropropoxyphene found in his body were consistent with Dr Kelly taking twenty-nine or thirty Coproxamol tablets and that the only way these drugs could have got into his body was by him ingesting them. There was a plentiful supply on hand. Mrs Kelly, who suffered from arthritis, kept them and Dr Kelly was thought to have taken them from her store.

The police did not show the knife to Dr Kelly's widow or his daughters. Instead, Mrs Kelly was shown a photograph of the knife found beside the body. It was a knife that Dr Kelly had owned since he was a boy, which he kept in the desk in his study along with a collection of pocket knives. It was found to be missing after his death. His daughters said that it was not unusual for him to take the knife when he went for a walk.

Professor Keith Hawton, Professor of Psychiatry at Oxford University and the Director of the Centre for Suicide Research, visited the site of Dr Kelly's death.

"It occurred in an isolated spot on Harrowdown Hill," he said, "in woodland about forty or fifty yards off the track taken by ramblers. The site is well protected from the view of other people . . . What struck me was it is a very peaceful spot, a rather beautiful spot and we know that it was a favourite – it was in the area of a favourite walk of Dr Kelly with his family."

This and the other circumstances of Dr Kelly's death led Professor Hawton to believe that Dr Kelly took his own life.

He had read Dr Hunt's report and seen photographs of Dr Kelly's body, and concluded that the injuries to his wrist were consistent with suicide, even though the ambulance crew and others said that there was not very much blood at the scene. The fact that Dr Kelly had removed his glasses, his cap and his watch also suggested suicide. There were no signs of violence on his body, other than the obvious injury to his wrist, that would indicate that he had been involved in some sort of struggle or a violent act. There was no sign of the trampling down of vegetation and undergrowth in the area around the body. So Professor Hawton concluded that it was highly unlikely that others were involved. Certainly, if someone had forced Dr Kelly to take Coproxamol, there would have been signs of a struggle. He was not drugged and force-fed the tablets either. While a sample taken of Dr Kelly's lung was not tested for volatile liquids such as ether, no traces of stupefying substances were found in his blood. Based on his examination of the evidence of the pathologist and the biologist, Professor Hawton also ruled out the possibility that Dr Kelly was force-fed Coproxamal elsewhere, then brought to the scene.

"I think that taking all the evidence together, it is well nigh certain that he committed suicide," he said.

According to Assistant Chief Constable Page, around 500 people were interviewed during his investigation into the death of Dr Kelly; 300 statements were taken; 700 documents were seized and numerous computer files examined to determine whether there was any criminal dimension to Dr Kelly's death. As it seemed out of character for Dr Kelly to commit suicide, the investigation focused on whether he was being blackmailed, but could find no evidence of it.

However, the Hutton Inquiry into the death of Dr Kelly also heard from David Broucher, the United Kingdom's Permanent Representative to the Conference on Disarmament in Geneva, who had met Dr Kelly in connection with his duties. He had wanted to pick Dr Kelly's brains about Iraq's compliance with the biological weapons convention, asking him why the Iraqis were courting disaster by not cooperating with the weapons inspectors and giving up whatever weapons they might have had in their arsenal. Dr Kelly said that he was in touch with the Iraqis but found himself in an ambiguous position. He had assured the Iraqis that if they cooperated with the weapons inspectors they had nothing to fear. However, he had come to believe that the invasion of Iraq might go ahead anyway and the Iraqis would think that he had lied to them. He said he did not like working for the Ministry of Defence and wanted to go back to working for the weapons research establishment at Porton Down.

Broucher asked Kelly directly what would happen if Iraq was invaded. According to Broucher: "His reply was, which I took at the time to be a throw-away remark – he said, 'I will probably be found dead in the woods.'" This raised the possibility that he had been murdered by Iraqi agents.

"I did not think much of this at the time, taking it to be a hint that the Iraqis might try to take revenge against him, something that did not seem at all fanciful then," said Broucher. "I now see that he may have been thinking on rather different lines."

The Hutton Inquiry concluded that Dr Kelly had committed suicide, but others were not satisfied with this conclusion and called for a formal inquest into Dr Kelly's death. Former assistant coroner Dr Michael Powers QC said that the cuts would not have caused Dr Kelly to bleed to death and the dose of Coproxamol in his body was normal. He was backed in this view by trauma surgeon David Halpin, epidemiologist Andrew Rouse, surgeon Martin Birnstingl, radiologist Stephen Frost and Chris Burns-Cox, who specializes in internal general medicine.

"Suicide cannot be presumed, it has to be proven," said Dr Powers. "From the evidence that we have as to the circumstances of his death, in particular the aspect of haemorrhage, we do not believe that there was sufficient evidence to prove beyond reasonable doubt that he killed himself."

He also found it suspicious that, while there were twenty-nine pills missing from the packs found nearby, there was comparatively little Coproxamol in his body. The inquest should not have been left to Lord Hutton, he said, as he is not a coroner.

"Any unnatural death has to be investigated properly," said Halpin. "This has not."

In their twelve-page submission, Powers, Halpin et al. concluded: "The bleeding from Dr Kelly's ulnar artery is highly unlikely to have been so voluminous and rapid that it was the cause of death. We advise the instructing solicitors to obtain the autopsy reports so that the concerns of a group of properly interested medical specialists can be answered."

Norman Baker MP uncovered information showing there were no fingerprints on the knife the scientist apparently used to slash his wrist, even though he was not wearing gloves.

The two members of the ambulance crew who arrived at the scene were also surprised at Hutton's conclusion because the small amount of blood they saw around the body was inconsistent with the cut on his wrist being the cause of death.

"I just think it is incredibly unlikely that he died from the wrist wound we saw," said paramedic Vanessa Hunt. "There just wasn't a lot of blood. When someone cuts an artery, whether accidentally or intentionally, the blood pumps everywhere. I just think it is incredibly unlikely that he died from the wrist wound we saw."

"Everyone was surprised at the outcome of the Hutton Inquiry," said fellow paramedic Dave Bartlett. "I would have thought there would have been more blood over the body if someone had bled to death."

Outside in the cold, vasoconstriction would slow the blood loss, it has been argued. But it has never been made public how much blood Dr Kelly had actually lost.

Over the years, Hunt and Bartlett have been to the scenes of dozens of attempted suicides where somebody has cut their wrists. In only one case has the victim been successful.

"That was like a slaughterhouse," said Hunt. "Just think what it would be like with five or six pints of milk splashed everywhere." If you slit your wrists, that is the amount of blood you would have to lose if you are going to die."

They were also amazed by the number of policemen at the scene.

"Some were in civilian clothes and others in black jackets and army fatigues," said Hunt. "I thought it might have been a firearms incident as there were the guys from the special armed response units."

When they first saw the body, Bartlett assumed that the man had hanged himself. It was only after they had checked for a pulse, shone light in the eyes and put electrodes on the chest to check for heart activity, that he noticed that the left sleeves of his jacket and shirt had been pulled up to just below the elbow and there was dried blood around his left wrist.

"There was no gaping wound," said Hunt. "There wasn't a puddle of blood around. There was a little bit of blood on the nettles to the left of his left arm. But there was no real blood on the body of the shirt. The only other bit of blood I saw was on his clothing. It was the size of a 50p piece above the right knee on his trousers."

Hunt found this strange.

"If you manage to cut a wrist and catch an artery you would get a spraying of blood, regardless of whether it's an accident," she said. "Because of the nature of an arterial cut, you get a pumping action. I would certainly expect a lot more blood on his clothing, on his shirt. If you choose to cut your wrists, you don't worry about getting blood on your clothes. I didn't see any blood on his right hand . . . If he used his right hand to cut his wrist, from an arterial wound you would expect some spray."

Bartlett agreed.

"I remember saying to one of the policemen it didn't look like he died from that [the wrist wound] and suggesting he must have taken an overdose or something else," he said.

He recalled being called to one attempted suicide where the blood had spurted so high it hit the ceiling.

"Even in this incident, the victim survived. It was like *The Texas Chainsaw Massacre* and the guy walked out alive. We have been to a vast amount of incidents where people who have slashed their wrists, intentionally or not. Most of them are taken down the hospital and given a few stitches then sent straight back home. But there is a lot of blood. It's all over them."

Bartlett does not buy the overdose theory either.

"If they showed me photos showing a lot of blood and said he had massive amounts of drugs or another substance in his body and that killed him, I would accept it," he said. "But until then there has to be some doubt."

The reaction of the paramedics was matched by the experts. Professor of intensive care medicine, Julian Blon, joined Dr Powers in a letter to *The Times*, saying: "Insufficient blood would have been lost to threaten life. Absent a quantitative assessment of the blood lost and of the blood remaining in the great vessels, the conclusion that death occurred as a consequence of haemorrhage is unsafe."

The ulnar artery is not the main artery in the wrist where the pulse is taken, but a small artery below the little finger, which is hard to locate and lies deep within the wrist.

Martin Birnstingl, former president of the Vascular Surgical Society of Great Britain, consultant at St Bartholomew's Hospital in London and one of the country's most respected vascular surgeons, said he believed it was "extremely unlikely" for Kelly to have died by simply severing the ulnar artery. He explained that arteries have muscles around them that will constrict when severed to prevent life-threatening loss of blood.

"It would spray blood around and make a mess," he said. "But after the blood pressure started to fall, the artery would contract and stop bleeding."

This view is supported by Dr Bill McQuillan, a former consultant at Edinburgh's Royal Infirmary who for twenty years has dealt with hundreds of wrist accidents.

"I have never seen one death of somebody from cutting an ulnar artery," he said. He pointed out that lying in a warm bath might encourage more bleeding, but in the open air the artery would simply close down. "I can't see how he would lose more than a pint of blood."

The two paramedics are concerned by something else they read in the Hutton report. Dr Kelly's body, it said, was found with his head and shoulders "slumped against a tree". Lord Hutton said he had seen a photograph showing his body in that position. The first person to find Dr Kelly, Louise Holmes, agreed that he was resting against a tree. But when Hunt and Bartlett arrived, Kelly was lying flat, some feet from the tree. Had someone moved him? Had his body been searched? None of the police officers at the scene admitted touching the body.

Norman Baker said that the Hutton Inquiry had "blatantly failed to get to the bottom of matters".

"The most important unanswered question is why he would have wanted to commit suicide, which still hasn't been addressed," said Baker.

Baker pointed out that it is unlikely the scientist would have decided to kill himself by "slitting a rather hidden artery in his hand". According to Dr Rouse, committing suicide by slitting the wrists in a fifty-nine-year-old man with no previous psychiatric history is extremely rare. Only one person is thought to have killed themselves this way in 2003 – Dr Kelly himself.

One witness told the *Observer* that, even if you accepted that Kelly's mental state was desperate enough for him to take his own life, it is inconceivable he would have chosen such an uncertain method.

"He was a scientist, a highly intelligent man. If he had chosen to kill himself, he would have opted for something certain, like hanging himself or throwing himself under a train. He would not have risked surviving. I can't believe he would have chosen to cut one small artery and take some pills. The outcome would be too uncertain."

Baker is also puzzled by the fact that, while Dr Kelly supposedly took twenty-nine Coproxamol tablets, only "a quarter of one tablet" was found in his stomach. Mai Pedersen, Dr Kelly's former US Air Force interpreter in Iraq and a close friend, said that he could not have swallowed twenty-nine tablets because, due to a disorder, he "had difficulty swallowing pills". She also said he could not have cut his wrist because an injury to his elbow had left his arm too weak to cut steak. He would have to have been a "contortionist" to have killed himself in the way the Hutton Inquiry claimed, she said.

Dr Powers is even more perplexed that the written records of the Hutton Inquiry, including witness statements, were to be kept secret for thirty years, while all medical records, including the post-mortem report and the photographs, would remain closed for seventy years.

"Supposedly all evidence relevant to the cause of death has been heard in public at the time of Lord Hutton's inquiry," said Dr Powers. "If these secret reports support the suicide finding, what could they contain that could be so sensitive?"

However, Dr Andrew Falzon, a consultant forensic pathologist with the Forensic Science Service, warned that the views of those who have not studied forensic pathology, even if they are medically trained, needed to be treated with caution.

"People who are not trained to look at causes of death will perceive things differently," he said. "It's hard for them to believe certain things can happen."

Kelly's heart disease and overdose meant a smaller loss of blood could kill him than that required to kill a healthy person: "You are going to succumb to a smaller volume of blood loss than if you were a twenty-year-old with a healthy heart. The heart vessel is already deprived of oxygen because of the blockage of the vessels. With the loss of blood, there is less oxygen to the heart. Throw in the toxic level of drug, that makes the heart more sensitive to cardiac arrhythmia [an electrical disturbance] which causes sudden death. I'm sure bleeding from the ulnar artery can kill you."

Dr Andrew Davison, a forensic pathologist with Cardiff University, agreed.

"You only have so much blood going around," he said. "If you have a heart condition you can't afford to lose as much blood as a healthy person."

According to Professor Derrick Pounder, head of forensic medicine and a forensic pathologist at the University of Dundee: "It may be that there are several factors in a death. In this case, we know he had taken more than a therapeutic dose of drugs, and that he had some pre-existing heart disease. We have three factors in the death that are known to the public. The cause of death is likely an interplay between the three."

Professor Peter Vanezis, senior consultant in forensic medicine to the armed forces, also attacked Hutton's critics.

"These people are more clinicians and are obviously surprised that a person can kill themselves like that," he said.

He also said the lack of large amounts of blood in the wood where Kelly was discovered could also be easily explained: "It was outside, it could have gone into the soil."

Forensic pathologists Chris Milroy of Sheffield University and Guy Rutty of Leicester University say that it is hard to judge blood loss at the scene of a death as some blood may have seeped into the ground. Milroy also said that Kelly's heart condition may have made it hard for him to sustain any significant degree of blood loss.

The Oxfordshire coroner, Nicholas Gardiner, who had adjourned the inquest when the Hutton Inquiry was announced, considered the issue again in 2004. After reviewing evidence not presented to the Hutton Inquiry, Gardiner decided there was no need for further investigation. However, a public inquiry has only replaced an inquest in three other cases. In each of them multiple deaths had occurred. The incidents were the Ladbroke Grove rail crash in 2000 where thirty-one people died; the 311 deaths connected with Dr Harold Shipman; and the thirty-six lives lost when the Hull trawler *Gaul* sank in the Barents Sea in 1974. And that case was reopened in 2004.

The mystery deepened in August 2010, when Dr Richard Spertzel, the former head of the UN Biological Section who worked closely with Dr Kelly in Iraq in the 1990s, wrote to Attorney General Dominic Grieve saying that Dr Kelly was on a hit list in the final years of his life.

"I know that David, as well as myself and a couple of others, were on an Iraqi hit list," he said. "In late 1997, we were told by the Russian embassy in Baghdad. I had no idea what it meant but apparently David and I were high on the priority list."

He and Dr Kelly were told that they were "numbers three and four" on the list during an inspection trip in Iraq.

"David just being associated with the work he'd been doing for the UK government would have made him a high target," Dr Spertzel said.

He also agreed with the doctors who said that it was almost impossible to kill yourself in the way described in the Hutton report.

"My concern about David Kelly's death is exactly what the doctors are saying now – that is, it's virtually impossible to commit suicide by slashing your wrist in that way," he said. "It just doesn't make sense. It seems to me that they [the British authorities] are intentionally ignoring all this. Something's fishy."

Some forensic pathologists back this view. Sir Barry Jackson, past president of the British Academy of Forensic Science and one of the doctors who wrote to ministers, said: "In my experience from thirty years as a practising surgeon I find it difficult to agree with the cause of death as listed on his death certificate."

Dr Elizabeth Driver, a solicitor and Fellow of the Royal College of Pathologists, agreed.

"As a pathologist I cannot understand how Dr Kelly could have died from blood loss of a severed ulnar artery," she said. "It makes no medical sense. Little is known about the medical facts because the post-mortem has been kept secret. There are obvious questions which were not addressed in the inquiry."

In his book, *The End of the Party*, political commentator Anthony Rawnsley claimed that Geoff Hoon, defence secretary at the time of Dr Kelly's death, "planned to make a speech about the Kelly affair that he told friends could trigger the instant downfall of the prime minister", after he was unceremoniously dumped from office in 2006. Hoon visited Dr Kelly's widow shortly after his death.

There were also extraordinary claims that the Thames Valley Police had stripped the wallpaper from the sitting room in Dr Kelly's home after he was reported missing, but before his body was found. Meanwhile, Janice Kelly and her daughters were forced to wait in the garden. There is speculation that they were sweeping the room for listening devices. The police refused to comment.

Dr Halpin received an anonymous and carefully worded letter from someone claiming to be a relative of a former colleague of David Kelly at the Ministry of Defence, saying that Kelly's colleagues had been "warned off" attending his funeral.

The doctors seeking to reopen the coroner's inquest managed to obtain a copy of Dr Kelly's death certificate. Near the top of all British death certificates is a box headed "Date and place of death", where the doctor or coroner should enter the exact location of a death, if it has been established. Dr Kelly's certificate gives his date of death as 18 July 2003. Then, instead of giving place of death, it says: "Found dead at Harrowdown Hill, Longworth, Oxon" – implying that he might have died elsewhere and his body merely found on Harrowdown Hill. Strangely, the death certificate was completed five weeks before the end of the Hutton Inquiry. Nor is it signed by a doctor or coroner as it should be.

"This death certificate is evidence of a failure properly to examine the cause of Dr Kelly's death," says Dr Powers. "It is evidence of a pre-judgment of the issue. In a coroner's inquest the cause of death would not be registered until the whole inquiry had been completed. As we see here, the cause of death was registered before the Hutton Inquiry had finished. This is remarkable. To my mind it is evidence that the inquiry into Dr

Kelly's death was window dressing because the conclusion had already been determined."

Chief Inspector Alan Young of Thames Valley Police, who headed the investigation into Dr Kelly's death, did not even give evidence to the Hutton Inquiry. Then, in 2008, a Freedom of Information request revealed that the police helicopter with thermal-imaging equipment sent to search for Dr Kelly on the night he disappeared did not detect his body even though, at 2.50 a.m. on 18 July 2003, it flew directly over the spot where his body was found less than six hours later. Yet the pathologist who took Dr Kelly's body temperature at 7 p.m. on the day his body was found determined that Dr Kelly could still have been alive at 1.15 a.m. on 18 July – just ninety-five minutes before the helicopter flew over that patch of woodland when the body would have been warm enough to be picked up by the helicopter's heat sensors.

In his 2007 book, *The Strange Death of David Kelly*, Norman Baker said that Kelly was almost certainly murdered. Both the police investigation and Hutton Inquiry failed to resolve numerous discrepancies and anomalies in the physical, medical and witness evidence. Baker concluded that Kelly's death was probably a revenge killing by supporters of Saddam Hussein. It was then disguised as a suicide by Thames Valley Police, who appeared to have known of an assassination plot in advance, because the British government was fearful of the political consequences.

In October 2010, the post-mortem report was made public by the new government. In it, Dr Hunt stated: "It is my opinion that the main factor involved in bringing about the death of David Kelly is the bleeding from the incised wounds to his left wrist. Had this not occurred he may well not have died at this time. Furthermore, on the balance of probabilities, it is likely that the ingestion of an excess number of Coproxamol tablets coupled with apparently clinically silent coronary artery disease would both have played a part in bringing about death more certainly and more rapidly than would have otherwise been the case. Therefore I give as the cause of death: 1a. Haemorrhage;

1b Incised wounds to the left wrist; 2. Coproxamol ingestion and coronary artery atherosclerosis."

Dr Powers refused to accept the finding, but Julian Blon reversed his previous position, saying: "Any one of the injuries or disease processes identified – had it existed by itself – would not have been sufficient in itself to cause death. When you assemble it together, you get a different picture . . . The information provided satisfies me that this was suicide."

9/11

O N 9 SEPTEMBER 2001, two planes full of passengers crashed
into the Twin Towers of the World Trade Center in New
York, causing them to collapse. A third passenger plane ploughed
into the Pentagon in Virginia; a fourth – possibly destined to
crash into the White House or Capitol Building – came down in
a field in Stonycreek Township, near Shanksville, in Somerset
County, Pennsylvania. This presented investigators with three
massive crime scenes. Each presented its own difficulties.

In Pennsylvania a makeshift morgue was set up at the
National Guard Armory at the Somerset County Airport by
D-MORT, the Disaster-Mortuary Operation Response Team.
The team is part of the US Department of Health and Human
Services' national disaster medical system set up under the 1996
federal Aviation Disaster Family Assistance Act. Heading the
team at Stonycreek was forensic anthropologist Paul Sledzik, the
curator at the Armed Forces Institute of Pathology's National
Museum of Health and Medicine in Washington, DC, who has
worked on numerous murder cases.

Some seventy-five people went to work, including X-ray
technicians, anthropologists, forensic pathologists, dentists and
experts on DNA analysis, to assist Somerset County coroner
Wallace Miller in the identification of the thirty-three passengers
and seven crew members. The D-MORT workers' job was to
attempt to document every piece of tissue, no matter how small.
By walking or crawling over the crash site and by sifting dirt
through mesh screens, D-MORT workers recovered even tiny
samples that, despite their size, would be analysed and identified.
Afterwards, the remains were transferred to the Armed Forces
Laboratory at Dover, Delaware, for further tests.

Miller had asked everyone involved, particularly those working in the evidence recovery and search efforts at the crash site,

to consider the dignity of the victims and the feelings of their families.

"We give the site the dignity and respect it commands," said Miller. "These people are loved ones of family members . . . We respect that and embrace it."

Miller was among the very first to arrive after the 10.06 crash on the sunny morning of 11 September. He was surprised at the small size of the smoking crater.

It looked, he said, "like someone took a scrap truck, dug a ten-foot ditch and dumped all this trash into it".

As coroner, Miller had only handled two homicides in his twenty-year career – a domestic murder-suicide and the case of a woman who killed her husband after he refused to take her rattlesnake hunting.

After about twenty minutes, he said, he stopped being a coroner because there were no bodies at the scene.

"It became like a giant funeral service," he said. He found himself honoured and humbled to preside over what has become essentially an immense cemetery stretching far into the scenic wooded mountain ridge that he considers to be the final resting place of forty national heroes.

When the FBI arrived, the crash site became an FBI crime scene and agents clambered over it clad in white suits to protect them from jet fuel and possible biological hazards posed by human remains. Investigators drained a two-acre pond about 1,000 ft (300 m) from the crater where the jetliner slammed into the ground. It was full of plane parts, personal belongings and human remains.

When the FBI left, the crash site became the coroner's crime scene again. Miller said that he could not guarantee to identify the remains of all the passengers or that investigators would find every last trace. The first victim was identified nine days after the incident when a tooth was matched to a dental record. Others were identified in the next few days.

"The identifications we have made for now have been mostly through dental records and fingerprints," he said. "We're also using radiology records, and we can find surgical work such as hip replacements."

Fingerprint specialists examined tissue and dentists examined teeth, fillings or wire from dental braces that had been collected for comparison with X-rays and other records obtained from relatives of the crash victims. Anthropologists and X-ray technicians did the same with bones, looking for evidence of healed fractures, past injuries or surgeries.

As part of the identification process, the FBI insisted that DNA matches be used as a final confirmation. Victims' families were asked to provide items such as the victims' hairbrushes, toothbrushes, used razor blades or licked postage stamps, so that medical investigators at the Armed Forces Institute of Pathology's DNA-identification laboratory in Rockville, Maryland, could glean samples to draw final DNA matches. Blood samples from close relatives were also taken. The FBI also hoped that DNA links would help them identify the hijackers, whose identities at that point were concealed by the fake IDs they had used when boarding the plane.

The victims and the killers together constituted about 7,000 lbs (3,175 kg) of human flesh, most of which was cremated on impact. Some 1,500 mostly scorched samples of human tissue, totalling less than 600 lbs (272 kg) or about 8 per cent of the total, were recovered by the hundreds of searchers who climbed the hemlocks and combed the woods in the following weeks.

Dr Dennis Dirkmaat, a professor of forensic anthropology at Mercyhurst College in Erie who was called in to assist, said: "We would expect in a crash as horrific as this that there would be extreme fragmentation."

He assisted the FBI and evidence recovery teams at the crime scene, which was marked off in grids of 20 × 20 yards (20 × 20 m). When they were located, debris and remains were marked, photographed and then collected. Personal effects were then transferred to the FBI.

Dirkmaat's goal was to get the biological material off site as soon as possible, leaving law enforcement officers to handle the non-biological remains. Most of the plane had disintegrated into jagged metallic nuggets, mangled and melted into irregular shapes, little bigger than children's marbles.

"It's always very troubling in the terms of putting a human face on this," Dirkmaat said. "It's hard to put into words . . . We feel really badly about what happened. But we have a job to do for the families, and we have to do the best job we can."

The Boeing 757, still heavily laden with jet fuel, had slammed almost straight down at about 575 mph (925 km/h) into a rolling patch of grassy land that had long ago been strip-mined for coal. The impact spewed a fireball of horrific force across hundreds of acres of towering hemlocks and other trees, setting many ablaze. The fuselage burrowed straight into the earth so forcefully that one of the black boxes was found 25 ft (7.6 m) underground.

There was a range of people on board. Aged twenty to seventy-nine, they came from New York City, Honolulu, Manalapan in New Jersey and Greensboro, North Carolina. They were energetic salespeople, ambitious college students, corporate executives, lawyers, a retired ironworker, a waiter going to his son's funeral, a four-foot-tall disabled-rights activist, a census worker, a fish and wildlife officer, a retired couple who were volunteer missionaries, a former collegiate judo champion, a retired paratrooper, a weightlifter, a flight attendant who had been a policewoman, a female lawyer who had a brown belt in karate, a 6 ft 5 in. muscular rugby player who was gay and a former college quarterback.

Herded to the back of the plane, they used mobile phones or the on-board phones to call 911 and contact loved ones. Only then did they discover that the hijacking of United Airline's Flight 93 from Newark to San Francisco was not an isolated incident. Four passengers in particular – Todd Beamer, Tom Burnett, Mark Bingham and Jeremy Glick – would be hailed as heroes because their phone conversations provided the most detailed account of the passengers' plan for a life-or-death charge for the cockpit after the terrorists had seized control.

Beamer, a thirty-two-year-old account manager for a Silicon Valley software firm, made a lengthy 911 call to Lisa Jefferson, a veteran operator outside Chicago. As the plane lurched and passengers screamed, Beamer, a devout Christian, and his seatmates recited the Lord's Prayer. Jefferson joined in. More screams were heard while Beamer and others recited the twenty-third psalm: "Yea, though I walk through the valley of the shadow of death, I will fear no evil . . ."

Then Beamer said: "Are you guys ready? Okay. Let's roll!"

The cockpit voice recorder that records the last thirty minutes of every flight was recovered at the crash site. Most of the tape is taken up with the howling wind created by a plane travelling fast at low altitude. But the recording also includes the seven-minute death struggle in which muffled voices are heard screaming and cursing in both English and Arabic as the plane plunges towards the earth. The families of the victims were allowed to listen to the tape, something that is not normally made public. The recording opened the possibility that some of the victims were killed before the plane hit the ground. Investigators who recovered remains from the crash site brought possible stab wounds and lacerations to the attention of FBI pathologists. But the FBI said that "the catastrophic nature of the crash and fragmentation" left them unable to draw conclusions.

The crime scene was in a scenic stretch of the Appalachians – 70 miles (113 km) south-east of Pittsburgh and 170 miles (274 km) north-west of Washington, DC. It was settled more than a thousand years ago by the Monongahela, and crisscrossed by trails of the Shawnee, Iroquois and Delaware tribes. Then Europeans – German, British, Dutch and Italian – arrived here to hunt and trap, then to settle. In the late 1700s, a German named Christian Shank built a mill on the Stonycreek River, and a town grew up that took his name. It was supposed to become the hub of commerce, but remained a tiny community of 245 people, who describe it as a place that time forgot, in the middle of nowhere. They farmed and fished and hunted, cut timber, mined coal and made steel. They built many churches where they were taught to help out one another when crops went bad, when fires and floods hit their neighbours, when loved ones were taken away by death.

When Flight 93 hit this isolated spot, it was suddenly overrun by the FBI, the state police, a federal disaster mortuary team, the Red Cross, the National Transportation Safety Board, officials of United Airlines and the news media. Almost instantly, informal church networks and local telephone trees were activated and a cascade of hot casseroles, pots of coffee, cold drinks and clean clothes materialized at the crash site. An estimated 5,000 people, mostly Pennsylvania natives, came from across the country to help. Meanwhile, the deep gash in the earth was being excavated, examined and sifted. The nearest thing to a local victim was the Reverend Larry Hoover, a Lutheran pastor in Somerset County who also ran a family lumberyard. He and his wife Linda owned 8 acres (32,000 m^2) of woodland with a secluded cabin that was their weekend retreat and their planned retirement home. Their thirty-four-year-old son Barry lived in a sturdy old stone cottage on the property. The shock wave from Flight 93 crashing just a few hundred yards away spewed debris through the woods with such force that it blew out all the windows and doors, and shook the foundations. Human remains were still being found there months later.

The identification process took five months. Ten victims were identified through dental and fingerprint records. All forty were identified by their DNA and four additional DNA profiles were isolated. These belonged to the terrorists – Ziad Jarrah, Ahmed Al Haznawi, Saeed Al Ghamdi and Ahmed Al Nami.

When the identification process was over, the site was restored and a memorial to those who died was built there. The remains of passengers and crew that were identified were released to the families for burial, entombment or cremation, depending on families' preferences. Unidentified remains and those yielding no DNA information were interred in the county under the auspices of the coroner. The remains of the hijackers would remain in the custody of the FBI. Death certificates for the forty victims record their deaths as homicides, while the hijackers' death certificates call their deaths suicides.

Despite the numerous phone calls from the doomed aircraft and the evidence from the crime scene itself, a number of conspiracy theories had grown up around the crash of Flight 93. Sceptics claimed that the plane was hit by a heat-seeking missile from an F-16 jet fighter or an electronic pulse from a mysterious white plane seen in the vicinity by at least six witnesses. It was said to have been flying at 34,000 ft, but later to descend to 5,000 ft to examine the crash site.

It has even been suggested that there were no terrorists on board or that the passengers were drugged. A wilder theory is that the passengers from the other planes that were downed on 9/11 were loaded on to Flight 93 so the government could kill them, or that the passengers colluded with the hijackers to bring the plane down.

There was indeed a jet in the vicinity. It was a Dassault Falcon 20 business jet owned by the VF Corporation of Greensboro, North Carolina, a clothing company that markets Wrangler jeans. The VF plane was flying into Johnstown-Cambria airport, 20 miles (32 km) north of Shanksville. According to David Newell, VF's director of aviation, the Federal Aviation Administration's Cleveland Center contacted co-pilot Yates Gladwell when the Falcon was at an altitude "in the neighbourhood of 3,000 to 4,000 ft" – not 34,000 ft.

"They were in a descent already going into Johnstown," Newell adds. "The FAA asked them to investigate and they did. They got down within 1,500 feet of the ground when they circled. They saw a hole in the ground with smoke coming out of it. They pinpointed the location and then continued on."

One of Flight 93's engines was found "at a considerable distance from the crash site," according to Lyle Szupinka, a state police officer on the scene who was quoted in the *Pittsburgh Tribune-Review*. This is interpreted by one conspiracy-theory website to mean that "the main body of the engine . . . was found miles away from the main wreckage site with damage comparable to that which a heat-seeking missile would do to an airliner".

Experts on the scene reported that it was only a fan from one of the engines that was recovered in a catchment basin, downhill from the crash site. The catchment basin was just over 300 yards

(275 m) south of the crash site, which means that the fan landed in the direction the jet was travelling.

"It's not unusual for an engine to move or tumble across the ground," said Michael K. Hynes, an airline accident expert. "When you have very high velocities, 500 mph or more, you are talking about 700 to 800 feet per second. For something to hit the ground with that kind of energy, it would only take a few seconds to bounce up and travel 300 yards."

According to the *Pittsburgh Post-Gazette* of 13 September 2001: "Residents and workers at businesses outside Shanksville, Somerset County, reported discovering clothing, books, papers and what appeared to be human remains . . . Others reported what appeared to be crash debris floating in Indian Lake, nearly six miles from the immediate crash scene."

One website says: "On September 10, 2001, a strong cold front pushed through the area, and behind it – winds blew northerly. Since Flight 93 crashed west-southwest of Indian Lake, it was impossible for debris to fly perpendicular to wind direction . . . The FBI lied."

Another concludes: "Without a doubt, Flight 93 was shot down."

But Wallace Miller, Somerset County coroner, said that no body parts were found in Indian Lake. Human remains were confined to a 70-acre (0.3 km^2) area directly surrounding the crash site. Paper and tiny scraps of sheet metal, however, did land in the lake.

"Very light debris will fly into the air, because of the concussion," said former National Transportation Safety Board investigator Matthew McCormick. Besides, Indian Lake is less than 1.5 miles (2.4 km) south-east of the impact crater – not 6 miles (10 km) – easily within range of debris blasted skyward by the heat of the explosion from the crash. The wind speed on 11 September 2001 was 9 to 12 mph (14 to 19 km/h), blowing from the north-west – that is, towards Indian Lake.

Flight 93 was not the only plane downed that day. After firefighters doused the flames of American Airlines Flight 77 at the Pentagon and the survivors had been evacuated, the crash site became a crime scene and the gruesome task of crime scene investigation was begun by National Capital Response Squad and the Joint Terrorism Task Force. A chunk of the aircraft's nose cone and the nose landing gear was found in the service road between rings B and C of the Pentagon. A seat from the cockpit was discovered intact, while the two black boxes were found near the hole punched in the outer wall of the building. The cockpit voice recorder was too badly damaged to retrieve any information, but the flight recorder did yield some useful data.

Part of a driver's licence with the name "ALHAZMI" on it was found among the rubble. It was thought to belong to Nawaf al-Hazmi, one of the hijackers. Personal effects belonging to the victims – including a watch face, a piece of shirt and a burnt handkerchief – were also found and sent to the Joint Personal Effects Depot at Fort Myer.

All fifty-eight passengers, four flight attendants and both pilots on board, as well as 125 occupants of the Pentagon, had died. Only one of those who perished made it to hospital. The rest were killed at the crash site.

"There were so many bodies, I'd almost step on them," said Kevin Rimrodt, a Navy photographer surveying the Navy Command Center after the attacks. "So I'd have to really take care to look backwards as I'm backing up in the dark, looking with a flashlight, making sure I'm not stepping on somebody."

Some bodies were intact. But mostly only pieces of tissue were to be found. All were badly burnt, making identification difficult.

Under the authority of the FBI, remains of the victims at the Pentagon were taken to a temporary morgue in the Pentagon's north parking lot, where they were photographed, labelled and then refrigerated. The debris was also collected there for more detailed examination and bagging and tagging as evidence. The remains were then transported to Davison Army Airfield at nearby Fort Belvoir, and from there to Dover Air Force Base, Delaware, where a large mortuary had been built for use in wartime. FBI agents accompanied the remains during transportation to maintain the integrity of the crime scene evidence.

About 250 people, including fifty medical examiners from the Armed Forces Institute of Pathology (AFIP) and fifty members of the FBI's disaster team, went to work at the mortuary to identify the remains. A computerized tracking system assigned numbers to each victim. As most of the victims were military personnel, the family services divisions of each branch of the military collected dental and medical records, and contacted the families of the victims to compile DNA reference material.

The remains were first scanned for the presence of unexploded ordnance or metallic foreign bodies. Then attempts were made to identify the remains from fingerprints, dental records and X-rays. Where possible, full-body radiography was used to identify fractures or other damage prior to death that might have shown up in the medical records. After that an autopsy was performed by one of the twelve forensic pathologists on hand to determine the precise cause and manner of death. Forensic anthropologist Dr William C. Rodriguez tried to determine the race, sex and stature of each victim. Forensic dentistry experts from the Department of Oral and Maxillofacial Pathology compared any teeth or jaw parts to dental records. For eight days a full complement of AFIP forensic specialists worked twelve-hour shifts to complete the operation. However, in most cases, identification was problematic as the specimens were usually unrecognizable body parts mixed with debris from the aircraft and the building.

Tissue samples were then sent to an Armed Forces DNA Identification Laboratory (AFDIL) in Rockville, Maryland, for DNA analysis. Teams of forensic scientists, under the direction of Demris Lee, technical leader of the Nuclear DNA Section, began the task of generating DNA profiles of the victims. Their work included not only the Pentagon crash victims, but the victims of the Somerset County crash as well. Every one of the organization's 102 DNA analysts, sample processors, logistics staff and administrative personnel were involved, collecting, tracking and analysing DNA samples, and gathering and logging DNA reference material to prepare DNA reports. For eighteen days following the terrorist attacks, AFDIL employees worked on twelve-hour shifts, seven days a week. By the time the formal identification effort ended on 16 November, they had identified the remains of 184 people who died in the Pentagon or aboard Flight 77, plus the five hijackers who were identified by a process of elimination. Their remains were returned to the FBI. DNA profiles identified two of the hijackers as brothers – Nawaf and Salem al-Hamzi.

More conspiracy theories have grown up around the attack on the Pentagon. Firstly, sceptics draw attention to the 75 ft (23 m) wide entry hole in the building's exterior wall, visible for twenty minutes until the facade's collapse, and the 16 ft (5 m) wide hole in Ring C, the middle ring of the Pentagon. These, they claim, are far too small to have been made by a Boeing 757, which is 125 ft (38 m) wide and 155 ft (47 m) long. It must have been made by a smaller plane or, perhaps, even a missile.

However, a forensic reconstruction of the incident, using CSI evidence from the crash site, showed that one wing hit the ground before the plane reached the building and sheared off. The other hit one of the Pentagon's load-bearing columns and was torn away. Only the fuselage actually penetrated the wall, according to Mete Sozen, a professor of structural engineering at Purdue University.

"If you expected the entire wing to cut into the building," said Sozen, "it didn't happen."

Sceptics also point out that some of the Pentagon's windows, even those just above the point of impact were found intact. Again, this is thought to prove that the Pentagon was hit by a smaller plane or a missile. However, the Pentagon is a military establishment, thought to be a prime target for a terrorist attack, and has blast-resistant windows.

The idea that it was not an airliner that hit the Pentagon is refuted by CCTV footage and blast expert Allyn E. Kilsheimer, the first structural engineer to arrive at the Pentagon after the crash, who helped coordinate the emergency response.

"I saw the marks of the plane wing on the face of the building," said Kilsheimer. "I picked up parts of the plane with the airline markings on them. I held in my hand the tail section of the plane, and I found the black box . . . I held parts of uniforms from crew members in my hands, including body parts."

The crime scene investigation at the World Trade Center was even more complicated due to the large number of victims, the large area affected around the crash site and the multiple disasters of the crashing planes and the collapsing buildings. While it was known who was on the planes, there was no manifest of who was in the buildings. They were joined by firefighters, police officers and other emergency personnel, some of whom died when the buildings came down. It was not even known how many were dead. On 13 September, the estimate stood at 4,947. This rose to 6,714 by 24 September. Now it is thought that 2,606 people on the ground were killed, along with eighty-seven on American Airlines Flight 11, which hit the North Tower, and sixty on board United 175, which hit the South Tower – making 2,753 in all. The investigators were also put under pressure by Mayor Rudy Giuliani, who said that he wanted Ground Zero cleared by the time he left office on 31 December.

The attack on the World Trade Center not only produced many more victims than any disaster in modern American history, but the destructive forces unleashed were far worse than any other disaster on American soil. First, there was the explosion of jet fuel, then the extreme heat from the fires. After that there was the crushing force of thousands of tons of steel and concrete falling from a great height. The destruction was so great that the flight recorders of neither plane were found at the crash site.

Given the extent of the destruction, Ground Zero could not be sealed off like other crime scenes and volunteers swarmed over the debris, which was soon known as "The Pile". Rescue workers found bodies strapped to what was left of airplane seats and discovered the body of a flight attendant with her hands bound with plastic handcuffs, presumably put on by the hijackers. Sometimes when they found a body, they simply marked it and burrowed further into the debris in the hope of finding survivors. But again, the bodies of most of the victims had been torn apart. Body parts were put in body bags and taken to refrigerated trucks that were parked in several places around the 16 acre (65,000 m^2) site.

Working in the tangle of concrete and steel from the shattered buildings, investigators found wallets, luggage, blackened computer keyboards and shards of furniture. The landing gear of Flight 175 was found on top of a building on the corner of West Broadway and Park Place, an engine was found at the intersection of Church and Murray Street and a section of the fuselage landed on top of World Trade Center 5, a smaller building nearby.

A passport belonging to Satam al-Suqami, one of the hijackers, miraculously survived the crash and landed on the street below. The passport, soaked in jet fuel, was picked up from the street by a passer-by who gave it to a New York City Police Department detective shortly before the South Tower collapsed.

In the days after the attacks, hundreds of forensic pathologists, anthropologists, dentists and doctors, many of them volunteers, flocked to three huge tents outside the East Side Manhattan headquarters of the medical examiner's office. There they pored over body parts both large and small, taking fingerprints and tooth prints and X-rays, seeking a match with a list of those missing. They made hundreds of relatively quick identifications in the first weeks and months.

Then began a more laborious process. The medical examiner's office collected hair and saliva samples from thousands of families, and set about trying to extract DNA from almost 20,000 body parts collected from more than two million tons of debris. Initially, they used standard DNA analysis, but soon the scientists were forced to develop new forensic techniques where they attempted to establish a profile from degraded DNA extracted from tiny fragments of bone and tissue.

By 2005, they had stretched the technology to its limits. By then, 1,588 of the victims had been identified, leaving 1,161 unaccounted for. The city was left with 9,720 unidentified body parts, which biologists freeze-dried and stored, in the hope that someday new technology will allow them to be identified. Nevertheless, work continued. In November 2006, after the families provided fresh DNA samples, body parts were identified belonging to Karen Martin, a flight attendant on Flight 11 who had been stabbed by the hijackers; passenger Douglas Stone, who was a New York businessman; and another male passenger whose name was withheld at his family's request. More human remains were also found in a utility manhole near Ground Zero. And in April 2007, examiners using newer DNA technology identified another Flight 11 victim. The remains of two hijackers, probably from Flight 11, were also identified and removed from Memorial Park in Manhattan. The remains of the other hijackers have not been identified.

A three-month search of two dumptrucks' worth of debris recovered by demolition workers from the top of the Deutsche Bank building near Ground Zero yielded seventy-two new fragments of human tissue in 2010. This resulted in the identification of twenty-five new victims using a DNA profiling technique called single nucleotide polymorphisms, or SNPs – the first time this was used in forensic analysis.

Conspiracy theorists believe that the Twin Towers – and the smaller World Trade Center building nearby, which collapsed later – were not brought down by the impact of the planes but were wired with explosives as the lobbies of both of the towers were visibly damaged before the towers collapsed. According to one website: "There is NO WAY the impact of the jet caused such widespread damage 80 stories below. It is OBVIOUS and irrefutable that OTHER EXPLOSIVES (. . . such as concussion bombs) HAD ALREADY BEEN DETONATED in the lower levels of tower one at the same time as the plane crash."

However, a study by the National Institute of Standards and Technology (NIST) showed that plane debris sliced through the utility shafts at the North Tower's core, which became a conduit for burning jet fuel. This travelled down the elevator shafts, disrupting the elevator systems and causing extensive damage to the lobbies. According to first-person testimony, some of the elevators plummeted down the lift shafts and crashed into the ground floor.

"The doors cracked open on the lobby floor and flames came out and people died," says James Quintiere, an engineering professor at the University of Maryland and a NIST adviser.

Another website pointed out that kerosene does not burn hot enough to melt steel, so the burning fuel could not have caused the collapse of the building. It is true that, while jet fuel burns at 800°F to 1,500°F (427°C to 816°C), steel melts at 2,750°F (1,510°C). However, the steel frames did not need to melt for the buildings to collapse. They just need to lose some of their structural strength, which happens at a much lower temperature.

"I have never seen melted steel in a building fire," said retired New York Deputy Fire Chief Vincent Dunn. "But I've seen a lot of twisted, warped, bent and sagging steel. What happens is that the steel tries to expand at both ends, but when it can no longer expand, it sags and the surrounding concrete cracks."

And jet fuel was not the only thing burning, notes Forman Williams, a professor of engineering at the University of California, San Diego. He said that the inferno caused by the burning fuel was intensified when the carpets, curtains, paper and other combustible material inside the buildings caught fire.

"The jet fuel was the ignition source," said Williams. "It burned for maybe ten minutes, and the towers were still standing in ten minutes. It was the rest of the stuff burning afterward that was responsible for the heat transfer that eventually brought them down."

NIST also said that a great deal of the spray-on fireproofing insulation was knocked off the steel beams that were in the path of the crashing jets, leaving the metal exposed to the heat, while pockets of fire hit 1,832°F (1,000°C).

"Steel loses about 50 per cent of its strength at 1,100°F," said senior engineer Farid Alfawakhiri of the American Institute of Steel Construction. "And at 1,800°F it is probably at less than 10 per cent."

Puffs of dust were seen coming out of the sides of the building as it collapsed – a sure sign that explosives had been detonated, some conspiracy theorists say. But this can be explained in another way.

Once each tower began to collapse, the weight of all the floors above the collapsed zone crashed down on the floor below. Unable to carry the weight, that floor would then collapse on to the floor below. This progressive collapse would cause a chain reaction that engineers call "pancaking". No explosives are required for the collapse to continue.

As each floor pancaked, the air inside would be expelled with enormous force, carrying pulverized concrete and other debris with it.

"When you have a significant portion of a floor collapsing, it's going to shoot air and concrete dust out the window," NIST lead investigator Shyam Sunder told the magazine *Popular Mechanics*. "Those clouds of dust may create the impression of a controlled demolition, but it is the floor pancaking that leads to that perception."

Seismographs at Columbia University's Lamont-Doherty Earth Observatory 21 miles (40 km) north of Ground Zero recorded the shock waves of the buildings collapsing.

"The strongest jolts were all registered at the beginning of the collapses, well before falling debris struck the earth," reports the website WhatReallyHappened.com.

Prisonplanet.com said that this was "indisputable proof that massive explosions brought down" the towers as the sharp spikes of short duration were consistent with a "demolition-style implosion".

However, the seismologists at Lamont-Doherty pointed out that the earlier jolts were caused by the planes hitting the towers and that the spikes associated with the collapse, rather than being of a short duration, were spread over forty seconds. Examined in detail, they start small and then grow larger as the buildings fall to the ground.

"There is no scientific basis for the conclusion that explosions brought down the towers," said seismologist Arthur Lerner-Lam.

Seven hours after the two towers fell, the forty-seven-storey World Trade Center 7 collapsed. According to 911review.org: "The video clearly shows that it was not a collapse subsequent to a fire, but rather a controlled demolition."

Indeed, a preliminary report by Federal Emergency Management Agency (FEMA) said there was relatively light damage to World Trade Center 7 before it collapsed. However, further research by NIST revealed that the building was far more damaged by falling debris than the FEMA report indicated.

"The most important thing we found was that there was, in fact, physical damage to the south face of building 7," said NIST's lead investigator Shyam Sunder. "On about a third of the face to the centre and to the bottom – approximately ten stories – about 25 per cent of the depth of the building was scooped out."

NIST also discovered previously undocumented damage to the building's upper storeys and its south-west corner. Investigators believe a combination of intense fire and severe structural damage triggered a progressive collapse, where failure of part of the building put a strain on other parts, bringing the whole structure down. Videos of the collapse show cracks, or "kinks", in the building's facade just before the two penthouses disappeared into the structure, one after the other. The entire building fell in on itself, with the slumping east side of the structure pulling down the west side.

Other factors include the exceptionally large loads the columns were carrying. The removal of just one of them would cause the building to collapse. There were also trusses transferring the load from one set of columns to another. These communicated the stress caused by damage to the columns on the south side to the rest of the building.

There had been no firefighting at World Trade Center 7 as the New York Fire Department were concentrating on the Twin Towers where 343 of their firefighters and paramedics were killed. It burnt for seven hours before it collapsed. Investigators believe the fire was fed by tanks of diesel that were used to fuel emergency generators. Most tanks throughout the building were fairly small, but a generator on the fifth floor was connected to a large tank in the basement via a pressurized line. Together these factors combined to bring the building down.

It seems that crime scene evidence once again refutes the conspiracy theories.

7/7

A T ABOUT 8.50 A.M. on 7 July 2005 – often known as 7/7 in the style of 9/11 in the United States – there were three almost simultaneous explosions on the London Underground. The first occurred on a train in a tunnel on the Circle Line between Liverpool Street and Aldgate stations. The second was on the Circle Line just outside Edgware Road and the third was in a tunnel on the Piccadilly Line between King's Cross and Russell Square. Then at 9.47 a.m., there was a fourth explosion on the upper deck of a number 30 bus in Tavistock Square, less than 500 yards (460 m) from Russell Square tube station. Fifty-six people, including the four bombers, were killed by the attacks, and about 700 were injured. The attack also left four crime scenes for the police to investigate.

Much of the evidence of the crime and its perpetrators came from CCTV footage. At 3.58 a.m., a light-blue Nissan Micra was caught on CCTV on Hyde Park Road in Leeds, on its way to the M1. This car had been hired by Shehzad Tanweer and was thought to have been carrying Tanweer, Mohammad Sidique Khan and Hasib Hussain. Hyde Park Road was close to 18 Alexandra Grove, where a bomb factory was later discovered.

At 4.54 a.m., the Micra stopped at Woodall Services on the M1 to fill up with petrol. Tanweer went into the station to pay. He was wearing a white T-shirt, dark jacket, white tracksuit bottoms and a baseball cap. He bought snacks, quibbling with the cashier over his change. Then he looked directly at the CCTV camera and left.

Thirteen minutes later, at 5.07 a.m., a red Ford Brava was seen entering the car park at Luton station. Jermaine Lindsay was alone in the car. He got out and walked around, then entered the station and looked at the departure timetable. Afterwards, he moved the car a couple of times. Initially, there were just a few other cars in the car park, but more arrived.

The CCTV showed the Micra arriving at Luton at 6.49 a.m. It parked next to the Brava. All four men got out. They opened the boots of the cars and were seen to move items between them. Each put on a large rucksack that appeared to be full. It looked like they were going camping.

At 7.15 a.m., Lindsay, Hussain, Tanweer and Khan entered Luton station and went through the ticket barriers together. Six minutes later, CCTV caught them on the platform waiting for the Thameslink service to King's Cross. They were casually dressed and apparently relaxed. Tanweer's posture and the way he pulled the rucksack on to his shoulder as he walked suggest that he found it heavy. It was later estimated that in each rucksack there was between two and five kilograms of high explosive. For some reason, Tanweer was now wearing dark tracksuit bottoms.

The King's Cross train left Luton station at 7.40 a.m. with the four men on board. There were conflicting accounts of their behaviour on the train. Some witnesses report noisy conversations; another says he saw two of them standing silently by the doors of the train. The four stood out a bit from the usual commuters due to their rucksacks and casual clothes, but not enough to cause suspicion as it was the beginning of the summer tourist season and Luton station serves the nearby airport.

A delay on the line meant that the train arrived slightly late at 8.23 a.m. At 8.26 a.m., CCTV spotted them on the concourse between the overground Thameslink platform and the Underground system. Four minutes later, four men fitting their descriptions were seen hugging. They appeared happy, even euphoric. Then they split up. Khan took the westbound Circle Line train. Tanweer went eastbound on the Circle Line train, while Lindsay took a southbound Piccadilly Line train. Hussain also appeared to walk towards the entrance to the Piccadilly Line.

CCTV at Liverpool Street station at 8.50 a.m. showed commuters bustling to get on the train. It pulled out of the station. Seconds later smoke billowed from the tunnel. This was greeted with shock and confusion on the platform as people made for the exits.

Forensic evidence suggests that Tanweer was sitting towards the back of the second carriage with the rucksack next to him on the floor. The blast killed eight people, including Tanweer, and injured 171 others.

At Edgware Road, Mohammad Sidique Khan was also in the second carriage from the front, near the standing area by the first set of double doors. It was thought that he was also seated with the bomb next to him on the floor. Shortly before the explosion, he was seen fiddling with the top of the rucksack. The explosion killed seven, including Khan, and injured 163 people.

On the Piccadilly Line, Jermaine Lindsay was in the first carriage as it travelled between King's Cross and Russell Square. It is unlikely that he was seated as the train was crowded. There were 127 people in the first carriage alone, making it difficult to work out the position of those involved. Forensic evidence suggests the explosion occurred on or close to the floor of the standing area between the second and third set of seats. The explosion killed twenty-seven people, including Lindsay, and injured over 340. The force of the explosion in the confined space of the deep tunnel of the Piccadilly Line shattered windows and left charred and twisted metal. Soon after the blast, one young policeman staggered from the scene at Russell Square station and said: "I don't know what heaven looks like but I have just seen hell."

Hussain did not get on the Underground. Instead, at 8.55 a.m., he walked out of the station on to Euston Road. Mobile phone records show that he tried unsuccessfully to contact the other three bombers on his mobile over the next few minutes. He appeared relaxed and unhurried. Five minutes later, he walked back into King's Cross station and bought a nine-volt battery from the WHSmith's store there. Then he visited the McDonald's on Euston Road, leaving after ten minutes.

At 9.19 a.m., Hussain was seen on Gray's Inn Road. Around this time, a man fitting Hussain's description was seen on the number 91 bus travelling from King's Cross to Euston Station, looking nervous and pushing past people. At Euston, he changed to a number 30 bus, which was crowded as – due to the other bombs – the Underground was now closed. The official story then was that there had been a power surge. Forensic evidence indicates that Hussain sat on the upper deck, towards the back, with the bomb next to him in the aisle or between his feet on the floor. However, a man answering his description was seen earlier on the lower deck, fiddling repeatedly with his rucksack.

The bomb went off at 9.47 a.m., killing fourteen people, including Hussain, and injuring over 110. It remains unclear why the bomb did not go off at 8.50 along with the others. It may be that Hussain was intending to go north on the Underground from King's Cross but was frustrated by delays on the Northern Line. Another possibility is that he was unable to detonate his device with the original battery. After he had returned to King's Cross to buy a new one, he could not get back on the Underground because it was then closed.

After the first bombs went off at 8.50 a.m., rumours about a power surge, a crash or suspicious packages on the Underground circulated. The police and emergency services were quickly on the scene. At 10.19 p.m., Hasib Hussain's family called the emergency Casualty Bureau and reported that he was missing. By then, the survivors and the bodies of the dead had been removed and the investigation of the crime scene had begun with a finger-tip search that lasted more than two weeks.

In the tube line between King's Cross and Russell Square, the temperature soared to 140°F (60°C) due to the oxyacetylene cutting gear they were using and because the tunnels' ventilation system was blocked off to prevent clues being blown away. In this hot, dusty, dangerous and claustrophobic atmosphere, 100 ft (30 m) underground, CSI officers were plagued by rats and fumes from the aging tunnels which, at 11 ft (3.4 m) wide, were barely larger than the train. At first, they could work no more than twenty minutes at a time before resurfacing to gulp in fresh air and water. As conditions settled over the days, they managed two-hour shifts.

The crime scene investigation quickly bore fruit. At 11.40 p.m. on 7 July, the police exhibits officer telephoned the investigators to say that, along with many other personal items, membership cards in the name of "Sidique Khan" and "Mr S Tanweer" had been found at Aldgate. The following day, at 11.59 p.m., Khan's credit card was found at the site of the bombing in Edgware Road. He was now tied to two crime scenes.

On 9 July, police searching for clues at the bomb sites found further items linked to Tanweer and Khan. It seems that they had been on the periphery of earlier investigations by the security services. The next day, a driving licence and other ID bearing the name of Hasib Hussain were found at Tavistock Square. Further investigation linked him to 18 Alexander Grove in Leeds.

In the early morning of 12 July, the police searched premises in the West Yorkshire area, including the homes of Khan, Tanweer and Hussain, and 18 Alexandra Grove. On 19 November the previous year, Khan and Tanweer visited Pakistan, staying there until 8 February 2005. In May, the group rented a flat in 18 Alexandra Grove from an Egyptian chemistry graduate student at Leeds University, who subsequently returned to Egypt. Lindsay had met this man at Leeds Grand Mosque in November 2004; 18 Alexandra Grove was next door. The ground-floor flat in a two-storey block was in a student area, so the bombers would not have stood out. When the police searched it on 12 July, they found much of the bomb-making equipment still in place, making it a fresh crime scene. It is not clear whether the bomb-making equipment had been left there deliberately, or whether someone was supposed to have cleared up and failed to do so. The DNA of three of the bombers – Khan, Tanweer and Hussain – was found in the bomb factory.

On 12 July, the police also received a report of four men who had been putting on rucksacks at Luton station on the 7th. They had already worked out that the three bombed Underground trains were roughly equidistant from King's Cross when the bombs went off. They then identified four men carrying rucksacks on the CCTV footage from King's Cross. The same four men were seen on the CCTV footage from Luton station. And Tanweer was identified from a photograph held by the Driver and Vehicle Licensing Agency.

The Nissan Micra was then found in the car park at Luton station. Four nail bombs – explosive devices of a different kind from those in the rucksacks – had been left inside, along with four containers of bomb-mixture and four detonators. These were disposed of at the scene with controlled explosions. The Micra had a parking ticket on it. The Brava did not and had been towed away. It was registered to Lindsay and, in the car pound, a 9 mm handgun was found inside it.

On 13 July, Jermaine Lindsay's wife reported him missing and the police searched his home in Aylesbury. The following day, property belonging to Khan was found in Tavistock Square, tying him to a third crime scene. However, the police publicly confirmed only the identity of Tanweer and Hussain. The next day, property belonging to Lindsay was found at Russell Square and, on the 16th, the police confirmed the identity of Khan and Lindsay.

By 21 July, DNA profiling had identified their remains at the bomb sites and the mutilated state of their corpses indicated that they had been close to the bombs when they went off. It was assumed that they were suicide bombers as no evidence of remote-controlled detonators had been found at the bomb sites. And in the bomb factory at Alexander Grove, there was no indication that they had been trying to build remote devices. Later, in a video shown on Al Jazeera on 1 September, Khan said that he intended to martyr himself in a terrorist attack.

Khan's video statement was broadcast together with a statement by al-Qaeda's deputy leader Ayman al-Zawahiri supporting the attacks. In a second video, broadcast on 19 September, Zawahiri went further, stating that al-Qaeda "launched" the attacks.

"London's blessed raid is one of the raids which Jama'at Qa'idat al-Jihad [a faction of al-Qaeda] was honoured to launch," he said. "In the Wills of the hero brothers, the knights of monotheism – may God have mercy on them, make paradise their final abode and accept their good deeds."

However, while there is no firm evidence to corroborate this claim, if al-Qaeda did not directly support the attack, the 7 July bombings were certainly inspired by its ideology.

Initially, because of the force of the explosions, it was thought that plastic explosives had been used. But no residue was found at the crime scenes. Traces of high explosives were found at 18 Alexander Grove, along with chemical residues, bulbs, wires and batteries. However, containers of a mixture of black pepper and hydrogen peroxide, used as the main charge, were found in the bath, while traces of the high explosive HMTD (hexamethylene triperoxide diamine) were found on a cooker in the kitchen.

The bombs appeared to be home-made and the ingredients used were all readily available and not particularly expensive. The first purchase of materials identified was on 31 March 2005. No great expertise was required to assemble a device of this kind and the instructions can be found on the internet, but the government's *Official Account of the Bombings in London on 7 July 2005* says that "that the group would have had advice from someone with previous experience given the careful handling required to ensure safety during the bomb-making process and to get the manufacturing process right". The mixtures would have smelt bad enough to make the room very difficult to work in. Tanweer and Lindsay both bought face masks from shops and the internet. The net curtains were taped to the walls so that the bombs could be made without being seen when the windows were opened. The fumes had killed the tops of plants just outside.

The mixtures would also have had a strong bleaching effect. Both Tanweer and Hussain's families had noticed that their hair had become lighter over the weeks before the bombing. They explained this as the effect of chlorine from swimming pools as the two men regularly went swimming. Shower caps were also found at the Alexandra Grove crime scene, which may have been used during the manufacturing process to try to prevent this. The official report says that the bombers would have probably have carried out at least one test explosion.

Forensic examination of their bank accounts indicated that the group was self-financing. Even with their trips to Pakistan, bomb-making equipment, rent, car hire and UK travel, the overall cost of the 7/7 bombings was less than £8,000.

Tickets found at 18 Alexander Grove suggest that they made one reconnaissance trip in mid-March. Khan, Tanweer and Lindsay appear to have made a dry run on 28 June, travelling from Luton to King's Cross early in the morning and getting on the Underground. They were picked up on CCTV near Baker Street tube station later in the morning and returned to Luton at lunchtime. Lindsay was found to have a chart of times taken to travel between stations.

During the investigation, the police took over 12,500 statements. There were over 26,000 exhibits of which over 5,000 were forensically examined. The police seized 142 computers along with thousands of exhibits relating to associated hardware and software, and they went through more than 6,000 hours of CCTV footage. All this led to the conclusion that Hasib Hussain, Mohammad Sidique Khan, Shehzad Tanweer and Jermaine Lindsay were responsible for the bombings in London on 7 July 2005.

However, there are sceptics who do not believe the official version and campaign to have the crime scene evidence released. They claim that eyewitnesses have stated that there was another explosion on a Hammersmith & City Line train travelling towards Liverpool Street. And an eyewitness interviewed by CNN on 7 July 2005 described an explosion on her Circle Line train travelling from Aldgate towards Liverpool Street – in the opposite direction from the Circle Line train mentioned in the official report.

There were conflicting stories about the acknowledged bombings. An eyewitness said they saw a hole in the carriage and "the metal was pushed upwards as if the bomb was underneath the train". Another described the hole as being "twisted upwards". There is also speculation that the explosion at Aldgate was really caused by a power surge, as originally reported, as there is no CCTV footage of Tanweer getting on the train and no eyewitnesses who said they saw him. And why was the property of Mohammed Sidique Khan found at Aldgate and Tavistock Square, when he was supposed to have died at Edgware Road?

To add fuel to conspiracy theories, it is alleged that Rudy Giuliani was staying in a hotel in Liverpool Street at the time and was notified of the bombing while everyone else was being told that there was a power surge. Benjamin Netanyahu, former prime minister of Israel (although he was re-elected later, in 2009), then finance minister, was also in town. It is said that he was warned to stay in his hotel and not travel to the City for a meeting before the first bomb went off. This led to the theory that the bombings were orchestrated by Mossad or the CIA.

Sceptics also point out that Jermaine Lindsay's property was only found on the crime scene on the Piccadilly Line after his wife had reported him missing and his home had been searched. No eyewitnesses saw Lindsay on the platform or on the train. How did he manage to put a large rucksack on the floor when the carriage was full to capacity? And why was Lindsay not identified from his DVLA picture on 12 July, when Tanweer was?

Again, there is no CCTV footage of Khan getting on the train and, sceptics say, there are indications that there was more than one explosion at Edgware Road. They also suggest that there was more than one explosion in Tavistock Square, possibly a controlled explosion to get rid of a suspicious "microwave box". One of the witnesses, a young radiation therapist named Richmal Marie Oates-Whitehead, was found dead in her Shepherd's Bush bedsit seven weeks later in supposedly mysterious circumstances.

The July 7th Truth Campaign says that these matters cannot be cleared up until all the crime scene evidence is released.

THE UNREFORMED JACK UNTERWEGER

O N THE CHILLY September morning of 15 September 1990, the naked body of a woman was found on the bank of the Vitava River near Prague in what was then Czechoslovakia, now the Czech Republic. She was lying on her back with her legs open in a sexually suggestive position, although she was covered with twigs, leaves and grass. There was a gold ring on her finger and a pair of grey stockings tied around her neck. She had been beaten and stabbed as well as strangled. There were bruises all over her body, indicating that she had put up quite a struggle. But she had not been raped. Her tampon was still in place and there was no semen on her body or at the crime scene. She had been killed recently, probably the previous night.

A search of the crime scene unearthed no clues to her identity. But further along the river, women's clothing was found. It appeared to be the right size for the dead woman. A wallet was also found carrying the ID of Blanka Bockova.

It transpired that Ms Bockova worked at a butcher's shop in Prague. According to acquaintances, she was a party girl, who turned the occasional trick. But she was a not a professional prostitute. The night before her body was found, she left work and went for a drink in the upmarket bars in Wenceslas Square. She met some friends. At around 11.45 p.m., they headed home. But Blanka stayed behind talking to a well-dressed stranger who appeared to be aged around forty. She was not seen alive again. Blanka Bockova died sometime between midnight when she left the bar and 7.30 a.m. when her body was found. The stranger she had been talking to was an obvious suspect, but the police had no clue who he was.

About five weeks later, in Graz, Austria, over 200 miles (320 km) to the south, a prostitute named Brunhilde Masser vanished. She was last seen on 26 October 1990. Prostitution is legal in Austria and sexually motivated murders were rare. At the time, an average of around one prostitute a year was killed. However, that was about to change. On 5 December, another prostitute, Heidemarie Hammerer, disappeared from Bregenz, near the border of Switzerland and Germany. Then, on New Year's Eve, hikers came across her body in the woods outside the town. She was fully clothed and lying on her back with her stomach covered with dead leaves.

When the police arrived at the crime scene, they found that the victim appeared to have been naked when she was killed. Afterwards, she had been redressed, then dragged through the woods. Fortunately, the cold winter weather had preserved the body. Heidemarie's legs were bare and the pathologist determined that she had been strangled with her own pantyhose. The cause of death was recorded as asphyxiation.

A piece had been cut from her slip with a sharp instrument, such as a knife. The missing piece was found in her mouth. It had been used as a gag. There were bruises on her wrists, indicating that she had been restrained with handcuffs or a tight ligature. The bruises on other areas of her body showed she had been beaten. No semen was found in, on or around the body. However, she had been killed elsewhere and any sexual discharge outside the body could have been washed away by the elements. She still wore her jewellery, so robbery did not seem to be a motive. The only clue to the killer was the presence of several red fibres on her clothing that did not match anything that she wore. These were collected and sent to a lab for analysis.

On 4 January 1991, five days after Heidemarie Hammerer's body was found, other hikers stumbled across a badly decomposed corpse in a forest north of Graz. The naked body of a woman had been left in the bed of a stream and, again, covered with leaves. Her buttocks had been partially eaten by animals. The pathologist was able to determine that she had been stabbed and possibly strangled with her pantyhose. But the advanced state of decomposition made it difficult to determine the cause of death with certainty. Her clothing, handbag and other personal property were missing. Yet she still had her jewellery. Eventually, police identified the victim as Brunhilde Masser, who had gone missing in Graz ten weeks before. Her murder was linked to that of Heidemarie Hammerer and the Federal Police took over the investigation. They tried to track down Brunhilde's and Heidemarie's last customers and discovered that, on the night she disappeared, Heidemarie had been seen with man wearing a leather jacket and a red scarf but the clue led nowhere.

Two months later, another prostitute disappeared in Graz. Elfriede Schrempf was last seen on her usual corner on 7 March 1991. Two days later, a man phoned the Schrempf family home and mentioned her by name. He railed against prostitutes and made threats, then hung up. A little later, he called again and repeated the exercise. He was not heard from again.

The Schrempf family's phone number was unlisted, but Elfriede always carried it with her. Unless a close friend or relative was playing a dreadful prank, Elfriede had either run off with the man who had made the call, or he was her kidnapper or murderer.

While the Austrian police did not know about the murder of Blanka Bockova in Prague, they did tie the disappearance of Elfriede Schrempf to the murders of Brunhilde Masser and Heidemarie Hammerer. But still they had no real leads. Then on 5 October 1991, hikers found the skeletonized remains of a woman in the forest outside Graz. All that was left of her clothing was a pair of socks. Again she was covered by leaves, although it was autumn in any case. The remains were soon identified as those of Elfriede Schrempf. But the crime scene rendered no clues as to her killer.

Then four prostitutes – Regina Prem, Silvia Zagler, Karin Eroglu and Sabine Moitzi – disappeared from the streets of Vienna in under a month. While the police laid on extra patrols, they had no new crime scenes to investigate. But on 20 May 1992, Sabine Moitzi's remains were found. Three days later, someone came across Karin Ergolu's body. Both had been dumped in forested areas outside of Vienna; both had been strangled with articles of their own clothing. Moitzi was only wearing a jersey, pulled up to expose her breasts. Her clothing was found nearby, along with her handbag, though her money was missing. Ergolu was naked and had been subjected to blunt-force trauma to the face. Her handbag was missing, along with her clothing, except for her shoes and a body stocking. This had been forced down her throat.

According to the Austrian press, this was a clear sign that a serial killer was on the loose. They dubbed him the "Vienna Courier". However, the police resisted the idea, emphasizing the different modus operandi of the killer in each case. However, sixty-nine-year-old former detective August Schenner had been following the murders in Vienna, Graz and Bregenz in the press. Until he retired nearly five years earlier, he had been with the Criminal Investigation Department in Salzburg. He called his former colleagues to tell them that the killer's MO reminded him of a murderer he had once arrested.

Back in 1974, he had investigated two murders. One of the victims had been eighteen-year-old Margaret Schäfer. Her friend and fellow prostitute Barbara Scholz told the police that she and a man named Johann "Jack" Unterweger had robbed Schäfer's house. Then they had lured her into a car and taken her into the woods. Unterweger had tied Schäfer's hands behind her back with a belt from her coat. He had beaten her, stripped her and demanded certain sexual acts. When she refused, he hit her on the head with a steel pipe. Then he strangled her with her bra, leaving her naked body face up in the forest, covered with leaves – a crime scene strikingly similar to those of Blanka Bockova, Brunhilde Masser, Heidemarie Hammerer, Elfriede Schrempf, Sabine Moitzi and Karin Ergolu.

Schenner had arrested Unterweger. Under questioning, he had broken down and confessed to the murder of Schäfer. Dr Klaus Jarosch, a forensic psychologist who examined him, had proclaimed him a sexually sadistic psychopath with narcissistic and histrionic tendencies.

"He tends to sudden fits of rage and anger," said Jarosch. "His physical activities are enormously aggressive with sexually sadistic perversion . . . He is an incorrigible perpetrator."

In court, Unterweger said that when he hit Margaret Schäfer, he had seen his mother before him and had been consumed by a murderous rage. His mother Theresia had been a prostitute; his father an American soldier he had never met. From the age of two, he lived in a one-room shack with his grandfather, an alcoholic who beat him. From the age of five, he was drinking schnapps. His aunt, another prostitute, was murdered by a client. When he was sixteen, he had been arrested for assaulting a prostitute. This was significant as attacks on prostitutes were rare in Austria. He also had a rap sheet that included stealing cars, burglary, pimping and receiving stolen goods. He had also forced a young woman into acts of prostitution, and then took back the money. His fifteen prior convictions also included rape. By then he had taken the sobriquet "Jack" because of his fascination with Jack the Ripper.

In the second case that Schenner had been investigating, another prostitute, Marcia Horveth, was strangled with her stockings and a necktie. Her mouth had been covered with adhesive tape and her body was thrown into Lake Salzachsee near Salzburg, where Schenner had found her. As Unterweger had already been sentenced to life in prison, he was not charged with murder. But Schenner, who interviewed him, was certain that Unterweger was responsible, despite his denials.

Although Unterweger had been illiterate before he went to prison, he taught himself to read and spent every minute poring over books. Before long, he was editing the prison newspaper and a literary review. His poems, short stories and plays began to circulate in the outside world. In 1984, his short story "*Endstation Zuchthaus*" – "Terminus Prison" – won a prestigious literary prize and his prison memoir, *Fegefeuer – eine Reise ins Zuchthaus (Purgatory – a Journey to Prison)* was a bestseller.

"I wielded my steel rod among prostitutes in Hamburg, Munich and Marseilles," he wrote. "I had enemies and I conquered them through my inner hatred."

Fegefeur begins with a sense of existential despair. "My sweaty hands were bound behind my back with steel chains snapped around my wrists. The hard pressure on my legs and back makes me realize that my only escape is to end it. I lay awake, removed from the liberating unconsciousness of the sheep. Bathed in shit, trembling. My miserable small dreams are a daily reminder. Anxiously I stare into the unknown darkness of the still night outside. There's security in darkness. I try to divert my thoughts from wondering about the time. I ask only for the immediate moment, for in that lies my strength. It's still night, already late into the night, getting closer to morning."

As a result, Unterweger was hailed as a literary talent and a campaign was launched to have him freed. He was paroled, just a few months before Brunhilde Masser was murdered. However, it would need crime scene evidence to pin any crime on Unterweger, who was now a celebrity. His plays were being produced. *Fegefeur* was made into a movie. Unterweger was much in demand at parties and opening nights. He had his pick of women and drove around Vienna in a Ford Mustang with the number plate "W-JACK 1".

Unterweger promoted himself as an expert on murder, writing about it and talking about it on television. Naturally, he turned his attention to the Vienna Courier. After interviewing the investigators and prostitutes on the street, he announced that a serial killer was at work. But he himself was put under surveillance. The police had been following him for just three days when he flew to Los Angeles to write articles about crime there for an Austrian magazine. During his five weeks away, the murders in Austria stopped.

In charge of the investigation was Dr Ernst Geiger, one of the most experienced detectives in the Austrian Federal Police. He knew that he either had to eliminate Unterweger from the investigation or build a case against him. Geiger's first job was to place Unterweger at the scene of the crime. He got hold of Unterweger's credit card records and began to trace his movements. They placed Unterweger in Graz in October when Brunhilde Masser was murdered and in March when Elfriede

Schrempf disappeared. He was in Bregenz in December when Heidemarie Hammerer vanished. And he resembled the man in the leather jacket with whom she was last seen.

He was also in Vienna when Regina Prem, Silvia Zagler, Karin Eroglu and Sabine Moitzi disappeared. Unterweger's credit card records also put him in Prague the previous September. He said he had been researching an article on prostitution there. The Austrian police contacted the Czech authorities and learnt that his visit had coincided with the unsolved murder of Blanka Bockova. Found in the woods, covered in dirt and leaves, and strangled with her own undergarment, her murder bore the same signature as the Austrian victims.

Unterweger was questioned by the very investigators that he had interviewed in connection with the Vienna Courier. He admitted seeing prostitutes, but denied knowing any of the victims. He offered no alibis, but then the police only had the most tenuous of circumstantial evidence to connect him to the crime. And now that Unterweger knew he was a suspect, he was on his guard and he responded with a series of articles about the investigators' mishandling of the case.

The husband and son of Regina Prem, whose body had not yet been found, received phone calls from an unidentified man on their unlisted numbers. He accurately described what Regina was wearing the night she went missing. He then said that he was her executioner and that God had told him to do it. She had been left in "a place of sacrifice" with her face "turned toward hell".

He also said: "I gave eleven of them the punishment they deserved."

This sent a chill through the police. It meant there were more victims than the eight they were currently investigating.

Three months later, in January 1992, Prem's husband found five empty cigarette packets of the brand his wife smoked stuffed into his mailbox. With them was a photograph of Prem's son that she had carried in her purse.

Geiger questioned the Austrian prostitutes that Unterweger visited. They told him that he liked them to wear handcuffs during sex. He tracked down the BMW that Unterweger had bought when he was released from prison, but had since sold. In it, crime scene investigators found a piece of hair fragment that they sent to the lab for analysis. At the Institut für Rechtsmedizin in Berne, Switzerland, forensic scientist Manfred Hochmeister found enough skin on the root to produce a DNA profile using the polyermerase chain reaction technique to magnify the sample. It matched that of Blanka Bockova.

The DNA match allowed Geiger to get a warrant to search Unterweger's apartment in Vienna. There they found a brown leather jacket and red knitted scarf, which they seized. They also found a menu and receipts from a seafood restaurant in Malibu, California, along with photographs of Unterweger posing with female members of the Los Angeles Police Department. Geiger contacted the LAPD and asked about unsolved murders. At the time, they were investigating three seemingly linked killings in the city.

All of the victims – Shannon Exley, Irene Rodriguez and Sherri Ann Long – had been prostitutes. They had been beaten, sexually assaulted with tree branches, strangled with their own bras and had been left out in the open. And all of them had been killed during the time that Unterweger had been in Los Angeles. Of course, the LAPD knew all about Unterweger. He had introduced himself as a European journalist researching an article on prostitution and asked for a police escort to the red-light district. Were these three women the other murder victims that the man who had called Regina Prem's husband and son had boasted about?

Receipts recovered from Unterweger's apartment showed that Unterweger had stayed in seedy hotels near where the victims had last been seen alive. And in his article on prostitution in Los Angeles, Unterweger had written chillingly: "Real life in LA is dominated by a tough struggle for survival, by the broken dreams of thousands who come to the city and an equal number who leave, sometimes dead."

Meanwhile, analysts at the University of Berne found that fibres from the red scarf taken from Unterweger's apartment were consistent with those found on the body of Heidemarie

Hammerer. While they could not definitely identify the scarf as the source, it was enough for Geiger to get an arrest warrant.

When the police arrived at Unterweger's apartment, he was not there. Unterweger had gone on a holiday with his girlfriend, Bianca Mrak, a pretty eighteen-year-old who had met him in a wine bar where she worked as a waitress. She was flattered by the attention of this famous man and she moved in with him.

Friends told Unterweger of the police interest, while the newspapers announced his imminent arrest. He fled to the United States with Bianca and contacted the Austrian papers. Then he offered the police a deal. He would return to Austria and face questioning if the arrest warrants were withdrawn.

"My flight was and is no confession," he said in his open letter to the authorities in Vienna. He went on to say that there was no way they could prove anything against him. Fate was punishing him for his past.

One magazine, *Erfolg*, made him an offer for the exclusive story of his flight. Another journalist called and asked Unterweger whether he had forced Bianca to go with him. He put her on the line and she said that she was travelling with Unterweger of her own free will and they were having a wonderful time.

Unterweger then claimed that he had an alibi for each of the murders. He was at a book reading event on the night one woman had disappeared. In another case, he was not even in the city at the time. The police were manufacturing evidence against him because they were angry that he had been given parole. He would remain a fugitive until he could be guaranteed a fair hearing. On one point, he was adamant – he was not going back to prison.

Bianca needed some money and asked her mother to wire some cash to her in Miami. Her mother promptly informed the police. They alerted the US authorities via Interpol. Three deputy US marshals and an agent from the Bureau of Alcohol, Tobacco, and Firearms staked out the branch of Western Union in South Beach.

They had a photograph of Unterweger, but he had lost weight. When he and Bianca approached the Western Union office, they almost did not recognize him, but the prison tattoos on his arms gave him away. When the marshals moved in to arrest him, Unterweger took flight. He ran into a restaurant and out the back. But the officers cornered him in a car park, handcuffed him and took him downtown.

Unterweger had been arrested in Miami on a technicality – he had not declared that he was a convicted murderer to immigration officials. When he learnt this, he became quite cheerful, joking with the officers and saying that he would put them in his next book. However, when one of the officers mentioned the murders in Austria, Unterweger began to sob.

Bianca took the police to the rented rooms where she and Unterweger were staying. A search turned up Unterweger's travel journal. It was clear from the pages that he was contemplating murdering Bianca.

It was not immediately certain whether he should be extradited to Austria or transferred to California. In Austria he could be tried for all eleven murders, while in California he could only be tried for the three in Los Angeles. So Unterweger plumped for California. Blood, hair and saliva were taken for DNA testing. His DNA matched semen taken from one of the victims in California, but she also had semen from six other men in her vagina. The only other evidence against him were the hotel receipts that Geiger had provided, putting him in the vicinity of the murders. It was not much of a case. But when the Los Angeles cops who had flown to Miami to question Unterweger pointed out that he faced the death penalty in California, Unterweger quickly changed his mind and agreed to be deported to Austria. He believed that he still had Austrian public opinion on his side. The physical evidence the police had was flimsy. He believed he could beat the rap and on 28 May 1992 he was on a plane to Vienna.

From jail he continued writing to the press, protesting his innocence and giving interviews. He told *Profil* magazine: "Would I be so stupid and so mad that during the luckiest phase of my life, in which I've done theatre productions, played a role onstage, organized a tour, and made many wonderful female friends, I would go kill someone each week in between?" He also kept a prison journal of his thoughts and wrote poetry about the time he'd been free. In his letters to the press he said he could prove he was innocent, but he gave nothing away.

Then, parts of a skeleton were found that were identified as the remains of Regina Prem, a year after her disappearance. Like the other victims, she had been left in the woods, but no clothing or jewellery were found. After being left exposed to the elements for so long, the cause of death could no longer be determined.

Geiger got in touch with the FBI and enlisted the help of Gregg McCrary at the Behavioral Science Unit at Quantico, Virginia. Working with details of the crime and the crime scene, he studied the sequence of murders, looking for deviation from the pattern. If Unterweger was responsible for all eleven murders, he was a rarity. Serial killers usually go about their business in a confined geographical area. They rarely travel internationally to commit their murders and a defence attorney could easily find an expert to say that. Nevertheless, McCrary spotted a consistent pattern in the crime scene details and the modus operandi.

"We had a similar victimology and manner of disposal," he wrote in his book, *The Unknown Darkness*. "Most of these women had been prostitutes and were left outside, with branches or foliage placed over them. We had no semen left on or in [most of] those bodies. The cause of death for those on which we could tell was strangulation, but some bodies were too decomposed to make a determination. Most had restraint bruises on their arms and wrists. No one had seen them getting into a car, so this offender had been careful. There was an absence of any indication of sexual assault. The trace evidence was next to none as well, and he appeared to have a calculated MO. He was smart and he was organized."

McCrary also fed details of the murders into the database for the Violent Criminal Apprehension Program. At that time, it carried the details of 10,000 to 12,000 homicide cases. Using fifteen cross-referenced criteria for the search, he ended up matching the eleven killings for which Unterweger was thought to have been responsible with just one other murder. The killer in that case had already been convicted.

"It would be highly unusual to have more than one guy engaging in this specific type of behaviour during this same time period," said McCrary. Whoever had done one of the eleven unsolved murders had probably done the rest.

Unterweger's movements fitted the timeline of the murders. The modus operandi – the MO – in the murder of Margaret Schäfer, which he had admitted, matched the others. But one piece of crime scene evidence was the clincher. Lynn Herold, a forensic scientist at the Los Angeles Crime Lab, examined the knots that had been made to tie the ligatures used to strangle the three prostitutes in California. The knot was complicated and it matched the knots in the pantyhose used to kill several of the victims in Austria.

In Graz in June 1994, Unterweger went on trial for the seven murders in Austria, along with the one in Prague and three in Los Angeles. Despite the gravity of the accusations, he still managed to garner public support through interviews where he would brag that he would win.

Detective Jim Harper and Lynn Herold came from Los Angeles to testify. Gregg McCrary flew in to show that the behaviour shown in the eleven murders was consistent with the behaviour Unterweger had exhibited in the murder of Margaret Schäfer. The prosecution also had a psychiatric report about Unterweger's sadistic criminal nature and character witnesses who would testify to his deviant nature. Then there was the crime scene evidence – Blanca Bockova's hair recovered in Unterweger's old car, numerous red fibres from Brunhilde Massar's body that were consistent with fibres from Unterweger's red scarf, the knots and scene where the bodies had been found.

In court, Unterweger was well dressed and charming. He asked the jury not to judge him on his past crimes. He admitted that he had been "a primitive criminal who grunted rather than talked and an inveterate liar", who "consumed women, rather than loved them". But he had been rehabilitated.

"I'm counting on your acquittal," he said, "because I am not the culprit. Your decision will affect not only me but the real killer, who is laughing up his sleeve."

The trial lasted two and a half months. His charm swayed the jury, but he could not counter the crime scene evidence. He was found guilty of nine counts of murder – one in Prague, three in Los Angeles and five in Austria. In the other two cases in Austria, the victim's bodies had been too decomposed to determine the precise cause of death. He was sentenced to life in prison. That night, he committed suicide at Graz-Karlau Prison. He hanged himself with a rope made from shoelaces and the elastic from his prison jumpsuit, using the same intricate knot he had used on the murdered prostitutes – thereby confirming his guilt. But as he died before an appeal could be heard, under Austrian law, he is officially considered innocent.

CONCORDE CRIME SCENE

A T 2.44 P.M. ON 25 July 2000, an Air France Concorde, Flight 4590 with the tail number F-BTSC, was taking off from Runway 26 Right at Charles de Gaulle International Airport outside Paris on a charter flight to New York's Kennedy Airport with 100 passengers and nine crew members on board. But as it careened down the runway approaching take-off speed, fire burst out from under the port wing. As burning fuel plumed from the wing tank, engines one and two on the port side surged and lost power.

A fire warning went off in the cockpit and the captain ordered the flight engineer to shut down engine two. However, engine one recovered. Concorde had already passed V_1 speed, that is the speed that the plane can still take off if an engine fails. The take-off continued and Concorde managed to claw its way into the sky. But the landing gear would not retract and, with engine one surging and producing little power, the plane was unable to gain much height or speed. Unable to climb or accelerate, the aircraft maintained a speed of 200 knots (230 mph; 370 km/h) at an altitude of 200 ft (60 m). The heat of the fire began to melt the metal in the port wing, which began to disintegrate. Engine one surged again, but this time failed to recover. As all the thrust was coming from the starboard engines, the right wing lifted, causing the plane to bank. The power was reduced on engines three and four in an attempt to level the aircraft. The pilot tried to make for nearby Le Bourget airport, but with falling airspeed he lost control. The plane crashed into Les Relais Bleus Hotel in the small town of La Pattie d'Oie de Gonesse near the airport, killing all 109 people on board and four people on the ground.

The Bureau Enquêtes-Accidents (Accident Investigation Bureau) was informed of the accident minutes later and an investigation was launched. Investigators would minutely examine the wreckage and comb the runway as they would in any plane crash. What made this a crime scene investigation was that, in 2008, five people were charged with manslaughter in connection with the crash.

The plane had taken off from Runway 26 Right. Normally, Concorde used Runway 27, but work on it had been underway for the previous three weeks. An examination of the runway found various debris and marks under the aircraft's flight path. These included parts of the water deflector from the left main landing gear and pieces of one of Concorde's tyres showing a transverse cut approximately 12.5 inches (32 cm) long.

On the shoulder of the runway was a strip of metal about 17 in. (43 cm) long. Its width varied from $1^1/_8$ to $1^3/_8$ in. (29 to 34 mm) and it had holes drilled in it. Some contained rivets. On visual inspection, the piece appeared to be made of light alloy, coated on one side with a greenish epoxy and on the other side with what appeared to be red aircraft mastic used on hot sections. But it did not appear to have been exposed to high temperature. Investigators quickly realized that this was not part of the Concorde.

Further down the runway, investigators found a small piece of Concorde's number five fuel tank measuring 12.5×12.5 in. (32×32 cm). It showed no signs of impact damage. An inboard alloy part, identified as the brake servo valve cover, from the left main landing gear, was also found. It was covered in soot and had clearly been overheated. There were also signs that it had been deformed on impact. Further on, a piece of concrete 4 in. (10 cm) wide and 10 to 14 in. (25 to 30 cm) long had been separated from the runway and there were signs of an explosion. A black scorch mark was found surrounding the detached chunk.

At 3,000 yards (2,800 m) from the runway threshold, the left runway edge light was broken. Small pieces of it were found nearby. The marks on the ground showed that it had been broken by Concorde's left main landing gear. The mark of a deflated tyre with incomplete tread ran from 1,974 yards (1,805 m) to 3,000 yards (2,800 m) down the runway. This ran parallel to the direction of the runway at about 12.5 ft (3.8 m) from the centreline until around 2,400 yards (2,200 m) when it began to diverge. By the time it disappeared at about 2,560 yards (2,340 m), it was 26 ft (8 m) from the centreline. It corresponded to the right front tyre of the aircraft's left landing gear. Further on, some irregular tyre tracks from the left landing gear were noted up to the broken edge light at 3,000 yards (2,800 m). After that point, the tracks became intermittent and then disappeared at about 3,100 yards (2,830 m).

There were marks on the runway at around 1,990 yards (1,820 m), probably made by kerosene. Soot, produced by the incomplete combustion of kerosene, was found from 2,035 yards (1,860 m) onward. These deposits were large and dense up to 2,515 yards (2,300 m), then became less dense and rich in carbon up to the taxiway at 3,030 yards (2,770 m). The traces were on average 23 ft (7 m) wide. They were initially centred on the damaged wheel ground mark and progressed towards the left as the plane veered from the centreline.

There was a further sooted area after the taxiway up to the broken light. Between 3,174 and 3,461 yards (2,902 and 3,165 m), there was more soot on the grass along the edge of the runway, indicating that there was extensive flame after the aircraft became airborne.

In the mile after the end of the runway, near the extended centreline, other debris was found. One piece was identified as coming from a repair on the left inner elevon, the moveable control surface at the back of the delta wing. Also found were the tail cone anti-collision light, a severely fire-damaged inspection panel from the wing's lower surface and seven inspection panels identified as coming from the upper surface of the left wing but which showed no signs of fire damage.

Beyond that, investigators found another inspection panel from the upper surface of the left wing that also showed no signs of fire. There was also a fire-damaged piece of duct and fire-damaged structural parts that appeared to have come from the tail cone of the aircraft.

The tar had melted on the roofs of buildings in the freight zone and more debris was found there. Burn marks on the ground were also visible and a wheat field was damaged by fire 1.5 miles (2.5 km) from the end of the runway.

As the doomed flight continued, the plane shed more debris. Investigators found on the ground two hydraulic shut-off valves, one damaged by fire. Then there were two lower inspection panels from the engine casing, one melted, the other intact; debris from the wings, in particular fuel tank parts; a fire-damaged hydraulic line; and another inspection panel from the left main landing gear.

Leading up to the crash site, many small pieces of metal, honeycomb components, pieces of riveted structure and parts of the rear fuselage were found. Most of these parts showed traces of fire.

Examination of the crash site itself revealed that the aircraft had struck the ground heading 120 degrees left, practically flat with little forward speed. After the impact, it broke apart and debris spread generally to the south. The wreckage was extensively burnt. Only the front parts of the aircraft, together with a few pieces of the fuselage scattered over the site, escaped the fire on the ground. Most of the wreckage, with the exception of the cockpit, remained within a rectangle measuring 110 yards (100 m) long by 55 yards (50 m) wide. Parts of the air intake for one engine, a wheel, the front left door sill and a hinge from the aircraft's famous droop nose were buried in the ground.

Near the hotel, impact marks were found in the asphalt. The right main landing gear was found nearby. Examination of the locking mechanism of the side strut of the left main landing gear showed that the landing gear was down and locked at the time of impact. But a 12 in. (30 cm) spacer that keeps the left main landing gear in alignment was missing. It was found, later, that it had not been replaced after recent maintenance.

The hotel itself was almost entirely flattened. Panels from fuel tank five were found inside. The outer part of the left wing, with the outer elevons still attached, was found melted on the ground. Nearby was the inner part of the wing with engines one and two still attached. The fin was resting on it with the rudder nearby. The left inner elevon was found beneath the two engines, still linked to part of the wing. It is normally located between the engines and the fuselage. The engines themselves were resting on a water tank 5 ft (1.5 m) in height. Many wing parts were found nearby, including the lower surfaces of tanks six and ten.

Parts of the cockpit had hit an electric power transformer. The pilots' seats, the throttle levers and the autopilot were found there. It was possible to recognize the aisle between the cockpit and the cabin. One of the flight recorders – the QAR, or quick access recorder – was found there. The nose landing gear was found nearby, extended.

The QAR and the other two flight recorders were recovered within four hours of the crash. The QAR's box was crushed and its magneto-optical disc was deformed. But the memory card, visible through the half-torn casing, seemed to be in good condition. Two of the three memory cards had been torn off at impact. The third was still in place and it contained all the information the crash investigators needed.

The cockpit voice recorder showed signs of fire and impact damage, but it was possible to recover a transcript of everything that was said in the cockpit from take-off to crash. The flight data recorder was also damaged on impact and showed signs of exposure to fire. It was taken to the Bretigny Flight Test Centre, where it was opened. The tape was in position and the winding mechanism appeared to be in good condition. However, there were black marks on the tape, various mechanisms and the inside of the casing. Once it had been cleaned with distilled ethyl alcohol and patched up where it had begun to tear, it gave a read-out of reasonable quality.

The wreckage of the passenger cabin was found mixed with the debris from the hotel. The seats and most of the victims were found in the same area. None were alive. Engines three and four were found to the right of the passenger cabin.

The central instrument panel showing the engine speeds, fuel flow and exhaust gas temperatures were also found. The lever that operated the nose and visor and the landing gear selector were in the down position. All the landing gear was down.

The engines showed no signs of fire damage before the crash. Engine one showed signs that it had hit a hard object before it hit the ground. Engine two showed signs of damage from a soft object. It was determined that both were turning much slower than engines three and four.

Wheel one was burnt, but the wheel and tyre showed no signs of damage before the crash. Wheel two was also burnt, but part of the tyre was missing. It also had not been burnt before the impact. Nor had wheel five, which was found intact. Wheel six was intact and not burnt.

A partial reconstruction of the aircraft took place between 1 October 2000 and 31 January 2001. However, due to the condition of the wreckage, not much was learnt this way. It was not possible to reconstruct the surfaces located near the landing gear well, nor the majority of the right wing. But a melted piece appeared to have some small punctures.

The seats from the cockpit showed that the crew was in position for take-off with the flight engineer between the captain and the flight officer. Passengers were in the seats assigned to them on boarding. Their seat belts were fastened.

The lower surface of the port wing showed signs that it had been exposed to flame and the dry bay between the fuel tanks showed that it had been exposed to very high pressure after take-off. This was thought to have been caused by the combustion of kerosene inside the wing. It was noted that the alloy used to make the majority of the structure of the aircraft weakened rapidly when exposed to high temperatures. At around 572°F (300°C), it is six times weaker than at normal working temperatures.

The investigators concluded that the fire under the port wing had started between V_1 and V_r, rotation speed – that is, the speed where the plane actually takes off. On impact, the plane was engulfed in fire so intense that exposed plastic parts of the nearby hotel were melted. Firemen from Le Bourget were the first on the scene, but due to the scale of the fire they were only able to limit its spread and attend to the injured. Paris Charles de Gaulle Rescue and Fire Fighting Service then turned up with twelve vehicles, including six with foam firefighting systems. They poured more than 180,000 litres of water and 3,800 litres of emulsifier on to the flames. With the help of reinforcements from neighbouring fire stations, they managed to get the fire under control after three hours. It was clear that no one on board could have survived.

The examination of the wreckage told the same story as had been captured on film and seen by eyewitnesses. The first phase of the take-off was completely normal. But during the final acceleration, several people heard explosions. The first was followed by the appearance of a flame under the wing, between the left engine casing and the fuselage a few seconds before the plane took to the air.

Some people reported seeing pieces fall on the runway immediately after the first noise of explosion. Several people said that the conflagration began with a small flame like that from a blowtorch. It then grew much wider, enveloping the left engines, and longer until it was the length of the fuselage. The flame was accompanied by thick black smoke. According to some observers, the plane swerved slightly to the left, but then stabilized slightly off the centreline of the runway.

After take-off, numerous small pieces were seen to fall from the aircraft. After passing the airfield's freight zone, the aircraft was no longer climbing. The angle of attack seemed to be constant and the landing gear remained extended. It flew over the RN 17, the road outside the perimeter of the airfield at around 200 ft (60 m), then made a sharply banked left turn. After turning nearly 180 degrees, it went nose up and struck the ground with its left wing. There was a conflagration followed by one or more explosions.

Other Concorde cabin crew said that, given their experience, the crew of Flight 4590 could not have failed to notice the significant changes in the aircraft during take-off. They would have noticed the engine surges, the lateral and longitudinal accelerations and the strange smell.

Investigators noted that Concorde's tyres had burst on fifty-seven occasions – twenty-seven on British Airways' planes and thirty on those of Air France. Nineteen of these tyre bursts were caused by foreign objects on the runway. In twelve cases, the wing had been damaged and in six the fuel tanks had been penetrated. But none had resulted in the rupture of a tank, a fire or a significant loss of power in two engines.

On 14 June 1979, Air France's F-BVFC was taking off from Washington Dulles Airport, when tyre six deflated and lost its tread. This caused tyre five to burst, leading to the destruction of the wheel. Debris thrown up caused small punctures in tanks two, five and six. After some unsuccessful attempts to retract the landing gear due to the failure of the hydraulic system, the crew landed the aircraft back at Washington, DC, twenty-four minutes later.

On 9 August 1981, British Airways' G-BOAG was taking off from New York's Kennedy Airport when tyres one and two burst, leading to minor penetration of tank five. Tyre five burst when G-BOAB was taking off from London Heathrow on 5 November 1985, causing damage to the landing-gear door. Tank five was penetrated, probably by a piece of the door mechanism.

On 29 January 1988, G-BOAF was taking off from London Heathrow when it lost ten nuts from wheel three. A bolt punctured tank seven. Tyre four burst on G-BOAF when it was landing at London Heathrow on 15 July 1993, damaging the gear door mechanism. Tank eight was damaged, probably by a piece of this mechanism. The tyre burst when the braking system jammed. Then tyre two burst when G-BOAB was taxiing at London Heathrow on 25 October 1993, again due to the braking system jamming. There was damage to the water deflector and tank one suffered minor penetration, probably from a piece of the deflector.

Four of these events occurred during take-off. One was caused by an object on the runway. In two cases the tyre burst occurred for reasons that were not determined. In the other case, it was due to a tyre deflating while the aircraft was rolling at high speed. One of these events resulted in an aborted take-off. In the three others, the aircraft took off, then returned to the airport to land instead of proceeding to its destination.

By far the most serious was the accident that had taken place at Washington, DC, on 14 June 1979. Most of the structural damage resulted from the impact of pieces of wheel rim on the wing. Three tanks, whose skin is just $^1/_{20}$ in. (1.2 mm) thick, were penetrated, one by a piece of rubber from a tyre. The resulting leaks lost fuel at a rate of four gallons a second. It was considered that the risk of a fire was low and it was not necessary to install protection for the underside of the wing. In the later accidents, the tanks were not penetrated by pieces of the tyre itself but by debris dislodged by the tyre, and modifications were made.

After the crash in 2000, tests were made to see what would happen to tyres if they were damaged by a curved metal strip similar to the one found on the runway afterwards. At a Goodyear technical centre in the United States, the tyres were installed on the side of a trolley. A load of about 25 tons was applied to each tyre. The sample strips were stood on edge on a concrete surface and a truck towed the trolley over them at 6 mph (10 km/h). With the strip in that position, it was flattened by the tyre. But in other positions it cut into the tyre. Eventually, a position was found where it cut the tyre in a similar way to the piece found on the runway at Charles de Gaulle airport.

Further experimentation showed that if the rupture took place at 60 metres per second (216 km/h; 134 mph), a piece of tyre weighing 2.5 kg would be flung off. At higher speeds, heavier pieces were thrown off. These would hit the underside of the wing at up to 65 metres per second (234 km/h; 145 mph).

The metal strip found on the runway did not come from Concorde. It was clearly part of a plane so investigators set about trying to find the aircraft it had come from. The piece was a wear strip from an engine fan reverser cowl. It was suspected that this came from the DC-10 operated by Continental Airlines that had taken off from Charles de Gaulle Airport five minutes before Concorde, bound for Newark, New Jersey. Only one plane, an

Air France Boeing 747, had taken off in the interim. Investigators headed for Houston, Texas, home of Continental.

They examined the plane and the aft support of its fan reverser. The lower left wear strip, which was about 17 in. (44 cm) long, was missing. This would not be noticed when the fan-reverser cowl was closed. The support was painted with green epoxy primer like that found on the metal strip on the runway after Concorde had crashed. The position where the missing part should have been was covered in red mastic, also like the runway strip. Some rivets were still in place. The right wear strip appeared to be an original part, but another of the left wear strips had been replaced and the level of wear on the strip adjacent to the missing strip exceeded the tolerances specified by the manufacturer.

The lower right wear strip was missing a rivet and the strip itself was distorted. Compared with the original part, the strip was too long and prevented the fan door from closing. There was considerable wearing around the other strips. The investigators asked Continental to remove the reverser cowls and put them in storage.

According to the manufacturer, the disassembly and repair of the wear strips is classified as a "minor repair". It requires no special tools and requires no particular inspection after completion. New wear strips are made in the workshop. Shims are supposed to be placed between the strip and the cowl, but these are often left out, leaving too much play between the forward and aft cowls. Investigators found this to be the case on a number of aircraft. In normal conditions, this was satisfactory. But during take-off when the engine is at maximum thrust, the pressure inside the cowl is very high, which could explain the loss of the wear strip.

The plane's maintenance log shows that the left wear strips on engine three were replaced in Tel Aviv by Israel Aircraft Industries during a routine check on 11 June 2000. Further work on the engine's reverser cowl was carried out in Houston, where the lower left wear strip was changed. The technician who completed the maintenance report said that he had noticed a twisted wear strip that was sticking out of the cowl.

It is not easy to spot that the wear strip is missing when the cowl doors are closed. But the cowl doors on engine three were opened at least once between 9 July and 3 September 2000. None of the maintenance documents refers to the wear strips during this period.

The strip found on the runway was subjected to examination at the laboratory. It was found to be made of an alloy of titanium instead of stainless steel as the manufacturers specify. Along with the twelve rivet holes needed to hold it on, it had another seventeen holes that had been filled in with epoxy. Black marks on it and debris found jammed in one of the rivets were subjected to spectroscopic analysis and were found to be similar to the material of Concorde's tyres.

More laboratory tests showed that the primer and mastic on the strip found on the runway were the same as those found on the aircraft's cowl. Drill holes in the cowl correspond to those on the strip, though some of the rivets still in place in the cowl did not correspond to those on the strip. These were thought to have been left behind from a previous strip. However, the torn and unstuck areas of the mastic did correspond and the investigators concluded that the strip found on the runway did indeed come from the Continental Airlines DC-10.

The investigators also examined the two pieces of tank five found at the crash site and the three pieces found on the runway. At the crash site, one piece had a hole in it, which showed that the impact occurred from the outside towards the inside of the tank, from the left to the right and more or less from the rear towards the front. The puncture showed a clear petal-shaped structure, indicating a high-energy penetration not due to the final impact. Analysis was unable to provide details of the penetrating object, but its probable trajectory shows that it could have come from the left main landing gear.

However, the pieces found on the runway showed clear signs of rupture – from inside outwards. This excludes the possibility that it had been caused directly by a puncture and a great deal of theoretical work and practical experimentation had to be done to explain it. It was then calculated that, in principle, if a fuel tank was hit by a heavy object that did not rupture it, a pressure wave would be transmitted through the fuel inside that could rupture the tank at a weak point.

Tests were done at Centre d'Essais Aéronautiques de Toulouse – the Toulouse aeronautical test centre – where they fired pieces of tyre at test boxes containing a liquid with similar characteristics to kerosene. One was made out of a panel from tank five, taken from a Concorde while the plane was suspended from service following the crash. It was not possible to make a box that completely represented tank five as the material it was made out of, AU2GN, was no longer available.

Due to the large number of variables, it was not possible to reproduce the rupture of the tank found in the accident, but measurements taken during the tests demonstrated that it was possible to rupture the tank that way. A piece of tyre weighing just 4.5 kg travelling at a speed of around 140 metres per second (504 km/h; 313 mph) – easily achieved by a tyre burst when the wheel was rotating at speed – could have caused such a rupture.

Tank five was loaded with 7.2 tons of fuel before take-off. After the accident, the gauge indicated that two tons were left in the tank. This meant that several dozen kilograms of fuel were leaking from the tank every second – ten times greater than the loss of fuel after the accident in Washington, DC. This would mix with air and catch fire. But what ignited the fuel?

A surge in the engine can cause a flame in the air intakes. But this was rejected as the source of the ignition because the engine surge happened after the fuel streaming from with ruptured tank caught fire.

A spark from an electrical circuit in the main landing gear, damaged by debris from the burst tyre, could have been the source of ignition. Such damage was noted in the Washington incident. However, modifications were made after that incident and no further damage to the cables there was reported.

The fuel could have been ignited on contact with the hot walls of the engine or with gas coming out of the reheat (afterburner).

Yet there was no trace of fire damage on the engines. However, the fan blades of engine one showed signs of damage from impact with small pieces of stainless steel, while damaged fan blades in engine two showed it had been hit by something soft. There had been nineteen cases of damage to engines due to tyre debris; six led to a loss of thrust during take-off.

The surge and subsequent loss of thrust from engine one was thought to have been caused by the debris it sucked in, while the surge in engine two was blamed on hot gases entering the engine. Engine two was then closed down and the fire handle was pulled in an attempt to douse the fire. Engines three and four experienced a surge, too. But this was due to the roll and high angle of attack. All damage to the engines was found to have come from their impact with the ground.

Attempts were made to retract the landing gear. In the cockpit voice recorder, a voice can be heard saying "the landing gear is not retracting" and "I'm trying". Examination of the wreckage did not bring to light the cause. But there were indications that the hydraulic system had failed.

It was also calculated that, if the pilot had aborted the take-off, the plane would have still being travelling at between 74 and 115 knots when it reached the end of the runway – with similarly catastrophic results. The landing gear would have collapsed and, with a fire under one wing, the whole plane would have burst into flames immediately.

The Operations Manual for Concorde said: "The decision to abort take-off before V_1 must only be taken in case of a significant loss of thrust or fire on an engine, or with the certainty that the aircraft will be unable to fly (loss of an essential structural element, for example . . .). In all other cases it is preferable to continue the take-off" and "In case of a failure on take-off, no action will be taken before 400 feet AAL [Above Aerodrome Level], apart from ensuring the track and gear retraction."

A study of the safety record of Concorde showed that the rate of tyre problems on take-off had reduced from one in 1,500 to one in 8,000 over the lifetime of the plane due to modifications.

But that compared with one in 100,000 for an Airbus A340. And 50 per cent of the incidents were caused by foreign bodies.

An examination of the bogie on the left main landing gear, which had recently been replaced, revealed that the spacer was missing from the axle. This meant that the bogie could move from side to side. The electrical wiring was long enough not to snap. The hydraulic pipes could have ruptured, but that would only have led to the loss of braking and would. not have been a factor in the crash. Usually, the forces on the bogie would bring it back into alignment and no cases of bogie "shimmy" had been reported on Concorde. Besides, examination of the bearings and brakes on the other wheels showed them to be in a normal condition, and there was no evidence of damage to the other tyres.

In theory, the absence of the spacer could have caused the aircraft to deviate from its straight-line path, tyre overheating and slower acceleration than normal. Study of the marks on the runway, as well as calculations of the trajectory and acceleration made on the basis of the data from the flight recorders, show that this was not the case. The path of the plane was straight until the loss of thrust on engines one and two. The temperature of both the right and left bogies was the same and nothing abnormal was noticed when the plane was taxiing. The acceleration down the runway for the first 1,310 yards (1,200 m) was perfectly normal and there were no identifiable tyre marks coming from Concorde before that point.

The plane was slightly overweight, starting its take-off weighing 185,880 kg, while its maximum take-off weight is 185,070 kg. But it was concluded that this had no significant effect on the take-off and acceleration distances.

The investigators concluded that at 1,860 yards (1,700 m) from the threshold of the runway, around where the first parts of the water deflector were found, tyre two ran over the metallic strip. In the following half-second, a clean, short noise was heard on the cockpit voice recorder. The noise was thought to be the sound of the tyre running over the strip. This is where the strip and a large piece of the tyre were found.

At 1,980 yards (1,810 m), the first marks from tyre two were noticeable on the runway. The piece of the bottom of tank five and the first kerosene stain were found at 1,990 yards (1,820 m). At 2,025 yards (1,850 m), the first marks of very dense soot were seen. This led to the conclusion that a large quantity of fuel leaked out before the fire broke out. A change in the background noise was heard, resulting from the ignition of the flame, which was then spotted by the controller in the tower. The heading changed slight, probably due to the burst tyre and the aerodynamic disturbance caused by the fuel leak and the fire.

The captain then turned the rudder slightly to starboard to compensate for the plane's slight move to port. The flight officer said: "Watch out."

Engines one and two suffered their first loss of thrust as their "go lights" went out in the cockpit. The captain pulled back on the control column at 2,095 yards (1,915 m). There was a slight yaw to port, then the nose gear lifted off the runway. The rudder was moved further to starboard and the plane side-slipped to port. By then, those on board would have felt a strange sensation of lateral movement due to the lack of thrust. There would have been unusual noises, a luminous glow and a strange smell permeating the cabin.

Engine one's "go light" came back on. The flight engineer announced the failure of engine two and began the fire-control procedure. Engine two briefly sparked back into life, delivering around 15 per cent of its normal thrust. The "go lights" on engines one, three and four went out – a normal reaction to the relaxation of the shock absorber on the left main landing gear.

Shortly afterwards, engine one suffered a second surge, this time caused by the ingestion of hot gases or kerosene, aided by the aircraft's peculiar angle of attack. As engine two picked up speed, its auxiliary air intake opened, allowing the further intake of hot gases. This caused a further surge, leaving the aircraft powered only by the thrust from engines three and four.

At this point, the aircraft was about 25 yards (22.5 m) from the runway centreline and wheel six ran over the runway edge light. No components of the light were identified in the debris inside the engines, so it seems to have played no part in the crash.

When the aircraft was airborne, the fire alarm sounded, followed by a warning gong. On the radio, someone, probably among the crew of aircraft waiting to take off, was heard to say: "It's really burning, eh?" Then a few seconds later: "It's burning and I'm not sure it's coming from the engine."

After three seconds in the air, the flight engineer said: "Shut down engine two."

The captain called for the engine fire procedure. The thrust lever was moved to the stop position and engine two's fire handle was pulled. Two seconds later, the flight officer drew attention to the airspeed, which was then 200 knots, when V_2, or the take-off speed, was 220 knots. Engines one, three and four went into "contingency mode", which automatically boosts the thrust on the remaining engines if one or more loses power. But engine one took seven seconds to respond due to the solid fragments inside it.

Another three seconds passed before the captain ordered the retraction of the landing gear. The speed was still 200 knots. The radio altimeter indicated 100 ft and the rate of climb was 750 ft a minute. In the next few seconds, the controller confirmed that there was a plume of flame behind the aircraft.

Engine one was then producing 75 per cent of its nominal thrust and the reheat kicked in. The flight officer acknowledged the controller's message, while the flight engineer drew attention to the problem with retracting the landing gear. The smoke detector went off in the forward lavatories. It was thought that smoke from the left engine that ran the air conditioning circulated into the cabin. The sound of the alarm was recorded on the cockpit area microphone, indicating that the cockpit door was open during take-off, then a common practice on Concorde.

The flight engineer repeated: "The gear." Then a gong was heard alerting the crew to low oil pressure due to the shutdown of engine two. Two seconds later, the flight engineer again repeated: "The gear." The red wheel light came on indicating a loss of pressure in tyre two. In this case the procedure requires that the landing gear is not retracted. Nevertheless, two seconds later, the captain ordered "gear retraction". Three seconds after that, engine two's fire alarm sounded again, along with its associated gong. The flight officer then said: "I'm trying." This was thought to have been in response to the captain's order to retract the landing gear.

At the same time, the flight engineer said: "I'm firing."

The captain asked: "[Are] you shutting down engine two there?"

The flight engineer replied: "I've shut it down."

Seconds later, the flight officer said: "Airspeed."

The airspeed was still only 200 knots when the normal climb-out speed was 220 knots. Over the next seven seconds, airspeed increased to 211 knots. Then the flight officer announced: "The gear isn't retracting." This was thought to be due to the failure of the left main landing gear door to open fully.

By then, the flame had been established for thirty-five seconds. Engine one surged again. Then engine two's fire alarm sounded one more time. It continued to sound until the end of the flight.

The ground proximity warning system sounded: "Whoop, whoop, pull up." This was heard three times. The nose was up at five degrees. The radio altimeter read 165 ft and the rate of descent was about 160 ft a minute.

There were disturbances in the fuel flow to engine one and the temperature of its exhaust. Eight seconds later, rudder control was switched to manual, leading to the loss of yaw auto-stabilization. By then, engine one was decelerating and only engines three and four remained in operation, causing the plane to bank to the left. The thrust was reduced to counter this, but this caused them to surge due to the disruption of the airflow caused by the yaw and the angle of attack, which was now twenty-five degrees. By then, the fire had destroyed vital control surfaces. Even if all four engines had been operating at that point, the damage caused by the fire to the structure of the wing and the flight controls would have caused the plane to crash.

The crew had been drilled in what to do in the event of an engine failure during training and in the flight simulator. They knew the importance of speed with Concorde, especially on the runway. But they were not prepared for a double engine failure on the take-off run. Thought to be a highly unlikely event, this scenario was not covered in training. After noticing the loss of thrust on engines one and two, the flight engineer said the word: "Stop." Then, noting that engine one was recovering, he announced: "Failure eng . . . failure engine two." He was plainly in a state of agitation.

But it was too late to stop the take-off. The sideways movement of the plane threatened to carry it off the runway and the captain decided to get it into the air as soon as possible. Engine two was shut down by the time they got to 400 ft (122 m). Alarms sounded, but the crew had no way of grasping the overall reality of the situation. All they could do was react instinctively to what they knew was an extremely dangerous situation. They were in no way to blame. The accident report noted: "Each time the situation allowed, they applied the established procedure in a professional way."

A great deal of tank five had melted so it was not possible to determine exactly how it had ruptured. But it was thought that it burst due to the pressure wave caused by the impact of a large piece of the tyre – though this had never been seen on a civil aircraft before. However, this does not explain the loss of fuel from tanks two and six. No debris was found from them on the runway. It was thought that the fire might have damaged the bottom of these tanks during flight.

It was not possible to determine how the leaking kerosene caught fire. However, the accident report noted that the runways at Charles de Gaulle airport were only inspected on average twice a day, instead of three. And there was no systematic research into where the recovered debris came from. This would hardly have helped F-BTSC as the metal strip that caused the accident had been shed by an aircraft that had taken off just five minutes before. The maintenance technicians who left the spacer off Concorde's bogie came in for criticism. But the oversight, though serious, did not contribute to the accident.

It was the loss of the wear strip from the thrust reverser door on the Continental Airlines DC-10 that was responsible. That fell off due to the lack of rigorous maintenance. Over a period of little more than a month, it had been replaced, then became detached and twisted and had been replaced again. This time the replacement part had not been made in accordance with the manufacturer's specifications and fell off on 25 July 2000.

The accident report was published in 2002. Six years later, Concorde's chief engineer Jacques Herubel, the head of the Concorde division of the French aircraft manufacturer Aérospatiale Henri Perrier, former employee of the French airline regulator Claude Frantzen, mechanic for Continental Airlines John Taylor and Continental maintenance manager Stanley Ford were charged with manslaughter. The trial began in January 2010. The prosecutors maintained that Aérospatiale had been aware of the design flaw that left the plane's fuel tanks vulnerable since the accident in Washington, DC, in 1979. Working for France's civil aviation authority responsible for the aircraft's safety, Frantzen also knew of Concorde's design flaw. Air France was not prosecuted and began a civil action against Continental after paying out $150 million in a settlement with the families of the victims.

After a trial that lasted five months, Continental Airlines was convicted of involuntary manslaughter and fined nearly $300,000. John Taylor, who made and installed the faulty wear strip, was given a fifteen-month prison sentence that was immediately suspended. Concorde returned to service briefly, but was then withdrawn permanently in 2003.

THE DEATH OF PRINCESS DI

O<small>N</small> 31 A<small>UGUST</small> 1997, Diana, Princess of Wales, died as a result of injuries sustained when the car in which she was a passenger collided with a pillar in the Pont de l'Alma road tunnel in Paris. Her lover, Dodi al-Fayed, and the driver of the Mercedes-Benz S280, Henri Paul, were pronounced dead at the scene of the accident. The Princess of Wales was still alive following the crash but barely conscious. She was taken to the Pitié-Salpêtrière Hospital. Following emergency surgery she was pronounced dead at 4 a.m. local time. Al-Fayed's bodyguard Trevor Rees-Jones was taken to the same hospital with very serious injuries and after extensive treatment was released on Friday, 3 October. He was the only survivor. The media blamed the paparazzi who were pursuing the car. Several of them were arrested at the scene of the accident and charged with failing to render assistance to persons in danger – an offence in France.

An eighteen-month French judicial investigation concluded that the crash was caused by Henri Paul, who was driving under the influence of alcohol and drugs. He lost control of the car at high speed after colliding with a Fiat Uno. The investigating magistrates said that Diana and Dodi would have survived if they had been wearing their seat belts. They also decided to take no action against the paparazzi, saying: "Their behaviour is an issue for them, and the people they work for, about the moral and ethical rules of their work. But it does not constitute a breach of the penal law."

However, Dodi's father, Egyptian-born Mohamed al-Fayed, then the owner of Harrods and the Ritz hotel in Paris, insisted that the deaths of the princess and his son were the result of a conspiracy by the British establishment to save the monarchy from the embarrassment of a potential marriage between the mother of a future king and a Muslim.

It is alleged that Diana feared death in a car accident. Her one-time bodyguard and lover Barry Mannakee died in a motorbike accident shortly after being dismissed from his post when the affair was discovered. Diana told her voice coach Peter Settelen that she thought Mannakee had been murdered. Then ten months before her death, she wrote to her butler Paul Burrell claiming that "my husband is planning 'an accident' in my car, brake failure and serious head injury in order to make the path clear for him to marry". The letter was reproduced in Burrell's book, *A Royal Duty*. Burrell said that she had written it as an "insurance policy" in case of her death.

Mohamed al-Fayed also said that Princess Diana was frightened. A few weeks before her death, she told him that she had been threatened by Prince Philip. "Diana told me personally during a holiday in the south of France, 'If anything happens to me, make sure those people are exposed. The person who is spearheading these threats is Prince Philip'," al-Fayed said.

According to former MI6 agent Richard Tomlinson, British intelligence was planning a hit at the time. In a sworn deposition, he claimed the MI6 officer Dr Nicholas Bernard Frank Fishwick, who was in charge of Balkan operations, showed him plans to assassinate the Serbian leader President Slobodan Milosevic "by causing his personal limousine to crash".

"Dr Fishwick proposed to arrange the crash in a tunnel," said Tomlinson, "because the proximity of concrete close to the road would ensure that the crash would be sufficiently violent to cause death or serious injury, and would also reduce the possibility that there might be independent, casual witnesses. Dr Fishwick suggested that one way to cause the crash might be to disorientate the chauffeur using a strobe flashgun, a device which is occasionally deployed by special forces to, for example, disorientate helicopter pilots or terrorists, and about which MI6 officers are briefed during their training." Tomlinson noted that the scenario bore "remarkable similarities to the circumstances and witness accounts of the crash that killed the Princess of Wales, Dodi al-Fayed, and Henri Paul".

Mohamed al-Fayed had claimed that Diana's planned assassination became urgent when it was discovered that the mother of the heir to the throne was pregnant by his son Dodi. The pregnancy was confirmed by a French police officer who spoke anonymously to the *Independent on Sunday*. The officer went on to say he had papers to substantiate his claim and said the pregnancy was not revealed at the time because it had nothing to do with the investigation into the cause of the deaths after a car crash. Mohamed al-Fayed went on to claim that the crash was an assassination ordered by Prince Philip and carried out by MI6 because the royal family "could not accept that an Egyptian Muslim could eventually be the stepfather of the future king of England".

In an attempt to clear up these accusations, the Metropolitan Police began an investigation in January 2004 called Operation Paget. In December 2006, the Metropolitan Police Commissioner Lord Stevens published its 832-page report, which examined the crime scene evidence. The police used laser techniques to create an extremely detailed computer representation of the Pont de l'Alma underpass and its approach. Collision investigators of the Metropolitan Police Service and the Transport Research Laboratory then used this model to interpret the physical evidence left at the scene of the crash, such as tyre marks and the spread of vehicle debris. This showed how the Mercedes entered the underpass and crashed, supported by a comprehensive technical examination of the wreckage of the car, which was stored in containers outside Paris.

It was initially alleged that the speedometer of the Mercedes was stuck at 192 km/h (119 mph). However, the manufacturers insisted that the speedometer would have reverted to zero after the crash brought the car to a halt, as the French investigation had found. A photograph of the dashboard of the crashed car and the testimony of the investigating officer Captaine Francis Bechet confirmed this. However, when officers from Operation Paget examined the wreckage, they found that the needle was pointing to 231 km/h (144 mph), but the needle could be moved manually and would remain where it was placed. Neither the French investigators nor officers from Operation Paget found any physical marks or indentations on the face of the speedometer that would allow one to ascertain the reading on the instrument at the point of impact. The needle sometimes makes an indent on the speedometer face following a violent impact. All the other instruments on the dashboard had returned to zero, leaving no indication of their reading at the time of the crash.

After crash tests of similar Mercedes saloons, the manufacturers estimated that the speed of impact with the thirteenth pillar of the tunnel was 65 mph (105 km/h) +/– 5 per cent. The measurement of the tyre marks confirmed this.

Forensic accident investigator David Price examined the wreckage and went to the scene of the crash. He also studied the French crash report, and consulted the French technical experts and technicians from Daimler Chrysler who made the Mercedes. Examining the Mercedes brakes, he found the brake-pad sensor was out of position and road dirt had worn away where the sensor made contact, causing the warning light to flicker on and off, as reported by Olivier Lafaye, the car's previous driver. The French examination had found that, "no fault capable of triggering the brake warning light on the instrument assembly was found". However, the misplaced brake-pad sensor would have had no effect of the braking capability of the vehicle.

There were traces of water in the brake fluid. The French investigators found that this was due to prolonged exposure to air and would, again, have had no effect on the vehicle's braking capability. The French investigators were puzzled that the gear selector was not in place. David Price concluded that it had been removed by the rescue services at the scene of the accident to give them more space.

Some of the car's fuses were missing or blown, but none that controlled any critical systems. Some of the wiring was damaged, but none showed signs that they had been chaffed or had failed before the crash.

Captaine Bechet reported that the right front tyre was deflated when he examined the car at Nord Garage, MacDonald Boulevard, on 1 September, but when French technical investigators examined the car in October, it was inflated to 30 psi (2.1 bar). Price found a small cut in the side wall of the car. The tyre was no long airtight and when it was inflated to 32 psi (2.2 bar) it deflated to 10 psi (0.7 bar) within an hour, and to zero sometime within the following three hours. He concluded that, if the tyre was inflated to 30 psi, it must have been inflated shortly before the French experts had examined it. The nature of the cut indicated that it had been caused by damaged bodywork during the crash.

The tyre treads were in very good condition and had no abnormal wear. This indicated that there was no serious misalignment of any suspension components immediately before impact with the pillar. The condition of the tyre treads was also consistent with the limited skid marks found at the scene of the crash.

The engine had taken the brunt of the impact and had shattered. Examining the pieces, Price found no signs of engine seizure, which could have contributed to the crash. The French technical experts dismantled the gear box and concluded that the only damage present had resulted from the crash. It was not possible to establish which gear the car was in when the crash occurred.

Although the steering had been badly damaged in the collision, there was no indication that it had malfunctioned beforehand. Damage to the steering wheel and column indicated that it was turned about ninety degrees to the right from the straight-ahead position at the moment of impact. This would have resulted in the steered wheel being turned to the right by about seven degrees because of the steering ratio.

The wheel left alloy rub marks on the edge of the kerb. There was no abnormal wear on the tyres indicating that the wheels were misaligned. However, in October 1996, shortly after the Mercedes was purchased, the owner reported its poor handling to the dealer. It was checked by the dealer, who found nothing wrong, and returned it. The car was stolen in April 1997. When it was recovered, minor repairs were made. The steering geometry and wheel alignment were checked and minor adjustments were made. No further reports of unsatisfactory handling were made.

The headlights had been dipped at the time of the crash and photographs of the vehicle showed that the brake lights remained illuminated. There was no evidence that there had been anything attached to the car that would have affected its control. No signs of adhesive or drilled holes were found. And there was no unusual wiring, other than that for a telephone system that had been fitted at the request of the owners, Etoile Limousines. Indeed, nothing considered likely to have affected the control of the car during the run-up to the crash was discovered. Price found no anomalies or points of interest in his examination of any of the other components of the car and there was no sign of interference with the vehicle.

The car was not one that Diana and Dodi had used before. They had two other vehicles on hand when they left the Ritz hotel that night to return to Dodi's apartment in Rue Arsène Houssaye, just off the Avenue des Champs-Élysées, near the Arc de Triomphe. However, Philippe Dourneau, Dodi al-Fayed's regular chauffeur in Paris, accompanied by Kieran Wingfield, had left in the Mercedes Dodi and Diana had arrived in from the front of the Ritz, followed by Jean-François Musa in the backup Range Rover, in an attempt to draw off the paparazzi. A second Mercedes S280 was called to the back of the Ritz in the Rue Cambon.

At 12.20 a.m., Diana and Dodi left in the back of this car. Trevor Rees-Jones was the front-seat passenger. Henri Paul, the head of security at the Ritz, had been seconded as driver. This was not his usual job, but he had been on at least four driving courses in Germany run by Daimler-Benz, where he was taught anti-hijacking procedures and how to force another vehicle off the road. Friends said he drove slowly and carefully. He had gone for a medical for his pilot's licence a week before he died and there was no sign that he drank excessively. But when his flat was searched, the police found a cupboard containing various aperitifs – Crème de Cassis, Ricard, Suze, port – which had been partly drunk. There were also unopened bottles of beer, red wine and champagne.

On a table in the lobby there were several unopened aperitifs bottles – Martini Bianco, Vodka, Pinot, Suze and fortified wine. In the refrigerator there was one bottle of champagne and two small bottles of beer. And in the kitchen cupboard there were opened bottles of Ricard, Bourbon and Martini Bianco. His doctor had prescribed the anti-depressant Prozac, Noctamide to treat his insomnia, Tiapridal to prevent him dwelling on his personal problems, and Aotal, also known as Acamprosate, which causes a dislike of alcohol. He took Tiapridal and Aotal when he was working to prevent him drinking. On certain occasions, when Paul was freed from his professional constraints, or when he was on holiday, he did not take this medication and drank alcohol in reasonable quantities, though always in a social context. His doctor permitted this as he did not have the clinical signs of being an alcoholic. However, these drugs were prescribed because Paul feared he might be dependent on alcohol. Other prescription drugs were found in his apartment.

At the time of his death, Paul was found to have been carrying 12,645 French francs in cash, which was worth about £1,254. This did not appear to have been withdrawn from any of his bank accounts. In all, he had approximately 1,245,000 francs (£124,500) in fifteen bank accounts, along with shares worth 431,485 francs (£43,148), and had deposited 430,000 francs (£43,000) in the last eight months of his life. Mohamed al-Fayed claims that this is evidence that he was in the pay of MI6. However, Claude Garrec, Henri Paul's closest friend, said that it was commonplace for him to have large sums of money because of the services he provided for wealthy clients at the Ritz. His parents said that their son received tips of 5,000 francs (£500) from customers. Garrec said that Paul received tips of anything from 1,000 francs (£100) to 10,000 francs (£1,000) – "the sums were limitless, depending on what help or services Henri Paul organized," he said. These tips were always paid in cash.

Asked about the cash he had on him at the time of his death, Garrec said: "I can say that I had seen him with larger sums on previous occasions. He told me that he needed to have cash at his disposal to assist Ritz clients and VIPs, as he was often required to pay upfront for services or purchases that they had asked him to make. Henri Paul told me that rich people never had money on them. He would be reimbursed by the Ritz, which would bill the client."

In his evidence to Judge Hervé Stéphan, the examining magistrate who headed the French investigation, ex-MI6-man Richard Tomlinson said: "I should point out that it is very common for national security services to try and recruit members of security staff in the big hotels as they are very well placed to pick up information . . . I should explain that only MI6, Mossad and the CIA pay their informants, unlike other countries, including France, who would never pay such sums to their informants. The French intelligence services can pay foreign informants, but not French nationals, and not that much money."

Henri Paul was born in Brittany and was a French national.

In the computerized telephone book in Paul's office and the hard copy he kept at home were the names of police stations, police officers and names and telephone numbers for two people with the letters DST next to them. DST stands for *La Direction de la Surveillance du Territoire*, the organization that deals with espionage, terrorism, the protection of the French economy, serious and organized crime, and the non-proliferation of nuclear, biological and chemical weapons. However, according to the records of calls from his home phone and his mobile from midday on Saturday, 30 August 1997, to 12.30 a.m. on Sunday, 31 August, he did not call the numbers associated with the DST.

According to investigative journalist Gerald Posner, citing a source in the United States' National Security Agency, Henri Paul had a meeting with a member of France's *Direction Générale de la Securité Extérieure*, or DGSE – the equivalent of Britain's Secret Intelligence Service (SIS), commonly known as MI6 – on the night of the accident. He was a paid informant who passed information on important guests, particularly foreign diplomats, at the Ritz. But the meeting that night did not concern the Princess of Wales.

"I was told the subject did come up but only in general conversation," said Posner. "It was pure coincidence that this meeting took place on the same day as the crash occurred."

Posner also said that Paul was paid 12,560 francs.

The DGSE denied all knowledge of Henri Paul. But was he working for MI6? Richard Tomlinson told Judge Stéphan: 'I cannot say for sure that it was Henri Paul but I am positive that it was a Frenchman working in the security department of the Ritz Hotel. I am certain that this money originated from MI6. This is speculation on my part, but if he was an MI6 informant, it would be quite normal for him to receive money."

Tomlinson said that two experienced SIS officers, who knew Henri Paul, arrived in Paris shortly before 31 August 1997 and "most probably met Monsieur Paul shortly before his death", Tomlinson said in a sworn statement to Judge Stéphan. One of them was Richard Spearman, who had been the personal secretary to the Chief of MI6, David Spedding, before he was posted to Paris the month before the accident. The British Diplomatic Service List did show that "Mr R. D. Spearman" had been posted to the British Embassy in Paris as "First Secretary (Political)", arriving in his post on 26 August. However, records showed that he had applied for the post in the autumn of 1996 and he had begun pre-post training, including taking French lessons, in May 1997, before Dodi joined Diana and his father in St Tropez for a holiday in July 1997. He also arrived in Paris before anyone outside Mohamed al-Fayed's organization knew that Diana and Dodi would be in Paris on the weekend of 30 August. That Saturday was, coincidentally, Spearman's birthday and he went out to dinner with his wife.

The other SIS officer Tomlinson named was Nicholas Langman. He was on leave in Britain that weekend. Officers from Operation Paget obtained corroborating statements from the relatives with whom he was staying. Both Spearman and Langman said that they had never knowingly met or communicated with Henri Paul at any time, either socially or professionally. On a second visit to Tomlinson, the officers from Operation Paget said that he did not know where Spearman and Langman were that weekend and never said he did. He merely thought their movements were suspicious, but later accepted that "these suspicions would appear to be unfounded".

Tomlinson said that a plan to assassinate Princess Diana had been drawn up by MI6. He told Judge Stéphan: "The plan was fully typed, and attached to a yellow minute board, signifying this was a formal and accountable document. It will therefore still be in existence."

He also told Judge Stéphan: "MI6 are frequently and routinely asked by the royal household (usually via the Foreign Office) to provide intelligence on potential threats to members of the royal family whilst on overseas trips. This service would frequently extend to asking friendly intelligence services (such as the CIA) to place members of the royal family under discrete surveillance, ostensibly for their own protection."

And, according to Tomlinson, "one of the 'paparazzi' photographers who routinely followed the Princess of Wales was a member of 'UKN', a small corps of part-time MI6 agents who provide miscellaneous services to MI6 such as surveillance and photography expertise".

SIS officers stationed in Paris who were interviewed by investigators with Operation Paget said that no SIS officers knew that Diana and Dodi were in Paris that night until after the crash. Most SIS officers were on leave at the time as business in Paris closes down in August. No SIS officer knowingly met or communicated with Henri Paul, and no SIS officer had the use of a white Fiat Uno like the one seen in the tunnel at the time of the accident.

Officers from Operation Paget met the SIS IT systems controller and searched the service's database. According to Lord Steven's report: "The searches showed no trace on any intelligence or informant database of Henri Paul, or any codename or description fitting or apparently referring to Henri Paul or someone in his position at the Ritz hotel before the crash in August 1997. Records were checked back to 1990."

They also checked all the telegrams that passed between the SIS station in Paris and their headquarters in London between 14 July 1997, when Dodi arrived in St Tropez, and 14 September, two weeks after the crash. The telegrams had numbers that were generated automatically and the sequence between those two dates was complete. They found no reference to Henri Paul or anything relating to the crash.

Officers from Operation Paget made a further search for references to Paul in later telegrams. One reference was found. Dated 18 November 1997, some two and a half months after the crash, the telegram sent from the SIS station in Paris to London Headquarters said: "The Ritz Hotel still crawling with members of the Brigade Criminel [*sic*] of the Police Judiciaire investigating the Princess of Wales' death," and added a comment: "Presumably as Head of Security there Henri Paul had been a contact of DST and they would have such a capacity again."

Plainly, the SIS station in Paris did not know Henri Paul before the crash and did not expect their headquarters in London to know him. Nevertheless, Tomlinson insisted that he had seen an operational file detailing Henri Paul's involvement with Operation Battle, an attempt to recover hi-tech weapons from the former Soviet Union, in 1992. Meetings took place in the Ritz hotel. Officers from Operation Paget gained access to the file, but could find no reference to the Ritz or anyone who could be identified as Henri Paul.

It appears that Henri Paul only knew of the visit of Diana and Dodi on 29 August and, with other members of staff, made arrangements to greet them the following day. However, his boss, Franz Klein, who was in day-to-day control of the Ritz, knew ten days beforehand that Dodi and his "girlfriend" would be visiting Paris at the end of the month.

On the morning of 30 August, Paul played tennis with his friend Claude Garrec, driving through the Alma tunnel on the way to the court. Afterwards they went to the Café Pelican near Paul's apartment for a drink. While Garrec had a beer, Paul drank cola. Paul was not meant to have been on duty that weekend, but he told his girlfriend Badia Mouhib on the telephone that he could not see her that evening. Later, he was seen leaving his flat in the company of a young blonde woman. After the crash, a young blonde woman, aged about twenty-five, turned up at the Ritz asking for "Monsieur Henri". Paul's parents also said a young blonde woman who gave her name as Françoise turned up at Paul's flat in the days following the accident asking for something by which to remember him.

At 3 p.m., Paul drove Dodi al-Fayed's Range Rover to Le Bourget airport and collected the staff accompanying the couple and their baggage, which he took to Dodi's apartment in the Rue Arsène Houssaye. Dodi's usual chauffeur, Philippe Dourneau, collected Diana and Dodi in a hired Mercedes S600, accompanied by Trevor Rees-Jones, Dodi's principal bodyguard.

Security staff were on duty at the Ritz to deal with the paparazzi and Paul asked another chauffeur, Jean-François Musa, to be on duty outside the Ritz at 5 p.m. Henri Paul asked Musa to drive Dodi al-Fayed to Repossi jewellers in Place Vendôme opposite the Ritz, which he did. At about 6 p.m., Paul told Musa to drive the Range Rover for the rest of the evening, while Philippe Dourneau drove the Mercedes S600.

At around 7 p.m., Paul told night security officer François Tendil, who had just come on duty, that he was finishing work for the day. Diana and Dodi had already left the hotel by then and Paul told him that the couple were not expected to return. They had gone to Dodi's apartment, where they drank champagne, and they had a reservation at the restaurant Chez Benoit. If there was any change of plan, Paul said he could be contacted by mobile phone. He then left the Ritz.

At 7.30 p.m., Paul was seen in the Bar de Bourgogne in the Rue des Petits Champs near to his home. However, the staff there said they did not see him that night. The owner of a bar called Le Champmeslé, about 55 yards (50 m) from the Bar de Bourgogne, did see Paul. He came in for a short time around 9.30 p.m., but did not have a drink. He did not appear to be drunk and arranged to meet up with friends at the Bar de Bourgogne at around midnight.

As Dodi and Diana could not shake the large posse of paparazzi, they had decided not to eat at Chez Benoit and returned to the Ritz instead. Tendil called Paul, who returned to the hotel at 10 p.m. The couple decided not to eat in the hotel restaurant and had food brought to them in the Imperial Suite, while their bodyguards went to the Bar Vendôme in the hotel, where Paul later joined them.

"He got himself a drink at the bar and came to sit down with us," said Trevor Rees-Jones. "He had a drink, I do not know what it was, but it was yellow-coloured . . . After a while, Paul had another drink."

According to the bill and the barmen at the Bar Vendôme, Paul drank two Ricards. The instructions came from Dodi al-Fayed that Paul should arrange for a third car to be waiting at the rear of the hotel in the Rue Cambon. The two cars at the front of the hotel would act as decoys. No instructions were given as to who would drive the third car and it is not clear at which point Paul took it upon himself to drive. There was no reason to think that Paul was drunk and none of the security officers or senior staff at the hotel objected, though Trevor Rees-Jones thought it was a bad idea to head off in a single car with no backup. Dodi did not even want to take Rees-Jones with him, but agreed when the bodyguards dug their heels in.

Bodyguard Kieran Wingfield told the French enquiry: "I noticed that Henri Paul had just smoked a cigar, I could smell it on his breath. I am positive, he did not smell of alcohol and his behaviour was perfectly normal."

Later, he told Operation Paget: "He wasn't drunk. There was no slurring of his words and when he walked up the corridor he wasn't falling around. He was quite tactile – he would touch your arm when he was talking to you – and he stood very close to me. I don't smoke and neither does Trevor and I was close enough to smell cigars on him but not drink."

Wingfield then went down to the front of the hotel to give the paparazzi the impression that Diana and Dodi would be coming out in fifteen minutes.

Jean-François Musa was worried by the choice of Paul as the driver of the third car, but only because he did not have a "Grande Remise" licence, the special licence to drive limousines.

At 12.17 a.m., CCTV caught Henri Paul leaving the Rue Cambon exit of the Ritz with Diana, Dodi and Trevor Rees-Jones. Paul took over from chauffeur Frédéric Lucard who had delivered the car. Before he drove away, Lucard heard Paul say to the photographers: "Don't try to follow us; in any case you won't catch us."

Then he drove off.

Off-duty physician Dr Frédéric Maillez arrived on the scene almost immediately after the crash. He noted that the driver was "stuck in the twisted metal and had no illusions about his condition". At 12.32 a.m., Sergeant Xavier Gourmelon of the Fire Service, who was trained in medical emergencies, made his initial assessment and noted that the driver was in cardiac arrest, trapped, inaccessible and apparently dead. Eight minutes later Dr Armaud Derossi with Service d'Aide Médicale Urgente, or the Urgent Medical Aid Service, also noted that the driver was dead. His body was taken directly to the mortuary at the Institut Médico-Légal (IML) at 2 Place Mazas, Paris, where it was given the identification number 2147. Dodi al-Fayed was pronounced dead at the scene and was also taken to the IML mortuary where his body was given the identification number 2146. The Princess of Wales and Trevor Rees-Jones, who were both still alive at the scene, were taken to the Pitié-Salpêtrière Hospital for emergency medical treatment.

Deputy Public Prosecutor Maud Coujard turned up at the scene and requested Professor Dominique Lecomte, an expert on the list of the Paris Court of Appeal, to carry out a full autopsy of Henri Paul to ascertain the circumstances and causes of death, and to seek any evidence of an offence. Commandant Jean-Claude Mulès, an officer with the Brigade Criminelle who was present at the scene of the crash, also attended the post-mortem. Professor Lecomte found that Paul had no lesions to the organs, notably the heart or brain, that would suggest a pre-existing condition. The injuries found were primarily traumatic in nature with "a rupture of the spinal cord and rupture of the descending aorta". She also noted multiple fractures, primarily to the spinal column, the ribcage, pelvis and legs, that were consistent with trauma.

But there were some discrepancies in the post-mortem report. Professor Lecomte recorded Paul's body weight as 73 kg and height as 1.72 m, while Commandant Mulès recorded his body weight as 76 kg and his height as 1.67 m. Professor Lecomte told the French investigation that the autopsy began at 8 a.m., but told Operation Paget that it was 8.30 a.m..

Peter Vanezis, a professor of forensic medical science called in by Mohamed al-Fayed, criticized the post-mortem, saying that the place on the body from which blood samples had been taken was not recorded. Nor was it mentioned whether the blood had been stored in appropriately refrigerated conditions, while samples of the urine, vitreous humour and bile that had been taken were not analysed.

The blood was divided into two and sent to two different laboratories. One sample showed a high level of alcohol.

"A high blood alcohol in one sample may occur for a number of reasons other than from the intake of the appropriate amount into the body to give such a high level," said Professor Vanezis. "The action of bacteria in blood, the presence of high sugar, sampling from an area close to the stomach or from the portal vein may all give an exaggerated inordinately high reading. There are well-documented cases with high alcohol levels with no evidence that the appropriate amounts of alcohol to account for such levels had been ingested."

In a letter to Mohamed al-Fayed, Patrice Mangin, professor of legal medicine and director of the Institute of Legal Medicine at Lausanne University, also pointed out the shortcomings of the post-mortem report. While it had been said that Paul had been consuming alcohol to excess for up to a week before the crash, the autopsy report did not include biological analyses of the liver, or even the pancreas or other viscera.

"In such a case, it seems to me of the most elementary investigation," he said.

He also noted the high levels of carboxyhaemoglobin in the blood – caused by inhaling carbon monoxide – which Professor Lecomte and independent toxicologist Dr Gilbert Pépin had not been able to explain.

On 4 September 1997, a second post-mortem was performed by Dr Jean-Pierre Campana, a pathologist, on the orders of Judge Stéphan, who was present along with Dr Pépin and three police officers. The judge did this because the blood alcohol levels recorded by the police toxicologist Dr Ivan Ricordel had come as a surprise. However, Dr Pépin confirmed that they were correct. In this case, the blood was taken from the femoral artery in the thigh. Professor Lecomte had taken her blood samples from the heart and the chest.

In the blood samples from the first post-mortem, Dr Ricordel had found a blood alcohol level of 1.87 grams per litre – this was well over the French drink-driving limit of 0.5 grams per litre and the British limit of 0.8 grams per litre. Dr Pépin found 1.74 grams per litre less than two hours later, after Dr Ricordel's findings had been contested by Mohamed al-Fayed and his lawyers.

Dr Pépin was asked by the examining magistrate to do a full toxicology report after the second post-mortem. Again he found a blood alcohol level of 1.74 grams per litre. There were high levels of alcohol in his stomach and urine. Pépin also found traces of prescription drugs in his system and a very high level of carboxyhaemoglobin in his bloodstream. It was thought that Paul inhaled carbon monoxide produced by the triggering of the airbags in the car. This also explained why the level in the cardiac or chest cavity blood – 20.7 per cent – was much higher than that found in the femoral blood – 12.8 per cent – as the heart and chest are much closer to the lungs and Paul would only have breathed in the carbon monoxide from the airbags in the last moments of his life. During the crash he would have breathed in involuntarily and the gas would have been forced into his lungs. Some of the carboxyhaemoglobin would also have been produced by the cigars he smoked. The air in the middle of Paris – like that in any big city – would contain carbon monoxide and there was also the possibility that the samples were contaminated in the laboratory.

The experts employed by Mohamed al-Fayed dismiss this explanation. They said that Paul could not have breathed in enough carbon monoxide from the airbags as he died instantly. Nor did he smoke heavily enough, and if he had the levels of alcohol and carbon monoxide found in his blood before the crash he would have been seen staggering in the CCTV footage from the Ritz. If Henri Paul drank as heavily as was alleged, there would have been damage to his liver. But the second autopsy showed that his liver was perfectly healthy. While Prozac and Tiapridal, which Paul was prescribed, were found in his blood, albendazole was found in samples of his hair. Albendazole is a drug used to treat intestinal worms, not a condition Paul was known to have been suffering from. This raised the possibility that the samples being tested did not come from Henri Paul, but rather from an alcoholic who had committed suicide by inhaling the exhaust from a car. However, carboxyhaemoglobin levels found in the blood of suicides is usually around 50 per cent, not the 20 per cent found. Nevertheless, DNA tests were ordered by Judge Thierry Bellancourt, who had taken over the case in France. These established that the blood did, indeed, come from Henri Paul.

Although it is clear that the two Ricards that Paul drank after his return to the Ritz would not have caused the high level of alcohol in his blood or left him incapable of driving, the obvious conclusion was that he had been drinking between 7 p.m. and 10 p.m. when he was away from the hotel. It is estimated that he could have drunk six measures of Ricard in that period.

According to Mohamed al-Fayed, there were ten CCTV cameras along the route taken by the Mercedes, including one above the Alma tunnel itself, but no footage from those cameras had been forthcoming. On the orders of Judge Stéphan, Lieutenant Eric Gigou of the Brigade Criminelle followed the route and found that there were indeed ten cameras along the way, but they were mainly security cameras trained on the entrances to buildings. Most did not belong to the Parisian authorities but to

the owners of the buildings and were operated privately by them.
None of the footage captured by them was relevant.

There was a traffic-monitoring camera above the underpass
in the Place de l'Alma. It was operated by the Compagnie de
Circulation Urbaines de Paris – the Paris Urban Traffic Unit.
But that department closed down at about 11 p.m. It had no
night-duty staff and made no recordings. Officers in the Police
Headquarters Information and Command Centre could continue to view the pictures shown by the traffic camera in real
time, but could not control it. And there was no reason for those
in the overnight control room in Paris to be viewing that camera
before the crash.

There were no known video recordings or photographic
images of the Mercedes on its final journey between the Ritz
hotel and the Alma underpass. No official images surfaced and
no unofficial ones appeared in any media. There was evidence
that the French investigators took steps at an early stage to identify any such evidence but were unable to find any.

Mohamed al-Fayed also maintained that there was a speed
camera that would have taken a flash photograph of the
Mercedes, if it had been speeding. Officers from Operation
Paget found that there was no speed camera in the Alma tunnel
at the time. The paparazzi had flash cameras, but they were
following the car, not in front of it. An eyewitness to the crash,
who was walking near the entrance to the tunnel, said that he saw
no speed cameras nor any police officers carrying out speed
checks. The Brigade Criminelle recorded the location of all
portable speed cameras in use that night and officers from
Operation Paget were satisfied that they were all elsewhere and
none of them produced any pictures relevant to the enquiry.

A letter from Lewis Silkin, Mohamed al-Fayed's solicitor, to
the coroner said: "Another photo apparently exists which was
taken by a vehicle in front of the Mercedes in the tunnel showing Mr Paul and Trevor Rees-Jones."

Officers from Operation Paget believed that the photograph
in question was one of the two shot by Jacques Langevin at the

rear of the Ritz in Rue Cambon, not in the Alma underpass. They found no photograph of the Mercedes entering the tunnel.

Eyewitnesses said that they saw a vehicle that stopped the Mercedes taking the exit on the Cours Albert 1er – the route a driver would normally have taken to the Rue Arsène Houssaye – forcing it into the Alma tunnel. But officers found their evidence conflicting. However, they concluded that a motorcycle was in a position that would have made it difficult to take the exit. The collision investigator assigned to Operation Paget also concluded that the Mercedes was going too fast to take the exit. By the time the Mercedes reached the slip road, the driver had already lost control. But it would have been possible to exit there if he had slowed down as there were no other vehicles blocking the slip road.

A driver named François Levistre said he saw a bright flash of white light in the tunnel before the crash. However, Operation Paget concluded: "It is questionable whether he could have seen the detail of what he claimed to have seen inside the underpass."

Levistre recounted a large amount of detail seen in his rear-view mirror while driving through an underpass at speeds of around 120 to 125 km/h (74 to 78 mph). He was also negotiating the slip road to join the main carriageway, an action that would have required his full attention, regardless of his speed. His wife, who was in the car with him, contradicted parts of his account. The French enquiry discounted François Levistre's evidence.

Another eyewitness, Brian Anderson, described seeing a flash immediately before hearing a bang or explosion and the screeching of car tyres. He could not be specific about the location or source of the flash, saying he only saw it "out of the extreme corner of my left eye".

The consultants at the Transport Research Laboratory carried out a technical reconstruction of the collision and concluded that the Mercedes was between 60 and 105 m (200 and 345 ft) from the beginning of the underpass when the driver, Henri Paul, began to perceive the hazard presented by another vehicle, such as the Fiat Uno, and saw the need to take avoiding action.

Allowing for human reaction times, the driver began to respond to the hazard of an obstruction 30 to 60 m (100 to 200 ft) before entering the underpass.

The chain of events that led to the crash started some way from the entrance to the underpass. By the time the Mercedes approached the thirteenth pillar, the collision was inevitable. The physical evidence of tyre marks, vehicle debris patterns, points of collision from the scene and the marks identified on the Mercedes car supported this view. So if there was a bright light inside the underpass near the Mercedes, and particularly near the thirteenth pillar, it could not have caused the crash. Curiously, Anderson was adamant that he had not seen the white Fiat Uno that other eyewitnesses insist was at the scene.

Other witnesses spoke of seeing bright flashing lights outside the underpass, but none described a blinding effect. Many eyewitnesses who would have been in a position to see a powerful light or flashes made no reference to them.

The examination of vehicle debris at the scene in the Alma underpass, together with samples taken from the Mercedes door, side panels and wing mirror, indicated that a white Fiat Uno was involved in the crash. Immediately afterwards, it was seen emerging from the tunnel being driven in an erratic fashion. The driver never came forward and, although the French enquiry checked 4,668 similar vehicles, it was never identified.

Of particular interest was the white Fiat Uno belonging to James Andanson, a photojournalist who had been in St Tropez that summer photographing the Princess of Wales. On 4 May 2000, his body was found in his burnt-out BMW in a forest in the south of France. The official verdict was suicide, but Mohamed al-Fayed maintained that Andanson was working for the SIS and had been murdered by them as part of the cover-up. Or, if he had committed suicide, it was because his conscience was troubled by the part he had played in the deaths of Princess Diana and Dodi al-Fayed.

However, Operation Paget found no evidence to place him in Paris on the night of 30 August. He was at his home in Lignières, some 170 miles (274 km) south of Paris, and left at about 4 a.m.

on Sunday, 31 August 1997, to fly to Corsica for a prearranged appointment. His wife, Elisabeth Andanson, corroborated his alibi. There was no evidence that his Fiat Uno was in Paris either. It also seems to have been in Lignières. The French authorities carried out forensic tests on paint and bumper samples taken from his Fiat Uno and compared them to samples taken from the wreck of the Mercedes. Their conclusion was that, although the bumper material and some of the paint samples were compatible, there was no damage to the Uno, so the car was eliminated from their enquiries.

Officers from Operation Paget looked into the circumstances surrounding Andanson's death. When the fire brigade put out the fire, they found Andanson's headless body in the driver's seat. The head lay between the two front seats. Although this sounded suspicious, Eric Baccino, the pathologist who attended the crime scene, said that his head could have been detached by the intense heat of the blaze. There was a hole in the left temple. But no missile or projectile was found. During the autopsy, no subdural bleeding was found and Professor Baccino concluded that the hole in James Andanson's head was caused from the inside by the intense heat, and not from the outside by a blow or foreign object. Dr Richard Shepherd, adviser on pathology to Operation Paget, confirmed this explanation.

The French pathologists also noted that the "residual muscular masses at the cervical level and the level of the buttocks have a pinkish colouration such as those found during carbon monoxide poisoning, which signifies that the person was alive at the time the fire started". The post-mortem also found no evidence of violence.

A helicopter was used in the crime scene investigation and aerial photographs revealed that there was only one set of tyre tracks heading into the scene – those of the BMW. There was no evidence that anyone else had been involved in his death.

The vehicle registration plates had been destroyed in the fire. The vehicle was identified through a serial number etched on to one of the windows. The examining magistrate then ordered an examination of the burnt-out vehicle to determine the cause of the fire.

Stéphane Calderara, Guillaume Cognon and Philippe Malaquin of the Institute of Criminal Research of the National Gendarmerie carried out the examination. They reported: "We proceed with testing for the presence of inflammable products using a hydrocarbon detector. This proves positive in the area of the front floor pan . . . It should be noted that nothing is discovered that would indicate a criminal act."

The car had been doused with petrol and set on fire. An accidental or technical cause for the fire was ruled out.

Andanson had made preparations for his suicide. That morning, he left at home his wallet, Cartier watch, mobile telephone and his attaché case, all things that he would have normally carried. At some point during the day, he posted a letter to Sipa Press agency asking for all of his photographic royalties to be put into his wife's name. The letter was stamped at the Lignières Post Office on 4 May 2000 and arrived at the agency the next day.

His bank statement revealed that his bank card was used to make a purchase of 608 francs – about £60 – at the Géant Service Station in Millau at 3.36 p.m. There were no precise details of what he purchased, however the French investigation concluded the value of the transaction was more than was necessary to fill the fuel tank of his car. Andanson was known to carry fuel containers in his vehicle. Millau was just 12 miles (19 km) from Les Louettes in the commune of Nant, where the burnt-out car was found. Andanson had stayed at the Hotel Campanile in Millau across the road from the petrol station two months earlier when he had been on a photographic assignment 550 yards (500 m) from Les Louettes.

James Andanson would normally have had numerous appointments recorded in his diary for the coming days and weeks. However, his appointment with Sophie Deniau at 4 p.m. was the last. She arrived at Sipa in Paris as arranged, waited for an hour, then left.

Long-standing friends and associates interviewed during the French investigation said that Andanson had talked of committing suicide and described the manner in which he would do so. Jean-Gabriel Barthélémy, a photographer who had known Andanson since 1972, said that when they were in Gstaad, Switzerland, together ten years earlier, Andanson had told him that if anything happened to his wife he would kill himself by pouring petrol from a canister in his car boot and lighting it with the end of his cigar. He said that Andanson often talked about committing suicide and of his worries about the financing of his son's career as a racing driver.

Franck Doveri, a friend of twelve years, saw Andanson in Klosters a month before his death. During a conversation with another photographer whose wife had left him, Andanson said that if his own wife ever left him he would put a bullet in his head.

Sophie Deniau, who bought photographs from Andanson, recalled a conversation with him on 18 April 2000 – sixteen days before he died – where he said that if anything were to happen to a member of his family he would not be able to live with himself and he would commit suicide by sitting in his car with a good cigar and setting fire to himself.

Christian Maillard of Sipa Press, a friend of James Andanson since 1988, said that during a conversation about ten days before his death, Andanson had told him that he was thinking of committing suicide by creating an explosion in his car. Maillard told him not to say such things, but Andanson insisted that he would be able to do it.

During the French investigation into Andanson's death, a tape was recovered from his home. On it, he stated that he was unhappy and that he worried about his son's safety and how he would continue to finance his motor-racing career. During 1999, Andanson had personally sponsored his son to the tune of 750,000 francs (£75,000).

Elisabeth Andanson was sure that her husband's death was suicide.

"Frankly and honestly I think he did it for professional and financial reasons," she told the police. "There were the far-reaching changes in the press which worried him a lot and about which he was right to be worried. Our son had become champion of France a year after starting out in motor sport and that involved expenditure. Furthermore, my husband was having trouble adapting to the changes in the press, in which the use of digital technology was one of his concerns. My husband started to age, and he was tired. Even though he expressed his concerns to me fairly often, he never followed my advice."

When Elisabeth Andanson was told of Mohamed al-Fayed's claim that her husband committed suicide because of his conscience over the deaths of Princess Diana and Dodi al-Fayed, she said: "You tell me that it has been suggested that James committed suicide because he had been involved in the accident that cost the lives of Diana, Princess of Wales, Dodi al-Fayed and Henri Paul and he felt guilty: that is absurd, and it is people who do not know the facts that must have said that. I had never heard of this."

Six weeks after Andanson's death, his offices at the Sipa news agency were robbed by three armed men. One of them shot the security guard through the foot. Forcing those present to reveal the security codes, they searched the second and third floors. They took the Visa and Eurocard of Marek Kaserzyk, a Polish computer programmer working at Sipa Press at the time, and forced him to reveal his PIN numbers. They also took his mobile phone and his laptop. Before leaving the scene, they looked around for the bullet that had gone through the victim's foot and took it away with them.

It was alleged that the robbery had been carried out by the security services, that only material belonging to Andanson had been taken and that the French police never investigated the crime. Operation Paget found that computers, scanners and camera, worth 540,000 francs (around £54,000) were stolen, but nothing belonging to Andanson was missing. The French police arrested what they described as ordinary criminals who were linked to a series of similar robberies. They were arrested

during another robbery and had previous convictions. One of
them was carrying the mobile phone he had stolen during the
Sipa raid and had the same gun. There was no evidence that the
security services were involved or that Andanson worked for the
SIS. Goskin Sipahioglu and his wife, who owned Sipa Press, said
that the raid on their offices had nothing to do with the deaths of
Diana or James Andanson. It was more likely that the criminals
were looking for some compromising photographs of a particular French celebrity, although he did not name the person.
Sipahioglu told Operation Paget that, at the time of the burglary,
Sipa Press was in dispute with a television personality he named
as "Arthur". "Arthur" had been photographed in the company
of a girl and had made threats towards Sipa Press in an attempt
to stop the photographs being published.

There was yet another crime scene involved in the death of
Diana. On 1 September 1997, the office in the London home of
Lionel Cherrault, a French photographer based in Britain, was
burgled. Cherrault also worked with Sipa in Paris and specialized
in pictures of the royal family. Credit cards, cheque books, £50
and 400 French francs were taken, along with a computer whose
hard-disk carried many of his photographs.

At 1 a.m. the previous morning, Cherrault had been woken by
a call, from the owner of Sipa, who told him about the car crash.
He considered going to Paris, but decided against it. A short
while later he got a call from British photographer Mark
Saunders, a colleague in Florida, who told him that a contact was
offering pictures of the crash. He asked Cherrault if he was interested in getting copies. Cherrault told him that he was and
Saunders said that he would get back to him in three or four
hours. Cherrault and his wife Christine waited up, but Saunders
did not call and Cherrault did not receive any photographs.

Detective Sergeant Freeman, the investigating officer, visited
the scene and wrote in the crime report: "The VIW [victim or
witness] has for the last sixteen years, been almost exclusively
photographing the royal family and has in recent years concentrated his efforts on the Princess of Wales. The computer equipment contained a huge library of royal photographs and appears

to have been the main target for the perpetrators. It appears too much of a coincidence that the burglary took place when it did to not be connected with her death. The property stolen indicates that the thief would have prior knowledge of the house or the VIW's business in that an older Apple computer was left at the scene whereas the standard computer burglar tends to take all computers which are present."

DS Freeman confirmed that he had said this.

"I consider that, on reflection, the comment was appropriate, given the facts as I saw them at the time the entry was made," he explained later.

According to Cherrault, when a crime prevention officer, Detective Constable William Kemp, came round on a follow-up visit, he said: "I am assuming you are not recording this conversation. I have examined your report. I have to tell you that you were not burgled but targeted."

"You mean the grey men?" said Cherrault, meaning intelligence agents.

The policeman replied: "MI5, Flying Squad or hired local hoodlums."

He also said: "Not to worry, your lives were not in any danger." Nevertheless, this upset Christine Cherrault who broke down in tears.

When questioned by officers from Operation Paget, DC Kemp denied mentioning MI5, the Flying Squad or hire hoodlums, but admitted saying something along the lines of what Cherrault had said.

"By this I meant that I was unhappy with the fact that it seemed to be too much of a coincidence that Diana had died in a car crash twenty-four hours before the burglary of a royal photographer," he said.

One of the stolen credit cards was used to make a call to Ireland and a stolen cheque, made out for £920, was presented at a bank in Suffolk.

The burglar had tried to take Cherrault's BMW but was foiled by the security system. Instead, he took Christine Cherrault's Mitsubishi Cruiser people carrier to transport the stolen items. It was found the following evening, parked near to the Stonebridge Park estate in north-west London, a few miles from the scene of the burglary. Cherrault was surprised when he heard that no fingerprints had been found in the vehicle, even though it had been used for the school run.

A DNA profile was later obtained from a cigarette butt found in the recovered vehicle. This matched a forty-two-year-old man who was a known criminal and had numerous convictions for theft and other offences. He was a drug addict and suspected crack cocaine dealer who lived with his mother just 300 yards (275 m) from the Cherraults' home. Early that year, he had been living with a man who had convictions for aggravated burglary just 400 yards (365 m) from where the Mitsubishi Cruiser was abandoned.

When the suspect was arrested, he denied being involved in the burglary and the theft of the vehicle, explaining that he may have accepted a lift in the vehicle not knowing it was stolen. A file was submitted to the Crown Prosecution Service (CPS), but the CPS recommended that no further action should be taken against him. There was no indication that the security services were involved.

Mohamed al-Fayed claimed that the offices of Darryn Lyons, the owner of the Big Picture Agency who had received pictures of the crash by ISDN line, had been burgled at around 11 p.m. on 31 August 1997. Operation Paget found that this was not true. However, on 4 September 1997, Lyons returned late to his office at night to find it in darkness. He called the police because, after a news item on television said the Big Picture Agency was trying to sell the photographs, the company received threatening phone calls. Like other agents, he had been sent photographs of the crash, but he decided not to publish them and handed the hard drive containing the photographs to the police. On 4 September, the police found that no property had been taken and there was no sign of a forced entry, but the cause of the power outage could not be identified. Again, there was no evidence of any involvement of the security services.

According to Mohamed al-Fayed, Princess Diana's body was embalmed in France before it was shipped back to conceal the fact that she was pregnant with Dodi's child. Operation Paget concluded that no pregnancy test was carried out in France or in Britain. The authorities had no requirement, or reason, to carry one out. There was nothing unusual about the embalming process and no reason to believe that it was done to conceal a pregnancy.

"The evidence shows that all involved in the decision to embalm the Princess of Wales believed it was necessary to make her body presentable before viewing," the Stevens Report concluded. "Jean Monceau, an experienced French embalmer, believed this was the only way to ensure the Princess of Wales was presentable. He discounted the use of dry ice or mortuary cleansing because of the extent of her injuries."

The report found that there was no evidence the Diana was pregnant or that she intended to announce her engagement to Dodi al-Fayed, beyond Mohamed al-Fayed's claim. Nor was there any evidence that Diana and Dodi were murdered by MI6 on the orders of the Duke of Edinburgh.

According to Mohamed al-Fayed, the matter could be cleared up by the Central Intelligence Agency and the National Security Agency, the United States' electronic eavesdropping service at Fort Meade, Maryland, which admitted having more than a thousand pages of information on Diana on file, but refused to release them on the grounds of national security. It is thought that the United States' interceptions of Diana's telephone conversations were shared with British intelligence and the royal family, and could have provided the motivation for her assassination.

THE MURDER OF MARILYN MONROE?

A T AROUND 4 A.M. on 5 August 1962, the naked body of one of the world's most beautiful woman was found face down in her bed at 12035 Fifth Helena Avenue in the Brentwood area of Los Angeles. Marilyn Monroe was dead. The coroner, Theodore Curphey, concluded that she had died from acute barbiturate poisoning and recorded her death as a "probable suicide". However, observation of the crime scene led others to a different conclusion. Sergeant Jack Clemmons, the first police-man to arrive at the scene, believed that she had been murdered.

Marilyn's body had been found by her psychoanalyst Ralph S. Greenson. The actress had tried to commit suicide before and there had been concern that she might have overdosed earlier in the evening. The previous night, her press agent Pat Newcomb had slept over, waking around noon. Marilyn had not slept well and was tetchy. Her day began with a series of threatening phone calls. An anonymous woman called to say: "Stay away from Bobby, you bitch."

At the time, her affair with President Kennedy had ended and his brother Robert Kennedy, the attorney general, had stepped into his shoes.

Marilyn had summoned Dr Greenson to her house and spent most of the afternoon with him, apart from the time she went for a drive with her housekeeper, Eunice Murray. While Marilyn had been alert in the morning, Greenson found her drugged and depressed. It is thought that she had taken Nembutal, the trade name of the barbiturate pentobarbital, prescribed for insomnia. Her prescription had just been filled by her physician Hyman Engelberg. Dr Greenson had been trying to wean Marilyn off Nembutal, moving her on to chloral hydrate as a sedative.

But Marilyn was dependent on Nembutal and there was plenty around the house.

Pat Newcomb left Marilyn's house at between 5.30 and 6 p.m., followed by Dr Greenson at around seven. Marilyn had just broken off her engagement to her former husband Joe DiMaggio – the couple had planned to remarry. At 7.15 p.m., DiMaggio's son Joe Jr called to discuss the broken engagement. He said that Marilyn sounded fine. Afterwards, her mood was elevated and she called Dr Greenson to tell him about the conversation.

The actor Peter Lawford phoned at about 7.45 p.m. to invite Marilyn to a party he was having at his beach house. He said she sounded heavily drugged. Her speech was slurred and became increasingly incomprehensible. He claimed that he had to shout her name into the phone a few times when she did not respond to his conversation and that some of the things she said could be construed as suicidal. According to Lawford, who was married to Patricia Kennedy, the sister of the president, Marilyn said: "Say goodbye to Pat, say goodbye to the president, and say goodbye to yourself, because you're a nice guy."

The call ended abruptly. Lawford tried to call her back, but got the busy signal. Concerned, Lawford called Eunice Murray, who was staying the night, on a different line and asked her to check on Marilyn. She returned to the telephone and told Lawford that Marilyn was fine. Unconvinced, Lawford was tempted to go around to the house but was persuaded not to by his friend and lawyer Mickey Rudin in case his presence there attracted bad publicity. Her behaviour at the studios had become increasingly erratic and the filming of *Something's Got to Give* had been suspended after she had turned up for just twelve of the thirty-five days of shooting. Earlier that year, Marilyn had famously sung "Happy Birthday" to President John F. Kennedy at Madison Square Garden in a dress that showed off her magnificent figure. Veteran diplomat Adlai Stevenson described the outfit as "skin and beads – only I didn't see the beads". Kennedy responded by saying: "I can now retire from politics after having, ah, 'Happy Birthday' sung to me in such a sweet, wholesome way." This public exchange fuelled speculation that they were having an affair. Nevertheless, Lawford kept phoning.

However, according to Eunice Murray, who overheard her on the phone, Marilyn sounded happier.

"Marilyn came to her bedroom door," said Murray. "I was sitting in the living room. And she said, 'Good night, Mrs Murray. I think I'll turn in now.' And she closed the door."

But at some point during the night, Marilyn called her friend, actress and model Jeanne Carmen.

"She wanted me to bring her over a couple of sleeping pills because she didn't have any," said Carmen. "I had had a few drinks and I just didn't think I could make it over there without getting arrested. So I said, 'Marilyn, I can't come over.'"

Rudin claimed that he called Eunice Murray at around 8.30 p.m. and asked her to check on Marilyn. Eunice said that she checked and Marilyn was fine. At around that time, Marilyn was thought to have spoken to her hairdresser Sidney Guilaroff and told him that she knew a lot of dangerous secrets about the Kennedys. Her lover, the Mexican writer-director José Bolaños, also said he called around 9.30 p.m., claiming that she told him "something shocking . . . that would shock the whole world". During the conversation, he said Marilyn laid down the phone without hanging up because she heard some kind of disturbance at her door.

Eunice Murray said that she walked past Marilyn's bedroom and saw light under the door at 10 p.m., but decided not to disturb her. This is puzzling as the deep-pile carpet would have prevented any light from showing. Natalie Trundy, who was at a concert at the Hollywood Bowl with her future husband, Monroe's publicist Arthur P. Jacobs, said that Jacobs had to leave hurriedly after Rudin informed him that Marilyn had overdosed. According to Donald Spoto, author of a 1993 biography of Monroe, Jacobs left to handle the press.

Lawford was out of the loop. Around 11 p.m., he called his friend Joe Naar who lived close to Marilyn and asked him to go to her house to make sure she had not overdosed. But just as Naar was getting ready to leave his house, he got a call from

Rudin telling him not to go as Marilyn had been given a sedative by Dr Greenson.

At midnight, Eunice Murray again said that she saw a light under Marilyn's bedroom door. This time she knocked, but got no reply. She said that she tried the door, but it was locked. Others said that there was no functioning lock on the door. Worried, she called Dr Greenson. Later, she said she went back to bed after seeing the light under the door at midnight, only calling Dr Greenson at 3 a.m. after seeing that the light was still on.

When Dr Greenson arrived, he tried to break open the door but failed. So he went outside to look through the French windows. He saw Monroe lying on the bed holding the telephone, apparently dead. The French windows were locked, so he broke the glass, opened the door and checked Marilyn for signs of life. He then called Dr Engelberg. There was some speculation that an ambulance might have been called to the house at this point and later dismissed.

When Dr Engelberg arrived, he also examined Marilyn.

"She was sprawled over the bed, and she was dead," Dr Engelberg said. "I took out my stethoscope to make sure her heart wasn't beating. Checked her pupils because that's one of the sensitive ways to tell if a person is dead or not. I said she was dead. Which, of course, Dr Greenson knew anyway, but I had to go through the motions."

Dr Engelberg told investigators that he waited up to half an hour before calling the police. Asked why there was a delay, Dr Engelberg said: "We were stunned. We were talking over what happened. What she had said."

At 1 a.m., Rudin told Lawford that Marilyn was dead, but the police were not called until after 4 a.m. Dr Greenson and Dr Engelberg told the police that Marilyn died at around 12.30 a.m. They later amended that to 3.50 a.m.

When Sergeant Clemmons arrived at around 4.30 a.m., Dr Greenson and Eunice Murray led him to Marilyn's bedroom where he found her face down on the bed.

"She was lying face down in what I call the soldier's position," said Sergeant Clemmons. "Her face was in a pillow, her arms were by her side, her right arm was slightly bent. Her legs were stretched out perfectly straight."

It immediately struck him that she had been placed that way. He had seen a number of suicides. He knew that an overdose of sleeping tablets usually causes victims to suffer convulsions and vomiting before they die in a contorted position.

"It was not a suicide," Clemmons later told the BBC. "Marilyn Monroe was murdered and there's no question about it."

Marilyn was naked and her left hand was stretched out touching the telephone on the nightstand. It is not known who she had been calling. Also on the nightstand were a number of bottles of prescription drugs. Clemmons noted there was no drinking glass. Eunice Murray explained that there was no running water in the room. Marilyn was known to have trouble swallowing pills, gagging on them even when she had water to wash them down. Later, a glass was found lying on the floor by the bed, but police claim it was not there when the room was first searched.

The room was extremely tidy and there was fresh linen on the bed. Clemmons noticed that the housekeeper had done the laundry that night and questioned her about this odd behaviour. Appearing nervous, she said that she knew the coroner would seal up the house as a crime scene and she wanted to make sure everything was neat and tidy. Clemmons also noticed that Marilyn's body was in an advanced state of rigor mortis, which indicated that she had been dead for at least six hours. When questioned, the police noted that Eunice Murray was vague and evasive. She changed her story several times. Although she was a key witness, she took off to Europe and was not questioned again.

Clemmons found Engelberg and Greenson little more convincing. They claimed that Marilyn's body had been discovered some four hours earlier, but that they could not contact the police until 20th Century Fox's publicity department had given them the OK.

At 5.40 a.m., undertaker Guy Hockett arrived. He too noted that rigor mortis had already set in, indicating a time of death between 9.30 and 11.30. the previous evening. Later, he changed his estimated time of death to match the other witness statements.

Marilyn's body was taken to the morgue where an autopsy was performed by pathologist Dr Thomas Noguchi, the deputy medical examiner and coroner for the county of Los Angeles. In his report he remarked that he performed the post-mortem examination on the unembalmed body of a well-developed, well-nourished thirty-six-year-old Caucasian female weighing 117 lbs (53 kg) and measuring $65^1/_2$ in. (1.66 m) in length. She had bleached blonde hair and blue eyes. He noted a fixed lividity – a purplish discolouration that occurs when the blood is no longer being circulated by the heart – in the face, neck, chest, upper portions of arms and the right side of the abdomen. But he also noted a faint lividity in her back and the back of her arms and legs, which disappears with pressure. This would indicate that she had been laid on her back at some point after she was dead.

A slight ecchymotic area – that is, bruising – was noted in the left hip and left side of the lower back. There was no significant damage to the breasts. Dr Noguchi found a 3 in. (8 cm) horizontal surgical scar in the right upper quadrant of the abdomen and a 5 in. (13 cm) surgical scar above the pubic area. The mucus membrane around the eyes was congested, but there was no sign of bleeding or bruising.

Dr Noguchi then noted: "The nose shows no evidence of fracture. The external auditory canals are not remarkable. No evidence of trauma is noted in the scalp, forehead, cheeks, lips or chin. The neck shows no evidence of trauma. Examination of the hands and nails shows no defects. The lower extremities show no evidence of trauma."

He then cut open the chest and abdomen, and found no excess of fluid or blood inside. All the organs appeared undamaged and in the right place. Her heart weighed 300 g. The pericardial cavity around it contained no excess of fluid and everything was as it should be.

The right lung weighed 465 g and the left 420 g. Both lungs were moderately congested with fluid, but otherwise appeared healthy. The liver weighed 1,890 g. It was damaged where the gall bladder had been removed. There was a slight accentuation of its lobe pattern, but no haemorrhage or tumour was found. The liver temperature taken at 10.30 a.m. was 89°F (32°C).

The spleen weighed 190 g and showed some sign of abnormality, though no enlargement of the lymph nodes. The bone marrow was dark red in colour. The adrenal and thyroid glands appeared normal. The kidneys together weighed 350 g. The tissue was "moderately congested". The bladder contained approximately 150 ml of clear, straw-coloured fluid.

The brain weighed 1,440 g. There was no evidence of contusion or haemorrhage. The skull was not fractured. While the superficial vessels are slightly congested, there was no blood in the cavity and everything else appeared normal. The clavicle, ribs, vertebrae and pelvic bones showed fracture lines, but all the bones of the extremities were examined and showed no evidence of fracture.

"The external genitalia shows no gross abnormality," the autopsy report continued. "Distribution of the pubic hair is of female pattern." The uterus was of the usual size with no polyps or tumours. The cervix was clear with no cysts. The fallopian tubes were intact, though the ovaries showed some signs of disease.

The stomach was almost completely empty and contained no more than 20 ml of brownish mucus. Curiously, Dr Noguchi found no residue from the pills she was thought to have taken. She had no duodenal ulcers and her appendix was missing. However, her colon showed "marked congestion and purplish discolouration".

Blood was taken to be examined for alcohol and barbiturates. Her liver, kidneys, stomach and its contents, urine and intestines were saved for further toxicological study and a vaginal smear was taken. The toxicologist found high levels of Nembutal and chloral hydrate in her blood. It was estimated that she had taken thirty-eight to sixty-six tablets of Nembutal and fourteen to twenty-three tablets of chloral hydrate – enough to kill ten people. However, Dr Noguchi found no trace of capsules, powder or the typical discolouration caused by Nembutal in

Monroe's stomach or intestines, indicating the drugs that killed her had not been swallowed. There was no sign of a puncture wound, so they had not been administered intravenously. The only other way they could have got into her body was via a suppository or enema. But those would have had to have been prepared, if not administered by someone else. However, Dr Noguchi eventually put aside his qualms and accepted that the drugs must have been swallowed.

Just twelve days after her death, the coroner announced that her death was probably suicide. But suspicion lingered on. There were allegations that there had been a cover-up and in 1982, twenty years after she died, the Los Angeles District Attorney's office began to re-examine the evidence. The first question to answer was: was she murdered?

"We looked at the photographs of the death scene," said former Assistant District Attorney Mike Carroll. "Looked at autopsy reports. And had to talk to people because there were some areas that we could not really determine without talking to people."

Dr Engelberg was asked if he had prescribed the large number of pills found on Marilyn's nightstand.

"No. Only one had been prescribed by me," he said. "I was surprised to see at the side of her bed a large number of other sleeping pills."

Dr Engelberg said that he had only prescribed the Nembutal.

"I knew nothing about any chloral hydrate," he said. "I never used chloral hydrate."

If Marilyn had all those pills by her bedside, why did she call Jeanne Carmen to ask for more? And if she had deliberately overdosed, why had she left no suicide note?

Top forensic pathologist Dr Steven Karch said that major omissions in the toxicology report make it almost impossible to determine what killed her – and he did not rule out murder.

"I'm bothered by some of the inconsistencies in the reports," he said. "I'm particularly bothered by where the medicines came from. I don't know that they were hers. I don't know when they were taken, and I don't know what was in her body when she died because the toxicology is incomplete."

Karch thought that there had been a rush to judgement. Her death was thought to be a suicide almost from the moment she was found.

"The really strange thing is, it says barbiturate overdose death," he said. "How did they know it was a barbiturate overdose death at 4.45 in the morning?"

But for Mike Carroll it was a natural assumption to make at the scene.

"The bottles were there," he said. "She was unconscious. She had a history of overdose. In fact, she had a history of not only overdosing, but of being resuscitated."

However, Dr Engelberg played down the idea that Marilyn had made earlier attempts to take her own life.

"I'm not aware of any deliberate suicide attempt," he said. "I was only aware of the one time when she currently had too much to drink and had taken possibly slightly more than she should have. But that was not a serious attempt."

During his re-examination of the case, Carroll found no rush to judgement – there had been nothing hurried about Dr Noguchi's autopsy. Even so, he had the post-mortem report reviewed by an outside expert.

"He looked over the documents and he told us that this was a very competent and professional job considering the state of science at the time in 1962," said Carroll.

However, Dr Noguchi himself was not happy with his findings. Soon after, he decided to re-examine the tissue samples he had taken, but they were missing and have never been found. So was this evidence of a cover-up or, at the very least, deliberate destruction of evidence?

"Yeah, I think that's fertile grounds for people to say, 'Oh boy, we got it now. We have a smoking gun,'" said Carroll. "And my experience of the loss of material like that, it's unfortunately pretty common."

Carroll also interviewed a man named Rick Stone, who claimed that he was a paramedic in an ambulance called to Marilyn's house. He said he watched a doctor inject something into the dying movie star.

"He opened up a doctor's bag and took out a hypodermic syringe that was already filled and injected it into her heart," Stone said.

However, Noguchi had made a thorough search of Marilyn's body for needle marks, but found none.

"He put a needle in her heart," Stone later told CBS's *48 Hours*. "I guarantee it. I was looking right at it."

Set against Stone's account is the testimony of Ken Hunter, an ambulanceman who was believed to have been there that night. Asked whether a doctor plunged a needle into the area of Marilyn's heart, Hunter told Carroll: "That's bullshit."

No needle mark was found and the injection of a lethal dose of barbiturates would have left clear bruising.

Curiously, Hunter told Carroll that, when he saw her, Marilyn had been lying on her side, while Clemmons had found her lying face down and concluded that the body had been positioned, the scene manipulated and Marilyn had been murdered. Carroll dismissed Clemmons line of reasoning.

"His opinion was not based on any kind of personal, professional training or experience," said Carroll. "He was not a detective. He was not an experienced detective and certainly not a homicide detective."

Carroll concluded that the mystery surrounding what happened that night stems from the conflicting accounts given by Eunice Murray and the timeline of events.

"The investigator at the scene did have some concerns about Mrs Murray," said Carroll. "He thought that her answers were evasive, and that she might have either been distressed or hiding something."

The police were called at 4.25 a.m. on the morning of 5 August 1962, but allegations persist that Murray raised the alarm much earlier.

"There was some form of cover-up surrounding the circumstances of her death," said author Anthony Summers, who has written of the death of Marilyn Monroe in two books, *Goddess: The Secret Lives of Marilyn Monroe* and *Official and Confidential:*

The Secret Life of J. Edgar Hoover. At the centre of the cover-up were the Kennedy brothers.

Actress Jeanne Carmen had first-hand knowledge of Marilyn's affair with John F. Kennedy as it unfolded in Peter Lawford's Santa Monica beach house.

"President Kennedy and Marilyn were in bed when I went in to take my shower, just cuddle, cuddle, cuddle," she recalled. And she was not the only one who knew. FBI director J. Edgar Hoover had the place bugged.

Marilyn believed that, after he was re-elected, Kennedy would divorce his wife Jacqueline and marry her. This was not going to happen. As one Washington insider put it: "Marilyn Monroe was just another cup of coffee to Jack."

After the very public display of singing "Happy Birthday" in Madison Square Garden, Kennedy knew that he must distance himself from her and Robert Kennedy moved in.

"I think Marilyn Monroe was in love with John Kennedy for a while," said Jeanne Carmen. "Then I think she fell in love with Bobby."

In February 1962, Marilyn and Eunice Murray went to Mexico on vacation where they met Eunice's brother-in-law, Churchill Murray, who was living there with a group of openly communist Americans. She spent time with them, talking politics late into the night.

"Marilyn Monroe wasn't a dumb blonde," said Summers. "She devoured books on politics. She liked to talk to people about politics."

The conversations were monitored and the FBI opened a file on Monroe. It was the height of the Cold War and a woman who had access to the president and the attorney general, and was openly consorting with communists, was considered a security risk. Just months before the Cuban missile crisis, the FBI recorded Kennedy and Marilyn discussing the morality of atom-bomb testing over lunch at the beach house. What's more, Hoover did not get on with his boss, Robert Kennedy, who could not understand why his brother did not fire him.

"Discussing nuclear matters at a time of horrendous international crisis, if anything like that would have got out, it would have been enormously damaging to the Kennedys," said Summers.

On Saturday, 4 August 1962, President Kennedy was on the East Coast, while Robert Kennedy was in northern California. His host insisted that he was there the entire weekend, but the former chief of the LAPD Daryl Gates said that Robert Kennedy travelled to Los Angeles.

"Our records show that he was in Los Angeles and probably that information came to our intelligence function through the FBI," said Gates. But he did not think that Kennedy visited Marilyn. "Had he gone to see Marilyn that day, I think we would have known it."

However, Deborah Gould, Peter Lawford's third wife, said she was told that Robert Kennedy had gone to see Marilyn that day to end the relationship.

"Marilyn, from what Peter told me, knew then that it was over," said Gould. "That was it, over. Final. And she was very, very distraught and depressed."

According to Summers: "There was what you might call a benign cover-up, not a cover-up of a murder, but a cover-up to protect prominent people."

Jeanne Carmen said that Marilyn kept a diary, detailing her relationship with John and Robert Kennedy. No diary was found. Deborah Gould said Lawford told her that he had made an early morning sweep through Marilyn's house.

"He said he went there, he tidied up the place and did what he could before the reporters found out about the death," she said.

According to Summers, the FBI seized the telephone company's records, so he has never been able to discover who she was calling when she died. However, in the weeks leading up to her death, she called the Justice Department, where Robert Kennedy worked, eight times.

Most of the police records have also disappeared. They were "destroyed in compliance with departmental procedures," an official said.

But Dr Karch believes that the mystery can still be solved. All it would take is for someone to open her crypt at the Westwood Village Memorial Park Cemetery, take a few strands of her famously bleached-blonde hair and test it for poisons or paralysing drugs. Dr Karch was also interested in the drugs found at her bedside, saying that the peach-coloured pills in one bottle have never been identified.

Although Carroll's investigation did not go as far as opening the crypt, he concluded that she was not murdered by the Kennedys or anyone else.

"We uncovered absolutely no evidence of an intentional criminal act with respect to her death," he said. "No evidence of their involvement in her death ever came up with the exception that she was despondent. The cause of her despondency could have been one of the brothers. But in terms of involvement with a criminal activity, absolutely none."

Newly released papers say that Marilyn had secretly obtained a large stock of Nembutal and chloral hydrate. So her death was either suicide or an accident.

"If there was no murder, there was nothing to cover up except embarrassing information or connections," said Carroll. Although he admits that her death had political implications for the Kennedys, that lay beyond the scope of his investigation.

Theories of how Marilyn met her death abound. In 1985, the BBC produced the documentary, *The Last Days of Marilyn Monroe*, later shown in the United States under the title, *Say Goodbye to the President*. In it, Eunice Murray said: "When the doctor arrived, she was not dead."

Off camera, the narrator Anthony Summers heard her say: "Why, at my age, do I still have to cover this thing?"

In his 1993 biography of Monroe, author Donald Spoto concluded that Dr Greenson arranged for Marilyn to have a chloral hydrate enema to help her sleep, unaware that Hyman Engelberg was still prescribing Nembutal. According to Milton Rudin, on the night of her death, Greenson said: "God damn it. Hy gave her a prescription I didn't know about." The two drugs working together killed her.

Dr Engelberg was having marital difficulties at the time and failed to inform Greenson that he was still prescribing Nembutal. Spoto believes that the enema was administered by Eunice Murray who, like Greenson, had no idea that it would be fatal. Consequently, Greenson, Engelberg and Murray – the three people on the scene when the police turned up – all had reasons to avoid telling the truth to the authorities.

Spoto said that this account of Marilyn's death was supported by the autopsy report.

In Marilyn's blood count, "there were eight milligrams of chloral hydrate and four and a half milligrams of Nembutal," he said, "but in her liver there was a count of thirteen milligrams, a much higher concentration of Nembutal."

Spoto maintained that the ratio of Nembutal found in the blood compared to that in the liver suggested that Marilyn lived for many hours after the ingestion of that drug. While Marilyn was alive and mobile during the day, her body was metabolizing the Nembutal. It had ended up in the liver, which was removing it from her blood stream and beginning the process of excretion. The barbiturates that killed her were absorbed over a period of not minutes but hours. This was consistent with what Greenson called her "somewhat drugged" condition. That the final overdose was administered by an enema was indicated by the "purplish discolouration" of the colon.

According to Donald Wolfe, author of *The Last Days of Marilyn Monroe* in 1998, published as *The Assassination of Marilyn Monroe* in the UK, Marilyn knew something that could possibly bring down President Kennedy. She knew of his involvement with Sam Giancana, the mafioso who had helped him get elected in 1960. They even shared a girlfriend, Judith Campbell Exner. Wolfe said that Eunice Murray's son-in-law Norman Jefferies was also in Marilyn's house on the evening of 4 August. According to Wolfe, Jefferies claimed that between 9.30 and 10 p.m., Robert Kennedy and two other men came to the door and ordered them to leave the house. Jefferies said they went to a neighbour's home and waited until the men left at around 10.30 p.m. When they returned, Jefferies said that he saw

Marilyn naked, lying face down on her bed. She looked like she was dead. Eunice called an ambulance and then called Dr Greenson. Jefferies said he then saw Lawford and Pat Newcomb arrive at the house. In a panic, they called Robert Kennedy. The ambulance company chief said that Marilyn was in fact in a coma when the ambulance arrived. She was taken to Santa Monica Hospital, where she died. Her body was returned to her house as part of a cover-up.

Jefferies's account is partly corroborated by Marilyn's neighbour Elizabeth Pollard. She told police that she saw Robert Kennedy with two unidentified men approach Marilyn's house at about 6 or 7 p.m. One of them was carrying a black medical case.

According to Wolfe, Pollard's story was discredited by police and left out of their account of the investigation. However, Pollard was not alone. Anthony Summers said that she was playing cards with several friends who all recognized Kennedy when he drove up to Marilyn's house.

In 2005, former Los Angeles County District Attorney John Milner told the *Los Angeles Times* that Marilyn was not suicidal, citing tapes that she had recorded for Dr Greenson that Greenson had played him. The following year, CBS's *48 Hours* confirmed that Marilyn did have an affair with John Kennedy – and possibly Robert Kennedy – and that she was considered a security risk by the FBI.

Later FBI documents released under the Freedom of Information Act confirmed Marilyn's affair with Robert Kennedy and that he had promised to leave his wife and marry her. Among the documents, Australian film director Philippe Mora said that he found evidence that Marilyn was tricked into killing herself as part of a plot hatched by Robert Kennedy. It was in a report, dated 19 October 1964, written by a former FBI special agent and headed "Robert F. Kennedy". The agent maintained that she was given the means to fake a suicide attempt to gain sympathy and went ahead on the understanding that she would be found in time and have her stomach pumped.

Instead, those in on the conspiracy – Peter Lawford, Dr Greenson, Eunice Murray and Pat Newcomb – left her to die.

The motive was to silence Monroe, who had realized that Robert Kennedy was not going to leave his wife and threatened to go public about their affair. Monroe also believed that Kennedy had reneged on his pledge to "take care of everything" after her contract with 20th Century Fox was cancelled and they had "unpleasant words" on the phone.

The report says that that Lawford "knew from Marilyn's friends that she often made suicide attempts and that she was inclined to fake a suicide attempt in order to arouse sympathy". He had made "special arrangements" with Greenson, who wrote a prescription for sixty tablets of Seconal. This prescription was "unusual in quantity", the report says. Eunice Murray left the pills on Monroe's nightstand.

When Robert Kennedy returned to San Francisco, the report says, he "made a telephone call to Peter Lawford to find out if Marilyn was dead yet". Lawford called once and spoke to Monroe, "then checked again later to make sure she did not answer". According to the report, Eunice Murray then called Dr Greenson to tell him that Marilyn had taken the pills.

"Marilyn expected to have her stomach pumped and get sympathy for her suicide attempt," it continued. "The psychiatrist left word for Marilyn to take a drive in the fresh air but did not come to see her until after she was known to be dead."

Within forty-eight hours of Marilyn being found dead, the report says, Peter Lawford and Pat Newcomb flew to the Kennedy compound at Hyannisport, Massachusetts.

The former agent warned that he could not evaluate the authenticity of the information. However, the report was circulated to five top FBI officers, including J. Edgar Hoover and his deputy Clyde Tolson.

Mora said that he was not sure what to make of the report.

"Is all this the elaborate dirty tricks of Kennedy haters from decades ago, or are we getting closer to the historical truth?" he said.

Then in 2011 came the extraordinary claim that Marilyn had spent her last evening alive in Frank Sinatra's lodge on Lake Tahoe, Nevada, with Mafia boss Sam Giancana, who made a last ditch attempt to stop her going public about her affairs with the Kennedys. She had been flown there on board Sinatra's private jet.

The claim was made on tapes recorded by George Masters, Monroe's hair and make-up stylist, in the month before his death in 1998. The cassettes were found by his nephew, sixty-year-old sales consultant Jeff Platts. In a frail voice, Masters can be heard on the recordings saying: "The night before she died, the last time I saw her, was in Lake Tahoe at the Cal-Neva Lodge. She was there with Sam Giancana, who was the head of the Mafia."

Masters flew back to Los Angeles with Marilyn and dropped her off at her home at around 9 a.m. It has been documented that Marilyn had been at Sinatra's lakeside lodge two weekends before her death. According to Masters, she was called back for a one-to-one chat with Giancana, a friend of Sinatra.

Platt said: "George specifically told me that Marilyn spent the evening with Sam Giancana. The only other person he mentioned that was there was [the singer] Buddy Greco. No Frank Sinatra, no Dean Martin. George also said that the person she was really in love with at that moment was Sam Giancana."

On the tapes, Masters made clear why he thought she died.

"It was because of the Kennedys," he said. "I really think the FBI did it."

He also said that she had been moved both before and after she died.

"Did you know she was pronounced dead," he said, "and then they brought her back to the house, and she was still alive, and they took her back to the hospital, and brought her back home, and then the coroners came over, and they found her dead in another bed – somebody moved her?"

However implausible that may seem, even more bizarre conspiracy theories circulate. In one, Marilyn was pregnant. Although she had been seeing other men, she was sure that the father was either John or Robert Kennedy. After she called the Justice Department to tell Robert, he changed the phone number so she could not call again. Peter Lawford was left to sort out the mess. He took Marilyn to Lake Tahoe to have an abortion. There is even some suggestion that she was kidnapped and underwent the termination forcibly, but she was too full of drugs and booze at the time to tell the difference. She attended some orgies there with Lawford and Sinatra and was filmed, possibly to blackmail her into keeping quiet about her affairs with the Kennedys. By then, she was drinking champagne all day, after breakfasting on Bloody Marys and amphetamines.

An ambulance was seen outside her bungalow before the alarm had been raised. A helicopter was heard overhead and friends who tried to investigate her death independently received death threats.

THE OKLAHOMA CITY BOMBING

JUST AFTER 9 A.M. on 19 April 1995, a yellow Ryder Rental truck pulled into a parking area outside the Alfred P. Murrah Building, the US Federal Government complex at 200 NW Fifth Street in Oklahoma City. The driver stepped down from the truck's cab and casually walked away. Two minutes later, at 9.02 a.m., the truck exploded, destroying one-third of the nine-storey building, killing 168 people, including nineteen children, and injuring 800 more with 490 hospitalized. One unborn child was also killed. It was the most deadly act of terrorism on American soil before 9/11.

The blast was so powerful it lifted pedestrians from the ground. One Japanese tourist said that it was "worse than the worst quake because there was no initial warning, no noise to say something terrible is going to happen. It just hit."

The truck had been loaded with 5,000 lbs (2,268 kg) of home-made explosives. It created a fireball that briefly outshone the sun. Inside the building, a few lucky people had been away from their desks fetching coffee or delivering documents to another part of the building. But those in the offices above the blast stood no chance. The children's day-care centre next to the bomb was devastated. Upper floors fell on those beneath them, causing a progressive collapse that crushed everything and everyone below. The north side of the building crumpled, sending deadly shards of glass flying that maimed passers-by blocks away. The windows were shattered in 258 buildings nearby. The broken glass alone was responsible for 5 per cent of the deaths and 69 per cent of the injuries outside the Murrah Building.

The explosion made a crater 8 ft (2.4 m) deep and 30 ft (9.1 m) wide. Traffic signs and parking meters were ripped from the sidewalk. The blast damaged or destroyed 324 buildings within a sixteen-block radius. Ten collapsed at the time and a further thirteen were later condemned as unsafe. The explosion destroyed or burnt eighty-six cars, causing further explosions from the vehicles' gas tanks and tyres. It could be heard and felt up to 55 miles (89 km) away. Seismometers at Science Museum Oklahoma in Oklahoma City, 4.3 miles (6.9 km) away, and in Norman, Oklahoma, 16.1 miles (25.9 km) away, registered 3.0 on the Richter scale. Three square miles (7.8 km^2) of downtown Oklahoma City were devastated, leaving hundreds of people homeless and closing down scores of businesses; 50,000 people had to be evacuated. In all, the Oklahoma City bombing was estimated to have caused at least $652 million worth of damage. The Murrah Building, which had to be demolished, was alone worth $30 million.

Sirens blared as rescue workers rushed to the scene. The first were there within two minutes. Firefighters, ambulance men and volunteers alike clawed through the rubble to dig out the wounded and remove the dead. A command post was set up in a parking lot at NW Sixth Street and Harvey.

Immediately following the blast, the Oklahoma City Police Department Headquarters, which itself had been damaged, was evacuated. A bomb search was conducted, but no device was found. Civilian personnel were permitted to return to their assignments or go to a blood institute and donate blood. A temporary morgue was set up in the playground of the Murrah Building's day-care centre. Later it was moved to the first Methodist Church located at NW Fourth and Robinson.

A 10.28 a.m., it was reported that there might be another explosive device in the debris. Rescue crews and volunteers fled the scene. The police evacuated an area of four blocks. The police then seized the chance to secure an inner crime scene perimeter one block around the Murrah Building. Forty minutes later an outer perimeter was established several blocks further out. When no bomb was found, rescue operations resumed at 11.25 a.m. By then the police limited access to essential rescue, medical and construction workers, along with law enforcement personnel.

The FBI assumed jurisdiction over the crime scene, the collection of evidence and criminal investigation. Meanwhile, detectives began arriving at the command post. They attempted to locate and interview any person who may have been a witness to the explosion. They also searched the immediate area in an effort to locate surveillance cameras and went around the hospitals to locate and interview the injured. Five detectives were assigned to phone lines to gather information from the public calling to provide details on suspects. The Oklahoma City Police Department also assigned officers to liaise with the FBI and US Attorney's office.

Technical investigation officers arrived with the crime scene van. They brought with them all available crime scene tape, latex gloves, cameras, film and other supplies, such as disinfectant soaps and evidence bags. One entered the building to help rescue the children while others taped off the area and established a triage area. Photolab personnel began photographing the area and aerials shots were taken from a helicopter within the first hour. Technical investigations personnel were also assigned to the temporary morgue where they fingerprinted and photographed the victims. Some went to the homes of suspected victims to collect fingerprints for comparison. Over 1,100 photographs were taken.

The command post was moved several times, ending up in the parking lot of One Bell Central when Southwest Bell provided the command team with all the landlines from its building.

Sniffer dogs searched the rubble and specialist listening gear that could detect a human heartbeat was brought in. Every so often, the site would fall silent in an effort to locate anyone still living. The listening gear found one buried woman, Dana Bradley, as she cried for help. For five hours the twenty-year-old lay bleeding in a foot of water with her leg pinned under a pile of shattered concrete. It could not be shifted. The rest of the building threatened to collapse. Its shaking had already temporarily driven the rescue workers from the scene once. Dr Gary Massad then faced a terrible choice. He had either to amputate her leg or let her bleed to death. Worse, as an anaesthetic could induce a fatal coma, the amputation would have to be done while Dana was fully conscious.

Dana Bradley survived. She was dragged from the ruins and rushed to hospital. But she had lost more than part of her leg as a result of the bombing; she also lost her mother and two young children.

At 4.30 p.m., President Clinton held a press conference in Washington, DC, and declared the bomb site and its surroundings a Federal Disaster Area. He mobilized the National Guard. That Sunday, he attended a memorial service in the State Fairgrounds Arena and the police went on a recruitment drive. On Monday, 24 April, the police began releasing vehicles and personal effects from within the outer perimeter. Business owners were allowed limited access to survey damage and to begin repairs. The Oklahoma City Police Department and the FBI issued over 20,000 assorted access passes and released 432 vehicles from within the perimeter. Auto-theft investigators were brought in to identify the eighty-six cars destroyed by the blast and the ensuing fires.

Rescue and recovery work had to be halted several times as high winds threatened to topple damaged buildings. But over the next seventeen days, rescue crews sifted through the debris to remove rubble in search of victims. As bodies were located, police and personnel from the medical examiner's office placed them in the temporary morgue. Later, they were transported to the State Medical Examiner's Office for identification. There, teams of technical investigation personnel used fingerprints, DNA profiling, X-rays, and medical and dental records. Of the 168 dead, 109 were identified by fingerprints.

Between 19 April and 5 May, 165 bodies were recovered. The Murrah Building was demolished by implosion on 23 May. The bodies of another three victims were recovered on 29 May from an area deemed to be too unstable for recovery while the building still stood. Then on 30 May, a severed leg was found, leading investigators to believe there may be one more victim. It was eventually identified as the leg of Lakesha Levy, a female member of the Air Force who had been killed in the bombing. Levy's coffin had to be reopened so that her leg could replace another unmatched leg that had been buried with her remains. The unmatched leg had been embalmed, so it was impossible to identify the leg's real owner. Meanwhile, forensic teams from the FBI and Oklahoma City Police Department bomb technicians moved in to shift over 460 tons of debris, looking for crime scene evidence.

Some 238 personnel from the Oklahoma City Police Department were on duty at the site each day, along with 258 officials from seventy-three municipal agencies, eight sheriffs' departments, eight different state agencies and the National Guard.

Fifty-two persons were arrested on or near the site between 19 April and 5 May, mostly on misdemeanour charges including public drunkenness, trespassing, obstructing officers, traffic offences, curfew violations, outstanding warrants and one theft. Those arrested included several representatives of the media caught trespassing in unauthorized areas.

Twenty Oklahoma City police officers were injured in the incident, though only three were hospitalized. The remainder were treated and released or filed an injury report to document their exposure to smoke, dust and asbestos. Two officers were involved in vehicle accidents while responding to the incident. Following the demolition of the Murrah Building, one bomb technician was sent to hospital to be treated for stress and chest pains. To manage the Oklahoma City crime scene, the police put in 47,821 work hours, costing $1,122,726.

While the forensic teams went about the business of collecting crime scene evidence, there was no great mystery as to who had committed the crime. The man who had planted the bomb was in custody within ninety minutes. He had been arrested by veteran Oklahoma patrol officer Trooper Charlie Hanger on an entirely different matter. After the bombing, Hanger had initially been ordered to Oklahoma City, but was then told to stay on his normal patrol in Noble County. He was about 75 miles (120 km) away, near Perry, Oklahoma, when he saw a yellow 1977 Mercury Grand Marquis without any licence plates.

Hanger pulled the car over. In it was Timothy McVeigh. He was wearing a T-shirt with a picture of Abraham Lincoln on it and the words "*sic semper tyrannis*" – "thus always to tyrants". This is the state motto of Virginia and were also the words John Wilkes Booth shouted after he shot Lincoln. On the back, it had a picture of a tree watered by droplets of blood and a quote from Thomas Jefferson: "The tree of liberty must be refreshed from time to time with the blood of patriots and tyrants."

Hanger asked McVeigh why he had no licence plates. McVeigh said he had just bought the car. He had no bill of sale or insurance, explaining that they had been posted to his home address. But he did have a driver's licence. It carried the address of James Nichols in Decker, Michigan.

The officer then noticed that McVeigh had a gun under his jacket. He pulled out his own pistol and confiscated McVeigh's 9 mm Glock, along with a knife and an ammunition clip. McVeigh complained that he had a licence to carry a concealed weapon. Hanger pointed out that McVeigh's New York licence was not valid in Oklahoma. He handcuffed McVeigh and put him in the back of his patrol car. He then searched McVeigh's car and found a commentary by seventeenth-century English philosopher John Locke, copied by hand, asserting that a man has a right to kill anyone who would take away his liberty. Along with it was a photocopy of a passage from *The Turner Diaries*, a novel written by William Luther Pierce, founder of the white nationalist organization National Alliance, under the pseudonym Andrew Macdonald. A favourite of the far right, the book tells the story of white supremacists who blow up the FBI headquarters in Washington, DC, with a truck bomb one morning at 9.15, as part of a war to overthrow the federal government and exterminate African-Americans, Jews and "race traitors". The passage photocopied said the purpose of the fictional bombing was to wake up America.

Hanger then drove McVeigh to Noble County jail in Perry. On the way, McVeigh managed to hide a business card belonging to military-supply dealer Dave Paulson. On the back, McVeigh had written "TNT $5/stick need more" and "Call after 01 May, see if I can get some."

At Noble County jail, McVeigh was charged with four misdemeanours – failing to display current licence plates, failing to carry proof of insurance, unlawfully carrying a weapon and transporting a loaded firearm in a motor vehicle. Normally, these charges would have been dealt with quickly and McVeigh would have been out on bail. But the local judge was tied up in a protracted divorce case and his bail hearing was held over until 21 April.

The FBI profilers got to work, trying to work out who the bombers might be. The United States was unused to acts of domestic terrorism. Their first thought was that the culprits were the group of Islamic terrorists who had tried to blow up the World Trade Center in New York two years earlier. Another possibility was that the bomb had been planted by a drugs cartel and was aimed at the Drugs Enforcement Administration that had an office in the Murrah Building. Psychological profiler Clinton R. Van Zandt had been an FBI negotiator at the siege in Waco, Texas, where David Koresh and the Branch Davidians held off the federal authorities for fifty days. Van Zandt noticed that the day of the bombing, 19 April 1995, was two years to the day since the siege had ended with a fire and firefight that killed seventy-six people, including more than twenty children. Terrorism expert Louis R. Mizell Jr also noted that the date was the anniversary of the Battles of Lexington and Concord, the first military engagements of the American Revolutionary War, commemorated as Patriot's Day and revered by the growing militia movement. And 19 April 1995 itself was the day that white supremacist Richard Snell was executed for the murder of a pawn-shop owner who he believed to be Jewish. He also killed black Arkansas State Trooper Louis P. Bryant. It is also alleged that he plotted to blow up a gas pipeline near Fulton, Arkansas, and the Murrah Building in Oklahoma City.

Meanwhile, crime scene evidence came into play. When the truck exploded, the rear axle flew through the air and crashed into the hood of a Ford Festiva belonging to Richard Nichols, injuring his wife and nephew. The vehicle identification number on the axle and remnants of the licence place found on the mangled bumper led agents to Elliott's Body Shop, a Ryder Rental outlet in Junction City, Kansas. The truck had been rented to one Robert Kling. This was the name of a soldier who McVeigh had known in the army.

Eldon Elliott, the owner of Elliot's Body Shop, helped sketch artists produce two drawings – one of the man who rented the truck, the second of another man who had been in the rental office at the same time. The picture of the man calling himself Kling was recognized by Lea McGown, the manager of the Dreamland motel. She said he had arrived in a yellow Marquis. Later, he had parked a large Ryder truck in the motel's parking lot and he had signed in under the name Timothy McVeigh. It was odd that McVeigh signed in under his real name when he had hired the truck under an alias, but McGown had an explanation. The motel was used by prostitutes and their customers, and she had learnt how to spot men who signed in under a false name.

"People are so used to signing their own name," she said, "that when they go to sign a phoney name, they almost always go to write, and then look up for a moment as if to remember the new name they want to use. That's what he did, and when he looked up I started talking to him, and it threw him."

McVeigh had also given the address of James Nichols's farm in Decker that was on his driver's licence – and was now on the charge sheet at police station in Perry. The connection was made by the computer at the National Crime Information Center in Washington, DC, and soon FBI agents were on their way to Perry by helicopter.

Although McVeigh was the subject of a nationwide manhunt, his hearing on the gun charges were scheduled for that day – and he may well have been released. McVeigh was waiting outside the courtroom when the Sheriff Jerry Cook got a message that he was wanted for the Oklahoma City bombing. Officers simply led him back to his cell, saying: "The judge isn't ready for you."

Back in his cell, another prisoner asked McVeigh if he was the bomber. McVeigh ignored the question. Soon, he was taken to a room where two FBI special agents awaited. Special Agent Floyd Zims said: "You may have some information about the bombing. I'm going to read you your rights."

McVeigh asked for a lawyer. Meanwhile, a hostile crowd gathered outside. McVeigh's request for a bulletproof vest was denied. FBI agents obtained a warrant to search the home of McVeigh's father. As the address given on his driver's licence was that of James Nichols in Decker, Michigan, the FBI began looking for Nichols and his brother Terry, another former soldier that McVeigh had met in the army. Hearing that the FBI was after him, Terry Nichols turned himself into the police station in Herington, Kansas.

Searching Terry Nichols's home, the FBI found blasting caps and ammonium nitrate, a fertilizer often used in home-made bombs. There were also barrels made of the same plastic as fragments found at the crime scene, a drill that was shown to have been used to drill out a lock on a quarry from which explosives had been stolen, thirty-three firearms and telephone cards that McVeigh had used when shopping for bomb-marking equipment, along with books on making bombs and a copy of *Hunter*, another novel by William Luther Pierce, where a lone hunter murders interracial couples and Jews. FBI agents also found a map of Oklahoma City, marked with the place McVeigh had left his getaway car. James Nichols was also arrested, but released after thirty-two days due to lack of evidence. He was indicted on charges that he had helped his brother and McVeigh detonate a small test explosion on his farm. These indictments were eventually dismissed.

McVeigh was brought to trial on 24 April 1997. Forensic experts showed that traces of nitroglycerin and pentaerythritol tetranitrate, or PETN, an explosive used in detonator cord, had been found on McVeigh's clothes after his arrest. Prosecutors also presented evidence to show how, in the months before the bomb exploded, McVeigh set out to gather materials for it.

Frederick Alan Schlender, the manager of the Mid-Kansas Coop in McPherson, Kansas, testified that on 30 September 1994 someone resembling Terry Nichols had bought forty 50 lb (23 kg) bags of ammonium nitrate and another 50 lb bag on 18 October – over a ton in all. Schlender testified that the man "said he was a wheat farmer. It was an unusual transaction. It wasn't common for someone to buy a ton of ammonium nitrate."

When FBI agents searched Nichols's home in Herington, they found a receipt for one of the purchases. It had McVeigh's fingerprint on it. Prosecutors produced a handwritten note McVeigh left on the Marquis saying it had a bad battery when he had parked it in downtown Oklahoma City as his getaway car, ensuring that no one would tow it.

However, the prosecution produced no witnesses who had seen McVeigh in downtown Oklahoma City on the day of the bombing or making the bomb. The most damning witness against McVeigh was Michael Fortier, another buddy from McVeigh's army days. Fortier knew of McVeigh's plans, even making a reconnaissance trip to the Murrah Building in December 1994 when Christmas decorations hung outside the day-care centre. In the end, he refused to join the plot, but was sentenced to twelve years' imprisonment for failing to inform the authorities. Fortier's wife Lori, who also knew of the plot and made the fake South Dakota driver's licence McVeigh had used to rent the truck, also testified against McVeigh in exchange for immunity from prosecution.

McVeigh had visited Waco during the siege of the Branch Davidians in 1993, handing out anti-government leaflets and bumper stickers bearing messages such as "Politicians Love Gun Control", "Fear the Government That Fears Your Gun" and "A Man With a Gun Is A Citizen, A Man Without A Gun Is A Subject". It was alleged that the breaking of the siege by officers from the Bureau of Alcohol, Tobacco, and Firearms (BATF) sent McVeigh over the edge.

"He thought the [B]ATF agents, whom he blamed for the Waco tragedy, had their offices in that building," said the prosecutor Joseph Hartzler. "As it turns out, he was wrong."

But there was another reason he decided to bomb the Murrah Building.

"And second, he described that building as, quote, 'an easy target'," said Hartzler.

Testimony showed that McVeigh had also mixed in the same circles as Richard Snell, who was executed by lethal injection in Arkansas on the day of the bombing, and may well have known him.

The defence attorney Robert Nigh attempted to humanize McVeigh by introducing testimony about his war record. As the lead gunner in a Bradley Fighting Vehicle, he had won the Bronze Star during Operation Desert Storm in 1991. However, not all his service reflected well on him. He bragged that he had knocked an Iraqi soldier's head off his shoulders like a cue ball. After the Gulf War, McVeigh signed up for a twenty-one-day try-out for the Green Berets. He left after just two days.

The defence also used crime scene evidence, suggesting that the unmatched leg belonged to the mastermind who had planted the bomb. The medical examiner's report described it as a male leg clothed in dark socks and a size $7^1/_2$ military boot closed with a strap used by soldiers to fold their trousers into their boot-tops. The DNA of the leg did not match that of the seven dead who were found missing left legs. Since then the leg had undergone intensive forensic investigation by podiatrists, anthropologists and other experts the FBI had brought to Oklahoma.

The medical examiner had initially said that there was a 75 per cent probability that the leg was a man's, but test results proved otherwise.

"DNA analysis by the FBI has shown conclusively that the left leg is not male but female," Dr Fred D. Jordan, chief medical examiner for Oklahoma, said. He reported hair analysis by the FBI had shown that the victim was black. Tests indicated the woman's height to be about 5 ft 5 in. (1.65 m) and that she was between sixteen and thirty years old. The report also said that blue fragments that had been found embedded in the leg were of a blue plastic similar to that of the barrels the bombers had packed with the ammonium nitrate and fuel oil they had used as an explosive.

The defence also called Dr Frederic Whitehurst, the whistle-blower who condemned the work of Thomas Thurman in the Lockerbie case. He testified that the FBI's investigation of the bomb site and other key evidence had been sloppy.

Nevertheless, on 2 June 1997, McVeigh was found guilty on all eleven counts of conspiracy and murder – the US Department of Justice could only charge McVeigh for causing the deaths of the eight federal officers who died in the Oklahoma City bombing. The murder of the other 160 dead fell until the jurisdiction of the state of Oklahoma. As McVeigh was sentenced to death, the state of Oklahoma did not bring charges.

McVeigh was sent to the new Supermax prison at Florence, Colorado, where he shared a wing with Ted Kaczynski, the "Unabomber", who was serving four life sentences, and Ramzi Yousef, who masterminded the 1993 World Trade Center bombing that had killed six and injured over a hundred. Yousef had been in the Philippines at the same time as Nichols, leading some to believe that the two terrorist incidents were linked. In jail, Yousef made attempts to convert McVeigh to Islam.

On 26 April 2001, McVeigh wrote a letter to Fox News explaining why he had bombed the Murrah Building in Oklahoma City. He also gave extensive interviews to journalists Michel Lou and Dan Herbeck, which they used as the basis for their book, *American Terrorist*, again leaving no doubt that McVeigh was responsible for the outrage. In a letter to the *Buffalo News* published the day before he died, he said: "I am sorry these people had to lose their lives," he wrote. "But that's the nature of the beast. It's understood going in what the human toll will be."

He also denied that there was a mastermind behind the plot.

"For those diehard conspiracy theorists who will refuse to believe this, I turn the tables and say: show me where I needed anyone else," McVeigh wrote. "Financing? Logistics? Special-ized tech skills? Brainpower? Strategy? Show me where I needed a dark, mysterious 'Mr X'!"

Then at 7 a.m. on 11 June 2001, Timothy McVeigh was executed by lethal injection at the US Federal Penitentiary in Terre Haute, Indiana. In 1997, President Clinton had signed into law a bill preventing him, or anyone else convicted of the bombing, from being buried in a military cemetery. His body was cremated and his ashes scattered.

Terry Nichols also stood trial in a federal court. Although he was at home in Kansas when the bomb went off, he had robbed an Arkansas gun dealer McVeigh had befriended at gun shows to bankroll the bombing and had helped McVeigh prepare the bomb. His wife Marife testified that Nichols had travelled to Oklahoma City three days before the bombing, supporting the prosecution's contention that Nichols had helped McVeigh stash the getaway car. She also failed to provide an alibi for him on 18 April, the day the government alleged he helped McVeigh build the truck bomb at Geary Lake fishing park near Herington. A mail-order bride from the Philippines, Marife had arrived in the United States pregnant with another man's child. Two years later, the child was found dead with a plastic bag over his head at the Nichols' family farmhouse in Michigan. The death was ruled an accident.

After six days deliberation, the jury found Nichols guilty of one count of conspiracy to use a weapon of mass destruction, a capital offence, and eight counts of involuntary manslaughter as he had not actually detonated the bomb and no one had positively identified him as the purchaser of the ammonium nitrate. Unlike McVeigh, he had shown some signs of remorse and the defence argued that he had withdrawn from the plot before the bombing.

Nevertheless, he was sentenced to life without possibility of parole and sent to the Supermax prison at Florence, Colorado. Again, in a federal court, he had only stood trial for the murder of federal officials. He then faced a state trial for 160 capital counts of first-degree murder, one count of foetal homicide, first-degree arson and conspiracy. He was convicted on all counts, but the jury failed to reach a unanimous verdict on imposing the death penalty after he claimed he had converted to

Christianity. Nichols was sentenced to another 161 life terms without the possibility of parole, along with thirty-five years for first-degree arson and ten years for conspiracy. He was also ordered to pay compensation to the victims and fines that will never be paid. His wife divorced him and returned to the Philippines with their children.

THE ICEMAN

O N 19 SEPTEMBER 1991, two German hikers came across a curious crime scene high in the Alps between Austria and Italy. They found a mummified body sticking out of the glacier. At first, it was thought to be a modern corpse, but when it was taken to the morgue in Innsbruck it was found to be 5,300 years old. The iceman was soon given the name Ötzi after Ötz valley where he was discovered. On further examination, he was found to have an arrow head in his back and it became clear that he had been murdered. This made the murder of Ötzi the coldest of cold cases.

The dead man was about forty-five years old. Once around 5 ft 5 in. (1.65 m) tall and weighing 110 lbs (50 kg), when he was found he had shrunk to 5 ft 2 in. (1.57 m) and 84 lbs (38 kg). He also appeared to have been scalped. He had a full head of hair, but it was not attached to his head. There was probably nothing sinister about this. It appeared to have been caused by the action of freezing.

From the enamel of his well-preserved teeth, it was possible to deduce the minerals in the water he drank and the composition of the earth where his food was grown. These clues showed that he had been born and brought up in the Eisack Valley, near the present-day village of Velturno in the Italian Tyrol. When he grew up, he went to live in the Venosta Valley some 36 miles (60 km) to the west.

The bones of his legs indicated that he frequently made long walks over extremely hilly terrain. Some of his clothing had been preserved. His shoes were waterproof and made of various animal skins. The wide soles, seemingly made for walking on snow, were made from cow's leather; the instep from deer. The uppers were also made from domesticated cattle. There was fur on the outside and the shoe laced up. Dried tree bark and grass were stuffed inside for warmth. He had a goatskin loincloth, sheepskin leggings and a coat made from goatskin. These were sewn together with sinew. His leather belt had a pouch on it containing a bone awl, a scraper, a flint flake, which could have been used as a primitive knife, and dried fungus. He also had a bearskin cap with two leather straps and was carrying a mat woven from swamp grass that it is thought he used to protect himself from rain or snow.

As some of the clothes he wore came from domesticated animals, it is thought that he was a herdsman rather than a hunter. The cow's leather came from ancient cattle that used to migrate across that region of the Alps. However, he was also a man of some social significance as he had with him a precious copper axe made a thousand years before archaeologists had previously thought man had discovered copper.

Ötzi was also carrying a flint-tipped dagger and a little fire-starting kit – a birch-bark container holding embers wrapped in maple leaves, flint and pyrite for creating sparks, and so-called tinder fungus. However, he was curiously poorly armed to set off into the mountainous wilderness miles to the north of his home. Twelve of the fourteen arrows in his deerskin quiver were half-finished. The other two, which had arrow heads and fletching (stabilizing fins), were broken. And he was carrying a roughly shaped piece of yew 6 ft (1.83 m) long, thought to be an un-finished longbow that had yet to be notched and strung. A bowstring was found in the quiver, along with a tool made from an antler thought to have been used for sharpening arrow points. This led to speculation that he had left home in a hurry.

When he was first found, it was thought that he had slipped and frozen to death in the snow. There was also speculation that he had been the victim of a ritual sacrifice – perhaps to placate the gods that sent an asteroid crashing into what is now Austria around 3,000 BC. Then an X-ray found a dense triangular shadow in his left shoulder.

Ötzi was moved from Innsbruck to the South Tyrol Museum of Archaeology in Bolzano when a survey showed that he been found 101 yards (92.56 m) on the Italian side of the border. The body was housed in a custom-built refrigerator to stop him thaw-ing out. In 2005, after the hospital in Bolzano had acquired a new high-resolution, multi-slice CT scanner, his body was put on a special foam mattress, covered in ice and insulating blankets, and rushed by ambulance to hospital. After the ten-minute ride he was swiftly scanned and returned to his fridge. They could not risk him defrosting.

The scans showed a sharpened piece of stone, probably flint, that had made a $1/2$ in. (1.2 cm) gash in his left subclavian artery. This is the main circulatory pipeline carrying fresh oxygenated blood from the heart to the left arm. Uncontrolled bleeding would have led to a rapid death. There was a small tear in his coat that corresponded with the entry point.

The position of the arrow head indicated that his attacker was behind and below him. It was a shot that prehistoric hunters would use to bring down game. The arrow went clean through the bone and severed the artery. Immediately, blood would have gushed out, filling the space between the shoulder blade and the ribs. Ötzi would have suffered haemorrhagic shock. His heart would have started to race and he would have been drenched in sweat, even in the cold at 10,000 ft (3,000 m) above sea level. In a matter of minutes, he would have collapsed, lost consciousness and bled to death.

The wound indicates that he had been killed deliberately. Given that he had left home in something of a hurry, he seems to have been on the run from his killers. It seems that this was not his first run-in with them. There was a deep gash on his hand that had been inflicted some days earlier and was beginning to heal. He was carrying a type of fungus known to have anti-bacterial properties.

It is clear that he was not in good health when he set off up the mountains. The one surviving fingernail recovered from his remains showed that he suffered three significant episodes of disease in the last six months of his life, the last bout two months before to his death. His lungs were blackened, probably from breathing the smoke from camp fires. His ribs and nose showed signs of fractures that had healed and his hip joint showed evidence of aging. It had the type of small fracture that occurs after a lifetime of wear and tear. He had fleas and the eggs of the whipworm parasites were found in his intestines, causing diarrhoea or possibly dysentery. But he was not too ill to eat and there were small amounts of food residue in his intestines.

A day or two before his death, Ötzi had eaten a piece of wild goat and some kind of plant, and his very last meal was red deer and some cereals. The bran-like residues found in his digestive system contained barley and a primitive form of wheat known as einkorn. These were also found on his garments, indicating that the Neolithic settlement to the south of the Alps where he lived cultivated these grains. The small size of the wheat fragments found in the gut showed they had been ground. Indeed, small chips of mica from the grindstone were also found. The mica came from the Venosta valley where he had started his last journey. Tiny flecks of charcoal were discovered, suggesting that the ground grains had been baked on an open fire to make a primitive form of bread.

Archaeobotanists have analysed pollen and plant fragments to plot Ötzi's last movements. No less than eighty distinct species of moss and liverworts were found in, on, or near his body. The most prominent was the Neckera moss that still grows in the valleys to the south, close to known prehistoric sites. James Dickson of the University of Glasgow believes that the clump found in Ötzi's possession suggests that he was using the moss to wrap food. However, it is known that some ancient peoples used similar mosses as lavatory paper.

The pollen of the hop hornbeam, found in his digestive tract, strongly indicates that the Iceman's last journey began in the low-altitude deciduous forests to the south in the springtime when hop hornbeams were in bloom. But it seems he did not head straight up the mountain. Traces of pine pollen were found both above and below the hornbeam pollen. This suggests that Ötzi climbed up to where pine trees grow in mixed coniferous forests at higher altitude, then came down again to the lower altitude where the hop hornbeams flourished, before making his final ascent in his last day or two. It has been suggested that he was trying to avoid the steep, thickly wooded gorge of the lower Senales Valley, a vital detour if he was in a hurry – or being pursued.

When he reached a mountain pass now known as Tisenjoch, he would have paused to rest after completing the near vertical climb of 6,500 ft (2,000 m) from the valley below. To the north, he faced a desolate, glacier-riven landscape. He was found in a rocky hollow that would have afforded some shelter from the wind. It is not known if his enemies caught up with him or were already there waiting in ambush. But he never left that hollow alive. Snow and ice then embalmed him, preserving him for the next five millennia until a thaw finally released him from his icy grave.

The crime scene also provided a few clues to who the killer may have been. The shaft of the arrow that killed him was not found. Someone had pulled it out, leaving behind the stone arrowhead.

"I believe – in fact, I am convinced – that the person who shot the Iceman with the arrow is the same person who pulled it out," said Dr Eduard Egarter Vigl from the Department of Pathological Anatomy and Histology of the General Regional Hospital in Bolzano.

Dr Vigl argues that the shaft of a prehistoric arrow could be used to identify the archer in the same way that modern-day ballistics can link a bullet to a gun, so the killer pulled out the arrow shaft to cover his tracks. For the same reason, he did not run off with the valuable copper-bladed axe as its possession would implicate him in the crime. Consequently, the killer came from the same village or, at the very least, knew the victim. The motivation for the crime was not theft. It was something more personal.

Tom Loy, a molecular archaeologist from the University of Queensland, believes that more than one person was responsible for the death of the Iceman. He found microscopic specks of human blood on his leather coat, his knife and a broken arrow in his quiver, which Loy believes was the one his killer had pulled from his back. Using DNA analysis, he discovered the blood came from four individuals. The Iceman, Loy thought, had fought back against his attackers.

Alois Pirpamer, one of the climbers who found Ötzi, said that the Iceman had been clutching a knife in his right hand at the time of the discovery, indicating that, again, he was preparing to defend himself. The knife became detached when the body was pulled from the ice. On closer examination, Dr Vigl also found bruises on the body. However, *National Geographic* magazine pointed out that Loy's research had only been aired in the popular press, and sceptics in the academic community said the claims were impossible to assess unless they were published in the scientific literature and peer-reviewed.

The idea that Ötzi was attacked by more than one person chimes with the crime theory put forward by Walter Leitner, an archaeologist at the University of Innsbruck who is an expert in both archery and Stone Age culture. He believes the mountain-top murder was the last act of a political dispute that had begun down in the valley – and it was rivals in the Iceman's own tribe who finally succeeded in assassinating him.

According to Leitner's theory, Ötzi, with his copper axe, was top dog. But he was aging and younger men tried to overthrow him, first wounding him in the hand. Realizing that his reign was at an end, the Iceman fled, but was caught and killed on the mountaintop by his opponents. The reason that others in his tribe might had turned against him has also been discovered. Dr Franco Rollo of the University of Camerino examined his mito-chondrial DNA and found sequences associated with low sperm motility. This increased the chance of infertility. The aging Ötzi may have had no sons to succeed him and no family to defend him.

We will never know the name of the Iceman, or his killers. But their final confrontation in the Alps might now benefit future generations. Nuclear DNA has been extracted from a bone in his pelvis and his entire genome has been sequenced. While the search is on for his descendents, his mitochondrial DNA indicates that there won't be many of them. However, scientists now have a chance to study gene mutations over the last 5,300 years, which may shed light on hereditary aspects of diseases such as diabetes, hypertension and cancer.

THE ROMANOVS

IN MARCH 1917, Tsar Nicholas II was forced to abdicate the throne of Russia. Nicholas and the entire Romanov family were then arrested and held in the governor's mansion in Tobolsk, Siberia. After the Bolsheviks came to power that October, the Romanovs were moved to the Ipatiev House in Yekaterinburg, then dubbed "The House of Special Purpose".

The new Soviet government wanted to put Nicholas on trial, but Russia had been plunged into a civil war between the Red Army, who supported the new regime, and the White Army, who opposed it. In July 1918, the White Army threatened to take Yekaterinburg. The Bolsheviks could not risk Nicholas or his heirs falling into the White Army's hands and becoming a rallying point for opposition. So the decision was made to kill them. On the night of 16 July, Nicholas, his wife Alexandra, their four daughters Olga, Tatiana, Marie and Anastasia, their son Alexei, his physician Dr Yevgney Botkin, the cook Ivan Kharitanov, and servants Anna Demidova and Alexei Trupp were woken and told to dress. They were taken down to the basement where they were told they were going to be photographed. Instead, a firing squad led by Yakov Yurovsky, the local head of the secret police, burst in and shot them. Nicholas died immediately, but some of the women had jewels sewn into their corsets and survived the initial fusillade. They were finished off with bayonets. As the order had come from Lenin, the head of the new Soviet State, the executions were kept secret until two years after his death in 1924, when a Soviet version of a book by the White Russian magistrate and crime scene investigator, Nikolai Sokolov, published in the west as *The Sokolov Investigation of the Alleged Murder of the Russian Imperial Family*, was authorized. It was rewritten for publication in the Soviet Union by Pavel Bykov, the new chairman of the Ural Soviet.

Eight days after the murders, the Whites had taken over Yekaterinburg. As the court investigator for the Yekaterinburg Regional Court, it was Alexei Nametkin's job to look into the murder of the Romanovs. But as he drew his authority from the tsar – and it appeared that the tsar was dead – he dragged his feet. The military authorities suspected that he was doing this because he was afraid of the Bolsheviks, who still threatened Yekaterinburg, so Judge Ivan Sergeyev took over the case. There was then a consolidation of the administration of all Russian territory outside the control of the Bolsheviks. Power was concentrated in the hands of Admiral Alexander Kolchak at Omsk who, on 5 February 1919, put Nikolai Sokolov, the local examining magistrate, in charge of the case.

Sokolov first examined the evidence that Sergeyev had collected from the crime scene. These included pieces of wooden lath from the eastern and southern walls of the basement with bullet holes and bullets in them, usually from a Nagant-type pistol manufactured in Belgium for the Russians. There was also a bullet from an American Browning pistol. More bullet holes were found in pieces of wood taken from the floor. Some of the wood was stained with blood. Another Browning bullet was found in a floorboard, along with one from a Colt 45. Sokolov's book shows a photograph of eleven of the bullets recovered but he notes that not all the bullets were shown in the picture as Sergeyev had given some of them away. Detailed chemical analysis of the stains on the wood, including those in the bullet holes, made by both Sergeyev and Sokolov showed that they were made by human blood. Strands of dyed wool from clothing were also found in the bullet holes.

It was noted that there were no signs of violence in the upper floor of the Ipatiev House where the imperial family lived, but only in the rooms of the lower, basement floor, from which there was no escape. The only window was covered by a thick iron grate. It was sunk in the ground and concealed from the outside by a high fence.

If the imperial family and their retainers were indeed the victims killed in the basement, "there is no doubt that they were lured here from their living quarters on some false pre-text," Sokolov said. Consequently, the murders were plainly premeditated.

Sokolov concluded from the crime scene evidence that the murders were perpetrated with revolvers and bayonets. Evidence from the crime scene indicated that several people had been murdered as one person could not have changed their position in the room during the slaughter. The spread of the bullet holes and the bloodstains indicated that some of the victims were positioned along the eastern and southern walls, while others were nearer the centre of the room. Several were hit while they were already lying on the floor. Sokolov estimated that more than thirty bullets were fired as some of them would have remained lodged in the victims' bodies.

According to Sokolov, Nametkin looked into rumours that the imperial family had been rescued and, to conceal the fact, other people had been shot in the basement. The tsar's valet Chemodurov testified that Nicholas had a great deal of clothing with him that had disappeared. The reasoning was that, if the tsar had been rescued, he would have taken it with him. But it was known that many things were stolen by the guards, including the tsarevich's diary and his favourite dog, a spaniel named Joy.

Sokolov pointed out that the Tsarevich Alexei, a haemophiliac, had been ill throughout his time in captivity, but his medicines were found in the Ipatiev House. Why would these be left behind when the boy suffered from a life-threatening condition?

The killers took what they wanted and left behind anything that was of no use to them. More than sixty icons were found, including icons of Rasputin – the tsarina's favourite – and his inscriptions. Another was an icon of the Feodorov Mother of God. Alexandra Feodorovna, born a Lutheran, converted to Orthodoxy when she married the tsar. Chemodurov said: "The empress never went anywhere without this icon. To take the icon from the empress would be the same as taking her life." The diamonds had been removed from it, but the icon itself had been left behind.

Prayer books, hymnals and religious tracts were left in the Ipatiev House. Burnt bits of clothing and linen, the scorched remnants of handbags, purses, cases, buttons, brushes, needles, thread, articles of female handiwork and other items were found stuffed in the stove.

Holy pictures of Saint Simeon Verkhoturye and Saint Seraphim Sarovsky were found in a rubbish pit, along with a disfigured icon, bearing the tsarina's inscription: "Keep and preserve. Mama, 1917. Tobolsk." This icon was Alexei's last Christmas gift from his mother, which she had given him when they were still at Tobolsk and it hung above his bed at Yekaterinburg. Also found in the rubbish pit was an officer's cockade and a ribbon of St George. Chemodurov testified: "The ribbon of St George was taken from the emperor's overcoat. The emperor never parted with this overcoat and always went about with it."

Sokolov interviewed a man named Loginov, who said that a woman doctor named Golubeva, the director of a Bolshevik hospital train, told him that she had a pillow and some boots that had been taken from among the Romanovs' possessions. They had been given to her by Shaya Goloshchekin, the general administrator of Yekaterinburg.

In 1935, one of the assassins, Peter Yermakov, told American journalist Richard Halliburton that, two days before the murder, he had been assigned to find a place to bury the bodies. In the forest about 12 miles (19 km) north of Yekaterinburg, he found a place called the Four Brothers, named for the four towering pine trees that had once overlooked the site. Amid the swamps and peat bogs were the shafts of abandoned coal mines. Yurovsky brought the bodies there on the back of a truck. On the way, they met a party of twenty-five men on horseback and in peasant carts. Most were drunk. They were factory workers, some members of the new Ural Regional Soviet, who had been tipped off by Yermakov. He had promised them the four grand duchesses – the tsar's daughters – plus the pleasure of killing the tsar.

"Why didn't you bring them alive?" they complained.

Yurovsky placated the angry men and ordered them to move the bodies from the truck into the carts. While doing so, the workers seized the opportunity to rob the victims. Yurovsky put a stop to this by the threat of a summary firing squad.

The procession made its way slowly down the narrow track to the Four Brothers, only arriving there after sunrise. According to Yermakov, the bodies were stripped and the jewels discovered. Eight pounds (3.6 kg) of diamonds and other jewels were removed and, on the orders of Yurovsky, the corpses were flung down an abandoned mine shaft. But when word spread in Yekaterinburg that the Romanovs had been killed, the executioners feared their crime would be discovered. They retrieved the bodies. Two of them were burnt. But that took too long. So, deeper in the forest, a pit was dug. Rock was close to the surface there, so the executioners had to make do with a broad, shallow grave. The bodies were dumped in it, their faces smashed beyond recognition. They were doused with sulphuric acid, then covered with earth. Clearly, the killers hoped that the evidence of their crime would remain undiscovered for ever. This was very effective. Throughout the Soviet era, no one was sure what had happened to the Romanovs. As late as 1976, two British journalists, Anthony Summers and Tom Mangold, related in their book, *File on the Tsar*, the theory that the massacre at Yekaterinburg had been an elaborate fabrication. Only the tsar and his son had been executed. The Tsarina Alexandra, who was the granddaughter of Queen Victoria and German-born, and the rest of the family had been kept alive – no one knew for how long – as a bargaining chip in negotiations with the Germans, with whom the Soviets had only just made peace.

Years before, Sokolov had concluded that all the Romanovs were dead because a telegram had been intercepted, in which the Bolsheviks confirmed that the entire imperial family had been executed. Several eyewitnesses stated that they had seen the Romanovs and their entourage dead and nobody had seen them alive after that night. Most of those who visited the crime scene were convinced.

Pierre Gilliard, the children's Swiss tutor, who reached Yekaterinburg in August 1918, said: "I went down to the ground floor, the greater part of which was below the level of the ground. It was with intense emotion that I entered the room . . . Its appearance was sinister beyond all expression. The only daylight filtered in through a barred window at the height of a man's head. The walls and floors showed numerous traces of bullets and blows with bayonets. A first glance showed that an odious crime had been perpetrated there, and that several people had been killed."

He stayed on in Siberia to assist Sokolov in his investigations.

In October 1918, the English diplomat Sir Charles Eliot was sent to Russia to investigate the murder of the Romanovs. He inspected the Ipatiev House thoroughly and found seventeen bullet holes in the walls of the basement. But, he reported: "Browning revolver bullets were found and some of them were stained with blood. Otherwise no traces of blood were visible . . . There is no real evidence as to who or how many the victims were, but it is supposed that they were five, namely, the tsar, Dr Botkin, the empress's maid and two lackeys. No corpses were discovered, nor any trace of their being disposed of by burning or otherwise, but it is stated that a finger bearing a ring believed to have belonged to Dr Botkin was found in a well."

However, Carl Ackerman, a reporter with the *New York Times* who visited Yekaterinburg in November 1918, said he did not believe that the Romanovs had been killed there. While he found twenty bullet holes in the basement wall and some blood on the floor, there are "no pools of blood, and it seemed doubtful to me that seven persons should die such a horrible death and leave only small 'blood-clots' in the bullet holes and small bloodstains on the floor".

According to Sokolov, who did not arrive in Yekaterinburg until February 1919, Sergeyev, despite producing an otherwise detailed description of the crime scene, "did not notice the splotches of blood which I discovered on the south and east walls". Meanwhile, Sokolov's assistant Captain, Pavel Bulygin, said that there was "so much blood that it had even soaked through the floor and stained the ground beneath it. There was blood on the floor in every room through which the bodies had been carried, blood on the gate, blood on the front steps, and blood outside where the lorry stood waiting."

The *Times* journalist Robert Wilton, who visited Yekaterinburg in 1919, said: "So much blood had flowed that the marks of the redden-stained swabs were visible a year later."

Sergeyev's boss, General Mikhail Dieterikhs, wrote of investigators finding table linen, towels and napkins with a "large thick bloodstain", which the murderers had wiped their hands on. He also said that the bodies were burnt and that clothes, jewels and other personal possessions were found on the spot where this had happened. Near there, at the bottom of a mine permanently covered with 3 ft (1 m) of water, he found the carcass of Tatiana's dog, dentures and a finger. He concluded that there was no grave and that the bodies of the Romanovs had been utterly destroyed. He had to flee later that year when the Bolsheviks retook Yekaterinburg.

After examining the evidence that Sergeyev had collected and Ipatiev House, Sokolov went out in search of the bodies. He headed to the Four Brothers, which Dieterikhs had already visited. In the nearby village of Koptyaki, he talked to Nastasya Zykova. Early in the morning of 17 July 1918, she had been on her way to Yekaterinburg with her son Nicholas and his wife Maria. She had been carrying fish to sell in town while her son had been called up by the Red Army. When they passed the mine and approached the Four Brothers, they saw a procession of carts and what they took to be Bolsheviks. As soon as they were seen, two horsemen detached themselves from the cortege and rode up to them.

"Two horses rode to meet us," said Nastasya Zykova. "One was in sailor's uniform and I recognized him. He was the sailor Vagano from Verkh-Isetsk. The other was in army uniform – in soldier's greatcoat and military cap. The horsemen came towards us quickly with Vaganov in front, the soldier behind. As they came up to us, Vagano shouted: 'Turn back!' He took out his revolver and held it over my head. We turned our horses quickly.

Our wagon nearly turned over. They pranced about us and Vagano shouted: 'Don't look back . . . I'll shoot.' Our horse raced off with all the spirit that was in him. They escorted us, Vaganov all the while keeping his revolver over my head and crying: 'Don't look back, citizens . . .' In this fashion we raced to a place beyond which lies the Big Meadow. They continued with us for about half a verst [a third of a mile], or three-quarters of a verst, and then fell back. We did not look back, of course, after they told us."

They warned other travellers to turn back. An officer from Koptyaki named Lieutenant Andrei Sheremetevsky rode out with some peasants to investigate. They found the grass on an old pathway into the forest trampled down. They were about to go down the trail when a Red Army soldier came out armed with a rifle, two pistols, a sabre and grenades. He warned them that there was going to be bomb-throwing practice at the mine and ordered them to leave. The road was then closed until 6 a.m. on 19 July.

After the Bolsheviks withdrew from Yekaterinburg on 25 July, two peasants from Koptyaki went to Verkh-Isetsk and reported the shutting off of the mine to the military authorities there. Seven peasants from the village then went to investigate. They were followed by a local forester and, on 30 July, the court investigator Nametkin turned up, accompanied by Doctor Vladimir Derevenko, the valet Chemodurov and a number of officers. According to Sokolov: "Several valuable discoveries were made."

Nametkin found no bodies and left after half an hour. He did not even take the road to the Four Brothers, the way Yurovsky and the Bolsheviks had gone. Instead, they travelled back and forth by train as a railway line passed nearby. Sergeyev did not even bother to visit the mine.

Sokolov himself arrived there on 23 May 1919 and, on 6 June, excavations were begun on the orders of Admiral Kolchak. It was clear from Sokolov's questioning of local witnesses that the tracks of a truck had been seen heading to the mine as well. He discovered tracks that showed a truck had skidded near the mine and had almost fallen in. A truck that had been despatched to the local headquarters of the Cheka – the secret police, headed in Yekaterinburg by Yurovsky – returned on 19 July.

"The entire platform of the truck was stained with blood," said Peter Leonov, who worked in the garage at Yekaterinburg. "It was apparent that the platform had been washed and swept with a broom. But the blood, nevertheless, was clearly visible on the floor of the platform."

His brother Alexander, who also worked at the garage, said: "I remember very well that the platform had a large, washed bloodstain."

Many small bonfires were found around the mine whose smoke would have protected the horses from mosquitoes and gadflies. According to Alexander Zudikhin: "It was apparent that horses had been tied there; the trees were broken and chewed."

Nicholas Zubritsky concurred: "They had dug up the earth with their hooves. It seemed to me at the time that a smudge had been lit near a small pine to protect them from mosquitoes."

Sokolov found evidence of this – small pine boards what were charred. The forest was damp thereabouts and off-cuts of board would have been used as kindling. Rope was also found along with the remnants of boxes. Sokolov discovered that, on the day following the murders, an employee of the commissariat of supply, named Zimin, had appeared at the chemist shop of the Russian Company in Yekaterinburg and delivered a written requisition for sulphuric acid in the name of the local commissar, Peter Voikov, who was on Lenin's staff. On the evening of 17 July and during the day of 18 July, some 358 lbs (162 kg) of sulphuric acid was delivered to the mine in wooden boxes by soldiers of the Red Army and personnel from the commissariat of supply.

An engineer named Kotenev told Sokolov that he had been travelling out from Yekaterinburg towards Koptyaki on 18 July, when he was stopped at the level crossing near the mine. There he saw a truck carrying a large drum of gasoline.

"Gasoline is always put in such drums," he said. "I can tell you exactly the quantity of gasoline that the drum on the truck should contain. It was a 10 to 11 pood [360 to 400 lbs; 163 to 181 kg] drum."

The watchman at the level crossing said he saw it pass by at around 7 a.m., but it stopped about 1,050 ft (320 m) from the crossing,

"I did not see very well just what was on it," he said. "It looked to me as if there was drums or boxes on it."

After dinner he saw another truck pass by and stop in the same place.

"This time I saw clearly that in this truck they were carrying gasoline in drums. I took a mind to ask for some gasoline, got a bottle and went to the place the trucks were standing on the Koptyaki road; and this time I did see clearly what was on the first truck, the one that came first. On the second there were about three drums of gasoline, or maybe two. The drums were all of metal. There were about five people near the two trucks . . . I asked them to pour me out a little gasoline. They gave me a bottle."

The Bolsheviks had appropriated all motor vehicles in Yekaterinburg at the time, so the trucks could only have come from the Soviet garage.

Sokolov estimated, from the testimony of eyewitnesses, that about 40 poods (1,290 lbs; 585 kg) of gasoline were brought to the mine. Some way from the mine, there was evidence of two large bonfires.

He went on to list all the things that were found in the mine. These included religious miniatures, some smashed, and red and white pieces of wax and candles of the same colour and type as those found in the possession of the guard Ivan Starkov.

"Their household articles at Tobolsk included red wax candles," said Alexei Volkov, the tsarina's *valet de chambre*. "They had acquired such candles from the monastery and the cathedral."

There was a portrait frame made in leather and lined with silk, bearing the mark of "Edward Akkerman, Berlin". Members of the imperial household said that the family had many such frames, which they took with them when they travelled. The lady of the bedchamber Maria Tutelberg said that the tsar had a portrait of the tsarina in one.

A military badge that the tsarina wore on a bracelet was found, along with belt buckles belonging to the tsar and tsarevich; jewelled ladies' shoe buckles of the type worn by the tsarina and the grand duchesses – one of which had been exposed to intense heat; a lens from a pair of spectacles – the tsarina had been prescribed glasses in Tobolsk; the frame and holder from a lorgnette; two lenses from pince-nez of the type worn by Dr Botkin; false teeth – Dr Botkin wore dentures; a collar button; a scorched brush of the type Dr Botkin used to tend his beard and moustache; a tie clasp of the type Dr Botkin wore; scorched elastic and silk corsets including six pairs of front stays, side bones, clasps, fasteners and hooks of the quality worn by the tsarina, her daughters and the servant Demidova; more than forty pieces of burnt high-quality footwear; an iron boot guard; seven men's buckles from breeches and vests, all but one foreign-made; coil springs and a buckle from a man's suspenders that had been destroyed by fire; two badly scorched buckles from belts belonging to Demidova and either the tsarina or a grand duchess; six military-style buttons from the expensive Vunder plant in St Petersburg, damaged by fire; buttons and parts of button from the sleeves of the grand duchesses and the garter of the tsarina, damaged by fire; hooks, eyes and buttons from Brissac, dressmaker to the tsarina and the grand duchesses; pieces of cloth roughly torn from the apparel of the tsarina, the grand duchesses, Demidova and Dr Botkin, many half-burnt; burnt cloth from the tsarevich's overcoat; khaki-colour fabric from the tsarevich's knapsack; pieces of lead foil, four nails, a spent revolver bullet, two copper coins of two kopeck denomination – all things that Alexei collected and would be found in his pockets; an American suitcase key; parts of a small handbag or purse; a penknife; a safety pin; splinters of glass thought to come from a watch, small picture frame or smelling salt vial; a jewelled cross made of platinum, carrying emeralds, brilliants and pearls; a large brilliant weighing ten carats, made of platinum and green gold, and studded with diamonds – both the brilliant and the cross belonged to the tsarina, given to her by the tsar and his mother respectively; an earring made in platinum and gold, carrying a pearl and a brilliant, belonging to the tsarina; parts of a pearl and a broken gold ornament, thought to be the remains of the matching earring; parts of a very large pearl; thirteen round pearls thought to have come from a string – the tsarina and grand duchesses had many; parts of a broken gold and silver ornament with brilliants, thought to have been part of a brooch belonging to the tsarina; thirteen splinters from a very large emerald thought to have come from an egg belonging to the tsarina; two splinters of a sapphire; two brilliants, a ruby, two admandines and two adamants thought to have come from a bracelet belonging to the tsarina; two gold chains – the tsarina and grand duchesses had many; part of a gold ring that had been smashed; two parts of gold ornaments, thought to have come from an earring and a bracelet; a gold ornament with three diamonds thought to be an eyelet for fastening jewellery belonging to the tsarina; and topazes such as those worn in necklaces belonging to the tsarina and grand duchesses. Sokolov believed that all this jewellery was found in the mine because it had been sewn into the women's clothes. Alexandra Tegleva, the children's nanny and later the wife of tutor Pierre Gilliard, testified to this.

Also found in the mine were two bullets from a Nagant revolver; the steel jacket from such a bullet; twenty-four pieces of lead thought to be other bullets that had melted; a well-manicured human finger thought to have come from a middle-aged woman, cut off with a sharp instrument; two pieces of human skin thought to be from a hand; and the corpse of a female. A hole found in its skull was thought to have been the cause of death. The Romanovs English tutor Sidney Gibbs identified it as belonging to the Grand Duchess Anastasia. The valuables and remains had been covered with a thin layer of earth. Burnt splinters of bone from a mammal and greasy masses mixed with earth, possibly animal fat, were also found. But the fall of Admiral Kochak's government prevented Sokolov conducting any scientific experiments on them.

Sokolov concluded that the bodies of the imperial family and their retainers had been brought from the Ipatiev House to the mine on the morning of 17 July. Their clothes had been stripped from them, torn away and cut with knives. Several of the buttons were destroyed in the process and the hooks and eyes stretched. The concealed jewels fell out, but some remained unnoticed after being trampled into the ground. Some were smashed when hit by bullets or other hard objects. The corpses were then cut up. The pieces were put on bonfires, doused with gasoline and burnt. The bullets melted and human fat soaked into the ground. What remained of the bodies was destroyed with sulphuric acid. Their clothes were also burnt and whatever remained was thrown down the mine, which was half-full of water, and covered with earth.

But some anomalies remained. On 25 June 1919, Sokolov took a picture of the carcass of what he took to be Tatiana or Anastasia's dog. However, Professor Keith Simpson, pathologist of the British Home Ministry, said: "If you look at the picture with a magnifier, you see very little loss of fur. It is impossible that this carcass at first has been in the water for two or three months. No dog could have had so much fur after being in cold water for two of three months. After the frost period the dog would have been in the water for another two months, and this picture doesn't show that at all."

Sokolov entrusted the evidence he had gathered to General Pierre Janin, head of the French military mission to Siberia, who was returning to France. In his book, *Ma mission en Sibérie*, published in Paris in 1933, Janin wrote: "He [Sokolov] had gathered about thirty charred bone fragments, as well as some human tissue which was found in the stake, human hairs, a cut finger, which the experts recognized as a ring finger of the Tsarina, some small icons, the buckle of a belt that belonged to the Tsarevich, bullets of a revolver, etcetera."

At the end of June 1920, Janin wrote to Grand Duke Nicholas Nikolaevich Romanov, who was considered the spokesman of the Russian emigrants, asking what he should do with the items Sokolov had collected. The jewellery and other personal objects of the victims were given to Grand Duchess Xenia Alexandrovna, who divided them among members of the imperial family. The human remains were also entrusted to the Romanovs. Nobody has seen anything of them since. Sokolov himself turned up in Paris in 1921, after the end of the Russian Civil War, but seems to have made no effort to have the evidence examined scientifically. Nevertheless, he set about publishing his report of the investigation into the murder of the Romanovs. In it, he concludes that the corpses of the Romanovs had been completely destroyed by sulphuric acid and fire.

Yermakov confirmed this. He told Richard Halliburton that the bodies had then been burnt and the ashes thrown to the wind.

"We built a funeral pyre of cut logs big enough to hold bodies two layers deep," Peter Yermakov said. "We poured five tins of gasoline over the corpses and two buckets of sulphuric acid and set the logs afire . . . I stood by to see that not one fingernail or fragment of bone remained unconsumed . . . We had to keep the burning a long time to burn up the skulls.'

He went on: "We didn't leave the smallest pinch of ash on the ground . . . I put tins of ashes in the wagon again and ordered the driver to take me towards the high road . . . I pitched the ashes into the air – and the wind caught them like dust and carried them out across the woods and fields."

But in his book, *Poslednie dni Romanovykh* (*Last Days of the Romanovs*), Bykov told a different story. Expanding on Sokolov's work, he gave some intriguing clues as to where the bodies could be found: "Much has been said about the missing corpses, despite the intensive search . . . the remains of the corpses after being burned, were taken quite far away from the mines and buried in a swampy place, in an area where the volunteers and investigators did not excavate. There the corpses remained and by now have rotted."

In other words, the remains had survived the fires. They had been buried quite far from the mines in a swampy place where Sokolov had not searched.

In *File on the Tsar*, Summers and Mangold challenged Sokolov's conclusion that, in two days, even with a plentiful supply of gasoline and sulphuric acid, the executioners had been able to destroy "more than half a ton of flesh and bone" as Yermakov claimed. Home Office forensic pathologist Professor Francis Camps told Summers and Mangold that it was extremely difficult to burn a human body, saying that, "the corpse first chars, and the charring itself prevents the rest of the body from being destroyed". In modern-day cremation, corpses are put in closed gas-fired ovens that are heated to 1,800°F to 2,000°F (982°C to 1,093°C). Even then it takes one and a half to two hours to reduce a body to ashes. However, this equipment was not available in the Siberian forest in 1918.

Sulphuric acid performs little better. According to Dr Edward Rich, an expert from West Point, with "eleven fully grown and partly grown bodies . . . merely pouring acid on them would not do too much damage other than disfigure the surface. If there is enough acid, and a large enough vat to contain them, similar to a cannibal's pot, perhaps they could dissolve them. But you can't do it in three days." Both Professor Camps and Dr Rich agreed that teeth are virtually indestructible, but none had been found.

From 1924 to 1991, Yekaterinburg was called Sverdlovsk, after Yakov Sverdlov, Lenin's closest ally and the nominal head of state of the Russian Soviet Federative Socialist Republic, who officially authorized the execution of the Romanovs on behalf of the Central Committee. In 1976, the crime writer and former policeman Gely Ryabov was an official researcher and film-maker for the Soviet Interior Ministry. When sent to Sverdlovsk to work on a script for a film about the Soviet militia, he asked to be taken to the Ipatiev House.

As early as 1923, it had been dubbed "the last palace of the last Tsar". It then became a branch of the Ural Revolution Museum, or the Museum of the People's Vengeance. After this it was an agricultural college, and then, in 1938, became an anti-religious museum.

Ryabov was not the only one who wanted to see the crime scene. Party apparatchiks would arrive in large tour groups to pose before the bullet-damaged wall of the basement where the tsar and his family had been killed. In 1946, the house was taken over by the local Communist Party and used as administrative offices. Then in 1974, it was formally listed as a "historical revolutionary monument". However, to the embarrassment of the Soviet government, it gradually became a place of pilgrimage for people who wanted to honour the imperial family.

According to Ryabov, his visit had a profound effect on him.

"I felt that I, too, was responsible for all the cruelty which cannot be erased in my country's history," he said, "for everything that came with the great cataclysms which shook Russia. I decided it was my duty to discover the truth about the execution and the burial of the Romanovs and to tell people."

It was only just in time. In 1977, the head of the KGB, Yuri Andropov, convinced President Leonid Brezhnev that the Ipatiev House had become a site of pilgrimage for covert monarchists. So, as the sixtieth anniversary of the Russian Revolution approached, the Politburo declared that the house was not of "sufficient historical significance", and ordered its demolition. The task fell to the first secretary of the Sverdlovsk Communist Party, one Boris Yeltsin. The house was demolished that July. Yeltsin wrote in his memoirs that "sooner or later we will be ashamed of this piece of barbarism". After the fall of the Soviet State, the Church on the Blood was built on the site, now a major place of pilgrimage.

But by the time the Ipatiev House was demolished, Ryabov had already teamed up with Alexander Avdonin, a retired geologist and expert on the executions. They were joined by Michael Kochurov, another geologist. While the two geologists began covert fieldwork, Ryabov began searching the archives for material. He came across Sokolov's book and wondered whether it might offer up some clues. During his research, Sokolov had learnt that on 18 July 1918, two days after the murders, a truck left Yekaterinburg and went down the Koptyaki Road. At 4.30 the following morning, the truck got stuck in the mud. The railway guard at a small guard box where the road crossed the tracks said that men came to him, told him their truck was stuck and asked for railroad sleepers to make a bridge across the mud. They made the bridge and the truck left. By 9 a.m., it was back in its garage in Yekaterinburg. Sokolov had thoughtfully provided a picture of the bridge and Avdonin and Kochurov set out to find the spot where the truck had stopped.

The chief executioner Yakov Yurovsky was long dead, but Ryabov contacted his son Alexander, a recently retired admiral. He had a report that his father had originally submitted to the Soviet government describing the execution of the Romanovs and the disposal of their bodies. The report stated that after the execution the town's people had very quickly found out where they had been dumped, so they went to retrieve them from the Four Brothers mine.

"At about 4.30 a.m. on the morning of 19 July, the vehicle got permanently stuck," Yurovsky had written. "All we could do was either bury them or burn them . . . We wanted to burn Alexei and Alexandra Feodorovna, but instead of the last with Alexei we burned the Freilina [Demidova]. We buried the remains right under the fire, then shovelled clay on the remains, and made another bonfire on the grave, and then scattered the ashes and the embers in order to cover up completely any trace of digging. Meanwhile, a common grave was dug for the rest. At about seven in the morning, a pit 6 ft (1.8 m) deep and 8 ft (2.4 m) square was ready. The bodies were put in the hole and all the bodies generally doused with sulphuric acid, both so they couldn't be recognized and to prevent the stench from them rotting (the hole was not deep). We scattered them with lime, put boards on top, and drove over it several times – no traces remained. The secret was kept – the Whites never found it." At the end of his report, Yurovsky wrote the precise location of the grave. It was the spot where Avdonin and Kochurov had bored into the old road-bed and found beneath the surface traces of wood from the temporary bridge.

On 30 May 1979, Avdonin's team dug up the site and found human bones. They removed three skulls. When cleaned with water, they were grey and black and areas appeared etched with acid. The central facial bones of all the skulls were missing and some skulls had large round holes in them that could have been caused by bullets.

Because of the political repression in the Soviet Union at the time, their investigation into the murder of the Romanovs put them in danger, so after secret tests had been done on them in Moscow they decided to keep quiet about their find until the political circumstances changed. They reburied the skulls. When Mikhail Gorbachev became General Secretary of the Soviet Communist party and de facto ruler of the Soviet Union, he announced the policy of *glasnost* – "openness". In the new atmosphere, Ryabov wrote to Gorbachev in 1989 to ask for his help on a government level "so that all of this could be handled properly".

In 1991, the Soviet Union was dissolved and the new prime minister of Russia, Boris Yeltsin, called for an official investigation. In the meantime, the grave had been disturbed by the laying of a power cable. After three days of digging, investigators had unearthed around a thousand bones. It seems that a truck was run over the grave to pack down the earth, fracturing the bones. When a preliminary assembly was made – ironically in the shooting gallery of the local police headquarters – it appeared that they found the skeletons of four males and five females. On 17 July, it was announced that the bones in all probability belonged to Tsar Nicholas, his family and their servants. The male skeletons were all adults, so the body of the Tsarevich Alexei, who was thirteen at the time of his death, was missing, along with one of his sisters. Controversy surrounded which one. For years, rumours had circulated that the tsar's youngest daughter, the Grand Duchess Anastasia, had survived. In the 1920s, a young woman tried to commit suicide in Berlin. She had no papers and refused to identify herself. She was taken to a mental asylum where one of the other patients recognized her as a daughter of the tsar, the Grand Duchess Tatiana. But by 1922, several Russian émigrés began to believe that she was Anastasia. After leaving the asylum, she called herself Anna Tschaikovsky, later registering with the Berlin Aliens Office as Anastasia Tschaikovsky. In the United States in 1928, she began calling herself Anna Anderson to avoid the press. After the death of the tsar's mother, the Dowager Empress Marie, twelve of the surviving members of the Romanov family denounced her as an impostor. From 1938 to 1970, she fought to establish her claim to be Anastasia in the longest-running case to be heard in the German courts. The final judgment was that she did not have sufficient proof to claim that she was the grand duchess. She died in 1984.

In February 1992, US Secretary of State James Baker visited Yekaterinburg and Governor Edward Rossel asked him to send Western forensic experts to confirm the identification of the Romanov corpses. Dr William Maples from the University of Florida led a team of forensic specialists who visited Yekaterinburg in July 1992 and quickly determined that the bones belonged to the imperial family. It was then up to DNA to confirm their findings.

As grandson of Tsarina Alexandra's oldest sister, Victoria, Marchioness of Milford-Haven, the Duke of Edinburgh was one of the Romanov's closest living relatives. He gave a sample of blood that was compared to DNA extracted from the skeletons. The tests were performed by Dr Peter Gill at the Forensic Science Services at the Biology Research Science Laboratory in Aldermaston. Further tests were performed by Dr Mary-Claire King of the University of California at Berkeley and at the US Armed Forces Institute of Pathology in Rockville, Maryland. These tests were completed in the autumn of 1995. They confirmed beyond any doubt that the bones were indeed the skeletal remains of the imperial family and those of their retainers. Further tests were performed in 1998 when the remains of Tsar Nicholas's younger brother, Grand Duke Georgji, were exhumed, providing DNA that positively identified that the remains from the forest outside Yekaterinburg belonged to Nicholas II, with a certainty of a hundred million to one.

Meanwhile, Russian scientists used computer modelling to compare old photographs of the imperial family with the skeletons and demonstrated that the two missing bodies were those of the Tsarevich Alexei and his sister the Grand Duchess Maria, and not Grand Duchess Anastasia. After Anna Anderson died in 1984, her body was cremated. However, DNA was taken from part of Anderson's intestine removed during an operation in 1979, and retained by Jefferson Hospital in Charlottesville, Virginia. It was compared with that supplied by the Duke of Edinburgh and that removed from the bones of the Romanovs, and showed that she was not related. It is now thought that she was Polish factory worker Franziska Schanzkowska, who worked in a munitions factory during the First World War. Shortly after she heard that her fiancé had been killed at the front, a grenade fell from her hand and exploded. It injured her in the head and killed her foreman in front of her. In 1916, she was declared insane and was treated in two asylums. Then, in 1920, she was reported missing from her lodgings in Berlin.

The remains of the Romanovs were given a State funeral and Christian burial in 1998 in the St Catherine Chapel of Peter and Paul Cathedral in St Petersburg, where Russian monarchs have lain since Peter the Great. Two years later, the Romanov family were canonized by the Russian Orthodox Church for their "meekness during imprisonment and poise and acceptance of their martyr's death".

In July 2007, Sergei Plotnikov, a forty-six-year-old builder who is part of an amateur group searching for the remains of the missing Romanovs, was investigating a clearing surrounded by silver birch trees 6 miles (9.7 km) north of Yekaterinburg when the instrument he was using to prod the earth hit something hard.

"There was a crunching sound," he said. "This means you've hit coal or bone. My friend Leonid and I started to dig. We found several bone fragments. The first was a piece of pelvis. We then discovered a fragment of skull. It had clearly come from a child. We shouted over to the archaeologists. They began an expert search. My heart leaped with joy. I knew immediately that this was the kind of thing that happens only once in a lifetime. I also felt satisfied. I knew the Romanov children would finally be united with the rest of their family."

These two bodies had suffered the same fate as the Romanovs.

"It was clear they didn't die peacefully," said Plotnikov. "Their remains were very damaged. You could see that they had been covered in acid and burned with flames. What we dug up was in a very bad state. We didn't find any bullet holes. But it was clear from the bones that some kind of kerosene had been poured over them."

Russian archaeologists soon confirmed that the remains belonged to a boy of between ten and thirteen and a woman between eighteen and twenty-three. This would correspond to the thirteen-year-old Alexei and nineteen-year-old Maria. It was thought they were cremated because the killers wanted to make sure they were dead. There were accounts that Alexei and one of his sisters showed signs of life when the assassins lifted their bodies on to the back of the truck. This was confirmed by a Soviet memorandum that came to light in 1989.

Along with the bone fragments, Sergei Pogorelov, deputy director of the Sverdlovsk region's archaeological institute, and his team found pieces of Japanese ceramic bottles used to carry sulphuric acid poured on the Romanovs' corpses, and a hinge and wire that secured the wooden boxes holding the jars. They also recovered seven teeth, three bullets of various calibres and a fragment of a dress. Fires had been lit near the site. There was little doubt that they were the missing Romanovs, Pogorelov said.

Archaeologists had excavated practically the whole site in the 1990s, but then ran out of money. When they had to stop, they left behind an 86 ft^2 (8 m^2) patch of unexplored ground. This was exactly where the amateur team found the final remains. Tests carried out in Moscow and at the University of Massachusetts Medical School in Worcester, Massachusetts, on DNA extracted from the bones showed that they were, indeed, the Tsarevich Alexei and the Grand Duchess Maria. The following year, they too were laid to rest in the cathedral in St Petersburg.

In 2010, the Russian Supreme Court ordered the reopening of the criminal investigation in the deaths of the Romanovs after the prosecutor general's main investigative unit had closed it down, claiming that too much time had passed and those responsible were dead. The Supreme Court ruled that the deaths of the actual gunmen were irrelevant. The investigators were duty bound to set the record straight. So Yekaterinburg, it seems, is an ongoing crime scene.

MURDER AT FORT BRAGG

A T 3.33 A.M. ON 17 February 1970, Carolyn Landen, a telephone operator in Fayetteville, North Carolina, got a call
from a man with a faint voice who gasped: "My name is Captain
MacDonald . . . stabbing . . . need a doctor . . . MPs and an
ambulance at 544 Castle Drive . . . Hurry!"

"Is this on post or off post?" she asked.

"Damn it, lady . . . my family . . . it's on post!" he said.

"In that case I'm sorry, sir, but you'll have to call the military
police yourself. You see . . ."

Landen heard a clatter as the caller dropped the phone. She
kept the line open and dialled the military police at Fort Bragg,
gave the desk sergeant the address, then waited about three minutes until she finally heard a noise in her receiver.

"Is this Captain MacDonald?" she asked.

"Yes. Don't you understand, I need . . ."

"Just a minute, sir," she said, putting the call through to the
military police. Then she heard the desk sergeant ask: "Can I
help you?"

"Thank God," Jeffrey MacDonald said. "We've been
stabbed . . . people are dying . . . I may be dying . . . we need a
doctor and ambulance . . . 544 Castle Drive . . ."

"They'll be right there!"

Military policemen (MPs) Kenneth Mica and Dennis Morris
were out on patrol that night. The desk sergeant dispatched them
to a "domestic disturbance" at 544 Castle Drive, a one-storey
garden apartment within the perimeter of Fort Bragg. But the
base hospital would not send an ambulance until the MPs confirmed one was really necessary.

On the way to the crime scene, Mica saw a young woman wearing a floppy, wide-brimmed hat and a dark raincoat, standing in the rain just three blocks from Captain MacDonald's home. This struck him as peculiar. It was 3.55 in the morning. Had they not been on a call, Mica and his partner would have stopped to ask what she was doing there.

When they reached the address, half a dozen MPs were already outside the front door of the darkened house. Lieutenant Joseph Paulk, the duty officer, pounded on the door and got no response. The door was locked, so Sergeant Richard Tevere went around to the back where he found the rear screen closed, but the door itself open. Inside he found a charnel house. He rushed back to report and an ambulance was summoned from the base hospital.

The sight that greeted the MPs was gruesome. There was blood on the floor of the corridor that led to the bedrooms. In the master bedroom they found twenty-six-year-old Colette MacDonald. She was sprawled lifelessly on her back with her legs spreadeagled. She was clad only in a blood-soaked pink pyjama shirt, which was open. Her left breast was partially exposed. The rest of her chest was covered by the tattered blue pyjama top. There were stab wounds to her chest and neck, and a large pool of blood under her head. Both her arms were bloody and injured.

Lying next to her was her husband, Jeffrey MacDonald, a doctor with the Green Berets who are based in Fort Bragg. His head lay on her shoulder and his arm was stretched out across her body. He was wearing only blue pyjama bottoms. Mica knelt down beside him to check whether he was alive and heard him whisper: "How are my kids? I heard them crying."

Mica ran into the other bedroom where he found five-year-old Kimberley in bed under the covers. When he examined her with his flashlight, he found that her head had been battered so badly that a shattered piece of bone stuck out through the skin below her eye and there were stab wounds to her neck. Across the hall, two-year-old Kristen also lay dead on her bed. Soaked in blood, she had multiple stab wounds to her chest and back.

Mica went back into the master bedroom where MacDonald gasped: "I can't breathe. I need a chest tube." He passed out. Mica tried to revive him with mouth-to-mouth resuscitation. Then MacDonald came round.

"I realized someone was breathing in my mouth," said MacDonald. "And I opened my eyes, and I could see a ring of military police helmets circling me."

He pushed Mica away, saying: "Fuck me, man, look to my wife! Check my wife. Check my kids."

Mica asked him who did this. MacDonald replied: "Four of them. She kept saying, 'Acid is groovy, kill the pigs.'"

On the headboard of the bed next to Colette's dead body, written in blood, was the word "PIG".

MacDonald went on: "Three men . . . a woman . . . one man was coloured, he wore a field jacket, sergeant's stripes. The woman, blonde hair, floppy hat, short skirt, muddy boots . . . she carried a light, I think a candle."

Mica told Lieutenant Paulk about the woman with the floppy hat he had seen close to the crime scene.

"Don't you think we ought to send out a patrol?" he asked.

But the lieutenant was busy writing down everything MacDonald was saying.

The ambulance arrived and two medics put MacDonald on a stretcher. As they wheeled him down the hall, he tried to get off and had to be restrained.

"Goddamn MPs," he shouted. "Let me see my kids!"

When MacDonald reached Womack Army Medical Center Hospital, he was treated for injuries that included a collapsed lung. Otherwise his wounds were superficial, except for a one-centimetre stab wound to the chest and "several small puncture wounds that may have been from an instrument, such as an ice pick". He was given some mild sedatives before being questioned by members of the Army's Criminal Investigation Division (CID).

MacDonald told the CID that on the previous night his wife had gone to bed, while he remained reading in the living room. It had been a busy day. After his regular shift at the base hospital, he took his daughters Kimberley and Kristen to feed a pony he had bought them that Christmas. Then they went home, where he showered and changed into a pair of blue pyjamas. After a quick family dinner, Colette had headed off to her child-psychology class, while he put Kristen to bed. Worn out by the twenty-four-hour shift he had worked the day before, moonlighting at a civilian hospital, he had fallen asleep on the living-room floor watching TV. An hour later, Kimberley woke him and asked if she could watch her favourite programme, *Rowan & Martin's Laugh-In.* When the show was over, she went to bed. Forty minutes later, Colette came home. They had a glass of orange liqueur in front of the television. Colette, who was four and a half months pregnant with their first son, went to bed, MacDonald said. He was not ready to turn in, so he watched the Johnny Carson show, then returned to a Mickey Spillane novel he had been reading.

After a while, he was interrupted by Kristen crying. He made her a bottle of chocolate milk to calm her. Around 2 a.m., he finished the book. Then, after washing the dinner dishes, he went into the master bedroom where he found Kristen sleeping next to her mother. When he went to get in, he found that Kristen had wet the bed. So he carried the little girl back to her room. Not wishing to wake his wife by changing the sheets, he grabbed a blanket and went back into the living room to go to sleep on the couch.

The next thing he remembered, he said, was screaming.

"Jeff, why are they doing this to me?" his wife yelled.

And he heard Kimberley screaming: "Daddy, Daddy, Daddy!"

He sat up to find three people at the foot of the couch. One of them was a woman with long, stringy blonde hair and a big hat. She had a kind of light on her face.

"I don't know if it was a flashlight or a candle," he said. "I just remember that my instinctive thought was that, 'She's holding a candle. What the hell is she holding a candle for?'"

Then he remembered her saying: "Kill the pigs. Acid's groovy."

The black guy with the sergeant's stripes raised some kind of a weapon and hit him on the head. He struggled to get up and the man hit him again. He noticed then that there were three men and the woman kept repeating: "Acid is groovy, kill the pigs."

The two other men were hitting him. Then MacDonald said he felt a terrible pain in his chest.

"I grabbed this guy's whatever-it-was – I thought it was a baseball bat at the time," he said. "Meanwhile, both these guys were kind of hitting me, and all this time I was hearing screams. That's what I can't figure out . . . all I got a glimpse of was, was some stripes. I told you, I think, they were E6 stripes. There was one bottom rocker" – the lower patch on the back of a motor-cycle club's vest – "and it was an army jacket, and that man was a coloured man, and the two men, other men, were white."

In the struggle he kept feeling pains in his stomach and chest. Eventually, he let go of the club. Then he saw something that looked like a blade. As he fell, he saw the woman's knees and the top of her brown, muddy boots.

"The next thing I remember was lying on the hallway floor," said MacDonald. "I was freezing cold and it was very quiet. My teeth were chattering. I went down to the bedroom. I was dizzy, you know. I wasn't real alert. My wife was lying on the floor next to the bed. There was a knife in her upper chest. I took that out and tried to give her artificial respiration, but the air was coming out of her chest. So, I went and checked the kids . . . there was a lot of blood around."

When asked about his family, MacDonald wept profusely and struggled to compose himself.

"So, I went back into the bedroom. This time I was finding it real hard to breathe and I was dizzy. So I picked up the phone and I told this asshole operator that my name was Captain MacDonald and I was at 544 Castle Drive and I needed the MPs and a doctor and an ambulance. And she said, 'Is this on post or off post?' Something like that. And I started yelling at her. Finally, I told her it was on post, and she said: 'Well, you'll have to call the MPs.'

"So, I dropped the phone and went back and checked my wife again. Now I was – I don't know – I assume I was hoping I hadn't seen what I had seen, or I was starting to think more like a doctor. So, I went back and I checked for pulses. You know, carotid pulses and stuff. There was no pulse on my wife. I felt I was getting sick to my stomach and I was short of breath, and I was dizzy and my teeth were chattering cos I was cold. And so I didn't know if I was going – I assumed I was going into shock because I was cold. That's one of the symptoms of shock: you start getting chills."

He recognized that he was suffering another symptom – shortness of breath. "That's what happens when you get a pneumothorax" – air in the chest cavity, causing the collapse of the lung – "you think you can't breathe. I had to get down on my hands and knees and breathe for a while, and then I went in and checked the kids and checked their pulses and stuff. I don't know if it was the first time I checked them or the second time I checked them, to tell you the truth; but I had blood on my hands and I had little cuts in here."

He pointed to his mid-section. His head hurt, but he seemed to be thinking better, he said, and he went into the bathroom to look at himself in the mirror. It then struck him that he had not got anywhere with his phone call. He went back out into the hallway. By this time he was on his hands and knees.

"I went into the kitchen, picked up that phone and the operator was on the line. My other phone had never been hung up. She said, 'Is this Captain MacDonald?' I said, 'Yes it is.' And she said, 'Just a minute.' And there was some dial tones and stuff and then the sergeant came on. And he said, 'Can I help you?' So I told him that I needed a doctor and an ambulance and that some people had been stabbed, and that I thought I was going to die. He said, 'They'll be right there.' So, I left the phone; and I remember going back to look again. And the next thing I knew, an MP was giving me mouth-to-mouth respiration next to my wife."

MacDonald had told an intriguing tale, but the CID did not believe him. They had sent a young investigator, thirty-year-old William Ivory, to the crime scene. He arrived there at 3.50 a.m. – even before MacDonald had been carted off to hospital – and he found things that contradicted MacDonald's story.

In the small living room, a plant had been tipped over and a top-heavy coffee table was lying on its side – a position it would never assume in subsequent tests. But otherwise the living room was undisturbed, though MacDonald said he had struggled against three full-grown men in there. According to his testimony and his examination in hospital, he had been stabbed numerous times with a blade or ice pick, shredding his pyjama top. However, just a single fibre from his pyjamas was found in the living room. But, in the bedrooms, there were dozens. Several were found under Colette's body. Others were found under Kimberley's sheets. Two more were found in Kristen's room – one lodged under her fingernail. Under further questioning, MacDonald said that he had not been wearing the tattered pyjama top when he went to his daughters' rooms – he had already laid it over Colette.

The distribution of the blood around the house also raised Ivory's suspicions. A lot of it was found in the bedrooms. There was even a bloody footprint matching MacDonald's exiting Kristen's room. But only a drop too small to be typed was found on the hallway steps and none on the living-room floor where MacDonald said he had been attacked. A tiny fleck appeared on the front of one of the lenses of MacDonald's glasses, which were found near the living-room curtains. It was Kristen's. But MacDonald said he had taken his glasses off before he went to her bedroom.

Ivory found the tips of surgical gloves beneath the headboard where "PIG" had been written in blood. Would drug-crazed hippies such as those MacDonald described have had the foresight to purchase surgical gloves to conceal their fingerprints? Forensic tests would show that they were identical in composition to those MacDonald kept in a cabinet beneath the kitchen sink. Beside the cabinet, on the floor, Ivory discovered drops of blood that were the same type as that of Jeffrey MacDonald.

"My gut told me that what he told the investigators and what he told the military police could not possibly have happened in that house," said Ivory. The master bedroom, where Colette's body lay, was all too neat. "I looked at that and saw how everything was laid out. I saw a weapon over to the side. And the position of her body. On the headboard of the bed, the word 'PIG' was written in blood."

At 6.42 on the morning of the murder, outside the back door Ivory found an ice pick, an Old Hickory paring knife with a wooden handle and a piece of wood the size of a baseball bat with bloodstains on it. Forensic tests found that they had all been used in the murders. It was also discovered that all of them came from the MacDonalds' apartment.

Another damning piece of evidence was found in the living room – a March 1970 edition of *Esquire* magazine with smudges of blood on it. It carried an article about Charles Manson and his hippie "Family" who had killed Roman Polanski's wife Sharon Tate and several other people in a murderous rampage in Los Angeles six months earlier. Was this the origin of the murderous hippies that MacDonald said had killed his wife and daughters? There were eighteen points of similarity between the MacDonald and Manson murders, including the word "PIG" written in blood on the wall and a blonde hippy-style woman carrying a candle. Ivory believed that MacDonald had to look up the article after the murders to get his story straight.

MacDonald's own testimony over the next six weeks did not help him. Three times shortly after the murders he had said: "Be sure to tell the CID I took the knife out of my wife's chest."

But why was he so fixated on the knife? Investigators were all the more puzzled when tests showed that the knife had never been in Colette's chest in the first place. However, the bent Geneva Forge knife discovered in the bedroom was found to have made two slits in MacDonald's pyjama top. Colette had been killed by twenty-one wounds in the chest where an ice pick had been driven in to the hilt, though there were another sixteen wounds thought to have been inflicted by the Old Hickory paring knife found outside. She had also been hit around the head at least six times and both her arms were broken. Apparently, she had held them up in an attempt to defend herself.

Kimberley had also been hit on the head with a club at least six times. One blow had shattered her skull. Another, which had hit the left side of her face, was delivered with such force that it had splintered her nose and cheek. When she was near to death, she had been stabbed in the neck with a knife repeatedly. The blows were grouped so closely together that the pathologist Dr William Hancock could only estimate the number of wounds to be eight or ten.

Kristen had fifteen wounds from the ice pick in the chest, along with four knife wounds. She had been stabbed with a knife another twelve times in the back and once in the neck. One of her fingers was also cut to the bone, suggesting she had been holding up her hand to protect herself.

These were frenzied attacks. By comparison, MacDonald's injuries were minor. According to a staff surgeon, MacDonald's most serious wound was a "clean, small, sharp" incision in the right chest, which caused a partial deflation of a lung. This was easily remedied.

There was more damning crime scene evidence. Unusually, MacDonald and the members of his family all had different blood types. This allowed CID agents to put together a scenario that tracked the action around the apartment. According to the CID, a fight began between MacDonald and his wife in the master bedroom. Colette, they believed, struck the first blow, whacking her husband in the forehead with a hairbrush. MacDonald retaliated by clubbing her with a piece of timber thought to have been a slat from Kimberley's bed. Colette defended herself using the knife with the bent blade. Woken by the commotion, Kimberley appeared at the door of the master bedroom. Her brain serum was found in the doorway. It appeared she was struck, possibly inadvertently, during the furious altercation.

"We believe that the older girl was in the bedroom with them and got in the middle of the fight between them," said Ivory. "He swatted back and hit her on the side of the head and dropped her to the floor."

Believing Colette to be dead, MacDonald carried his wounded daughter back to her bedroom, where MacDonald placed her back in her own bed. Then he finished the job, stabbing and bludgeoning her. At the time, he was still wearing his pyjama top, which was splattered with Kimberley's blood.

"While he's doing that, his wife regains consciousness and goes to the baby's room and lays across her on the bed, obviously in an attempt to protect her," said investigator Peter Kearns.

Ivory said that MacDonald followed her into that room. "And he began beating her more there with the club. That's evidenced by blood sprays that were on the wall and on the ceiling."

After he killed his wife Colette and his daughter Kimberley, MacDonald came back into Kristen's bedroom where the child was still in her bed.

"And then he killed her," said Ivory. "And the only reason in the world that he killed her was because she was a witness. And she was old enough, she could say, 'I saw daddy hitting mommy.'"

After he had killed them both, MacDonald wrapped his wife's body in a sheet and carried it back to the master bedroom. On the way out, he left a footprint in Colette's blood.

"There are no ridge marks . . . so we can't say it's his. But all the configuration fits his foot," said Ivory.

He then had to inflict some wounds on himself that would appear life-threatening. So he took a disposable scalpel blade from his supply in the hallway closet. In the bathroom next to it, he cut himself between his seventh and eighth ribs, an area with few nerve-endings. The incision let air into his chest cavity and collapsed a lung. Now a victim himself, investigators said MacDonald then went about setting a stage to fit his story of an attack by drug-crazed hippies that he borrowed from the Manson murders. He went to the kitchen to get some surgical gloves. Donning them, he returned to the master bedroom, dipped his finger in Colette's blood and wrote "PIG" on the headboard – just as Manson's followers had at Sharon Tate's house. MacDonald then laid his pyjama top over his wife's chest and repeatedly stabbed through it with an ice pick. Finally, with the gloves still on, he threw the club, the ice pick and the Old Hickory knife out of the back door. He used the phones in the kitchen and master bedroom to summon help, messed up the living room and flushed the gloves and scalpel blade down the lavatory. Or he might have thrown them in the garbage as the CID allowed it to be taken away before they had inspected it.

In fact, the CID investigation was a disaster all around. The crime scene was not sealed off. Lieutenant Paulk admitted that he did not know how many military policemen had been inside the apartment. It is thought that twenty-six people tramped through the crime scene while evidence was being collected. Paulk had never attempted to compile a list of names and he left no one in charge to ensure that evidence was not disturbed when he left the apartment to call an ambulance and notify the provost marshal of the crime.

When the ambulance turned up, an ambulance driver moved other things around, encouraging the theory that MacDonald had staged the assault. He even stole MacDonald's wallet from under the noses of the MPs.

One of the first men on the crime scene picked up the receiver dangling from the bedroom phone to inform headquarters that the MPs had arrived. The phone was then wiped. Fingerprints were wiped clean off Kristen's baby bottle and other items after MacDonald had been taken to the hospital. In all, forty sets of fingerprints were lost, along with the bloody footprint, which was destroyed when they tried to remove it. A blue fibre found beneath Kristen's fingernail and a piece of skin taken from beneath one of Colette's nails were also lost. An army doctor attending the crime scene was allowed to remove the blue pyjama top and turn over Colette's body, disrupting fibre evidence. As mentioned, the garbage was taken away before it could be examined, allowing potentially critical pieces of physical evidence to be discarded.

"The crime scene handling by the Army CID in 1970 is now taught in military police and investigation schools as a primary example of a crime scene investigation gone mad. This is the worst example they could find," said MacDonald's lawyer.

While MacDonald claimed that his family had been attacked by four assailants, no attempt was made to close off the surrounding streets while a search was made. Soon after his arrival at 544 Castle Drive, Lieutenant Paulk himself noticed wet grass tracked in from outside at various places around the apartment, but did not know if this had been brought in by the attackers or by his own men. Some of them were not thinking straight because they were distraught as a result of the slaughter they had seen.

Despite the destruction of crime scene evidence, the CID formally read MacDonald his rights seven weeks after the murders. It was noted that he showed little emotion when questioned about his family. However, he did agree to take a polygraph, but ten minutes after leaving CID headquarters, he phoned to say he had changed his mind. The army responded by putting him under armed guard.

It would be three months before the army would convene an "Article 32" hearing – this is the military equivalent of a grand jury. MacDonald's mother hired a civilian attorney, a former American Civil Liberties Union lawyer from Philadelphia named Bernard L. Segal, to defend her son. Like the CID investigators, Segal was struck by his client's almost total lack of emotion when describing the night of the murder. It was only when MacDonald talked of discovering Kristen's mutilated body that he betrayed a flicker of feeling. Segal figured that doctors were trained to deal with horror, so had him evaluated by a Dr Robert Sadoff, founder of the American Board of Forensic Psychiatry. He found "possibly some latent homosexual conflicts", as well as "some narcissistic need to be famous or infamous". However, Dr Sadoff said that, overall, he was "fairly certain" that MacDonald had not killed his wife and children. His conclusion was one of the centrepieces of the defence.

Segal was then approached by twenty-two-year-old deliveryman William Posey who, while living in the hippie district of nearby Fayetteville, had a neighbour he knew only as "Helen". During a trip to the bathroom at around 4 a.m. on the night of the murders, Posey said he had looked out of the window and had seen a Ford Mustang pull in next door. In it was Helen and two or three males. About two weeks later, Helen told him that she was going to have to leave town because the police had been hassling her about her possible involvement in the MacDonald killings. She confided that she had been so high on mescaline and LSD that night that she could not remember what she had done. Posey also told Segal that Helen used to wear a blonde wig and a floppy hat, but after 17 February he never saw her wear them again.

At the Article 32 hearing, Segal seized the opportunity to question the CID's William Ivory about his cursory investigation of Helen, who had reportedly hung funeral wreaths outside her apartment and dressed in black on the day of the victims' funerals. It turned out that the CID knew all about Helen, whose full name was Helena Stoeckley. She was the daughter of a lieutenant colonel who had thrown her out of his house at the age of sixteen for using drugs. A heroin addict from the age of fifteen, she first bartered syringes stolen from the hospital where she worked as a volunteer, then traded sexual favours for the drug. Her name had come up in the investigation before. It was the name the CID put to the description of the woman MacDonald said he had seen.

The civil authorities also knew about Helena Stoeckley. Fayetteville narcotics agent Prince Beasley had been running her as an informant. When Beasley was told of the murders the following morning, he also identified Stoeckley.

"She was dressed that way last night, wearing a blonde wig. I saw her," he told his boss, Captain J. E. Melvin of the Fayetteville Police Department. "And one of the guys she was with last night was black, wearing a field jacket with stripes. That's not a combination you see just everywhere."

What's more, they had been in a blue Mustang fastback.

The owner of a grocery store and a customer testified that they had seen Stoeckley that morning. She appeared drugged and was with a black man in an army field jacket. The customer, Dorothy Averitt, had already had an encounter with the man. At nearby Hickory Trailer Court, he had swung a baseball bat and deliberately hit a baseball at her.

At 9 a.m., Joan Sonderson, the car hop at the Chute Drive Inn restaurant on Fort Bragg, found a woman answering Stoeckley's description asleep in one of the cars in the parking lot. When she asked her if she wanted coffee, the woman, who appeared drugged, declined. Then she said: "The MacDonalds were murdered last night. Did you know that?" Sonderson said she didn't. "And that MacDonald is in the hospital and his wife and children are dead?" A black man wearing an army fatigue jacket got out of the rear of the car. There was white man in the front of the car that Sonderson did not see well. After the woman and the black man used the lavatory, they drove off.

Stoeckley had given Beasley a tip off about a trailer in Hickory Trailer Court, near the grocery store in the vicinity of where the black and white couple had been seen. That afternoon, the trailer was raided and drugs were found. It had been rented by two white men and a black man wearing an army fatigue jacket with sergeant's stripes, who lived there. A neighbour recalled seeing the men coming to the trailer at about 5.30 a.m. that morning with a woman. One of the men had a small, foreign two-seater sports car – a rare sight in Fayetteville in those days. Cumberland County Sheriff's Detective John DeCarter saw a small foreign sports car crammed with people on Bragg Boulevard. MacDonald's defence team discovered that Raymond Cazares, another alleged member of the Stoeckley group, owned a small foreign sports car at the time of the murders.

MacDonald's defence team later compiled a list of sightings of Stoeckley and her cohorts. In the early evening before the murders, Colette MacDonald had attended her child-psychology class at the North Carolina University Extension Campus. As she left, teacher Edith Boushey saw Colette backed up against a wall by a young man she identified as Stoeckley's boyfriend, Greg Mitchell.

Around midnight, a group of people answering the description MacDonald gave of the intruders were seen in the Dunkin' Donuts on Bragg Boulevard in Fayetteville. The young woman appeared high on drugs. At 1.30 a.m., Marion L. Campbell saw a young, blonde woman with a floppy hat and a white man. He appeared to be "in another world". They were with a black man who wore an "olive drab or fatigue jacket". He did not appear to be drugged and seemed to be in charge. Some of them left in a van similar to one later seen in the vicinity of the MacDonalds' home. And sometime before dawn, the night man at Dunkin' Donuts saw a white woman and a black man come in. They had something on them that he thought was blood.

That night, First Lieutenant Edwin Casper II and his wife heard one female and at least two males moving through the yard behind their building from Bragg Boulevard towards the building where the MacDonalds lived. Two houses along from the Caspers, Captain James Shortill and his wife Rita noted that the time was 2.10 p.m. A few hundred yards from the MacDonalds' home, Captain Kenneth Lamb, a Green Beret, and his wife were woken by someone fumbling at their back door. By the time Lamb got there, they had disappeared.

Then at 308 Castle Drive – just half a block from the MacDonalds' – Jan Snyder was awoken by a car with a loud exhaust. Later it returned. It parked next to a jeep and the occupants got out and got into a Mustang. Two days after the murders, Greg Mitchell was stopped by a Fayetteville police officer for having a loud exhaust on his 1964 Plymouth. Mrs Snyder told a CID investigator about what she had seen. She was told that someone would come back and take a statement. No one did.

Between 1.30 and 2.30 that morning, Martha Evans was driving down Bragg Boulevard near the MacDonald residence when she saw a parked blue Mustang. Standing by the car was a woman with a broad-brimmed hat. There were at least two men with her.

After the raid on the trailer park, Beasley was warned off investigating the MacDonald murder case. "Cooperate with the army," he was told by Cuyler Windham, boss of the Inter-Agency Narcotics Bureau. Beasley knew that Stoeckley's apartment was full of candles. When he had first visited, he found a soldier lying naked with two nude women in a circle of lit candles. More candles were stacked in a wicker basket against a wall painted with the circle of the zodiac. He had also been told that Stoeckley carried an ice pick in her handbag.

As Stoeckley was his informant, it seemed quite reasonable to talk to her. That evening he headed to her apartment on Clark Street. No one was in. So he parked in a dark spot up the street and kept watch. At 2.30 a.m., he heard the blaring exhaust of Greg Mitchell's car approach. Stoeckley and five males got out. Mitchell was among them, but there was no sign of the black man with the fatigue jacket.

Beasley then blocked their car in the driveway and insisted on talking to Stoeckley. She was high on drugs.

"I know what you're looking for, Mister Beasley," she said. "You want to see my ice pick."

He told her that he had seen her with a black guy the previous night.

"You were wearing boots last night, and your wig and hat," he said. "The descriptions fit you and your black friend to a tee."

Stoeckley was tearful. Beasley got the impression that she had witnessed the murders, but could not talk because the others were there. He called the CID at Fort Bragg.

"Bad trip, bad trip," said Stoeckley.

"Don't say anymore now," said Beasley. "Wait until the army guys come. It's a Federal case. I don't have any jurisdiction." Nevertheless, he took the names of the men with her.

The CID did not turn up and he had to let them go, though privately he urged Stoeckley to call the CID the following morning.

Ivory had interviewed Stoeckley a few days after the killings, then again after hearing Posey's story come to light. Neither time did she say anything useful and she struck Ivory as a "space cadet". However, she said she was sure that she had not been inside the MacDonalds' house; she did not even know the address. It was 1970 and a lot of women wore blonde wigs and floppy hats – including Colette MacDonald. So inconsequential was the interview that Ivory did not take notes. Nor did he inform Beasley about the interview. Later, the FBI used Stoeckley as an informant in their search for the woman with the wig and hat that MacDonald had said he had seen. She was also interviewed and tape-recorded saying: "Acid is groovy, kill the pigs." But her photograph was not shown to MacDonald. Nor was he asked to listen to the tape.

"Is there any reason why you didn't make notes?" Segal asked Ivory.

"No particular reason," Ivory replied.

"Isn't it standard operating procedure when you are conducting an interview that's related to an enquiry into a triple homicide to make notes of interviews?" said Segal.

Ivory did not answer. As Segal cross-examined Ivory, it became clear that there had been no effective investigation of Stoeckley and her companions, who were also drug addicts. The CID had concentrated on finding evidence against MacDonald and ignored every other possible suspect.

"Has anybody checked the electric bill, gas bill and telephone bill for the particular apartment in which this lady lived?" asked Segal.

Ivory said that he did not know.

"Mr Ivory, you really can't say to us that Miss Stoeckley was being frank, open, and candid," said Segal. "She was following her rules, which are not to tell outsiders who her friends and associates are."

"She said to me she only knew them by their first names," Ivory replied

"Of course, the telephone company, gas company, and electric company and landlords don't generally function on the basis of just first names, do they?" said Segal, pressing the point.

"That's correct," said Ivory.

"That avenue of investigation might produce last names, might it not?" said Segal.

"That's correct."

"Is it fair to say that on the basis of what has been done up to now, it could not be considered that the investigation of Miss Stoeckley's whereabouts on 17 February is complete?"

"It is not complete."

Ivory had months to complete an investigation and, by the time of his hearings, Helena Stoeckley had disappeared. It also came out that MP Kenneth Mica, who had first seen the woman in the floppy hat on his way to the crime and had tried to get Lieutenant Paulk to have her picked up, had been ordered not to mention the incident during the hearings.

Segal pointed out that no signs of drugs or intoxication had been found when MacDonald was taken to the hospital. The very low level of alcohol in his system was consistent with the glass of orange liqueur that he had drunk with Colette earlier that evening.

Regarding his emotional and mental state, Dr Sadoff, who had examined MacDonald earlier, testified: "I feel that Captain MacDonald does not possess the type of personality or emotional configuration that would be capable of this type of killing with the resultant behaviour that we now see. In other words, I don't think he could have done this . . . He is a very warm person, and very gracious, and one whom, I must admit, I like."

Colonel Warren V. Rock, the head of the 4th Psychological Operations Battalion at the John F. Kennedy Institute of Military Assistance and thirty-year veteran who headed the Article 32 hearings, also ordered psychiatric testing at Walter Reed Army Hospital. The chief psychiatrist, Lieutenant Colonel Bruce Bailey, examined MacDonald, along with head of psychiatric consultation Major Henry Edwards and director of research psychiatry Lieutenant Colonel Donald Morgan. They found no sign of mental illness or derangement. MacDonald, they said, was a personable and engaging young man and they did not believe that he had lied about what had happened on the night of the murders.

The hearing was closed so the public did not hear of the incompetence of the crime scene investigation, though Segal made it his business to leak it to the press. He called a series of witnesses who testified that MacDonald was an "all-American boy". These were led by Colette's devoted stepfather, New Jersey egg salesman Freddy Kassab, who said what a wonderful husband and father MacDonald had been. With tears running down his face, he said: "If I ever had another daughter, I'd still want the same son-in-law."

Speaking for himself and his wife Mildred, he said: "We know full well that Jeffrey MacDonald is innocent beyond any shadow of doubt, as does everyone who ever knew him. I charge that the army has never made an effort to look for the real murderers and that they know Captain MacDonald is innocent of any crime."

Kassab then announced a $5,000 reward for information leading to the arrest of the real killers and began a campaign to have MacDonald freed.

"My wife and I have a right to show the whole country that the charges against Captain MacDonald are false," he said. Syndicated columnist Jack Anderson then took up the cause and wrote a column criticizing the army for closing the hearing to the public and press.

MacDonald's friends, neighbours and professional associates – many leading figures in the military and medical fields – said much the same. His former commanding officer, Robert Kingston, called him "one of the finest, most upright, most outstanding young soldiers and very devoted to both his wife and children". However, it did come out that MacDonald had been unfaithful when away on training missions, but Colette, it was said, knew nothing of these indiscretions.

In his report, Colonel Rock found that the charges against Captain MacDonald were not true, recommended that they be dismissed and that the appropriate civilian authorities take up the investigation of Helena Stoeckley.

Ivory said he was shocked: "Because I knew that there was enough evidence to put reasonable suspicion in anybody's mind that perhaps this guy had done that."

Many other people at Fort Bragg were not happy with Rock's report and, instead of dismissing the charges completely, General Flanagan merely dropped the charges due to insufficient evidence. This meant that they could be revived again at any time.

MacDonald and Kassab's campaign against the army investigations had raised the possibility of perjury charges. These had to be refuted and a second CID investigation was now underway.

This time it was in the hands of a seasoned investigator, rather than the rookie Ivory.

Knowing that feelings at Fort Bragg were running against him, MacDonald applied for an honourable discharge, sold off his family's possessions in a yard sale and moved to New York, where he rubbed shoulders with model, heiress and socialite Countess Christina Paolozzi Bellin and searched for a journalist who would pay for his story. Then he appeared on a television with broadcast journalist Walter Cronkite to complain about his treatment by the army, and on *The Dick Cavett Show* he made wisecracks about the army investigators.

"He knew how to do it, as we say in the talk show trade. He knew how to handle himself," Cavett said. But this was not how a man who had just lost his wife and children should appear, Cavett felt. "His affect is wrong, totally wrong. My affect was, 'Gee, to find your wife and kids murdered.' And even his answer to that was something like, 'Hey, yeah, isn't that something?' Almost sounded like Bob Hope. Very like Bob Hope."

Colette's family were watching the show that night and were disturbed by MacDonald's performance.

"All he spoke about was how his rights had been violated," said Colette's older brother, Robert Stevenson. "I don't think he once mentioned about, 'Let's get the murderers. My family's been killed.' But I remember him grinning like a Cheshire cat."

Kassab, until then MacDonald's most dogged defender, was put off by the sight on his son-in-law joking about so grave a subject as the murder of his stepdaughter and grandchildren. MacDonald humoured Kassab by telling him that he and some Green Beret buddies had tracked down one of the killers and put him "six feet under". Kassab later found out this was not true.

Then MacDonald made another mistake. He gave Kassab the transcript of the Article 32 hearings that his father-in-law had been requesting for months. Going through the testimony with a fine-tooth comb, Kassab found that MacDonald had said things that could not be true. For example, he said he had seen blood bubble from Kimberley's chest. But the room was dark and Kimberley had no chest wounds. MacDonald also claimed in testimony that he had sustained near life-threatening injuries. Kassab had visited MacDonald in the hospital less than eighteen hours after the attack and found him sitting up in bed, enjoying a meal and with very little in the way of bandages and dressing. He also discovered that some of MacDonald's Green Beret buddies had come to the hospital and they had drunk a bottle of cold duck – a mixture of red wine and champagne.

With the investigators, Kassab spent hours at 544 Castle Drive, going over the crime scene inch by inch, testing MacDonald's testimony against the crime scene evidence. MacDonald's staunchest supporter had now become his most resolute enemy.

"He sat around a table that I still have at home, where you can see the elbow marks as he smoked pack after pack of cigarettes, trying to decide how this happened, drawing the diagrams, plotting it with the X's where the bodies were, the differing blood types," said Colette's brother Robert.

"When I was faced with the evidence, put together with what I knew he had told me, nothing fit. Absolutely nothing," said Kassab.

MacDonald was astounded.

"It never occurred to me that Alfred Kassab would turn on me, to be quite honest," he said.

MacDonald's mother had sold her house to pay for his defence. Now he had to earn some money to pay her back. He began working as an emergency-room physician at the St Mary Medical Center in Long Beach, California, alongside his old friend Jerry Hughes, who had transformed the department into one of the best in the state. There he soon acquired the accessories of a swinging bachelor, including a marina-front condominium and a yacht.

An enthusiastic sportsman, MacDonald helped organize an inter-departmental softball competition at the medical centre. He also taught emergency medicine at UCLA Harbor General Medical Center and became a public speaker in the campaign against child abuse. An expert in CPR, he saved the lives of a number of policemen and was made an honorary lifetime member of the Long Beach Police Department. Once again, he was known, liked and extremely successful professionally. Meanwhile, CID officers were on his trail and they began to discover that the MacDonalds' marriage had not been as picture-perfect as had been made out.

Born in the Jamaica district of Queens, in New York, MacDonald had been both "most popular" and "most likely to succeed" at Patchogue High School. A quarterback in the high-school football team, he was handsome, intelligent and hard-working. He won a scholarship to Princeton University, moving on to Northwestern University Medical School. After graduating, he did his internship in the prestigious Columbia Presbyterian Medical Center in New York City. But it was a struggle. MacDonald was only nineteen when his high-school sweetheart, the intelligent and attractive Colette Stevenson, fell pregnant. They married a month before his twentieth birthday. Kimberley was born the following April. While MacDonald was at Princeton, Colette was at Skidmore College. Then, together, they moved to Chicago. Kristen was born while MacDonald was still at medical school.

After he had completed his internship in 1969, he joined the army and the family moved to Fort Bragg in Fayetteville, where he was assigned to the Green Berets as a Group Surgeon to the 3rd Special Forces Group that September. That Christmas, Colette wrote in a card sent to friends: "We are having a great, all-expenses-paid vacation in the army. It looks as if Jeff will be here in North Carolina for the entire two years, which is an immense load off my mind at least. Life has never been so normal nor so happy. Jeff is home every day at five and most days even comes home for lunch. By the way, been having such a good time lately that we are expecting a son in July."

But there was a cloud hanging over this idyllic marriage – MacDonald's persistent infidelity. The CID discovered that he had at least fifteen girlfriends, most while he was away from home, training with the army. Colette's sister-in-law, Vivian "Pep" Stevenson, said that Colette knew of the affairs and complained bitterly about them. The marriage was on the rocks.

"I give up," Colette told Stevenson. "I don't want to do this anymore."

Two days before the murder, MacDonald informed her of another upcoming trip. He would be away for three months, during the last stages of what was expected to be a dangerous pregnancy, travelling as a physician for the Fort Bragg boxing team. Colette was so upset she phoned her mother, saying she wanted to come home with the kids.

Even her death did not dull MacDonald's libido. A secretary at Fort Bragg told the CID that MacDonald had sex with her "as often as possible", while he stood accused of murdering his wife and kids.

MacDonald admitted that he was unfaithful throughout the latter part of their marriage.

"I did step out on Colette," he said. "None of which I am proud of."

But he had his excuses.

"I don't think they were real girlfriends," he said. "They were one-night stands. I never had a love affair with anyone where we planned weekends away or divorce. I wore my wedding ring. It was the temper of the times. I like women and I wasn't thinking of the consequences. I had high testosterone. Among guys around me and people in medical school and the service, I wasn't doing anything unusual. It was '68, '70, and a lot of things were exploding."

His wife knew, he said, but was not concerned.

"I essentially wasn't screwing around. It's not true. Colette had no fears or worries. There weren't any."

Not to be wrong-footed again, the CID tracked down Helena Stoeckley, who had already told Nashville police officers that she believed that she was a witness to the MacDonald murders. But she would only say more if given immunity from prosecution. This was refused. Nevertheless, she took a polygraph test. The man who administered it told the CID: "Miss Stoeckley is convinced that she was physically present when the three members of the MacDonald family were killed."

But those who knew her said that she was disturbed. At school, she had been a sad little girl who made up stories to get attention. One of those stories, it turned out, was the one she told Posey – that she had to leave town to get away from the cops. The police were not even looking for her. Stoeckley did leave Fayetteville two months later to go to a hospital for her drug addiction. By then she was taking heroin eight or nine times a day, as well as taking barbiturates, stimulants and psychedelic drugs. Her rehab did not last long.

The diagnosis was that she had a "schizoid personality". "The prognosis for this patient seems poor," the psychiatrist wrote on her discharge form.

The CID discovered that Posey also had a penchant for making up stories, including the one about seeing Stoeckley in a Mustang on the night of the murders. After failing a lie-detector test, Posey admitted that he was not sure about seeing Stoeckley that night, and the sighting of the Mustang, it appeared, came from a dream he'd had two months later.

Stoeckley's credibility as a witness was further undermined by Fayetteville narcotics agent Prince Beasley, who had been running her as an informant.

"Helena would do anything to get me to pat her on the back and act proud of her," Beasley said. "That's why she turned in some of her best friends."

Beasley volunteered to accompany a CID agent to Nashville, Tennessee, where Stoeckley had resumed her career as an informant for the police department. She seemed happy to see Beasley, but over the next two months told the CID a jumble of contradictory stories. She later told the CID that she was only doing what Beasley had advised her: "Tell them anything, just get them off your back."

The CID went back to their crime scene evidence, but Stoeckley's hair and fingerprints did not match any of those remaining from the crime scene, and she was cleared as a suspect. The CID then prepared a 3,000-page report, again naming MacDonald as the prime suspect. But lead investigator Peter Kearns still wanted to interview one more witness – another of

MacDonald's girlfriends that they had recently discovered. He needed the approval of a lawyer in the Washington headquarters of the army's judge advocate general. He picked twenty-seven-year-old Brian Murtagh, a native of Queens who reminded people of Woody Allen, and tried to bounce him into giving his approval.

Dumping a stack of papers on Murtagh's desk, Kearns said: "Don't bother to read, just sign here."

"I was green, but not that green," recalls Murtagh. "I told him to leave it."

As Murtagh plunged into the paperwork, Kearns kept bringing more material, including the crime scene photographs of Kimberley and Kristen.

"I was feeling sick looking at them," says Murtagh. "I must have made then some kind of emotional commitment that however long it took – whatever it took – I was going to do nothing that, either through act or omission to act, was going to see this guy get away with this."

By this time, MacDonald had admitted to his father-in-law that he and his buddies had not caught one of the intruders and killed him.

"I was keeping Freddy happy," he explained. "The man is a fanatic."

It made no difference. Kassab was now convinced that MacDonald had killed his daughter-in-law. But while the new investigation had turned up fresh evidence, Kassab and Murtagh were told repeatedly that they did not have enough to convict MacDonald. So Kassab took the case to the Justice Department and the CID's crime scene evidence was handed over to the laboratories of the FBI, who made an exception to their usual policy of refusing to examine evidence that had been tested by other government labs.

"It wasn't until Freddy and I went from New York down to Clinton, North Carolina, to swear out a citizen's arrest. That's when the federal government got off their duffs and got an indictment and a grand jury," said Kearns.

With the aid of Kearns, Freddy and Mildred Kassab presented a citizen's criminal complaint against Jeffrey MacDonald in April 1974. The Justice Department had grown tired of the pressure that Kassab was putting on them and handed the case over to Victor Woerheide, whose handling of last-resort causes had made him the Justice Department's "junkyard dog". Murtagh offered his services and, in August, a grand jury was convened in Raleigh, North Carolina. After seven months of testimony and evidence, in January 1975, it indicted Jeffrey Robert MacDonald on three counts of murder. Within the hour, MacDonald was arrested in California.

After a week, he was freed on $100,000 bail pending disposition of the charges. That May, MacDonald was arraigned and pleaded not guilty to the murders. District Judge Franklin T. Dupree Jr rejected the defence arguments that MacDonald had been denied a speedy trial, as guaranteed by the US Constitution, and that he stood in double jeopardy as he had already effectively been tried in the Article 32 hearing. He set a trial date. Bernie Segal went to the Fourth Circuit Court of Appeals, who stayed the trial, then dismissed the indictment on the grounds that MacDonald had not been given a speedy trial.

MacDonald said that the "nightmare was over". In fact, it was only just beginning. In May 1978, the US Supreme Court overturned the appeals' court decision and reinstated the indictment. In October, the Fourth Circuit rejected MacDonald's double jeopardy arguments and, in March 1979, the Supreme Court refused to review that decision. So in July 1979, nine and a half years after the murders, MacDonald finally came to trial.

In the meantime, Woerheide had died of a heart attack. His place would be taken by Assistant US Attorney James Blackburn, who was trying his first homicide case. He was a mild-mannered minister's son from Winston-Salem, who MacDonald described as "chickenshit". He used the case as a springboard to become the US Attorney of the Eastern District of North Carolina, but was later convicted of forgery, fraud and embezzlement.

Blackburn would be assisted by Brian Murtagh, who MacDonald called a "little viper, totally lacking in the social amenities". Murtagh had been in a courtroom only once before, as a co-prosecutor in an obscenity case that the government lost. He was later accused of withholding several critical pieces of physical evidence that would have proven MacDonald's innocence.

There were even claims that Judge Dupree was biased. James Proctor, a former Assistant US Attorney who had been involved in the MacDonald case, had been an associate in Dupree's law firm from 1967 to 1969. He was married to one of Dupree's two daughters, and fathered Dupree's first grandchild.

Bernie Segal was still leading for the defence but, as a long-haired, liberal Jewish Yankee it was thought he might not go down well with a North Carolina jury composed of the law-and-order types his polling favoured. So he took on as co-counsel Wade Smith, a banjo-playing local man who could ladle on the drawl. Smith was one of the top trial lawyers in North Carolina, and he and Segal devised a defence strategy based on a simple premise.

"Is it possible for a person to live a good life and all of a sudden, in one moment, slaughter and mutilate his children, stab his wife many, many times, and then live out his life and have nothing like that happen again?" asked Smith. "And it suggests to me a reasonable doubt about whether he did it in the first place."

To help pay for his defence, MacDonald tried to secure a book deal. His first choice as author was Joseph Wambaugh, the LAPD sergeant turned best-selling crime novelist. But this collaboration was scuppered at the first meeting.

"I had interviewed dozens and dozens of people who were survivors of horrific crimes – some immediately after the event, some many years later," recalled Wambaugh. "I had never, in all my experience, seen anyone describe an event like that in the almost cavalier manner that Dr MacDonald described it."

MacDonald settled on Joe McGinniss, the author of *The Selling of the President*, a best-seller in 1968. In 1979, McGinniss was writer-in-residence at the *Los Angeles Herald-Examiner* and read in the paper that the Long Beach Police Officers Association was giving a dinner dance to raise money for MacDonald's legal defence. McGinniss, a former journalist, remembered the case when it first hit the headlines nine years before. He contacted MacDonald, who offered him an interesting proposition. If McGinniss wrote a book about the case from the perspective of the defence, he could live with the defence team in North Carolina and be privy to all their plans, strategies and deliberations. In return, McGinniss agreed to pay a portion of the proceeds from the book – 26.5 per cent of the publisher's $300,000 advance and 33 per cent of the royalties – to MacDonald's legal fund. As part of this deal, MacDonald agreed he would not sue McGinniss for libel no matter what he wrote.

Segal had hired forensic scientist Dr John Thornton to examine the crime scene evidence, but the prosecution would not hand it over.

"I was stunned to get the government's response," said Segal. "The government's response is 'Dr MacDonald is not entitled to receive this evidence now because he didn't ask for it in time.' I didn't know whether to cry or to laugh."

Judge Dupree then intervened.

"In almost any state court, the examination of evidence in a murder trial would be given as a right to the defence experts," Segal complained. "But not with the Feds. It's up to the judge's discretion."

While the army's initial assessment of the CSI evidence had taken six months, Thornton was only allowed access to it for just a few weeks before the trial. Even then, Murtagh only allowed Thornton to examine the evidence one piece at a time in a small jail cell with boxes stacked all around the room. Handwritten lab notes made by army CID technicians were withheld, so the defence had very little idea of what they were looking at.

Dupree also prevented the defence from introducing Colonel Rock's report, which found that the charges against MacDonald were not true. This prevented Segal from airing the incompetence of the CID's investigation and their mishandling of evidence. Notes accompanying the report were also denied to the defence and they were not allowed to introduce into evidence the psychiatric evaluation of MacDonald, which suggested that someone of his personality type would not have been able to kill his wife and children. Dupree explained that since no insanity plea had been entered, he did not want the trial bogged down by contradictory psychiatric testimony from the prosecution and defence.

The defence were depending on the testimony of Dr Robert Sadoff and the government psychiatric witness that had appeared at the Article 32 hearings. Segal also wanted to call Dr Seymour Halleck, a well-known forensic psychiatrist. After examining MacDonald, Dr Halleck also pronounced him to have a stable, non-pathological personality who was not the type to commit murder. He was not allowed to testify.

Judge Dupree also disallowed the prosecution's request to introduce several reports from the military investigators that claimed MacDonald may have murdered his wife and two daughters in a drug-induced rage. Dupree considered they were biased and based on hearsay. There was no evidence of drugs or intoxication when MacDonald was examined in hospital soon after the crime.

Judge Dupree would only allow psychiatric testimony if MacDonald underwent another psychiatric examination with a psychiatrist selected by the judge. Segal had very little choice but to go along with this. Dr James Brussel was picked, who had made his name on the cases of the Boston Strangler and the "Mad Bomber" George Metesky, who had terrorized New York planting bombs in public places in the 1940s and 1950s. After Brussel's offender profile proved uncannily accurate in that case, the press dubbed him "the Sherlock Holmes of the couch".

Some considered him a charlatan. Authors Jerry Allen Potter and Fred Bost, who wrote the book *Fatal Justice* about the MacDonald case, said: "Brussel's dominant reputation was that of almost psychic criminalist with the power to describe a suspect without interviewing him, without seeing the crime scene, and without questioning witnesses. It was said that he often needed only to talk with police on the telephone to make his diagnosis . . . Brussel was also an innovative researcher into novel methods for controlling inmates in psychiatric institutions. Lamenting the frustrations of managing unruly patients and the cost of housing them in the late 1940s, Brussel and an associate instituted electric shock experiments on the brains of female inmates."

After a brief examination, Brussel declared that MacDonald was a homicidal psychopath. What the defence did not know was that the CID had been consulting Brussel on the MacDonald case for eight years. Far from being an independent expert witness, Brussel had gone on record to say that MacDonald was guilty eight years before he had ever met him.

The defence was not given a copy of Brussel's report before the trial, though Judge Dupree and Brian Murtagh got one. Judge Dupree then ruled that psychiatric testimony would not be presented to the jury because it would confuse the jurors. However, Brussel's report that characterized MacDonald as a twisted monster was placed into the trial record even though the reports of the other psychiatrists were not.

Dupree also allowed the prosecution to introduce the 1970 copy of *Esquire* magazine found at the scene of the crime. This, they contended, was where MacDonald got the idea of blaming the murders on a hippie gang. While there was a bloody fingermark on it, it was smudged so it could not be positively linked to MacDonald.

After nine years wrangling, the court case came down, once again, to the crime scene evidence. Key to the prosecution case was the so-called "pyjama folding experiment". Brian Murtagh asked the FBI's chief forensic expert Paul Stombaugh to fold the pyjama top so that the forty-eight small, smooth, round holes thought to have been made by an ice pick in the fabric matched the twenty-one wounds in Colette's chest. Stombaugh did so and produced photographs of the pyjamas with metal skewers representing the blows of the ice pick sticking out of a mannequin. Blackburn and Murtagh explained to the jury that this was clear proof that MacDonald's story was a lie and that he had covered his wife's body with the top and then repeatedly stabbed her through it with the ice pick.

Segal had no access to the laboratory notes from either Stombaugh's experiment or the original CID investigation, so the defence was at a severe disadvantage. However, Segal had discovered that Stombaugh, though head of the FBI's chemistry laboratory, had only one year of formal training in chemistry. The judge would not allow this information to be presented to the jury.

During cross-examination, Segal was able to get Stombaugh to admit that there were significant differences in the position of the pyjama top shown in the crime scene photographs, where it is on top of Colette's body, and its position in the photos of the experiment. In other words, Stombaugh had adjusted the position of the pyjama top to get the results he wanted.

Stombaugh's evidence was countered by the defence's forensic expert, Dr Thornton, who pointed out that, when subjected to violent, persistent stabbing, loose fabric like that of a pyjama top would move around, so subsequent stabbings would move the holes made by the first punctures out of alignment.

The defence also pointed out that the FBI experiment failed to take into consideration the thirty punctures and eighteen cuts in Colette's own pyjama top, which would have lain between MacDonald's pyjama top and Colette's chest if the prosecution's contention was correct. Stombaugh said he had not been asked to analyse the holes in Colette's pyjama top.

Later, the lab notes, released under the Freedom of Information Act, showed that the CID's forensic investigators had attempted the folding experiment, but found it could not be performed in a way that indicated MacDonald's guilt unless they abandoned the scientific criteria that Stombaugh had given them.

During the Article 32 hearings in 1970, MacDonald had said: "I let go of the club and I was struggling with these two people and I realized that, you know, I couldn't punch back. My hands were like bound up in my own pyjama top. I couldn't get them out of the sleeve or something . . . as I was struggling, I received another what seemed like fairly impressive blow on the side of my arm and said to myself, 'What do I do now?' Really I was just struggling, trying to get my hands free. My hands themselves were free, but the pyjama stop was around my wrist and between my wrist and just around part of my hand really. And in the struggle, I had hold of one of these hands – I don't know which one – and in the hand I saw a blade."

The pyjama top, MacDonald maintained, had been damaged in that attack. So in the courtroom, Blackburn and Murtagh staged a dramatic reconstruction of events. With a similar pyjama top wrapped around his hands, Murtagh tried to fend off a series of blows from Blackburn, who was wielding an ice pick. The prosecution showed that the resulting holes in the pyjama top were jagged and torn, not smooth and round like the holes in MacDonald's pyjama jacket. Also, during the re-enactment, Murtagh received a small wound on his left hand. But when MacDonald had been examined at Womack Hospital, he had no wounds on his arms or hands. The inference was that he had not been involved in a struggle as he claimed.

Dr Thornton then repeated the pyjama-folding experiment, using a ham, and testified that the pyjama top did not have to be stationary to give clean, round holes when stabbed with an ice pick. It could just as easily have been in motion.

Stombaugh also testified that the bloodstains on MacDonald's pyjama top indicated that the tears in the fabric occurred afterwards as the stains on either side of the tears matched. The implication was that MacDonald had already fought with Colette. Her blood had stained his pyjama jacket. Then he had lain it on her body and stabbed through it. The defence had been given no chance to examine any lab notes supporting this new theory. When Segal asked for the photographic evidence, Stombaugh was unable to provide it. Nevertheless, the prosecution was able to make this assertion and the defence had no way to refute it.

Years later, when the defence team finally got its hands on the lab notes through the Freedom of Information Act, they found that Janice Glisson, a technician at the army's forensic lab, had explored the same bloodstain theory and had come to a different conclusion. She had found that the stain edges on either side of the rips did not match, so the pyjama top was ripped before it was stained, not afterwards.

Stombaugh also claimed that he found a bloody hair from Colette's head entwined with a fibre from MacDonald's pyjamas. The defence knew nothing of this. The evidence had been provided by Murtagh, but he had not told Segal of its existence. Again the defence was wrong-footed and could not challenge the evidence. But they questioned how such damning physical evidence had not been produced nine years earlier.

Again, when laboratory notes were obtained through the Freedom of Information Act years later, it was clear that the CID combed through the physical evidence three times and found no hair entwined in a fibre. The bloodstained hair in question was not even Colette's, but that of Kimberley. And it was not entwined with fibres from MacDonald's pyjamas.

The prosecution said that MacDonald had left two bloody footprints on a blood-soaked bedspread he used to transport Colette's body from Kristen's room back to the master bedroom. After the trial, the defence learnt that the FBI laboratory had repeatedly tested the sheet looking for footprints and found none. Again, this information had been withheld from the defence during the trial.

Then there was the question of the murder weapon. MacDonald always maintained that he did not own an ice pick at the time of the murders. When interviewed in 1970, both Mildred Kassab and the MacDonald's babysitter, Pam Kalin, had told army investigators that there was no ice pick in the MacDonalds' apartment. The two women were questioned again in 1971 and 1972, when both still claimed that they had not seen an ice pick. But in 1979, after extensive interviews with Brian Murtagh, both changed their minds and suddenly remembered seeing an ice pick nine years after the event.

Another piece of damning evidence was the recording made of the military investigators' interview with MacDonald on 6 April 1970. The jury heard MacDonald's matter-of-fact – almost indifferent – description of the murders. Then, when his interrogators suggested that he had committed the murders, he became defensive, emotional and angry. He asked the investigators why they would think he would have murdered his pregnant wife and two daughters in cold blood for no reason when he had a beautiful family, a good job and everything going for him. The investigators then confronted him with what they had discovered about his extramarital affairs. The jury heard MacDonald respond blithely: "Oh, you guys are more thorough than I thought."

Despite this, the prosecution could not come up with a convincing motive for the murders. MacDonald had no history of violence or domestic abuse of his wife or children.

While the prosecution felt that they had very little chance of getting a conviction when they started out, their confidence grew.

"The strength of our case always was very simple," said Blackburn. "The physical evidence, the scientific evidence, his statements. That was our case."

Segal called Helena Stoeckley as a witness for the defence in the hope that she would confess to being one of the intruders that MacDonald claimed had entered his family's apartment, attacked him and murdered his wife and children. Over the past nine years, Stoeckley had made several contradictory statements regarding the murders. Sometimes she said she was involved; on other occasions she said she could not remember where she had been on the night of the murders.

In 1978, she had contacted the FBI and told an agent that she was involved with the MacDonald killings. At the time, she was being treated for depression in a hospital in Raleigh, North Carolina. It was noted that she had suicidal tendencies but, when she entered the hospital, she showed no signs of drug abuse.

Just before she was to give testimony, she was interviewed by the defence and denied ever being in the MacDonalds' apartment or ever seeing Jeffrey MacDonald – until she was confronted by him in court. But Segal decided to take a chance.

At the trial, she said that, on the night of the murders, she was with her boyfriend Greg Mitchell and a number of soldiers from Fort Bragg. She admitted that they were all taking drugs, but no amount of threats or cajoling could prevent her from telling the jury that she had been too stoned to remember where she had been between midnight and 4 a.m. on the night of the murder. She also admitted owning a floppy hat, a shoulder-length blonde wig and boots. But she had burnt the wig as it linked her to the murders.

"Just a four-hour gap between midnight and 4 a.m., she claimed to have a lapse of memory," said Segal. "It's absurd . . . She lied about whether she remembered what was going on but she lied out of a defensive need to protect herself. She knew the government was looking at her."

Segal then asked her why she had told six people that she had been in the MacDonald's house at the time of the murders. She said that she did not remember. These witnesses were on hand. Out of the jury's hearing, all six swore that Stoeckley said that she might well have been in the house. One of them was Detective Prince Beasley, who heard her say on the morning after the murders: "In my mind, I saw this thing happen." Two other police officers also heard her admit to being present when Colette and the children were murdered. And a friend heard her admit she was at the MacDonald apartment and held a candle while the crimes were committed. An army polygraph expert also confirmed that Helena said she was present at the crime scene and explained that the people she was with had decided to punish Dr MacDonald for refusing to give methadone to drug-addicted soldiers.

But Judge Dupree refused to let them give their testimony in open court. He noted Stoeckley's long history of drug abuse. Not only were Stoeckley's statements "clearly untrustworthy", he ruled, but "this tragic figure" had made most of them while heavily drugged, possibly while hallucinating. He did allow the other witnesses to testify, but they were not to repeat what Stoeckley had said about the murders. This was hearsay as, otherwise, Stoeckley could not be connected to the slaying. However, when she had been interviewed by the prosecution before the trial, she confessed directly to Brian Murtagh. This was again withheld from the defence despite legal requirements.

A number of character witnesses testified that MacDonald loved his wife and kids. But Brussel's psychiatric report had already destroyed his "golden boy" image and he was now seen as a raging maniac. Segal had no choice but to call MacDonald, who on the stand tearfully denied murdering his wife and children. Sometimes he was so overwrought that he could not speak. For the jury, this was a stark difference from the way he appeared on the tape the prosecution had played of the eerily detached young captain parrying his CID interrogators years earlier. It stretched their credulity.

Under cross-examination from Blackburn, MacDonald became combative but could offer no alternative explanation to the evidence that had been presented. This, on reflection, was a mistake.

"On cross-exam, I got real testy – no question," said MacDonald afterwards. "My mom used to tell me, 'You always look cool, except when you are really nervous. Then you get a little smile.' And that combination was not good for me . . . Bernie said I did fine. My mom, my secretary . . . all said I did fine . . . He said, 'You are the Establishment. You're a captain in the Green Berets. No one is more established than a person who volunteers for the army, then airborne and Special Forces. You are not a radical. You don't wear a ponytail. You never wore an earring. You don't have tattoos. You are exactly what that doctor's son is, exactly what that cop wishes he could be.'" A doctor's son and a cop were on the jury. "He said, 'This is the best jury money can buy. They will understand.'"

After six hours of deliberation on 29 August 1979, the doctor's son, the cop and the rest of the jury returned a guilty verdict on one count of first-degree murder for the death of Kristen and two counts of second-degree murder for the deaths of Kimberley and Colette. This was a shock for MacDonald. Only moments before, he had been considering whether to hire the *Queen Mary*, the ocean liner turned hotel moored off Long Beach, California, for his victory party. He was sentenced to three terms of life.

"He has himself to blame," said Murtagh. "If he had kept his mouth shut, we could not have convicted him."

But this was not the end of the matter. There would be a series of appeals that would turn over the crime scene evidence again and again. In the meantime, MacDonald's bail was revoked and he went to jail.

MacDonald's friends hired the retired chief of the FBI's Los Angeles bureau, Ted Gunderson. Within twenty-four hours, Gunderson told his new employers: "Has your boy been railroaded?"

He tracked down Prince Beasley, who had now retired from the Fayetteville Police Department after being found by the state police passed out drunk in the middle of an intersection. He then spent time in a veterans' hospital where he was diagnosed as suffering from progressive "non-psychotic organic brain syndrome". Among his symptoms were "confusion" and "confabulation" – that is, making up stories without realizing he was doing so. However, Beasley still had a line on Stoeckley, who had married and moved to South Carolina.

With MacDonald's approval, Gunderson sent a Canadian psychic to convince Stoeckley that she had fallen in love with MacDonald. The psychic told Stoeckley that he could "foresee a beautiful life" for them, if she helped clear his name.

With Stoeckley distracted, Beasley went to visit her husband, Ernie Davis, a violence-prone hippie now languishing in the Fayetteville jail on an assault charge filed by his wife. According to Davis, Beasley promised to post bail and fly him to Los Angeles, if he would tell Gunderson everything he knew about the MacDonald case. Once Davis was in Los Angeles, more sweeteners, including a prospective movie-and-book deal, were offered and he signed a statement reiterating the incriminating claims Stoeckley had made about the murders. In the end, all Davis got out of the deal was $21 for a bus ticket.

But Gunderson still wanted Stoeckley's signed confession. By then Davis was back in South Carolina with Stoeckley. He had jumped bail. Beasley tracked them down and arrested Davis. On the ride back to Fayetteville with Davis in handcuffs, Beasly let it slip that Davis had spilt the beans to Gunderson. A fight broke out. It ended with Stoeckley offering to tell all.

Beasley did not even stop in Fayetteville long enough to pick up clean underwear. He spirited Stoeckley on to the next flight to Los Angeles. She underwent a gruelling five days of round-the-clock interrogation. Ex-FBI agent Homer Young assisted Gunderson. He later admitted that Gunderson had employed "unethical means and tactics". There had even been "an element of duress" in Stoeckley's questioning. They offered her immunity from prosecution (which was not in their gift). She was told that she would be resettled in California with a new identity – a job, home and, yes, even a part in the forthcoming movie. As a result, Stoeckley signed a statement not only implicating herself in the murders but also naming five other members of what she called the "Black Cult" – one of whom actually murdered Colette and possibly one of the girls, too. The credibility of her confession was bolstered by the inclusion of certain details of the crime scene that had never been released to the public. She also underwent three polygraph tests, which concluded she was telling the truth.

"Helena said that she was there. She was chanting, 'Acid is groovy, kill the pig,'" said Gunderson. She even repeated this on national television later.

"I had a floppy hat that I used to wear all the time, I had on boots that night and as a joke I put on the blonde wig," she said.

In the late 1960s and early 1970s, there had been a very serious drug problem in the Fayetteville area. While there were only about 52,000 troops in Fort Bragg, some 200,000 soldiers moved through the base each year. Those heading for Vietnam left Fayetteville full of hope, fear, courage and patriotism. Many returned disillusioned and jaded. They had witnessed horrors. Some were injured, some damaged mentally by the experience, and many were addicted to drugs. It was estimated that 1,000 heroin addicts lived on the base, while 8,000 others were strung out on amphetamines or other hard drugs.

The city of Fayetteville was little better. With some 53,000 inhabitants, it was known as "Fayettenam". In surrounding Cumberland County, it was estimated that, of the 225,000 residents, 25,000, or 11 per cent, were drug offenders. A thousand of them were considered hard-core heroin addicts. The narcotics came in from Miami and New York, or directly from the Far

East. Pushers, pimps and hookers thrived. And there were casualties. In the autumn of 1969, a soldier on LSD leapt to his death from an upper floor of the post hospital. On a single day in the following January, two twenty-year-old soldiers died from drug overdoses. In May 1970, two soldiers died after overdosing on uncut heroin in the lavatory of a laundromat in Fayetteville. The heroin was so strong that CID agents found them with their syringes still dangling from their arms.

Fayetteville's Rowan Park was so notorious for its drug dealers that it was known as "Skag Park". Fayetteville City Council introduced a curfew and narcotics agents, police officers, deputies and CID men patrolled the area. The result was a riot. The police responded with tear gas. Gunshots were fired and there were multiple arrests.

Things were no better on the base. According to Fort Bragg's newspaper, the *Paraglide*, in 1969, the military police filled twenty-two pages of their "blotter" daily. There were numerous armed robberies, particularly on pay days. Soldiers began carrying concealed weapons to protect themselves. They had so many prisoners in the stockade on Armstead Street that the overflow slept on cots in the halls. In 1969, the CID's evidence safe was stolen and, downtown, drug users were caught breaking into a police car looking for drugs. Three days after MacDonald's Article 32 hearing began, a Fayetteville drug dealer was found dead inside the base. He was slumped over the steering wheel of his 1967 Cadillac with two bullets in the back of his head and bundles of heroin hidden in his socks. The following week, three soldiers and a Fayetteville youth were charged with kidnapping a young couple. They had tied the male to a tree and beaten him to death, then raped his fourteen-year-old female companion.

The month before the murders, someone broke into the apartment of Janice Pendlyshok in a building across the walkway from the MacDonalds' apartment. Nothing was stolen, but Janice's underwear was found scattered around the room and obscenities were scrawled on a mirror. On the night of the murders, she was awoken by her German shepherd dog and heard a woman screaming and two children crying.

MacDonald's neighbour, aviator James Milne, had his car broken into. Also on the night of the murders, he had seen robed figures carrying candles heading for the MacDonalds' house.

The army's policy towards drugs was draconian. Under the new regulations, traditional doctor-patient confidentially was revoked and army doctors were to report soldiers who used drugs.

"If you were a physician, an army physician, you were under orders to turn in drug-abusing patients," said MacDonald. Asked if he thought someone he turned in might have been involved, he said: "Sure, that's one of the thought processes we immediately went through, of course."

Many physicians on the base were concerned that, under the new policy, drug-addicted soldiers would avoid medical treatment and make the drug problem worse. Four months after the murders, the policy had to be changed. The commander of Fort Bragg, Lieutenant General John Tolson, offered an amnesty to any drug user on the post who would step forward to seek help. They were to be tended in a hippie-decorated "halfway house", a clapboard building in the post's old hospital area.

MacDonald was group surgeon for his unit and was also assigned to provide medical counsel for Green Beret heroin addicts. But he did little to endear himself to drug addicts on the post. One of his duties was to restrict the supply of drugs to improve his unit's performance. He also encountered addicts in the emergency room of Cape Fear Valley Hospital where he worked to pay off his medical school bills. After MacDonald treated a soldier who had overdosed just a month before the murders, the police were called and a heroin dealer – a black man – was arrested. The word circulated that MacDonald was a "fink". But MacDonald was used to threats from junkies.

The soldier's name was Robert Wallack. He had been brought into the hospital by two hippie types, Larry Cook and Thomas Brown, who were convinced that MacDonald had called the cops. Cook was a friend of Greg Mitchell and was either part of, or tight with, Stoeckley's crowd. He told the FBI that, on the night of the murders, he stayed in Murchison Road near the Hickory Trailer Court and across the road from the grocery store. Brown said he stayed the night in a house on Haymount Street. There is no Haymount Street in Fayetteville, but there is a Hay Street, which runs through the centre of the then drug-plagued Haymount district. A black-painted pad where Stoeckley and her crew performed satanic rituals was at 908 Hay Street.

MacDonald's defence team could not find any documents giving the name of the drug dealer who had been arrested. However, he was described as a black man "five feet nine inches [1.75 m] tall, weighing 160 pounds [73 kg], and age twenty-nine to thirty", while MacDonald described the man he said had attacked him as 5 ft 8 inches (1.73 m) and about 165 lbs (75 kg).

The day before the murders, a young corporal visited MacDonald and demanded that the doctor discharge him from the army because of his heroin habit. When MacDonald informed him that he had no power to do that, the man became abusive. Captain Jim Williams had to come to MacDonald's rescue. It took three men to eject the corporal. Williams warned MacDonald of the deteriorating reputation he had among drug users who had just come back from Vietnam. These men were armed and dangerous. MacDonald replied that he was not concerned. After the murders, Williams told the MPs about the corporal and MacDonald's reputation as a fink. The corporal was picked up, but he had an alibi.

Helena Stoeckley told author Fred Bost: "MacDonald was just one of several people giving the drug users a hard time . . . It's kind of like if you tell somebody that they're going to be cut off [from drugs] . . . they said, 'Look, you know it's happening to us now. It could be you next'."

A raid on MacDonald's home was planned. At first, "there was simply going to be a little pushing around," she said, "you know, and trying to get a point across . . ."

But then, according to Stoeckley, the group decided to "annihilate the MacDonald family" because of his refusal to treat opium and heroin addicts. The main target would be Colette, then her two children.

"Human sacrifice involving a pregnant woman is the most prestigious for the cult members," said Stoeckley, "followed by children, women, and lastly men."

MacDonald was to be spared, so that he could provide them with drugs.

Early on the night of the killings, Stoeckley said she phoned the MacDonalds' home. Colette answered. She said she was going out to a class, but her husband would be home later. The group then decided to stage a Manson-style murder, accompanied by a satanic ritual. At around 2 a.m., they drove to the MacDonald apartment in a blue Mustang, unaccountably forgetting to take any weapons with them.

Two male cult members went into the master bedroom to see to Colette. Three others woke MacDonald and tried to get him to sign a prescription for Dexedrine. But MacDonald was "belligerent", Stoeckley said. They roughed him up a bit and he agreed to call a friend who would get the drugs. It was a trick. Instead, he dialled the operator in an attempt to get them to call the MPs. When they realized what was going on, the men administered a second, heavier beating, while Stoeckley chanted: "Acid is groovy, kill the pigs, hit him again."

Afterwards, she went to the master bedroom where she said she only remembered seeing one person actually attacking Colette. It was her boyfriend, Greg Mitchell.

Just nineteen at the time, Mitchell was already a heroin addict when he came back to Fort Bragg from his first tour of Vietnam. After the murders, he did what few other soldiers did. He asked to be sent back to south-east Asia. While waiting to be shipped back, he had an argument with his mother and yelled that he had to go kill all the ten-year-olds he could find. Soon after, he took an overdose of heroin, but survived. He then went back to Vietnam, until he was cashiered for drug addiction in 1971.

Back in Fayetteville, he broke down and confessed that he had murdered people, begging God to forgive him. Later, he was seen near a farmhouse where the words "I KILLED MACDONALD'S WIFE AND CHILDREN" were freshly painted on an interior wall. He told friends that the FBI was

interrogating him about the MacDonald murders and confessed
to one of them that he had done it.

Crime scene evidence also implicated Mitchell. Mitchell had
type O blood, the blood type found on Colette's hands.
MacDonald's blood was type B. The hair found under the victims' fingernails was brown, like Mitchell's, while MacDonald's
hair was blond. Forensic experts also concluded that Colette had
been killed by a left-handed person. Mitchell was left-handed,
while MacDonald favoured his right.

Stoeckley also remembered that, while Mitchell was
bludgeoning Colette, one of the children was lying motionless
next to her. Stoeckley believed Colette was fighting to protect the
child. At the sight of blood she became hysterical and started
"ranting and raving". The two men returned to the living room.
Stoeckley followed. MacDonald was then lying unconscious, half
on and half off the couch. She went to Kristen's bedroom where
she saw the younger daughter apparently dozing peacefully.
After looking in on Colette again, she returned to the living room
and said to the others: "Let's get out of here. She isn't breathing
anymore." She then ran out of the house. When she left, she said,
she thought MacDonald was dead.

Unfortunately, Stoeckley's story did not coincide with
MacDonald's account and Gunderson wanted more. While
threatening her with forty years in jail if she did not cooperate,
he promised that any statement she made was strictly for use in
a movie. In December 1980, he wrung a second statement from
her. In this one, a sixth member of the cult was implicated in the
crime. His name was "Wizard". Her filmed confession also
revealed much about the official investigators and their motiv-
ations for framing MacDonald. The idea was to limit the scope
of the investigation to MacDonald alone and maintain the cover-
up of a lucrative CIA drug pipeline running from Vietnam into
military bases in the United States, using the body cavities of
dead American soldiers being returned home. MacDonald, it
appears, was the perfect patsy.

Asked why he believed Stoeckley's story, Gunderson said:
"Because she said that she tried to ride the rocking horse in the

small bedroom . . . and she tried to get on it and she couldn't because the spring was broken."

Why would that be significant? "Because the only people that knew that spring was broken on the rocking horse was the family, the MacDonald family."

However, crime scene photographs seem to show that none of the springs on the toy horse were broken.

So far Beasley had not been paid a nickel by Gunderson. And if a movie deal was going ahead, he feared he would be left out of it. So he began making his own plans. He got in touch a reporter on the *Fayetteville Times* named Fred Bost, who was himself a former sergeant major in the Green Berets. Stoeckley joined the project for 20 per cent of the proceeds and signed a contract for a $5 advance. Gunderson also wanted a piece of the pie. He told Beasley to take Stoeckley to the *Washington Post*. But she did not like the tone of the resulting article and recanted her confession. Now in a fragile mental state, she accused Gunderson of being "a member of the Mafia". In a letter to him, she wrote: "Never have I seen a bigger mockery made of justice, or such a shambles made of an investigation."

Gunderson was busy rounding up witnesses to corroborate Stoeckley's story. He tracked down one of MacDonald's neighbours, who had testified at the Article 32 hearing that, sometime on the night of the murders, she had glanced out her window and seen the tail lights of a passing car. Under Gunderson's prompting, she remembered that it was between 2 and 3 a.m. The car was a blue Mustang, just like the one Stoeckley said she had been riding in and William Posey had said he had seen. Two other vehicles were parked by the Mustang. One of them was a military jeep driven by a black man. It was a rainy night and the neighbour was observing the scene at a distance of 70 to 80 ft (21 to 24 m). Nevertheless, she described the man sitting in the Mustang's passenger seat.

"I remember him specifically because of his piercing, deep-set eyes and the sneer on his face," she said. "I could pick him out of a crowd today."

She was then shown drawings produced during a hypnotic session with MacDonald. Stoeckley identified the man in the picture she selected as Allen Mazerolle, a former friend and fellow cult killer. According to Stoeckley, he had stabbed MacDonald with an ice pick.

Meanwhile, in July 1980, the Fourth Circuit Court of Appeals overturned MacDonald's conviction – just has it had thrown out the indictment – on the grounds that he had been denied a speedy trial. He went back to work as a doctor in California and returned to his playboy lifestyle, buying a ski condominium and dating an actress, who also happened to be the daughter of the chairman of the US Parole Commission. Then, at age thirty-seven, he got engaged to a twenty-two-year-old airline stewardess. But after twenty months, the US Supreme Court reversed the Fourth Circuit ruling. Appeals for a reduction of his sentence also fell on deaf ears. Courts were not impressed by his lawyers' argument that "the 1970 murders constitute the only blot on his record". Nor did Stoeckley's statements help.

"She was like a light bulb which hadn't been completely wound in," said one judge. "She blinks back and forth."

By this time, Bernie Segal was worn out and resorted to teaching at a San Francisco law school while new lawyers prepared further appeals. Gunderson still hoped to talk round Helena Stoeckley, who by then was destitute, pregnant, and an alcoholic. The offer of an interview on CBS's *60 Minutes* did the trick. She also had something new to add – fellow drug addict Cathy Perry had participated in the murders as well.

"Cathy freaked out," Stoeckley said. "Even the guys had trouble controlling her."

Stoeckley went on to claim that one of the killers was an undercover CID – apparently an idea suggested by Gunderson – and that three and a half weeks prior to the murders she had stolen a bracelet from Colette's jewellery box. This came as news to MacDonald and the interview was never aired.

Along with Stoeckley, six other people confessed to the MacDonald murders.

"If you put everybody in that room who confessed," said Murtagh, "there would hardly be room in there for Jeff."

Nevertheless, the FBI checked them all out. Meanwhile, Gunderson withdrew from the case when a hole was found in the steering-fluid drum of his car. Stoeckley's cult was suspected. A former New York homicide detective was hired to replace him, but he quit after concluding that MacDonald had done it. Undeterred, MacDonald's friends took on another ex-cop to work the case. But his investigation was hampered by the alcohol-related death of the heroin-addict and murder suspect Greg Mitchell, Stoeckley's former boyfriend who she had fingered for the murder of Colette. Six months later, Stoeckley's half-naked body was found in a low-rent apartment complex in Seneca, South Carolina. She was thirty, and she and her baby had been subsisting on peanut-butter sandwiches. Her body was decomposing, but the baby, though dehydrated, survived.

Gunderson suspected she had been murdered.

"Helena was like a puppet on a string," said her husband, Ernie Davis, who was then doing a fifteen-year stretch for first-degree sexual assault. "She knew it was all lies, but she . . . said if she didn't tell them what they wanted to hear they'd bother her even more."

Two weeks before she died, both Gunderson and Beasley had received frantic phone calls from Stoeckley. She had been recently interviewed by the FBI and now she said she could see two men in black suits parked across from her apartment in Seneca, South Carolina. They were watching her every move, twenty-four hours a day. She told Gunderson and Beasley that she was scared and needed protection. And she told Beasley that she was now prepared to tell the whole story about the MacDonald murders, without demanding immunity. This would "blow the lid" off Fort Bragg. Gunderson told Beasley to go down to Helena's place as fast as he could, but before Beasley could arrange to take the trip, Stoeckley was dead.

However, the post-mortem said the cause of death was acute pneumonia complicated by cirrhosis of the liver. Nevertheless, Gunderson was convinced that she was silenced using one of the many covert, untraceable assassination techniques known to government intelligence agencies. Stoeckley's body was found on 14 January. She had died the day before. A satanist and CIA insider interviewed by Gunderson identified 13 January as an important date for satanists. It is considered the Satanic New Year as it is the thirteenth day of the thirteenth month. The number thirteen is all-important. Covens, for example, always have thirteen fully fledged members.

Gunderson believed that there were thirteen members of Stoeckley's coven, too, and named eight of them: the cult leader Francis Winterbourne, nicknamed "Wizzard", who was white and by then was deceased; Greg Mitchell, who was also deceased; Shelby Don Harris, who was then alive; Allen Mazerolle, also alive; Dwight Smith, nicknamed "Zig Zag", who was the black man MacDonald and others had seen, and was then living; Bruce Fowler; Helena Stoeckley, deceased; and Cathy Perry, who was then still alive.

According to Beasley, Stoeckley had told him that a new man named Candy had taken over leadership of the group and was teaching them about black witchcraft. Stoeckley informed on him, but when Beasley went to arrest him he found no drugs. However, he found Candy in a room painted black. In the stairwell there was a painting of Christ being fellated by a hippie.

When Beasley confronted Stoeckley about the arrest, she said: "I changed my mind. Candy's our man."

In the yard outside Candy's apartment, Beasley found a mutilated cat. Stoeckley explained the significance: "They'd hang a cat up in the room, slit its throat, and have sex on the floor in the warm blood, men on women, men on men, women on women, it didn't matter."

The deaths of Mitchell and Stoeckley were a setback for MacDonald, who now put his hopes on the book that Joe McGinniss was about to publish. The two men had become close during the four years McGinniss was preparing the manuscript. McGinniss stayed in MacDonald's condo; they ate, drank and played together. When they were apart, McGinniss wrote often, assuring MacDonald of his belief in his innocence.

"There could not be a worse nightmare than the one you are living through now," McGinniss wrote in one letter. "But it is only a phase. Total strangers can recognize within five minutes that you did not receive a fair trial . . . What the fuck were those people thinking of? How could twelve people not only agree to believe such a horrendous proposition, but agree, with a man's life at stake, that they believed it beyond a reasonable doubt?"

He told others, including MacDonald's mother, the same thing. He had been present at all of the meetings with the defence team, seen the exculpatory evidence new lawyers had unearthed and knew the case inside out. MacDonald was sure that Joe would give him the "ultimate vindication". He learnt different during an interview with Mike Wallace on *60 Minutes*, just weeks before the book hit the shelves.

Wallace asked MacDonald: "How would you feel if I told you that Joe McGinniss says you're a homicidal maniac?"

"Joe McGinniss?" said MacDonald. "I don't believe you."

"Well," said Wallace, "I have the manuscript right here."

The book, which would be entitled *Fatal Vision*, was damning. It detailed all MacDonald's infidelities and lies. And it related another chilling tale. In California, MacDonald took a girlfriend and her son on a trip on his yacht. But then, enraged by some incident so minor no one else could recall it, MacDonald grabbed the boy and threatened to crush his skull between the side of the boat and the dockside. In the end, MacDonald relented and threw the child in the water. The girlfriend rescued her child and fled.

"I will never forget that look in his eyes," said the boy, who was grown up when McGinniss interviewed him. "Kind of a fire."

"Something seems to happen to people when [they] meet a journalist, and what happens is exactly the opposite of what one would expect," said Janet Malcolm, author of *The Journalist and the Murderer*. "One would think that extreme wariness and caution would be the order of the day, but in fact childish trust and impetuosity are far more common . . . There are very few people in the country who do not regard with rapture the prospect of being written about or being interviewed on a radio or television program."

McGinniss still had to explain how a man that everyone agreed loved and cared for his wife and children could suddenly become a raging maniac and kill them. He discovered that, a year before the murders, MacDonald had taken some prescription diet pills to lose weight. According to the book, he was over-dosing on two or three pills a day, inducing an amphetamine psychosis that turned him into a criminal psychopath. Kristen wetting the bed precipitated an uncontrollable drug-induced rage – even though no drugs were found in his bloodstream in hospital.

McGinniss said that he changed his mind about MacDonald's guilt after the trial. But some had cynically suggested that the story of an evil monster masquerading as an upstanding doctor who had tricked people into thinking he was innocent for nine years would sell more books than a crusade to get an innocent man a new trial.

Fatal Vision was hailed by the critics as a true-crime master-piece. It shot to the top of the best-sellers list. A made-for-TV movie followed. When it aired on NBC over two nights in the autumn of 1984, it was watched by an estimated sixty million Americans and was the network's highest-rated non-sports show of the year. It won a Primetime Emmy and other awards. MacDonald was disappointed. He had wanted Robert Redford to play him and was not happy with the casting of Gary Cole in the lead role.

"I thought he was wooden," he said. "I thought I was more expressive than him."

However, there was a glimmer of hope. Cathy Perry, the woman Stoeckley had named as a cohort, confessed. But her story was shaky at best. She said that, when the intruders were subduing MacDonald, they injected him with a narcotic. None was found in his system. Then they went upstairs to the bed-rooms. The apartment had no second floor. There they had beat one of the two boys. The children were both girls. Perry herself admitted killing Colette. This contradicted Stoeckley's testimony.

She stabbed her stomach and legs. Colette's wounds were to the chest and neck. The rest of her body was undamaged.

Worse, Perry had been a diagnosed paranoid schizophrenic. In and out of mental hospitals, she heard voices and hallucinated. Then, when under the doctor's care and dosed with Thorazine, she became sufficiently coherent to tell the FBI that she had no knowledge of the crime. True, there were some holes in her story, but that only made it more believable, MacDonald's lawyers said when they filed a habeas-corpus petition for his release in 1984. The fact that her story was contradicted by MacDonald's own testimony was countered with an affidavit from a psychologist, saying that he might be suffering from retrograde amnesia.

The petition would not be unopposed. Brian Murtagh produced a sheaf of FBI reports giving alibis to Stoeckley's alleged accomplices. The most ironclad belonged to Allen Mazerolle, who MacDonald's observant neighbour had said she had seen sitting in the blue Mustang only moments before the killings and Stoeckley said had wielded the ice pick. Unfortunately, at the time, Mazerolle was in jail, charged with the possession of a thousand tabs of LSD. What's more, the records further showed that he had been arrested three weeks before by Prince Beasley, acting on a tip from his top informant, Helena Stoeckley.

"It's a devastating blow," MacDonald said after the Fourth Circuit denied his petition. "But I cannot and will not roll over and play dead." Meanwhile, to add insult to injury, Murtagh, whom MacDonald had called a "viper", was driving around with the customized licence plate VIPR.

Under their agreement, MacDonald could not sue McGinniss for libel, but he could sue for fraud and breach of contract. In August 1984, he lodged a $15 million lawsuit.

Gary L. Bostwick, MacDonald's lawyer in the civil action, compared the tapes McGinniss had made of his conversations with MacDonald with the passages in *Fatal Vision* that purported to be "The Voice of Jeffrey MacDonald" and satisfied himself that McGinniss had skilfully edited the material to make it seem that MacDonald had delivered "glib, non-stop soliloquies of self-adoration". The passages where MacDonald had expressed concern about the tragic deaths of his wife and children did not make the page.

Worse, MacDonald's edited thoughts were interspersed with the prosecution's case, which was recorded unchallenged by the evidence the defence had unearthed. "The results, Bostwick charged, were fictional and the book could not be legitimized as non-fiction," said Jerry Allen Potter and Fred Bost, whose book *Fatal Justice* is a repost to *Fatal Vision*.

A few days before the trial, McGinniss offered MacDonald $200,000 to settle out of court. MacDonald refused. The trial did not go well at all for McGinniss. Eleven jurors found against him. But one was opposed to awarding money to a convicted murderer. She would not be persuaded.

"The trouble had started early in the trial," wrote Janet Malcolm, "when [the juror who held out], an animal-rights activist, brought animal-rights literature to the jury room and wasn't able to interest the other jurors in her cause. She became the weird 'Other' to the majority, and they became the 'Oppressors' to her . . . they had scorned this woman at their peril and were now powerless against her."

With the jury hung, the judge declared a mistrial, but left the door open for a new trial. McGinniss then offered to settle for $325,000. MacDonald's team negotiated him up a little, but the huge legal bills he was incurring forced him to settle. And even a victory in the civil courts could not undo the impression, produced by the book and the TV film, that MacDonald was a dangerous psychopath.

However, MacDonald found he had a new champion. Veteran *New Yorker* writer Janet Malcolm published her book-length attack on McGinniss, *The Journalist and the Murderer*. That prompted the thought: if the attacks on MacDonald were so mercenary and self-serving, might he be telling the truth after all? The result was a series of articles and TV documentaries that sought to exonerate him. Fortunately, Helena Stoeckley's statements had been videotaped and now she confessed to the nation from beyond the grave.

Jeffrey Elliot, who had interviewed MacDonald for *Playboy* and testified for him at the McGinniss trial, said of MacDonald: "There's a sweetness about him . . . After meeting him, you would say, 'This is a travesty. This is a good, decent, kind, thoughtful man, and the system has failed.' You might be willing to do things to help him."

MacDonald, as ever, was charming and engaging.

'I am that overachiever personality," MacDonald told a visitor. "I set up a goal and say, 'That's the next goal' . . . I don't sit and bemoan fates and say, 'Woulda, coulda, shoulda' . . . I don't have deep insights into life . . . My skill is medicine . . . By me helping a person, I help myself. I hope that doesn't sound selfish . . . I think that's all good. It's how I am . . . an overachiever, a very good physician. I am not patting myself on the back. Please. I am telling what is a fact. People like me, and I work very hard."

The visitor noted that he nodded at his self-diagnosis and smiled in a cool and confident fashion.

"Generally speaking, I say to myself, 'You are a good guy. You didn't save your family, but that doesn't make you bad. And, generally speaking, you tell the truth. So stop beating yourself up,'" he continued.

While going over 10,000 pages of government documents, the new defence team found a pre-trial memo that implied that MacDonald's attorneys had not been given unfettered access to the crime scene evidence. Among the dozen cardboard boxes of evidence, there was one labelled "Black/Black & Gray Root/ Synthetic Hairs". Inside it was an envelope marked "Synthetic Hairs, Blonde". Inside that was a 22 in. (56 cm) long, blonde strand of artificial hair recovered from Colette's hairbrush mounted on an evidence slide. It was much too long to have come from one of the children's dolls as had been suggested. MacDonald maintained that this came from the wig worn by the woman who had chanted: "Acid is groovy, kill the pigs." His attorney, Harvey Silverglate, and Harvard Law School professor Alan Dershowitz agreed that access to this evidence had been unfairly denied to MacDonald and filed another habeas-corpus petition in 1990. However, an FBI lab report presented to the

Fourth Circuit showed that this hair was made from saran, which was used to make doll hair, not human wigs.

"Unless the defendant wants to maintain that Ken and Barbie did it," said a government attorney, "I don't see how this hair helps them very much."

The judges agreed.

"At some point," they ruled, "we must accept this case as final."

Like other celebrity prisoners, MacDonald was besieged by women. One came from Ohio and claimed that she had seen her lover killing Colette and the children in a fight over her. Another went to work on his behalf and tracked down a textile executive who said that saran was used in human wigs. Silverglate found documents showing that the FBI knew this and contended that the bureau had committed "fraud on the courts".

The Freedom of Information Act uncovered other evidence that had been withheld from the defence. More artificial hair had been found in Colette's hand. Segal had been led to believe that this was natural hair from MacDonald's head.

Short brown hair was found under the fingernails of Colette and the girls. This was not MacDonald's hair, which was blond, nor the hair of any of the house's inhabitants. It was most likely the hair of the killer. Not only was this evidence suppressed, a lab technician wrote in a note that the hairs "are not going to be reported by me". The army lab, it seems, was under pressure to keep quiet about anything that might help MacDonald.

A piece of skin was also found under Colette's fingernails. This was also thought to been from her killer. No fingernail scratches were found on MacDonald when he was taken to the hospital after the murders. Conveniently, the skin was lost by the army investigators during their mishandling of the evidence.

Two dark fibres were found on the piece of wood used to beat Colette. The prosecution maintained that these came from MacDonald's pyjamas. Years later, the defence team learnt that no fibres from MacDonald's cotton pyjamas were found on the club. There were two black wool fibres that matched wool fibres found on Colette's mouth. It seems they had adhered when she was struck with the club. But these black wool fibres did not match any garments in the MacDonalds' apartment. The FBI lab notes said they were "foreign". But the defence were denied access to the notes and the jury was led to believe that fibres from MacDonald's pyjamas were found on the club.

Three wax drippings were found at the crime scene. These did not match the wax of any of the fourteen candles in the MacDonalds' home. This substantiated MacDonald's story that the woman with his attackers was carrying a candle, and Stoeckley's story of using candles in her incantations and rituals. A burnt match was found in Kristen's room. MacDonald and his wife did not smoke and the match could have been used to light the candle MacDonald said he saw. A bloody syringe was also found at the crime scene, but it was lost by the CID lab before it could be examined. There was also a number of gloves with blood on them, but not enough to determine whose it was. It came to light that seventeen unmatched finger- and palm-prints had been found at the crime scene. However, the crime scene investigation had been so sloppy that exemplar fingerprints had never been taken from the children and those from Colette were poor because they were only taken after she had been embalmed.

Other things began to go MacDonald's way. Jim Blackburn had been to prison for embezzling from clients and was now working as a waiter. Joe McGinniss was being pilloried by the critics for plagiarism in his new biography of Teddy Kennedy. And Potter and Bost's book, *Fatal Justice*, had just come out. In 496 pages, it makes a point-by-point rebuttal of the prosecution's case and posits a conspiracy theory involving the army, the Justice Department and the FBI. The press was now sympathetic. An inspector general's report trashed the FBI's saran expert's testimony in an unrelated case.

Then in October 1997, the Fourth Circuit allowed the defence to introduce DNA evidence. Testing began in December 2000 but this was another blind alley. Test results released by the Armed Forces DNA Identification Laboratory in 2006 showed that neither Mitchell's nor Stoeckley's DNA matched that found at the crime scene. The DNA in hair found stuck to Colette's left palm matched that of Jeffrey MacDonald. A hair found in

Colette's right palm was her own. MacDonald's DNA profile also matched body hairs found on the top sheet of Kristen's bed and the bedspread from the master bed. However, three hairs – one found under the fingernail of Kristen, one from the bedsheet and one, a long pubic hair, found between Colette's legs – did not match the DNA profile of any MacDonald family member or known suspect. Someone else had been in the room. This provided the basis for another habeas-corpus petition, which was supported by an affidavit of retired US Marshal Jimmy Britt. He said that, in 1979, he was present when Helena Stoeckley told James Blackburn that she had been inside the MacDonald apartment where she and the others had gone to get drugs. Britt then remembered Blackburn saying to her: "If you testify to the things that you've just told me, I will indict you for first-degree murder." The following day, Stoeckley testified in court that she had no memory of where she was that night. Blackburn denied this. Despite pleading guilty to a number of felonies, including embezzlement, forgery and stealing several hundred thousand dollars from his law firm, and being disbarred and imprisoned, Blackburn went on to become a speaker who gives lectures on ethics to lawyers.

In March 2006, Donald Buffkin of Alabama filed an affidavit in which he claimed that on several occasions between 1980 and 1982, he drank at a bar with a man who claimed to have been involved in the MacDonald family murders. Buffkin identified the man as Greg Mitchell. The last occasion that Mitchell told him about the murders was just two weeks before his death. Two other men, Everett Morse and Bryant Lane, also claimed in affidavits that Mitchell confessed that he had committed the murder to them on separate occasions. A law clerk claimed that she spoke to the cashier of a 7-Eleven store near the MacDonalds' home, who said that she saw a group of hippies come into the store on the morning of the murders – though she did not report it for fear of her life.

After over thirty years in jail, MacDonald's fight for freedom continues in the hope that something in the crime scene evidence will clear his name. His case has already been appealed to the US

Supreme Court more than any other in history. MacDonald married again in 2002. At the behest of his second wife, he attended a parole hearing in 2005, but refused to admit his guilt. A tape made by Fred Kassab before he died in 1989 was played. In it he said: "I want to be sure he serves out his sentence the way it should be served out. I don't want him walking around the streets."

Colette's brother Robert said: "My joy in you, Mr MacDonald, is that you are the complete sociopath that you are. And that you're never going to admit what you did. And that I'm going to have the pleasure of knowing that you're going to stay here and rot in jail for the rest of your life."

Parole was denied. MacDonald's next scheduled parole hearing is in 2020. Otherwise, his release date is set for 5 April 2071, when he will be 127.

THE PENNSYLVANIA POISONER

IN AUGUST 1991, newly married thirty-two-year-old Robert Curley was renovating an old home for his new wife Joann when he became violently ill. He suffered intense burning pains in his hand and feet. After four days in the Wilkes-Barre General Hospital, Pennsylvania, he was diagnosed with Guillain-Barre syndrome, a neurological disorder, and released.

But the symptoms did not go away. Despite his wife's objections, Robert Curley was readmitted to Wilkes-Barre General in early September 1991, where the doctors now confessed they were baffled by his symptoms. These included burning skin, repeated vomiting, weakness, numbness and rapid hair loss. After ten days, he became agitated and aggressive. Eventually, he had to be tethered to his bed by leather straps as he writhed in agony. Heavy-metal poisoning was suspected, so he was transferred to the Hershey Medical Center where doctors could perform the appropriate tests. Elevated levels of thallium were in his system – up to 900 times the lethal dose.

His brain swelled up. He eventually fell comatose and had to be hooked up to a respirator. But nothing could be done. His wife, who was at her husband's side throughout his suffering, permitted the doctors to turn off his life support and, on 27 September 1991, he died. The couple were very close, friends recalled.

Thallium was not a common substance. It had been discovered by Sir William Crookes in Britain in 1861 and, in limited doses, it was used to treat gout, ringworm and sexually transmitted disease, until it was found to be carcinogenic. It was also used in rat poison but was eventually banned in 1984. However, Curley worked on a construction project at Wilkes University earlier that year. A search turned up five bottles of thallium salts in the chemistry laboratory's stockroom, but none of Curley's thirteen co-workers exhibited any symptoms of accidental thallium exposure.

At Curley's post-mortem, it was discovered that the thallium levels in his body were so high that he must have been poisoned deliberately. His death was ruled a homicide. The cause of death was given as severe hypoxic encephalopathy, where the brain is deprived of oxygen – a secondary effect of thallium poisoning. Forensic pathologist Cyril Wecht, best known for his criticism of the findings of the Warren Commission on the assassination of John F. Kennedy, said that Curley's brain had swelled up so much it pushed down into the spinal cord.

Initially, a disgruntled work colleague, who had access to the poison, was suspected. However, investigators from the Federal Occupational Health and Safety Administration did an inventory of the chemicals at the lab and determined that none was missing. Then investigators turned their attention to the Curley home, where Joann, his wife of thirteen months, lived with her daughter from a previous marriage. They were also found to have elevated levels of thallium in their systems, but not at toxic levels. Investigators also found several thermos flasks that Joann Curley said her husband used to take iced tea to work. These too tested positive for thallium. But with no suspects, the case went cold for three years.

Curley's life insurance paid out $297,000 to his widow. Two days before Curley died, she had also received over $1 million in a payout over the car accident that killed her first husband. Now she grew greedy and sued the university over her second husband's death. Naturally, the university and its insurers sought to defend themselves. Her mercenary attitude also looked suspicious to the police and it was up to them to prove that she had killed her husband.

This was a job for forensics. The authorities approached Dr Fredric Rieders of National Medical Services, a private toxicology lab in Willow Grove with extensive testing abilities, who would later appear as an expert witness at the O. J. Simpson trial.

He was asked to do a more thorough analysis of the tissues. The evidence was sparse. Rieders needed more samples, but Joann Curley agreed to allow her husband to be exhumed. Hair shafts were removed from various parts of Curley's body, along with fingernails, toenails and skin samples. What could they show? It was already known that Curley died due to the raised level of thallium in his body.

But Dr Rieders had a clever plan. He divided each hair up into small segments. The level of thallium in each segment was then determined by the use of atomic absorption spectrophotometry. This was a sophisticated technique where chemicals were used to break down each segment of hair into individual atoms. These were then excited by electro-magnetic waves and the spectrum of their absorption plotted. Each element has a characteristic absorption spectrum.

Working out how much thallium there was in each segment of hair, it was possible to draw up a timeline of Curley's exposure.

"Hair is, for many things, a timeline," said Rieders, a former Philadelphia assistant medical examiner. "It is a repository of what circulated in the body. If you take an aspirin, what will grow out of your head will be a strand of hair on which a tiny portion will have a little aspirin."

Since hair grows at an approximate rate of $^1/_3$ to $^1/_2$ in. (0.8 to 1.3 cm) per month, scientists can start at the hair's root, and work backwards in time. Some of the strands of hair from Curley's head were long enough to track the toxin back up to 329 days before he died, but Dr Rieders confined himself to the previous nine months.

Investigators had thought that Curley had been fed thallium in August 1991, fallen ill and then died. Instead, the timeline showed a series of spikes, indicating that Curley had been fed thallium over a long period. And they began before Curley had started work at the university. This proved that someone was poisoning him long before he took the job there. There was also a massive spike just a few days before his death, while Curley was confined to the Hershey Medical Center. This was con-firmed by readings from hairs from other parts of his body, and measurements from his fingernails and toenails supported this data. This again suggested that the poisoning was intentional – and the poison was being administered by someone who had access to him in hospital.

There were other oddities about the timelines. There were at least seven separate spikes when Curley had ingested thallium. When Rieders compared it to the events in Curley's life, he found that, except for the few days before his death, the thallium levels dropped when he was away from home or in the hospital. However, in the last few days of this time, his family had brought some food into the hospital for him and he had been left alone with his wife.

As the prosecution prepared for trial, they called in some other leading expert witnesses. The former chief medical examiner for New York City, Michael Baden, confirmed Rieders's findings. Baden had been chairman of the Forensic Pathology Panel of the House Select Committee on Assassinations that reinvestigated the John F. Kennedy assassination. He had also given evidence at the O. J. Simpson trial and helped in the investigation of the remains of the Romanovs. Then there was Cyril Wecht, author of several books about high-profile crime scene investigations.

"I was an expert, with Michael Baden and Fred Rieders, for the DA," said Wecht. "I was the only one to testify at the preliminary hearing and I went through the entire forensic pathology and toxicology stuff that the three of us had prepared. It was a beautiful case because it had to do with the sequential chronological testing of a hair from its follicle to its tip. It showed the peaks and valleys of his poisoning. When he was away, he had a valley and when he was home or with his wife, he had a peak."

Wecht's role was to interpret the toxicological findings relating to the cause of death.

"The forensic toxicologist can come up with the technical methodology and findings," he said, "but the pathologist is needed to talk about cause of death and relate it to the science and symptoms and critical episodes. It's a joint effort."

Acknowledging that the case against Joann Curley was largely circumstantial, District Attorney Peter Paul Olszewski Jr said he believed a conviction would be "difficult, difficult, difficult". Police said Joann was the only person with "constant and frequent access to the victim and to the food and drink consumed by the victim". But the case, it seemed, literally hung by a hair. The prosecution did not give details of the psychological profile that they had built up on Joann Curley, nor did they say how she had obtained the thallium. However, they believed that Robert Curley had discovered he was being poisoned in the days before he died. A registered nurse at the Hershey Medical Center told police that Robert Curley grabbed her by the arm the day before he went into the coma and said: "Please help me. My wife is trying to kill me. She is not as she seems."

In the end, the big guns of forensic toxicology were not needed. Confronted with this panel of experts and the forensic evidence that had amassed, the pressure was on thirty-three-year-old Joann Curley. In 1997, she made a plea bargain with the prosecution. She confessed to having murdered her husband with rat poison for the life insurance. In exchange for her confession – and saving the state the cost of a prosecution – she was given a sentence of ten to twenty years in prison. She has, so far, been denied parole.

ACKNOWLEDGEMENTS

WITH THANKS TO John Tucker and Vaneese Tucker for their hard work in researching this book.